W9-BDV-715

ALSO BY MERRITT IERLEY

*Travelling the National Road:*
*Across the Centuries on America's First Highway*

*With Charity for All:*
*Welfare and Society, Ancient Times to the Present*

*The Year That Tried Men's Souls:*
*A Journalistic Reconstruction of the World of 1776*

*A Place in History: A Centennial Chronicle of North Arlington,*
*New Jersey, Birthplace of Steam Power in America*

# OPEN HOUSE

# OPEN HOUSE

A Guided Tour

of the American Home

1637 – Present

Merritt Ierley

HENRY HOLT AND COMPANY    NEW YORK

SUSSEX COUNTY LIBRARY SYSTEM
MAIN LIBRARY
125 Morris Tnpk, Newton, N.J. 07860
Telephone: 948-3660

Henry Holt and Company, Inc.
*Publishers since 1866*
115 West 18th Street
New York, New York 10011

Henry Holt® is a registered
trademark of Henry Holt and Company, Inc.

Copyright © 1999 by Merritt Ierley
All rights reserved.

Published in Canada by Fitzhenry & Whiteside Ltd.,
195 Allstate Parkway, Markham, Ontario L3R 4T8.

Library of Congress Cataloging-in-Publication Data
Ierley, Merritt.
Open house: a guided tour of the American home, 1637–present /
Merritt Ierley. —1st ed.
p.   cm.
Includes bibliographical references and index.
ISBN 0-8050-4837-5 (hc: acid-free paper)
1. Architecture. Domestic—United States.   I. Title
NA7205. I35   1999                          97-47082
728'.0973—dc21                              CIP

Henry Holt books are available for special promotions
and premiums. For details contact: Director, Special Markets.

First Edition 1999

*Designed by Kate Nichols*

Printed in the United States of America
All first editions are printed on acid-free paper. ∞

1   3   5   7   9   10   8   6   4   2

To Abigail, Albertina, Ann,

Charlotte, Elizabeth, Grace, Harriet, Isabel, Ise,

Jane, Janet, Mary, Rebecca, and Sarah,

for letting us visit their homes

# Contents

# Acknowledgments

$G$ ratefully acknowledged are the many who have been profoundly helpful with this project.

My thanks in particular to *Karl Katz,* executive director, MUSE Film and Television, New York, N.Y., formerly chairman for special projects, Metropolitan Museum of Art, in consultation with whom this project was first conceived and without whose help it might never have been accomplished.

I am deeply appreciative of those who read and critiqued major portions of the manuscript and offered many constructive suggestions: *Edythe Harvey Cederlund,* former curator, Gore Place, Waltham, Mass.; *Katherine M. Córdova,* curator, Fairbanks House, Dedham, Mass.; *Peter Gittleman,* director of interpretation and public programs, Society for the Preservation of New England Antiquities, Boston, Mass.; *Willie Graham,* curator of architecture, Colonial Williamsburg Foundation, Williamsburg, Va.; *Scott P. Heyl,* executive director, Historic House Trust of New York City, New York, N.Y.; *Lonnie J. Hovey,* A.I.A., Vitetta Group, Philadelphia, formerly preservation coordinator, The Octagon, Washington, D.C., headquarters of the American Architectural Foundation; *Elizabeth B. Leckie,* curator, Historic House Trust of New York City, New York, N.Y.; *Karin E. Peterson,* associate director and curator, Antiquarian and Landmarks Society, Hartford, Conn.; *Anne M. Serio,* assistant curator, Division of Social History, National Museum of American History, Smithsonian Institution, Washington, D.C.; and *William E. Worthington, Jr.,* assistant curator, Division of the History of Technology, National Museum of American History, Smithsonian Institution, Washington, D.C.

Special thanks to *Ati Gropius Johansen* for the previously unpublished photograph of Walter and Ise Gropius and herself that appears in chapter 6; to *Loren Pope* for his personal recollections (Frank Lloyd Wright's Pope-Leighey House, page 216); and to *Dolores Malecki-Spivack,* architect and illustrator, for the wonderful original artwork she produced for this book.

I must duly acknowledge a mentor in absentia, *Abbott Lowell Cummings,* whose one-of-a-kind book, *The Framed Houses of Massachusetts Bay* (Harvard University Press, 1979), served not only as a personal tutor on the Early American house but as a model of what a book about houses should aspire to be. It was correspondence with him that affirmed the significance of the Fairbanks House as the "oldest living relative" (see footnote page 5).

Others who read portions of the manuscript or contributed materially include: Antiquarian and Landmarks Society, Hartford, Conn.: *Mary Beth Baker,* regional administrator • Charleston Museum, Charleston, S.C.: *Mary Giles,* assistant archivist, *Karen B. King,* education coordinator, and *Ernest Shealy* • College of William and Mary, Williamsburg, Va.: *Margaret Cook,* curator of manuscripts and rare books, Earl Gregg Swem Library • David Davis Mansion, Bloomington, Ill.: *Rebecca Landau,* curator • Friends of Hyde Hall, Cooperstown, N.Y.: *Jeffrey Bliemeister,* director, and *Douglas R. Kent,* former executive vice president and curator • George Read II House, New Castle, Del.: *Timothy J. Mullin,* curator, and *Denise August,* supervisor of buildings and grounds • Harriet Beecher Stowe Center, Hartford, Conn.: *Jo Blatti,* executive director, *Debra Fillos,* curator, and *Kristen Froehlich,* former curator • Maryland Historical Trust, Crownsville, Md.: Orlando Ridout V, chief, office of research, survey,

and registration • Merchant's House Museum, New York, N.Y.: *Mimi Sherman,* curator • Monticello, Charlottesville, Va.: *William L. Beiswanger,* director of restoration • National Park Service: *Phyllis Ewing,* curator, Martin Van Buren National Historic Site, Kinderhook, N.Y. • National Trust for Historic Preservation: *Craig S. Tuminaro,* historian, Frank Lloyd Wright's Pope-Leighey House, Mt. Vernon, Va. • Pennsylvania Historical and Museum Commission: *Dr. William N. Richardson,* administrator, Joseph Priestley House, Northumberland, Pa. • Sandwich Glass Museum/Sandwich Historical Society, Sandwich, Mass.: *Lynne M. Horton,* curator of history • Schifferstadt, Frederick, Md.: *Lou Anne Rayburn,* director, Schifferstadt Museum • Sinclair Lewis Foundation, Sauk Centre, Minn.: *Roberta Olson,* president, and *Joyce Lyng,* tour guide/supervisor • Society for the Preservation of New England Antiquities, Boston, Mass.: *Jane C. Nylander,* president, *Richard Nylander,* curator of collections, and *Lorna Condon,* archivist • The White House, Washington, D.C.: *Betty C. Monkman,* associate curator • Wyck, Philadelphia, Pa.: *John M. Groff,* executive director.

The following supplied historical data, chiefly through responses to the survey "The American Home and the Development of Domestic Technology" (see appendix 2), which was an integral part of the research for this book: American Architectural Foundation, Washington, D.C.: Eryl J. Platzer, director of The Octagon • Atlanta History Center, Atlanta, Ga.: Jenny Siegenthaler, head of Historic Houses and Gardens • Baker Mansion, Altoona, Pa.: Timothy C. Van Scyoc, curator • Baltimore City Life Museums, Baltimore, Md.: Louise E. Akerson, archaelogical curator, and

Victoria Taylor Hawkins, curator of objects • Bethel Historical Society, Bethel, Me.: Dr. Stanley Russell Howe, executive director, Dr. Moses Mason House Museum • Campbell House Foundation, St. Louis, Mo.: Jeffrey L. Huntington, executive director • Carter House Association, Franklin, Tenn.: Kim Finley, curator. Chrysler Museum, Norfolk, Va.: Roberta D. Whisman, manager, Adam Thoroughgood House • Church of Jesus Christ of Latter Day Saints, Salt Lake City, Utah: Margaret Adams, director, Beehive House • Cohasset Historical Society, Cohasset, Mass.: David H. Wadsworth, curator, Caleb Lothrop House • Colorado Historical Society, Denver, Colo.: Paula Manini, site administrator, Bloom Mansion, Trinidad, Colo. • Crawford County Historical Society, Meadville, Pa.: Leslie A. Przybylek, curator, Baldwin-Reynolds House Museum • El Pueblo de Los Angeles Historic Monument, Los Angeles, Calif.: Jean Bruce Poole, Historic Museum director • Florida Trust for Historic Preservation: Bonnet House, Fort Lauderdale, Fla.: Denyse Cunningham, curator • Gallier House Museum, New Orleans, La.: Mary Strickland, curator • Gay Mont, Rappahannock Academy, Va.: James S. Patton • Georgia Department of Natural Resources, Atlanta, Ga.: James E. Hall, manager, Vann House Historic Site • Grout Museum of History and Science, Waterloo, Iowa: Judy Burfeind, site manager, Rensselaer Russell House Museum • Henry Clay Memorial Foundation, Lexington, Ky.: Robert C. Magrish, curator • Hermann-Grima Historic House, New Orleans, La.: Jan C. Bradford, curator • The Hermitage, Hermitage, Tenn.: Marsha Mullin, curator • Hillforest Historical Foundation, Aurora, Ind.: Elizabeth A. Cook, executive director • His-

toric Hudson Valley, Tarrytown, N.Y.: Kate Johnson, curator, and Jennifer Anderson-Lawrence, site director, Philipsburg Manor; Maiken Nielsen, site director, Sunnyside • Historic Pensacola Preservation Board, Pensacola, Fla.: B. Lynne Robertson, museum curator • Illinois Historic Preservation Agency, Springfield, Ill.: Marilyn Ayers, site manager, Bryant Cottage; Ken Costa, acting site manager, Lincoln's New Salem; Dr. Donald P. Hallmark, site manager, Dana-Thomas House; Terry J. Miller, site manager, Grant Home/Washburne House; Carol Nelson, site manager, Carl Sandburg House; Sandy Stenger, capital projects coordinator; and Roger Wicklein, site manager, Menard Home • Indiana Division of State Museums and Historic Sites, Indianapolis, Ind.: Becky Smith, curator, Limberlost State Historic Site • John Greenleaf Whittier Home, Amesbury, Mass.: Frances C. Dowd, president and librarian • Johns Hopkins University, Baltimore, Md.: Mary Butler Davies, director, Homewood House Museum • Juliette Low Birthplace, Savannah, Ga.: Stephen L. Bohlin-Davis, curator • La Crosse County Historical Society, La Crosse, Wisc.: Brenda R. Jordan, administrative curator • Lyman House Memorial Museum, Hilo, Hawaii: Paul A. Dahlquist, curator • McFaddin-Ward House, Beaumont, Tex.: Jessica H. Foy, curator • Minnesota Historical Society, Saint Paul, Minn.: Janet Budack, site manager, Alexander Ramsey House; John R. Crippen, historic sites administrator; Tom Ellig, district manager, Meighen House/Forestville; Craig Johnson, site manager, James J. Hill House; Jim Mattson, site manager, Oliver H. Kelley House; Lee Radzak, site manager, Lighthouse Keeper's Dwellings; and Donald H. Westfall, site manager, Charles A. Lindbergh House • Missouri Division of State Parks, Jefferson City, Mo.: Hugh M. Brown, site administrator, Pershing Boyhood Home State Historic Site • Nathaniel Russell House, Charleston, S.C.: Robert A. Leath, assistant curator • National Park Service, Washington, D.C.: Elaine R. Clark, curator, Andrew Johnson National Historic Site, and Jon E. Taylor, historian, Harry S. Truman National Historic Site; Linda Norbut Suits, curator, Lincoln Home National Historic Site • New York City Historic House Trust, New York, N.Y.: Nancy Zeigler, development director, and Valerie Kalas • North Carolina Department of Cultural Resources, Raleigh, N.C.: Charlotte Carter, site manager, Charles B. Aycock Birthplace; A. Dale Coats, site manager, Duke Homestead; Ann Flanagan, assistant manager, Historic Bath; and Amy Hopkins, historic interpreter, Bennett Place • Oklahoma Historical Society, Oklahoma City, Okla.: Shirley Pettengill, site manager, Murrell Home/Drummond Home • Outagamie County Historical Society, Appleton, Wisc.: Jo Ellen Wollangk, curator • Peabody Essex Museum, Salem, Mass.: Robert E. Saarnio, curator, Early American architecture • Prairie Avenue House Museums, Chicago, Ill.: Janice C. Griffin, senior curator • Prestwould Foundation, Clarksville, Va.: Dr. Julian Davis Hudson, director • Robert E. Lee Boyhood Home, Alexandria, Va.: Virginia I. Bruch, research curator • San Antonio Conservation Society, San Antonio, Tex.: Ron Bauml, properties restoration manager • Shirley-Eustis House Association, Roxbury, Mass.: John B. Hermanson, director • Society for the Preservation of New England Antiquities, Boston,

Mass.: Ann Clifford, assistant archivist, and Nicole F. Nichols, education coordinator, Bowen House, Woodstock, Conn. • Tipton-Haynes Historical Association, Johnson City, Tenn.: Penny McLaughlin, director • The Trustees of Reservations, Windsor, Mass.: Jim Caffrey, superintendent, Bryant Homestead • Turner House, Hattiesburg, Miss.: David Sheley, director • Washoe County Parks and Recreation Department, Reno, Nev.: Betty Hood, curator, Historic Bowers Mansion • Western Reserve Historical Society, Cleveland, Ohio: Cynthia C. Miller, collections specialist • Wheatland, Lancaster, Pa.: Kathleen Bratton, executive director.

Still others to be acknowledged are Gretchen Bock, who suggested the title; Bill Becker, Custom Photo Graphics, Hillsdale, N.J., who processed all of the author's photographs; John Fredericks, Fredericks Fuel, Oak Ridge, N.J., who helped arrange for the artwork illustrating modern heating systems; and John Motta, AM Graphics, Closter, N.J., for typesetting of the questionnaire used in compiling the appendix.

Finally there are those to be acknowledged who are inevitably inconspicuous to the reader yet by their absence would be most conspicuous of all. That you wouldn't know how much they contributed is a tribute to their professionalism. But the author knows. So herewith a heartfelt thanks to my agent, *Faith Hamlin,* of Sanford J. Greenburger Associates; my editors at Henry Holt—*Beth Crossman, Darcy Tromanhauser, Kenneth Wright,* and *Mary Kay Linge;* and the project editor/copy editor, *Joyce O'Connor* (her second straight collaboration, by the author's personal request).

# Introduction

*Open House* is a visit to the American home as it has evolved from the beginning of European settlement to the present day.

The style and approach will be familiar to anyone who has taken a guided tour of a historic house, except that here it is not one but a chronological sequence of houses (all active house museums open to the public) that is visited, beginning with what is arguably the oldest surviving house in America—the home in Dedham, Massachusetts, that English settler Jonathan Fairbanks built for his family in 1637.

What was it like, this new home in a New World? From the point of view of the "modern" house, how modern was it for its own day? And what in turn were its origins?

From this starting point, we look at the American home through its technological development—its creature comforts like heat and light and indoor plumbing; through its significance as a reflection of a changing society; and finally through its evolution as architecture—that by which wood and brick and stone and mortar make a personal expression of this most fundamental of all architectural forms.

Although our visits conclude with two houses of the mid 20th century, these were forward-looking structures that encompass virtually all the significant change inherent in the average American home at the opening of the 21st century.

As befits its concept, *Open House* represents countless visits by the author to historic American dwellings. Along with new research, particularly into technological evolution, the result is a fresh and original look, with an emphasis on seeing the American house through the lives of those who first called it "home."

# OPEN HOUSE

# The House
# and American Life

The house, perhaps more than any other symbol of American life, fulfills the ideals of life, liberty, and the pursuit of happiness.

As for *life:* The house is a uniquely appropriate symbol, for it was to a starkly houseless landscape—a vast continent lacking anything that looked like a house to them—that the first settlers made their way. To be sure, native Americans had shelter, but it was not a very convincing sort to Europeans; and although the settlers' first structures (as at Plymouth) were hardly any better, if not less efficient, they were at least *houses.* And so, in conquering shelterlessness with their own definition of shelter, these first settlers left on the collective unconscious of American culture the preeminence of the house as a symbol of life in the New World.

*Liberty:* The house is a symbol of self-sufficiency (one's home is one's castle) and hence of independence, materialized in wood and bricks and concrete.

*The pursuit of happiness:* The house is the locus of the American dream and has long been the most conspicuous way of proclaiming personal success. As one climbs the economic ladder, one often also climbs the steps to a new and larger dwelling suitable to one's new station. Or one enlarges an existing but less conspicuous home to suit the purpose—as, for example, that single most famous of private American homes, a modest four-room farmhouse that became Mount Vernon.

Symbol of life, liberty, and the American dream: The American house is inextricably linked with the evolution of American life; for the same dynamics that shaped the nation, social and technological in particular, also helped shape the American house.

*The focus of this book is the American house as it has evolved since the beginning of European settlement, for that is what constitutes the prevailing concept of dwelling in America. Yet before there came a Fairbanks House or any other of its generation, there were, from time immemorial, the varied and often wondrous dwellings of the Native American. In recognition of that heritage, there appears here, in advance of any other, this photograph—the Acoma Indian pueblo in New Mexico (10th century), believed to be the oldest continuously inhabited settlement in the United States.* (Historic American Buildings Survey)

# CHAPTER 1

# The Genealogy of
# the House

## A FORTUITOUS ANCESTOR

The oldest living relative of the contemporary American house—suitably stooping at the shoulders and creaking at the joints—is the home that Jonathan Fairbanks built for his family in Dedham, Massachusetts, in 1637. The effects of time and hundreds of harsh New England winters have taken their toll. The aged house, with additions of later years, sags badly. As if in imitation of the cycles of freeze and thaw that have heaved it out of plumb, it has the look of some great ice sculpture that partly melted and then froze again in a surrealistic semblance of its original shape. Yet it is a tribute to its strong timbers that it stands at all. It was only seventeen years after the landing at Plymouth that this house was built, and it is the oldest extant dwelling of that first wave of English settlement. In fact it is arguably the oldest house of all—the oldest living relative of a most prodigious family.*

---

* The date of the Fairbanks House is commonly given as 1636. Abbott Lowell Cummings's authoritative *Framed Houses of Massachusetts Bay* cites it as 1637 and that is the date used here. The discrepancy owes to a long-perpetuated failure to adjust the date of Fairbanks's being accepted as a Dedham townsman—from March 23, 1636, under the Old Style (Julian) calendar to the New Style (the Gregorian, adopted by England in 1752), by which it would be March 23, 1637. It was presumably just after this date that Fairbanks undertook construction of his house. Other early houses still in existence—among them the John Humphrey, John Balch, Deane Winthrop, and Hoxie Houses in Massachusetts and the Adam Thoroughgood House in Virginia—are frequently ascribed dates contemporaneous with the Fairbanks. But recent scholarship (Cummings's in particular) strongly suggests that all are more recent than 1637 by anywhere from a year or two to perhaps a century or more. The Fairbanks House, its original structure almost completely intact (and never altered even to the extent of installing plumbing and electricity), is thus arguably the "oldest living relative" of the American house as it is seen in this book.

*The Fairbanks House, Dedham, Massachusetts: stooping at the shoulders. The central section, built in 1637, is flanked by additions dating to the early 19th century.* (Historic American Buildings Survey)

For various reasons, the Fairbanks House is a fortuitous ancestor from which to trace the genealogy of the American home. It is a wood-frame house, as are the vast majority of homes in America today; it is more or less average in size; as a household, it is easily recognizable by modern standards in its configuration of living, eating, and sleeping spaces; and it is quantitatively average by that basic yardstick, its taxable value: The earliest recorded tax valuation for Dedham, that of 1648, placed the Fairbanks home at £28, just above median for houses valued at from £2 to £45 (the latter amount being for the home of the minister, who in early colonial New England usually had the most sumptuous residence, relatively speaking, in town).

But what of the house as a place to live, and what of the people for whom this now ancient dwelling once bore the smell of fresh pine flooring or newly hung clapboard, much as a modern house the characteristic pungency of new carpet and fresh paint? To start with Jonathan Fairbanks himself: From what scant bits of information still exist, we know that he was a man of moderate means who grew up in the small village of Sowerby Bridge in Yorkshire, England, having been born at the very end of the 16th century. There is better information about his other vital dates: He was married in 1617 and died in 1668.

If he was born just before the end of the 16th century, say in 1598, this would have made him about thirty-five when, in the early to mid 1630s, he made the formidable decision to uproot his family and join the growing ranks of his countrymen who were seeking to establish new lives in the New World.

By that time Fairbanks and his wife, Grace, had six children—John, George, Mary, Susan, Jonas, and Jonathan, Jr.—ranging in age from late teens to infancy at the time the family set sail for America, probably in summer.

As a lot, their lives intertwined with colonial history much as many a similar family. John married in 1641; eventually, through primogeniture, he inherited the homestead and remained there the rest of his life. Mary in 1644 married the Metcalf boy from down the street; Susan married in 1647. Little Jonathan stayed in Dedham all his life and was nearly eighty when he died.

But alas, two of the Fairbanks children had unhappy endings. George drowned in 1682 after having moved to what is now Medway, Massachusetts, taking up the life of a farmer. Jonas moved to Lancaster, Massachusetts, then the frontier, in 1657 and had the misfortune to be in the settlement one day in February 1676 when the Indian sachem King Philip and fifteen hundred of his warriors swarmed Lancaster, killing at least fifty of the settlers, Jonas among them. By a twist of irony, one of Jonas's sons was killed in an Indian raid in 1697.

Distant fates unthought of, this was the family that set out from England, its immediate concern the safety of an ocean voyage. If winds and weather were on their side, they crossed in four and a half weeks; if not, perhaps in as much as two months. Once in America, the Fairbanks family made the Boston area

their temporary home until a permanent place of settlement could be decided upon. For the next year or two this temporary site provided shelter for the family and the possessions they brought with them, including a set of china, an oaken chest full of English goods, basic furnishings, bedding, and clothing.

After the family's arrival, Fairbanks began looking about for a permanent homesite. He found it just south of Boston, in a town created by the General Court of Massachusetts in July 1636 in response to petitions from colonists seeking homesites. Some starry-eyed among the petitioners had wished the town to be called Contentment. The court settled on Dedham, following the early New England custom of transporting place names from the homeland. Dedham is a village in East Anglia, from

*Built later in time (c1710–1720) is the Buttolph-Williams House in Wethersfield, Connecticut. With no additions over the years, it presents an appearance remarkably similar to what the Fairbanks House looked like originally, before its 19th-century additions.* (Photograph by the author)

which region a disproportionate number of the earliest Massachusetts settlers came. (It was East Anglia that contributed to the map of Massachusetts such place names as Attleboro, Braintree, Cambridge, Essex, Haverhill, Ipswich, Lynn, Malden, Norfolk, Sudbury, Suffolk, and Yarmouth.)

Fairbanks was not among the twenty-five original town fathers, those who were the first signers of Dedham's covenant; but on the recommendation of one John Dwight at the town meeting of March 23, 1637, Fairbanks was "accepted and subscribed" as one of Dedham's own and took his place among the governing members of the community. It was presumably

after this—during the spring, summer, and fall of 1637—that he built his house. The site was a twelve-acre tract, the usual grant in Dedham. The land was given the settler on condition he build within a reasonable period of time. Should he wish to sell, he needed the permission of the town. Fairbanks's lot was on East Street, somewhat removed from the center of the village; the most central lots went to the first signers of the covenant. His neighbors would be John Rogers and Timothy Dalton, the latter one of only five Dedham settlers with anything more than a rudimentary education. The lots, though spacious by later-day standards for a village, were greatly elongated, so

*Dedham Village, c1637. The Fairbanks property is the shaded area straddling both sides of East Street (the house itself being just to the left of the street). Two doors to the right are the Metcalfs; it was the Metcalf boy whom daughter Mary Fairbanks married in 1644.* (Dedham Historical Society, *Plan of Dedham, 1892*)

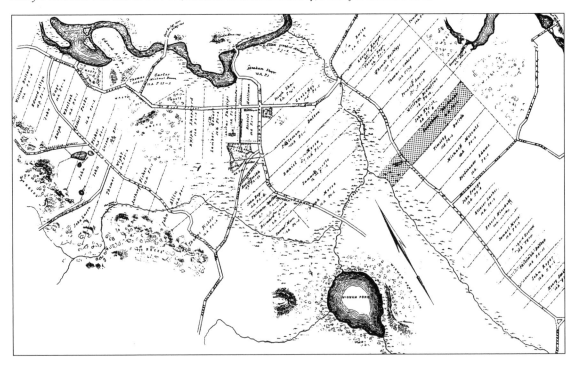

that the distance between neighbors was only in the hundreds of feet. The intent seems to have been to concentrate population and thus discourage attack by the Indians; and indeed, there is no record of any such attack in Dedham. But this arrangement was also typical of a medieval English town. Houses were built on "burgages," narrow strips of land with little frontage but enough depth to reach another lane in back.

On this site, with the help of experienced carpenters and masons and the assistance of neighbors in raising the frame of the house, much like a barn raising of more recent times, there went up a timber-frame house two stories high, with a dimension of 34 by 17 feet and four rooms in all. This is as much of the house as there would be in the years immediately to come. There would be a lean-to added in back c1660; enlargements in the early 19th century would increase the overall length of the house to 73 feet.

As accommodation for a family of eight, the original house of 1637 was tight by modern standards but larger than many of Dedham's first homes and considerably more spacious than those of the first settlers at Plymouth only a few years before. Most of those were one room, two at most, even for a family the size of Fairbanks's or larger, sometimes including relatives outside the immediate family.

The Fairbanks House had four rooms—two below, two above—conforming to a basic house plan that had been evolving in England. A massive central chimney dominated the interior. In front of the chimney was a tight, steep staircase to the second story (or perhaps at the outset only a ladder, the staircase coming later). To the right downstairs was the parlor;

to the left, and slightly larger, the hall. The latter designation may be perplexing to modern readers until analogy is made to the great hall of the medieval manor, from which this hall, though greatly diminished in size, was descended. This hall, like the great one, with its massive fireplace for cooking as well as heating, was the all-purpose room: for preparing meals, eating, working, gathering—"living" in its most active sense.

The parlor too was a "living room," also with a fireplace, but a more passive place for quiet conversation or perhaps to receive guests. This was the "best room" and would contain the family's best furniture—including the best bed: for, come nightfall, especially when there was a large family, the parlor turned into a bedroom, and this would almost certainly have been Jonathan and Grace's.

Upstairs were two rooms called chambers—in this case, hall chamber on the left, parlor chamber on the right. It was presumably upstairs that John, George, Mary, Susan, and Jonas slept; the infant Jonathan, at the outset, would have used a cradle in his parents' room. It may be that the girls had one room and the boys the other, but that is by no means certain. Families were used to doubling up and making the most of whatever space there was, with no concern for the kind of privacy that is taken for granted in the 20th century. Almost certainly there was not a bed for each child, nor necessarily a bed for any of them. It was common for children to sleep on the floor using a straw mattress and bedding that had been rolled up and stored away in the corner during the day.

The hall chamber had no fireplace, unlike the parlor chamber. This also may have prompted

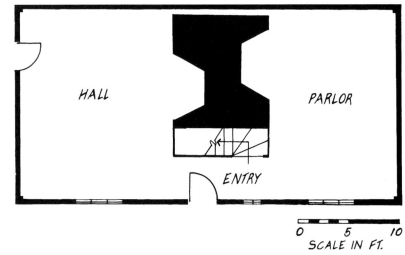

*The Fairbanks House: ground-floor plan. The all-purpose hall is just slightly larger than the parlor. The massive central chimney stack, as opposed to an end chimney, retained and radiated heat within the structure.* (Drawing by Dolores Malecki-Spivack, architect)

the children all to sleep in the latter. It may also be noted that an inventory of 1668 showed the hall chamber containing small tools; wool, linen, and cotton yarn; hops; and various odds and ends. But by 1668 all the children were grown and on their own, so the inventory would not in itself establish how the upstairs was used for sleeping when they were young.

Besides the four main rooms there was the loft, or attic, reached by a ladder and probably little used except for long-term storage. More useful was the cellar. It kept food relatively cool in summer and very cool but not frozen during the winter. Storage of food was the cellar's principal function, but it was not without 20th-century analogy in another respect. The same inventory of 1668, following Jonathan's death, showed the Fairbanks cellar to contain "2 vises and one turning lath and other small things"—the stuff of a basement workshop of later times. Beyond these simple amenities was the privy, somewhere out back.

This, in brief, was the house into which the

Fairbanks family moved one day in 1637, or possibly 1638. It was basically the modern, average middle-class house of its time. In size, shape, overall appearance, and general level of comfort, it was in keeping with what a family of similar circumstances would have enjoyed in England. The notion that early New England homes were "puritanical" in the sense of being austere is contradicted by this oldest surviving example. The first houses at Plymouth, to be sure, were in many cases barely hovels. As contemporary chronicler Edward Johnson wrote in his *Wonder-Working Providence,* some of the first settlers had to

burrow themselves in the Earth for their first shelter under some Hill-side, casting the Earth aloft upon Timber. . . .

In other words, a few of the houses (not all) were partially dug out of the earth; above ground, there was a simple superstructure of timber covered with thatch down to ground level. But these were understood to be temporary houses pending division of land into permanent homesteads. Little more than a decade later, it was taken for granted that homes were permanent and that living conditions ought essentially to equate with those left behind.

Looking at the external appearance of the Fairbanks House as of 1637, we find qualities that suit both our sense of the contemporary and Fairbanks's. As a two-story clapboard box with a chimney in the middle of the roof, it is like countless houses of the present day in virtually all areas of the country—what a real estate agent would list as a "Cape Cod" or a "Colonial." The principal differences are that the Fairbanks House has weathered clapboard (grayish in appearance) while the modern is usually painted (typically white, light gray, or some other light color) and that the windows are medieval-looking leaded casements with diamond-shaped panes of glass. That said, it must be noted that diamond panes are still fashionable today (occasionally as leaded glass but usually as simulations using plastic grillwork), and unpainted weathered clapboard siding on a house of this style is likewise in good taste. Taking the Fairbanks House as it originally looked, before it was considerably enlarged and before it started sagging, there is nothing about its appearance that would seem odd were it built today.

Whether Fairbanks's house was clapboarded at the time of construction is not clear. Dedham at first restricted clapboarding as a conservation measure; but on May 6, 1638, presumably after completion of the Fairbanks House, the village selectmen voted that "the Clapboarding of houses [is] set at liberty unto

*The Fairbanks House: the all-purpose hall* (top) *and hall chamber above it* (bottom)*. The hall fireplace reflects a modernization of the late 18th century—reduction in the size of the fireplace opening and relocation of the oven to the front. Otherwise, except for shelving, the room is essentially as it was in its earliest days. The upstairs chamber is shown fitted out for household work. This may well have been its original function since it is the other chamber that has a fireplace and that may have been the sleeping room for all of the children.* (Historic American Buildings Survey)

all men from this tyme forward." The clapboard on the Fairbanks House was hand-split lengths of cedar (some of which remains in place). These sections were considerably shorter than modern-day clapboard; and owing to the nature of hand splitting, they were not all even, giving a somewhat wavy appearance that sets off clapboard in its original form from its modern equivalent. The clapboard would have been left untreated, thus taking on a weathered appearance.

As for the roof: There is some evidence on which to conjecture that Fairbanks may have had thatch at first; but probably not, and even if so, shingles of cedar or pine would have been installed soon after construction, perhaps after the lifting of the ban on clapboard. Thatch was used on some early colonial homes. It can still be found on some houses in England, and at the time of American settlement was an exceedingly common roofing material for the vernacular house there. Thatch made a very good roof; if high-quality and properly installed, it might last fifty to sixty years. But that was in old England's wetter climate. Thatch is an obvious fire hazard when it becomes dry, as was more the case in America, and was quickly banned in towns and cities in the Colonies. Wet climate or not, it had also been banned in urban areas in England. Shingles fast became the norm for the vernacular house in America; larger, more expensive homes more often used slate or tile.

Thus to us today, as to his own contemporaries, the Fairbanks home of 1637 appears as a fairly representative sample of the vernacular dwelling. But in two respects it would have been noticeably modern to Fairbanks's generation. The clearest proclamation of up-to-

dateness, however, would perhaps escape the observer of today and be the least noticed; and that is its chimney. To appreciate this somewhat, let us go back to England a little more than half a century earlier:

> If ever curious [extraordinary] buylding dyd florish in Englande, it is in these our dayes. . . . There are olde men yet dwelling in the village where I remayne, which have noted three things to be marveylously altered in Englande within their sound remembraunce. One is the multitude of chimnies lately erected. . . . (Pastor William Harrison, of Essex, writing in Holinshed's *Chronicles,* 1577)

The chimney of the vernacular dwelling, as will be seen hence, was symbolically as well as literally an apex in the evolution of the house, and arguably a point of delineation between medieval and modern. It made possible much "marveylous alteration," most importantly a house of two (or even more) floors, since it was no longer necessary for the principal room—that containing the family hearth—to be open to the roof for the escape of smoke.

The second feature indicating "modern" would have been the windows, although on this point we have to allow some room for conjecture. We have no way of knowing, but given his relative means, we may guess that Fairbanks brought windowpanes with him from his house in Yorkshire. Window glass was expensive and far from common even in England. It was even rarer in New England in the early years of settlement; indeed, it was nearly unobtainable. Hence the need to bring glass along.

*Overcoatless: a half-timber house in England, with its more moderate climate.* (Drawing by Dolores Malecki-Spivack, architect)

Or, as advised Edward Winslow in a letter from Plymouth to prospective colonists back home in 1621: "Bring paper and linseed oil for your windows."

Oiled paper had often sufficed in England where there was not the means to possess glass; or, as in medieval times, a window was just an opening in the wall, protected only by a shutter or crisscrossed wattles and twigs. How many Dedham homes in 1637 had glazed windows, it is not possible to say. Certainly some homes; probably not all. But by mid century window glass was likely to have become common.

We have taken a look at the exterior appearance of the Fairbanks House. Now, suppose we figuratively remove that clapboard. We find not a skeleton framework, as would be the case with a timber structure of later date, but a house complete in its own right. The analogy is that of a man removing his overcoat; the body is already fully clothed, but not for the season that necessitates the overcoat. So too this house in harshly wintered New England. This same structure in England's more moderate climate did not need an overcoat (generally speaking, for there were some exceptions). It was sufficient for the house to be left in its traditional half-timber appearance—the look commonly associated with the typical Elizabethan cottage and its picturesque blend of exposed, dark-colored timbers in angular patterns interspersed with white plaster or herringbone brickwork. Half-timbering is perhaps most reflective of the English countryside but was characteristic of medieval and postmedieval northern Europe generally and Germany in particular.

Shorn of its overcoat, this was the Fairbanks House: a very typical half-timber structure looking for all the world like something transported from the English countryside. Half-timbering was a product of evolution in house building. It made no apology for having its basic structure showing; it took delight in it. Here were the thrust and stress and tension of architectural construction, manifested just as the thrust and stress and tension of life were, say, in a work of Shakespeare, whose Globe Theatre itself was half-timber.

In England, this unovercoated structure was sufficient. The space between the timbers was filled either with bricks or with wattle and daub. It was a time-honored—indeed, in the case of wattle and daub, eons-honored, going back to prehistoric times—method of construction. The climate generally required no further "attire," though here and there, in England, weatherboarding, the equivalent of what is now better known as clapboarding, was used. The early colonists in New England, and to a lesser degree the less northerly colonies, found the climate too severe. The cold of winter was more than traditional half-timbering could cope with; and heavy winds and pelting rains sweeping in from the ocean had an especially pernicious way with wattle-and-daub infilling. The recourse, almost universally, was to cover the structure with clapboard, or, in time, with shingles.

Underneath remained that same rugged, "stronge in timber" structure. Its appearance of ruggedness owes in part to existing wood-cutting technology.* This was the age of timber as opposed to lumber. Lumber is part of a later age, a machine age, that readily allows wood to be cut to precise and relatively small dimensions—into the traditional two-by-four, for example. In 1637 and for ages before, houses were built of hand-hewn timber. To hand hew a tree trunk into an 11- by 11-inch summer beam was one thing; to hand cut it all into two-by-fours was out of the question.

Hence the principal units of the frame were relatively massive pieces of timber. Lesser units—studs, joists, purlins, and so on—were sawed to lesser dimensions, but still of a size larger than would be produced later by mechanized sawmills.

This ruggedness of frame also dictated method of construction—mortise and tenon, which like wattle and daub goes back to prehistoric times. Nails were used as well—to attach the clapboard, for example. But clearly a few nails would hardly do for the junction of a 5- by 5-inch rafter with a 7- by 7-inch roof plate. The mortise was cut using auger and chisel. Into this went the tenon, sawed and chiseled. The juncture was then secured with a wooden peg known as a treenail.

The resulting simple yet sophisticated structure was the house that arrived with the first permanent settlers and that set the pattern for the most common of vernacular houses in America.

## FROM HALL TO HOUSE

Here we have had a brief look at a more or less typical early colonial house both inside and out: clearly modern, clearly up to date for its time. It had a chimney, fireplaces, upstairs and downstairs, an attic, a small cellar, and perhaps

---

* Sample structural components of the original Fairbanks House include summer beams, 10″ × 10″ and 11″ × 11″; roof plates, 7″ × 7″; rafters, 5″ × 5″; studs, 4″ × 6″. The summer beam was either bridging (lengthwise with the house) or binding (crosswise) and was a massive beam in the center of a room supporting the floor structure above. It is perhaps the most striking feature of an early colonial room because it is so unusual from a latter-day perspective; jutting down 10 or 11 inches, it can also be striking if one doesn't watch one's head.

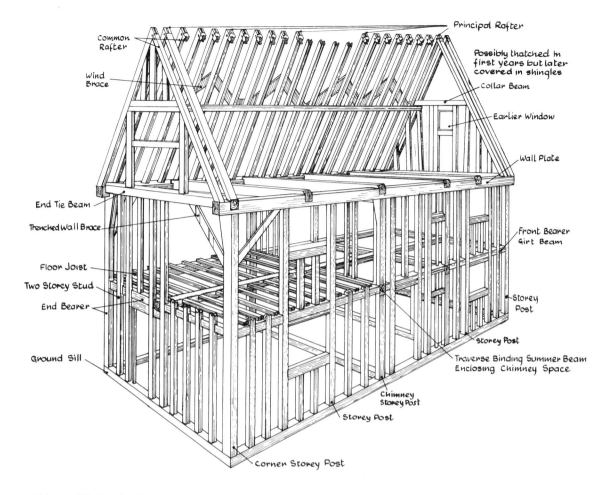

Principal Rafter

Possibly thatched in first years but later covered in shingles

Collar Beam

Earlier Window

Wall Plate

Common Rafter

Wind Brace

End Tie Beam

Trenched Wall Brace

Floor Joist

Two Storey Stud

End Bearer

Ground Sill

Front Bearer Girt Beam

Storey Post

Storey Post

Traverse Binding Summer Beam Enclosing Chimney Space

Chimney Storey Post

Storey Post

Corner Storey Post

(Above) *The Fairbanks House: internal structure. While it may appear to "stoop at the shoulders," the rugged timber frame of the Fairbanks House otherwise underlies its longevity. Its structural components include studs 4 by 6 in., rafters 5 by 5 in., and summer beams as large as 11 by 11 in., all assembled with mortise-and-tenon joints. The interstices in the walls are filled with wattle and daub, as in a typical English half-timber house, but the house has an "overcoat" of clapboard. The roof originally may have been thatch but was soon (if not at the outset) shingled.* (Illustration by June Strong. © Fairbanks Family in America Inc.)

(Right) *The housebuilder at work.* (Drawing by Dolores Malecki-Spivack, architect)

windows with glass panes in them; it was adaptable to the climate of its locale; and it was intended to be permanent in its construction (in retrospect, even more so than its builders might have imagined).

To understand how this was modern, and why the house was of this configuration, we must look back to what had been evolving for several centuries. This takes us to the medieval manor house, which, although hardly vernacular in its own right, gave a sense of direction to the shape of the simpler house.

While the manor had its other minor habitations (chiefly crude tenants' huts) and the manor house its lesser rooms, the great hall of the house was the center of life. Here congregated the many whose lives were wholly bound to the life of the manor. Here, in the great hall, they performed their many and often menial functions by daylight; here they took their meals; here by night they curled their weary limbs on whatever might serve for sleeping, be it a bench or the floor itself. Here also did the lord and his retinue hold forth, though to pass the night the lord and his lady often had private quarters. The focus of the hall and indeed of manor life was the open hearth—a great open bonfire in the middle of the room, tamed only by its stone bed and overlarge andirons, all in all a giant juxtaposition of the primitiveness of open fire against the grandeur of the great hall, its massive stone walls stretching up to a darkened timber ceiling, to louvers through which the smoke of the huge hearth managed, more or less, to find escape.

In its classic configuration, the great hall at one end had its dais, on which the nobility ate and in early times slept as well. Within the hall were long tables and benches at which the common people ate. Since this was also the sleeping room, the floor was strewn with rushes. Windows were few and, except in such cases as a bay window in back of the dais, were often unglassed; shutters had to suffice in cold and inclement weather.

At the end opposite the dais was a transverse passageway, screened off from the hall proper and connected to the main entrance on one side and a back entrance on the other. Sometimes the passageway was ceiled over, allowing for a minstrel's gallery above. The whole of the passageway came to be known as *the screens,* for the sometimes movable partitions that literally screened the passageway from the hall.

The hall in its earliest form was virtually self-sufficient; by the 14th century it had undergone a degree of evolution that would have eventual impact on the vernacular house. Beyond the dais, there came a wing that was exclusively the province of the lord and his family—the solar block. Unlike the hall, which was open from floor to roof to accommodate the open hearth, this area was usually two-storied; the rooms were either unheated or made use of small braziers. The solar was the private bedroom and sitting room of the lord and his wife and was always on the second floor. Underneath the solar was another private sitting room known as the *parlor,* a term derived from the name for the private room in a monastery set aside for outsiders and religious to converse. The solar block might also include a private chapel and perhaps a lady's bower. Curiously, *parlor* has remained a part of the nomenclature of the house to the present time. *Solar* has been so totally forgotten that most dictionaries do not even include its medieval sense; the modern term *solarium* derives from the Latin *sol,* 'sun', and has no connection whatever with the medieval *solar,* which probably comes from the French *sol,* 'floor', or *solive,* 'joist' or 'rafter'. However, it should be noted that such nomenclature was very fluid in the Middle Ages; terms like *bower, solar,* and *chamber* were not used consistently. Bower and chamber might be on the first floor or the second. In a peasant house, *chamber* usually meant a sleeping room if there was a separate room for this. It had this use in America for many years, as a second-floor bedroom.

On the other side of the screens came a service area consisting of the *pantry* (from French *pain,* 'bread') and the *buttery* (from French *bouteille,* 'bottle'). This was obviously the area set aside for processing and storing food and drink, although often a separate outbuilding served as a kitchen and some cooking was done at the open hearth.

Such was the great hall (and its dependencies)—a formidable and legendary place but not the epitome of comfort: cold and drafty in winter, clammy and smoky in summer, noisy much of the time. Hence custom and tradition changed. Even in the later 14th century, as observed in *The Vision of Piers Plowman,*

> Dull is the hall each day in the week where neither lord nor lady likes to sit. Now has every kingdom a rule requiring one to eat by himself in a private parlor or in a chamber with a fireplace and to avoid the great hall. . . .

Now, setting aside this essential layout for the moment, let us consider the housing of the common people, for clearly the great hall was the domain of the very wealthy. To the extent that retainers shared the hall, they account for a few of the common people; but what of the many? As was the case in Dedham, Massachusetts, in 1648, there is a tax valuation that gives us a clue—this one for the town of Colchester and nearby villages in Essex in 1301. Tax records show that the vast majority of residents had very simple houses. We may suppose that many were like those described early in the 16th century by Richard Carew as he cast his eye about Cornwall: the houses of the husbandman were

> walles of earth, low thatched roofs, few partitions, no planchings [floors] or glasse windows, and scarcely any chimneys, other than a hole in the wall [or roof] to let out the smoke.

In Colchester the goods and chattels of 384 houses (medieval taxation was based on personal property rather than real estate) were assessed for tax purposes, and this gives us at least some insight even though the houses themselves were not evaluated. Most of Colchester's houses were of one room only and seemed to have ranged downward from modest to subsistence-level. More than half of those recorded had no household goods worth enumerating, or only such basics as a bed or two and some cooking utensils, including andirons for their open hearths. At the other end of the scale, there were eighteen houses of three or more rooms and another twenty of two rooms. Among the most affluent eighteen of Colchester's residents was Roger the Dyer, whose house consisted of a central room with a fireplace, a sleeping chamber, a kitchen with its own fireplace, and a brewhouse that he apparently also used for his dyeing business. In its proportion of homes like Roger's compared with modest to subsistence housing, Colchester was probably typical of a town of the later Middle Ages.

To return to Richard Carew. "Walles of earth" may have been a reference to the clay daubing of wattle-and-daub timber huts or to walls of either turf or sod. Where it was plentiful, stone, mortared or unmortared, was also used for even meager huts. Thatch was predominant for roofs, although turf was sometimes used. Floors were of earth, often covered over with reeds or straw. If there was a window, it had no glass—at best, just a shutter or perhaps latticework. An open hearth was used for both cooking and heating. This had been the most basic house from time immemorial.

With the waning of the Middle Ages came the emergence of a class that was neither lord nor lowly laborer. The breakup of the manor system produced the small independent farmer—the yeoman, and just below him the husbandman—while newly developing villages and towns spawned increasing numbers of tradesmen. The 16th century was also a time of great economic growth in England. An expanding economy, producing greater affluence for the emerging middle class, in turn produced a building boom during the 1500s. New houses, with higher standards of comfort and convenience, were built; old ones were remodeled and updated. Thus the observation of William Harrison:

> There are olde men yet dwelling in the village where I remayne, which have noted three things to be marveylously altered in Englande within their sound remembraunce. One is the multitude of chimnies lately erected. . . . The second is ye great amendement of lodginge. . . . The thirde thinge they tell of, is the exchange of treene [woodenware] platters into pewter, and woode spoones into silver or tin. [Even] inferiour Artificers and most Fermers . . . have learned also to garnish their cubbordes with plate, their beddes with tapistrie, and silke hanginges, and their tables with fine naperie.

Just as their cupboards were coming to resemble those of knights and other wealthy sorts, even if on a very modest scale, so were the houses of the middle class. Let us look at the emerging "modern" house of the great majority through the first two of Harrison's observations.

First, as to a "multitude of chimnies": The legendary great hall, we may recall, had an open hearth—an indoor bonfire, in a sense, whose smoke made its way out through an opening in the roof. By the 14th century the fireplace was coming into use. At first it was just an opening in the wall to take the place of an opening in the roof. The theory was that the smoke would blow directly out rather than billow around the hall on its way aloft. And the theory was good as long as there was no wind to blow it back into the room. A better solution was found in constructing a chimney adjacent to the wall, and this led to the fireplace.

In more modest houses, the open hearth prevailed. Often there was not even an established exit for smoke, which had to make its way out an open door or through chinks in the roof. The result was all too often what Chaucer related of the home of the poor widow in his tale of Chanticleer and Pertelote: *ful sooty was hir bour and eek hire halle* (full sooty was her bower and also her hall).

An opening in the roof helped, but instead of louvers, often highly decorative on the manor house roof, there may have been only a barrel with both ends removed to serve the same purpose on the simpler house. An early step in the evolution of the chimney was construction of a simple canopy, or hood, over the hearth, placed so as to collect and conduct smoke out through an opening. It was sometimes of stone but more often timber and plaster; in the latter case, although hardly fireproof, it worked, with adequate precaution. Such fire hoods were still in use among some of the first settlers at Plymouth.

What made full chimneys practical was the flourishing, chiefly in the 15th century, of an old art that had been forgotten in England since Roman times—brick making. Stone could be, and was, used for chimneys, but largely in the homes of the wealthy. Bricks were cheaper and far easier to work with, and they began to make chimneys practical in all those new and remodeled homes that were part of the building boom of the 1500s.

A chimney allowed for a fireplace, which was considerably more efficient than the open hearth. More significantly, it also became unnecessary to keep a central room open to the roof to allow for the exit of smoke. Space above, which was heretofore wasted, now could become a second story. In the case of an existing home with an open central room, it was a matter of remodeling—attaching cleats to the posts and studs of the frame and running beams and joists across. The posts and studs of

the medieval house were normally the full height of the house. Once chimneys came into use and new houses were constructed with two stories, each story came to be built as a box of its own. Thus, as a generality, a house with studs two stories high is medieval; if the studs are one-story, it is postmedieval. (The cycle will repeat itself with balloon framing in the 19th century, but that is getting ahead of the story.)

The hall that was the nucleus of the great manor house was at first virtually the entirety of the house. As the manor house evolved, it subdivided, producing the solar block at one end and the service block at the other. Likewise, many of the homes of the emerging middle class, particularly in the 16th century, subdivided in much the same way, although on a far smaller scale. For a time there often remained a central core, open to the roof for the exit of smoke, as well as a service area and a parlor, one or both perhaps having lofts above. Since these, in effect, were separate structures attached to the hall, each might have its own separate roof. This produced a tendency toward elongation of the house. But the chimney was a counterforce tending toward compactness. If the chimney were in the center, it could heat two or more rooms from its single stack; and the house, instead of stretching out to gain living space, could gather itself around a central chimney and grow vertically, thus adding rooms by having a second floor.

Meanwhile, the function of the service area had been largely (and often entirely) absorbed by the hall, and the sleeping function of the solar block by the parlor. Although there were other variations, including one-room plans this was essentially the evolution of an English house to which one may look in seeking an ancestor of Jonathan Fairbanks's.

## STILL EARLIER BUILDERS

The vernacular house in America might have been predominantly of brick or stone, but it is not. From the start, timber has been the overwhelming favorite for building. Timber was clearly the most familiar form of construction among the earliest colonists, and it was the most suitable for a new continent that appeared to have boundless reserves. Wood, furthermore, has distinct advantages. Among standard building materials, it is the easiest to work with; it is versatile; it is light relative to its strength; it has inherent insulating properties; and it is the most economical: For those of the new middle class who could not afford stone or brick, wood was a very viable, and less costly, alternative.

We have looked at the basic timber house of the late medieval period and have seen its construction: an equipoise of massive timbers hewed into posts and beams and rafters and lesser timbers sawed as studs and joists and purlins, its framework interfilled with a wattle of stakes interwoven with sticks and twigs daubed over with clay or plaster. As recorded in 1577 by William Harrison,

our houses are commonly strong & wel timbered . . . in their walles they fasten their Splintes or radles, and then cast it all over wyth clay to keepe out the winde, which otherwyse woulde anoy them.

Yet use of wattle-and-daub timber construction already existed in Anglo-Saxon times and was described by Alfred the Great in the preface to his translation of Saint Augustine's *Soliloquies*. Although the purpose of the preface was to liken the acquisition of wisdom to the gathering of timber in the forest, it provides documentation of house building in the late 9th century:

Gaderode me þonne kigclas and stuþansceaftas . . . and bohtimbru and bolttimbru . . . þat he mage windan manigne smicerne wah, and manig ænlic hus settan . . .

Gathered me then short sticks and posts . . . and branch wood [bough timber] and building timber . . . so as to wind [wattle] many a fair wall, and erect many a splendid house . . .

While many stone churches (and at least one of timber) remain from the Anglo-Saxon period, the houses of the common people are decipherable only through what remains have been excavated. Some were crude stone huts, with roofs of thatch. But timber was probably more prevalent. These huts and houses were constructed with vertical posts and covered in some cases perhaps with planking but probably most often with wattle and daub—much the same as houses of the medieval period although using a more rudimentary form of timber framework. However, a notable advance over earlier construction was the use of a wooden sill around the perimeter, a distinct improvement over driving wall posts into the earth, as had been done since time immemorial. This may have been inspired by the setting of the mast in the keel by shipwrights; and indeed, there are many parallels between shipbuilding and house building, and probably a number of refinements of the latter owing to the former that are no longer obvious. It is the Anglo-Saxon period that shaped England's tradition of building with timber, and by the end of that period England was probably preeminent in Europe, if not in fact in the world, in timber construction. This is due partly to the fact that England's shipbuilding tradition carried over to timber construction, and partly to the fact that whereas Rome had more architectural impact on the Continent, helping to shape its greater stress on masonry construction, the Roman occupation of England had less impact overall and none on the common house, which remained essentially unchanged from what it had been before the legions of Claudius invaded in A.D. 43.

It is thus in prehistoric times that we must seek the earliest recognizable ancestor of the Fairbanks House. But first, there is the question of what constitutes a house. What primal level of complexity separates basic human habitation from the nests and habitats of the lower orders of creation?

A cave? Animals also use caves for refuge and the nooks and crannies of caves for hibernation. What separates very early humans is that they sometimes piled branches against the cave opening as added protection from the elements and as a crude barrier against unwanted visitors. This represents a degree of adapation, yet the cave was clearly not a house. There was no construction, hence no structure. The likely next step was a crude hut. Now human beings were using their heads as well as the arms that had heaped the branches. This hut probably

consisted of branches resting against one another, forming a wigwamlike structure. More important, these early builders perhaps took turf and mud and daubed it around the exterior. Now, however rudimentary, there was something that could be called a structure; and it was a better structure for the combining of the structural materials available. And furthermore, those who lived there enjoyed a certain degree of control over location instead of being at the mercy of geologic happenstance, as with a cave.

And yet this habitation was not one bit more complex, not one bit more sophisticated, than a bird's nest.

Perhaps in a moment of inspiration early humans found that by leaving forks at the ends they could interlink the branches; and then, having a way to assemble a simple, conical structure, they turned the branches into poles by stripping off the leaves. Smaller branches and brushwood were then interlaced among the poles to form primitive walls. Or they may have made the walls with stones, saving their branches and brushwood for the roof.

But was this a house? There was structure and there was synthesis; yet the materials that were used all remained in the form in which they existed in nature (save the stripping of leaves from branches). Humans had not yet done anything to change what naturally existed. They had not yet, through their own intellect, improved upon the bird's nest.

Now let us look at a prehistoric Dedham that shows the human being as architect and engineer. While there were similar villages as early as 1000 B.C. in England (and much earlier elsewhere), the remains of an Iron Age village, dating to about 300 B.C. near Glastonbury in

Detail of roof construction of the Fairbanks House showing use of mortise-and-tenon joint. Also clearly to be seen here are the carpenter's chisel marks (Roman numeral III) matching this purlin to its proper rafter. (Photograph by the author)

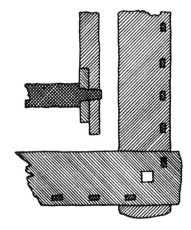

From the excavation of prehistoric Glastonbury, a mortised joint that was part of a rectangular hut. (Bulleid, *Glastonbury*)

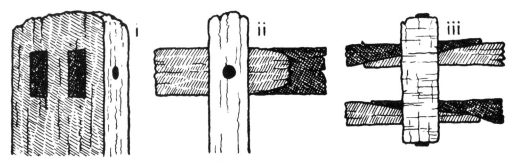

Three views of a mortised joint from prehistoric Glastonbury: parallel rails, iii, adzed to a wedge shape at their ends were inserted into mortise holes of a plank of oak, i, and then secured by an oak peg, ii—fulfilling essentially all the features of a mortise-and-tenon joint of later times except that in the later joint the tenons do not pass through. (Bulleid, *Glastonbury*)

southwest England, provide us with visual evidence not only of the evolution of the house but of how some of the most fundamental concepts of construction have remained with us fundamentally unchanged.

The village consisted mostly of round huts, a total of perhaps seventy that were actually used as habitations. They ranged in size from 18 to 28 feet in diameter. Here now we see the house as a distinct structure with walls and a roof. The walls, roughly 6 feet high, were constructed of wood posts driven into a base of clay about a foot apart. In between the posts were sections of framework known as *hurdles*, filled in with wattlework and covered with a daubing of mud or clay—basically no different than the wattle and daub of later half-timber houses. The roof consisted of poles serving as rafters (and perhaps, as well, cross members to counteract the outward thrust of the roof) and was covered with thatch. The entrance way was enhanced with a doorstep of stones. In the center of the hut was an open hearth, the smoke from which exited through a hole in the roof.

Round was basic—the shape of a simple stack of poles or branches. It was also less efficient in the use of space than a square or rectangle, which, however, required more complexity of technique to construct. At Glastonbury also were found remains suggesting a rectangular house: side sections, or hurdles, interspersed with upright poles, and nearby an oak beam—a beam, being straight, that could not have been part of a circular house. More notable is the fact that the beam had mortise holes along one side, parallel to the edge, the distances between the mortise holes matching

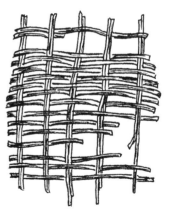

---

*The use of wattle and daub infilling at the Fairbanks House, and in still earlier homes of medieval Europe, in more primitive form goes back to prehistoric times. Wattlework* (top) *formed the walls of prehistoric Glastonbury huts; that the wattle was filled in with a plasterlike daub to create a solid wall is evident from the discovery of pieces of clay with indentations matching wattle found nearby. A section of wall at the Fairbanks House* (center) *shows that a certain similarity of structure not only existed then but continues to the present time in "wet wall" construction of plaster over lath. Construction similar to that in the Fairbanks House was still in use in the mid 19th century, albeit on a very limited scale. Shown* (bottom) *is a detail of wall at the Langholff House, Watertown vicinity, Wisconsin, built c1848. In this case it was construction known as* Fackwerk, *the equivalent of half-timbering, used by German settlers.* (Wattlework drawing by the author based on Bulleid, *Glastonbury;* Fairbanks House photograph by the author; Langholff photograph, Historic American Buildings Survey) the distances between the posts of the side sections. In other words, this was an ancient example of mortise-and-tenon construction, the mainstay of the half-timber house through the colonial period in America.

Also as in the later house was the apparent use of a very early form of wattle and daub. The hurdle-work sides consisted of twigs and branches interlaced among the upright poles—much the same as later wattle. That this was daubed over seems evident from the discovery of pieces of clay showing indentations identical to the wattle found.

So here we have an example of the house of the human architect and engineer. It was, by design, of a size and configuration appropriate to its use; it gave reasonably ample protection; it allowed for a hearth inside for heating and cooking; and it had such amenities as a doorstep.

At least some of Glastonbury's houses had front doors. One was a solid slab of oak, adzed to a thickness of from 1 to 1⅛ inches, with

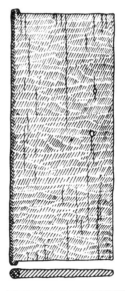

*A prehistoric front door from Glastonbury. The door was made of a solid slab of oak adzed to a thickness of from 1 to 1⅛ in. Pivots on the left side, top and bottom, served as primitive hinges.* (Bulleid, *Glastonbury*)

1-inch pivots on one side, top and bottom, that allowed it to swing open. Through that door, so recognizable yet so very ancient, let us now slip through time and see what the house will become once it has been transported to the New World.

# CHAPTER 2

# The House A-building

## The Building of a House, 1729

[Wednesday] June 25 [1729] Assisting in getting up ye boards & part of ye frame—
Matthias Ellis, Seth Stuart, Gamal[iel] Stuart,
Israel Tupper Junr, John Bodfish, Shuball Smith,
John Chipman, Edw Dillingham Junr, Seth Pope
Senr, Joseph [and] Peleg Fish.

A house a-building... this one in Sandwich, Massachusetts, the home of the Reverend Benjamin
Fessenden. A 1718 graduate of Harvard, Fessenden was ordained at Sandwich in 1722. In
1729 he undertook construction of a new house
of his own, employing both the professional help
of carpenters and masons and the volunteer
help of townspeople. Sandwich at the time was
a community of 136 families. In his diary, Fessenden kept a detailed record of the progress of

Drawing by Dolores Malecki-Spivack, architect

construction. It shows that work began in June 1729 and by October was essentially complete except probably for interior finish. This first entry, for June 25, refers to preassembly of sections of the framework.

The timber is cut from trees, oak and pine in particular, felled locally. The wood is then hewn to size with an adze and broadax. Frame members can be close to a foot square (corner posts, summer beams). Frame sections are assembled using mortise-and-tenon joints, pinned together with wooden pegs called treenails. There is generally no attempt to season the wood, except that wood for flooring may be the first cut so it has more time to dry before installation. Wherever a section of frame is to be attached to another during the raising of the frame, it is marked with a Roman numeral. A "VI," for example, takes three cuts with a straight-edged framing chisel, whereas a rounded Arabic "6" would be a practical impossibility with standard carpenter's tools. In effect, this stage of the building of the house is prefabrication of the basic structure.

[Thursday, June] 26 Stoning ye cellar—Joseph & Amos [Francis]

The start of construction of the cellar, presumably with uncoursed rubble stone. The cellar may be just a small section in one corner, as opposed to the full cellar of later times, and will be used primarily for storing food.

[Friday, June] 27 Stoning ye cellar—Joseph, Amos francis & Saml Oliver. pd franc[i]s 6 [pence], Oliv 1 [pence]. Setting ye Clamp of Brick—Deac[on] Tupper & his Sons Israel & Roland & Robin fuller pd a shill[ing]

While work continues on the cellar, other workers are setting up a clamp, or stack, of bricks for firing. The best of the bricks will be used for the chimney; others, perhaps, as infilling in the framework.

[Saturday, June] 28 Deac Tupper finishing ye clamp—Bringing up Timb[er] Lieut. Ellis & Grandf[ather] Lowe & Team—Deac Ellis, Brother Joseph, Amos francis, Robin fuller brought it up all.

Additional timber for completion of the frame—studs to space between the posts of the framework already assembled, purlins and rafters for the roof.

[Thursday, July] 3 Raised my House

Using poles, workers and townspeople raise the sections of framework assembled earlier—in the manner of a barn raising.

[Friday, July] 4 finished burning brick

[Saturday, July] 5 Carted boards—Bro[ther]s Joseph & Eph[raim], with Malachi's Oxen

Perhaps for the roof, which will then be covered with shingles of cedar or pine.

[Monday] July 7 Bro[the]r Joseph & Two Ephraims—carting stones with Seth fishs and Seth popes Oxen & brothers Horse

[Friday, July] 11 A very rainy day, ye Carpenters did not work

[Saturday, July] 12 Ye Carpenters at work

Perhaps now also a siding of hand-split cedar or pine clapboards nailed into the studs. This was still essentially the same post-and-beam construction as in the Fairbanks House. In some cases this outer covering consisted of vertical planking; but by far the most common sort was horizontal clapboard.

[Monday, July] 14 Ye Carpenters work

[Wednesday, July] 16 Carps at work—Deac Tupper, Isaac, Charles half a day—pd him all to half a crown—pd Amos francis 20 s[hillings] in full

[Friday, July] 18 Ye Carps at work—Bros wd not Work

[Friday, July] 25 Carted 2 loads of stones from Seth Fishs—Gershom Tobey loans Oxen

The stone is presumably for the foundation of the chimney.

(*Left*) William Fessenden, son of Benjamin: He made the house the Fessenden Tavern. (Photographs courtesy of the Sandwich Historical Society)

(*Right*) The house built by the Reverend Benjamin Fessenden in 1729 is believed to be the one indicated in this undated photograph, taken on Old Main Street in Sandwich, Massachusetts, in perhaps the 1870s or 1880s. The Reverend Mr. Fessenden became the minister of the First Parish Church of Sandwich in 1722 following the retirement of the Reverend Rowland Cotton and moved into the house Cotton had occupied near the church. He married in 1724 and by 1729 had three children (there would be four more). Wanting either a larger home or one more suitable to himself, Fessenden used the proceeds of a £250 settlement allowance to build, just up the street from the old parsonage, the house accounted for in his diary. After his death in 1746 the house passed to his widow, Rebecca. In 1789 the Fessendens' son, William (1732–1802), now the owner, turned it into a hostelry that became known as the Fessenden Tavern. It was renamed the Central House in 1857, and in 1915, by now having the additions at left and right shown in the photograph, became the Daniel Webster Inn, probably the best known inn on Cape Cod. The entire structure, including what is believed to be the 1729 house, was destroyed by fire in 1971.

[Tuesday, July] 29 Danl & Saml Wing at work—Deac Tupper & son Saml—laid [in the] P.M. found[ation] of ye chimney

[Wednesday, July] 30 Deac Tupper & son 4 tear [tier] of Brick

Work begins on the chimney itself. The mortar used in building it can be made by burning oyster shells. The shells are heated in a small kiln, which drives off the carbon dioxide, leaving a semblance of the shells as calcium oxide, or quicklime. This is then placed in a vat or pit and water is thrown on. A chemical reaction accompanied by a burst of steam produces a fine white powder, calcium hydroxide. When this is mixed with sand, it forms mortar; with the addition of horsehair, plaster for the walls and ceilings.

[Thursday, July] 31 Deac Tupper & son [worked] 2 thirds of a day—laid 6 course of brick [on the chimney]

[Saturday, August] 2 Carpenters at work

Perhaps now on some of the exterior trim—fascia, soffits, rake boards, door and window frames—which are nailed in place as opposed to the mortise-and-tenon construction of the timber framework.

[Monday, August] 4 Ye Masons at work—a good Days work—Stephen Nummock, bror & Eph

[Thursday, August] 7 Ye masons at work

[Saturday, September] 13 Ye Carpenters work to ye 16th Day of Aug. on my house at 7 s[hillings] pr Diem, amounts according to my computation to 25lb 9s, including the contingent bargain of 2 lb[.] In Sept ye work to ye 12th Day (since the commencement) amounts to £42. 12s. 9d.

[Saturday] Oct. 4 Ye Carpenters work at 7s pr Day comes to £56. 19s. 0d.

This concludes Fessenden's account. In its external appearance, the house would seem to be complete. Certainly it was habitable by the beginning of the winter season, so that any remaining interior work could be finished with less concern for the weather.

## BLOWS OF MALLETS
## AND HAMMERS

*The house-builder at work . . . the preparatory joint-ing, squaring, sawing, mortising, the hoist-up of beams, the push of them in their places, laying them regular, setting the studs by their tenons in the mortises according as they were prepared, the blows of mallets and hammers, the attitudes of the men, their curv'd limbs, bending, standing, astride the beams, driving in pins, holding on by posts and braces, the hook'd arm over the plate, the other arm wielding the axe, the floor-men forcing the planks close to be nail'd, their postures bringing their weapons downward on the bearers, the echoes resounding . . .*

WALT WHITMAN, the son of a carpenter,
"Song of the Broad-Axe"

At the same time that Fessenden's house was going up, echoes of hammers and mallets were resounding up and down the eastern seaboard and even into the hinterlands. The non-Native American population of the Thirteen Colonies when Jonathan Fairbanks built his house did not even reach 50,000. By 1700 it was more than five times that, and when Benjamin Fessenden was raising his frame, it was nearing a million. Many were newcomers to the New World; others were the products of natural population growth. As immigrants arrived and families grew and multiplied, the need for housing increased apace. Many were the new houses a-building; or in other cases, houses expanding to accommodate expanding families.

The Hempsted House in New London, Connecticut, for example. The Hempsteds were descendants of Robert Hempsted (c1600–1654), one of the original settlers of New London in 1645. It was Robert's son Joshua (1649–1687) who built the second (and existing) family homestead in 1678, the same year Joshua II was born. After the elder's death, the house passed to Joshua II, who married Abigail Bailey. They had nine children. Shortly after the birth of daughter Mary on July 29, 1716, Abigail died, though whether from complications or from illness is not known. It was a doubly tragic event in that the oldest son, Joshua III, aged eighteen, overcome by grief, took seriously ill and died following his mother's funeral (perhaps of the same illness?). This left Joshua II a widower responsible for eight children ranging in age from Nathaniel, sixteen, to the infant Mary. Joshua, contrary to the usual custom, never remarried. After Nathaniel, who married in his early twenties, died in 1729 at age twenty-nine, Joshua also raised Nathaniel's two sons.

It was Nathaniel's starting of a family that brought about expansion of the family homestead in 1728, exactly fifty years after it was built, although from a technical point of view the enlargement made the house a duplex since there were now two separate living units with two separate kitchens.

The original Hempsted House of 1678 has an appearance much like that of the Fairbanks House of 1637—clapboard, leaded windows like the original Fairbanks, a steeply pitched roof, an overall postmedieval ambience—but it is smaller than the Fairbanks, which had a central chimney flanked by a hall on one side and a parlor on the other. Here there is roughly half of that; the massive chimney abuts one wall, and the hall (there was no parlor) comprises most of the rest of the downstairs. This was a more modest home, but it offers a look at an interesting development in the evolution of the

SUSSEX COUNTY LIBRARY
NEWTON, NEW JERSEY

*Joshua Hempsted House,*
*New London, Connecticut*
*(1678/1728).*
(Photograph by the author)

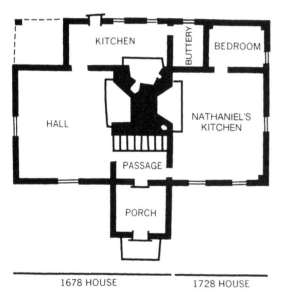

*Floor plan of the Joshua Hempsted House as enlarged:*
*The original 1678 house is from the chimney left, son*
*Nathaniel's addition of 1728 on the right. Space*
*identified here as "buttery" was added in the 1950s; the*
*original buttery is indicated by the dotted lines at left.*
(From Ronna L. Reynolds, *Images of Connecticut Life.*
By permission, Antiquarian and Landmarks Society,
Hartford, Conn.)

house. There is now a separate kitchen, in the form of a lean-to at the back. It was probably part of the original construction; and if not, it was added soon after. So we have evolution from the all-purpose hall; the kitchen as a separate entity was coming into use. We may suppose that meals were eaten in the hall, but not necessarily all the time. The kitchen is modest in size but has the usual immense fireplace of the time, so this would have been a *relatively* cozy room in cold weather, certainly warmer than the hall. Perhaps this kitchen served for many a winter repast or even just for sitting on a cold night.

On the second floor is the chamber that provided sleeping quarters for most of the family. When Joshua I built the house, he used the hall for himself and his wife as their bedroom, and the best bed was here, as, in a comparable way, for Jonathan and Grace Fairbanks it had been in their parlor. Joshua II, who was accustomed to sleeping upstairs, apparently remained there after becoming master of the house (and indeed the second floor generally became the more favored place for sleeping in the 18th century). There is also a full cellar as opposed to the corner-only that was the Fairbanks's.

So we have subtle but significant changes in layout and use. There is also evolution in construction. Gone now the "overcoat." The basic construction is still the same rugged mortise and tenon, post and beam as in the Fairbanks House. But the vestigial half-timbering has been superseded by what is essentially modern: on the outside, forming the outer fabric, oak and pine clapboard; on the inside, lath covered with plaster forming the interior wall. In between is insulation—in this case, as in many homes of the time near the coast, eelgrass from the beach. All things considered, such grass is reasonably good insulation; and with a high salt content, it also has fire retardant qualities. The windows are leaded casements.

One other exterior feature needs mention, and that is the "porch" (see photograph on page 30). The porch as seen here was not an uncommon feature of the postmedieval house in England (to be distinguished, both in size and function, from the "sitting out" porch that became popular during Victorian times; see chapter 4). Probably derived from the porch, so-called, of the medieval church, it was either an exterior shelter of the entrance way (as a projection of the chimney bay) or a form of vestibule just inside the front entrance. If exterior, it was commonly two-story and had a sleeping chamber on the second floor, as was the the case with the Hempsteds'. The projecting porch became popular (primarily in New England) in the second half of the 17th century; hence, there was none on the Fairbanks House

(1637), but there is on the original Hempsted House (1678). But this one is a re-creation, as are others from the same period. Postmedieval in appearance, these gabled projections were anachronisms in the 18th century as Georgian architecture became the fashion; and they were torn down if, in fact, the 17th-century house itself was allowed to stand.

Now let us look briefly at the enlargement of 1728, which extended the structure to the other side of the chimney, making a house roughly twice the size of the original. The first floor is mostly the kitchen, still very similar to the hall of the 17th century. In back, contiguous with the lean-to of the original house, is a small bedroom; upstairs, a large one. There is nothing atypical about the layout. But otherwise there are some striking features showing the evolution of the house even in just the past fifty years. Surely noticeable to the observer of 1728 was that the roofs of the two sections didn't match: One was higher than the other. The original 17th-century house continued the postmedieval tradition of a sharply raked roof. By 1728 roofs of lesser pitch were becoming more common—a trend that would continue until by the early 19th century a nearly flat roof was the "peak" of fashion. The disparity must have created something of a monstrosity, because Joshua saw fit to modernize his roof, adjusting its height to more or less equalize that of the new (in this case, like son, like father).

Another significant feature of the addition is its windows. By the early 18th century, leaded casements with their medieval-looking diamond-shaped panes were thoroughly passé. The double-hung sash window that is today so commonplace began appearing about 1700 and caught on almost overnight. So complete was the changeover that there is almost certainly not a single 17th-century house left in America with its original leaded casements intact; indeed, of even remnants there are precious few. Nathaniel Hempsted, born in 1700, naturally chose the new fashion and used double sashes on his side of the house.

As the 18th century wore on and a new generation of Hempsteds arrived along with a new generation of architecture known as Georgian, the house underwent further transformation to keep it up with the times. The porch was removed along with one remaining gable that clearly showed the house's 17th-century origin (Joshua had taken off another in making the roofs match), and those old-fashioned casements on Joshua's side were discarded in favor of double-hung sashes. What began as an asymmetrical, medieval-looking structure in 1678, a century later could pass reasonably well for a house of the new times—clean, symmetrical, dignified; if not really Georgian, at least Georgianesque.

Restored to roughly the original appearance that each side had when first built, the house still stands and is one of the country's most historic. Equally historic is the diary that Joshua II kept, beginning in 1711 and continuing until his death in 1758. Virtually every day, whether healthy or trembling with fever and chills, whether shaking with the biting cold of a frigid winter's night or torpid with the humid sultriness of the Connecticut shore in summer, he faithfully raised his quill to the self-imposed task of keeping a record of his time in meticulous detail. And since he wore so many hats—at some time or another he was farmer, surveyor, house carpenter, shipwright, attorney (before the day of law school and bar exams), stonecutter, coffin maker, gravestone engraver, merchant, whaleman, sailor, tradesman, justice of the peace, probate judge, overseer of widows, guardian of orphans—his diary is a remarkably complete yet remarkably crisp record of life in the 18th century.

It is also an account of what it means to be a home owner that transcends centuries of home owners' "oh what now?'s."

As for the 1728 improvement of his house, Joshua suggests there was more than just the size of his family to be reckoned with:

Thursd [July] 11 [1728]. a Thundr Shower In the Evening.

fryd [July] 12 fair. I was at home al d[ay]. foren[oon] mending ye house Stoping ye holes.

A month later there were apparently still some leaks:

Thursd [August] 8 Rainy most of the d. I was at home al day. Sowed Turnips & [worked] about ye Roof.

Mond [August] 19 Cloudy. I was at home al day about the Roof

Saturd [August] 24 fair. I was at home all day about the house. I finished Shingling the Roof where it was broke to put in the Coping plate.

At the age of fifty-two, Joshua was still tending to the equivalent of such modern chores as repainting the house—in this case applying pitch to the clapboard as a preservative:

Tuesd 18 [August 1730] fair hot. I was at home al day. I Tarred the Clabbords on the back Side of the Leantoo & mended it.

Wednsd 19 [August] fair hot. I was about home al day. I Tarred Some of the Clabords on the back Side my End of the Leantoo. they have been layed on above 20 years & are good.

Thurs 20 [August] fair. I was at home al day. I Tard ye E. End of house as high as ye Windows[.] 1. gall[on] tar {or pitch, used as a preservative on the clapboard].

A few years later, he was rebuilding some of the windows:

Saturd 14 [June 1735] fair. I was at home all day . . . fitting in glass and hanging a pr Casements that I have made ths week in odd hours.

He was still going strong at the age of sixty:

Thursd 10th [August 1738] fair. I was at home all day Shingling ye foreside of ye Stable.

Thursd 24 [August 1738] fair. I was in Town and bo[ugh]t 100 Cedar Clabbords 20s I pd for them.

By the venerable age of seventy-one the ills and afflictions of old age had finally caught up with Joshua Hempsted. Yet though he was hobbling about, he was still the caring steward of the old family homestead:

*"Thurs 20 fair. I was at home al day. I Tard ye E. End of house as high as ye Windows 1. gall tar . . ."*
—*Joshua Hempsted, diary, August 20, 1730. The Joshua Hempsted House, New London, Connecticut.* (Photograph by the author)

Mond 21 [August 1749] fair. I was about home able to Walk about, but Lame in my Legs arms Still. I workt a Little.

Tuesd 22 [August] fair. I had a poor night last night but little Sleep. when I Ly down my pain comes in my Shoulders & knees So that I am forced to Rise up & walk about to get Ease. 3 times up & down last night. I was at home all day Except that I went to Mr Shaws to get 100 6d [sixpenny] nailes. I am mending the back Side of the house Roof & Sides.

Stooping shoulders, aching knees, and all, Joshua Hempsted was still managing to keep up with the house at the age of eighty:

Wednsd 27 [September 1758] fair. Nathll bo[ugh]t for me as many cedar Shingles as comes to £3 6s 8d.

Saturd 30 [September] Cloudy Misty. . . . att home in the aftern[oon] Bundling up Shingles.

But that was as far as he could go. It was the last entry about the house in his diary. He died in December.

## ANOTHER TRADITION

Joshua Hempsted's house, characteristically New England, was a timber house in the English tradition. While timber was also common in the Middle Atlantic colonies, there was frequent use of stone as well, particularly by Dutch and German settlers. A quintessential example of a stone house is Elias Brunner's Schifferstadt, in Frederick, Maryland.

The Joseph Brunner family had immigrated in the late 1720s from Schifferstadt, Germany. Finding the land much as they had known it back home, they settled in the Monocacy Valley of Maryland and turned to farming with considerable success. Joseph's youngest son, Elias (1723–1783), in 1753 bought from his father a tract of 303 acres and thereupon set out to build the house that preserves the name of his German birthplace. The house was presumably completed in 1756, the date of a cast-iron

*Schifferstadt, Frederick, Maryland (1756).* (Photograph by the author)

stove that remains in place in an upstairs bedroom.

Schifferstadt is roughly 30 by 40 feet, built of sandstone with walls 2 feet thick. It represents what was familiar to the Brunners in Germany, and it is both a marvelously simple and marvelously practical design. The outer walls are stone, spanned by oak beams. In the center, also of stone, is a massive wishbone chimney—two separate stacks astride central halls on the first and second floors; just above the second floor these merge into one stack that rises through the roof. This design allows for a central hall on both the first and second floors. It is not a concept that has impact on the evolution of the house; but there are certain aspects of the layout of this house that do have long-range significance.

The emphasis on "through-ness" inherent in the wishbone chimney carries over to the layout as a whole: Windows on one side correspond with windows on the other; doors, with doors. This means cross ventilation—an evolving means of comfort. Comfort in this house, however, was most notably achieved through the use of stoves for heating. At the mid 18th century, most homes in America continued to rely, as they would for most of the next century, on fireplaces. In many cases the only real advance was the increasing use of coal burned in grates to make the fireplace more efficient, or a more modern configuration of the fireplace as espoused by Count Rumford (see chapter 3). But compared to the fireplace, the heating stove was a modern advance in comfort. Its cast-iron structure, once heated, continues to radiate heat even while the fire within fluctuates in temperature. Although set against a wall, it has presence by jutting into the room,

*This cast-iron stove dated 1756 at Schifferstadt is believed to be the only 18th-century stove in America remaining in its original location and condition. The stove abuts the chimney* (right) *and rests on a masonry base. It originally heated one large bedroom; as the family was growing, the room was partitioned into two using the stove to heat both sides. A gap was left between the partition (partly visible* at left) *and the stove for safety reasons.* (Photograph by the author)

its three or four sides plus top creating various planes all giving off heat in different directions, as opposed to the fireplace, which generates heat in only one direction.

Schifferstadt is presumed originally to have had two stoves upstairs and one down; the kitchen had an open hearth that could be used for cooking as well as heating. The stove remaining in place in an upstairs bedroom was cast by John Barr and Henry Stiegel at Elizabeth Furnace near Brickerville, Lancaster County, Pennsylvania. It is believed to be the only 18th-century stove in America remaining in its original location and original condition.

The stove is a "five-plate": three cast-iron plates as sides, another as the top, another as the bottom. What would be the sixth side of this rectangular box is open and abuts the chimney; through an opening in the wall the fire in the stove was tended from the central hall.

The house has two upstairs chambers, apparently for the children as well as for other household use. Elias and his wife, Albertina, slept in a first-floor chamber. In 1756 the family included sons Stephan, seven, and Peter, three. Another son, John, was born in 1759 and probably died in infancy; still another, also named John, was born in 1761.

Beneath the first-floor kitchen, and reached by means of an inside laddered passageway from the kitchen, is the *keller,* a vaulted cellar running the depth of the house that was laboriously excavated down to bedrock. It provided for year-round cold storage of foods, its suitably chilly temperature never wavering more than a few degrees between winter and summer. Iron rings that once held cured meats still protrude from the ceiling.

Outside there is an interesting contrast with the Hempsted House as remodeled in 1728: Here there is no attempt to simulate the stylish Georgian architecture that was now so much in vogue in the Colonies. But inside, there was practicality that transcends stylishness. Stove heating, with its greater comfort and efficiency, is one example. Cross ventilation is another, and the sizable *keller* still another.

There was also a kitchen sink. Here the point needs to be made that nothing comparable to the modern kitchen sink was yet in use. One generally used pails or tubs or basins for doing the washing in the kitchen and then emptied them outdoors. The sink in Schiffer-

*Although clearly primitive by modern standards, Schifferstadt's kitchen sink was a relatively rare convenience for its day. A slab of sandstone shaped to form a basin, it rested on the sill of a kitchen window and drained through a spout just below. Most kitchens relied only on buckets.* (Photograph by the author)

stadt's kitchen, to be sure, was still evolutional. It was a rectangular piece of sandstone scooped out to create a basin effect, and it sat on the sill of a kitchen window. The window did not need to be open. Water drained outdoors through a spout. There was as yet, of course, no running water in the house in the sense of modern plumbing; water used at this stone sink had to be brought in like water elsewhere. But the concept was there. A similar sink was in use at the Ephrata Cloister in Lancaster County, Pennsylvania, by 1745.

## THE EVOLVING TOWN HOUSE

By the eve of the Revolution, although America remained overwhelmingly rural, as it would until the late 19th century, city life was no longer an illusion. When Edward Johnson in the mid 1600s declared Boston already a "City-like Towne . . . whose continuall inlargement presages some sumptuous City" (Johnson's *Wonder-Working Providence*), it was somewhat before the fact. But Boston and the other centers of population were indeed continually enlarging. By the early 1770s the combined population of America's four largest cities was nearly double that of the entire settled East at the time Jonathan Fairbanks's home was built. Philadelphia, the largest of American cities, had some 33,000 residents; New York, 22,000; and Boston, 16,000. The South's largest city and commercial capital was Charleston with about 12,000 people.

The sound of hammers that accompanied this population growth was tending to become a little more concentrated. Joshua Hempsted's original house had no bounds imposed upon it. The house sat amidst sprawling farmland; and even when it was enlarged in 1728, there was still ample land and the house grew outward. Likewise Elias Brunner's sandstone fortress in the farmland of the Monocacy Valley, which spread outward with two additions in the early 19th century. But these growing cities were putting an increasing premium on available land as well as on walking distance as considerations in preserving compactness: and thus on the shape of the houses built there. Unlike the rural house that could expand sideways, the town house had to go backward or upward.

Row houses appeared relatively early in Boston, Philadelphia, and New York. In Charleston, South Carolina, likewise they could be found by the late 1600s. A disastrous fire there in 1740 pointed out the danger of having rows of houses, mostly wood frame, attached one to the other, and there evolved in Charleston the tradition of a narrow, detached house greater in depth than width (the so-called Charleston single house). Narrow houses also were dictated by the very narrow building lots in Charleston's first city plan, the "Grand Modell" of 1694.

It is one of these lots, No. 72, whose history—determined both through documentary research and archaeological excavation—provides another perspective for seeing the evolution of the house through the Colonial period. Lot 72 is what eventually came to be known as 87 Church Street, and by modern reference is just down the way from one of Charleston's most dominant landmarks, St. Phillip's Church. It is a very narrow parcel roughly 50 feet wide and 240 feet in depth and was granted to one Joseph Ellicott in 1694. Before the end of the year Ellicott had died, leaving the property, almost certainly undeveloped, to his son and two daughters.

Nothing more is known until the 1730s, when the property was now owned by John Milner. By at least 1737, Milner had built a house there and was operating as a gunsmith. Archaeological evidence shows that the house measured 24 by 18 feet and had a central entrance. Somewhat smaller in area than the Fairbanks House but without the latter's huge central chimney stack, Milner's dwelling had more usable space. It was apparently a two-story, wood-frame structure.

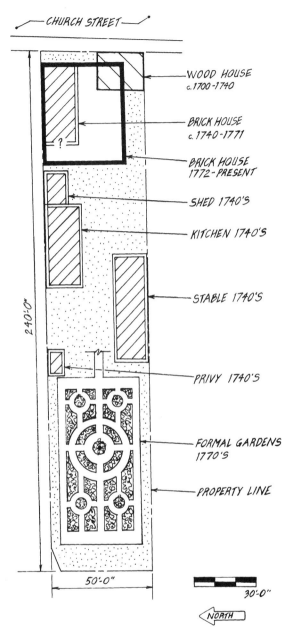

— CHURCH STREET —

WOOD HOUSE
c.1700-1740

BRICK HOUSE
c.1740-1771

BRICK HOUSE
1772-PRESENT

SHED 1740'S

KITCHEN 1740'S

STABLE 1740'S

PRIVY 1740'S

FORMAL GARDENS
1770'S

PROPERTY LINE

240'-0"

50'-0"

30'-0"

NORTH

*Lot 72 (87 Church Street) in Charleston, South Carolina: a sliver of colonial history. Created by Charleston's first city plan, the "Grand Modell" of 1694, lot 72 was the site of three different houses during the colonial period.* (Drawing by Dolores Malecki-Spivack, architect)

The fire of 1740 that devastated Charleston either destroyed or severely damaged Milner's house. Since much of his business was with the colonial government of South Carolina, maintaining and repairing arms, Milner filed a claim for reparation with the colony and was granted £154.

A new house of brick was built in the 1740s, this one abutting the north property line. It was 18 feet wide—less than half of Fairbanks's—but of greater depth (the exact measurement is not known). At about the same time, three outbuildings were constructed, and they survive to the present time—the kitchen, the stable, and the privy. A well, lined with barrels, may date from this period or earlier. There is archaeological evidence of three wells from three different periods—the earliest with a simple casing of barrels, the next a wooden box frame with barrel casing, and the last a brick well.

After the elder Milner's death in 1749, John Milner, Jr., carried on the gunsmithing business until 1768, when heavy debts forced him to sell the property. It was bought in 1770 by wealthy rice planter Daniel Heyward, who in 1771 sold it to his son, Thomas.

Thomas Heyward (1746–1809; commonly known as Junior to distinguish him from other Thomases in the family) was single when he bought the property but probably had a bride in mind when he demolished the small, brick Milner house and began construction of a rather elegant dwelling considerably larger than its predecessor. Late Georgian, brick, and 42 by 48 feet, this was a town house with spacious rooms, twelve in all, with large windows and high ceilings to ease the sultriness of Charleston summers. As for the winters, while they were hardly as severe as elsewhere in the Colonies, there was a still rare means of warding off the chill: the use of coal grates in the fireplaces. The coal came from England as ballast in ships and was then sold for a price that made it a luxury only the well-to-do could afford. For those who could, it was plainly better than wood in its greater heat and greater ease of tending. Heyward's wealth also showed in the built-in closets. As of 1772, few houses had even an occasional closet for china or linen. The Heyward House has two closets in each fireplace wall of a major room. These signified affluence not only in the additional construction expense but in the possession of enough worldly goods to make them useful. In other respects the house was usual for its time. The brick kitchen retained from the earlier house was a separate outbuilding, typical of the South. The privy was in back. The stable was also a carry-over from Milner's ownership.

As a town house this was also a place with the amenities of town life. Shortly after the house was built, a theater opened just up the street, and very nearby was the Parker and Hutchins variety store. Down the street by 1775 were a milliner and a doctor; across the street, a stationer and bookbinder; and just up a way an assembly room for dancing and fencing classes.

Heyward clearly did have a bride in mind; he married in 1773, likely while some construction work was still going on; and while he and Elizabeth Mathews Heyward also spent much of their time at their plantation, White Hall, near Beaufort, they used the house on lot 72 in Charleston frequently, especially during the peak social seasons.

Yet circumstances beyond the coming and going of the seasons had far more profound

*Thomas Heyward, Jr.* (Library of Congress)

*The Heyward-Washington House, Charleston, South Carolina (1772).* (Photograph by the author)

*Use of coal was still rare in America in the late colonial period. One instance of use was in the Heyward-Washington House and its fireplaces with coal grates. The coal came from England as ballast in ships and was a luxury only the well-to-do could afford. For those who could, it was a convenience worth the price.* (Photograph by the author. By permission of the Charleston Museum, Charleston, South Carolina)

*At Schifferstadt (left), the arch form was a pragmatic element of design: It incorporated a wishbone allowing for a single chimney shaft as an outlet for separate flues straddling an upstairs central hall. In the entrance hall of the Heyward-Washington House (right), the arch is a function of refinement, an expression of the full flowering of the architecture of the Century of Enlightenment.* (Photographs by the author; Heyward-Washington House, by permission of the Charleston Museum, Charleston, South Carolina)

consequence on how much Heyward would get to use his elegant town house over the coming years. His election to the Second Continental Congress took him to Philadelphia, where he was among the signers of the Declaration of Independence. He then served as a captain of artillery in the state militia, was captured, and was held as a prisoner of war until 1781.

During the first president's tour of the South in 1791, Charleston rented Heyward's house and made it George Washington's official residence during his time in South Carolina. Hence it is known today as the Heyward-Washington House. Heyward sold it in 1792 and retired to his plantation.

In the houses of the Fairbanks, Hempsted, Brunner, and Heyward families, covering both the time and geographic spans of colonial America, we can clearly see the progression of the house from postmedieval to premodern. When Thomas Heyward put his house on the market, dramatic changes in household technology were already taking place in Europe, England and France in particular—changes that would eventually have great impact on the comfort and convenience of daily life in America.

*Other traditions: Although English colonial architecture had the most significant impact on the shape and direction of the American house, other traditions—Spanish and French, in particular— are also a part of the American colonial heritage. For example: the Gonzalez-Alvarez House, St. Augustine, Florida (Spanish, early 18th century), Figs. 1–2, and the Bolduc House, Ste. Genevieve, Missouri (French, 1740), Figs. 3–4. Somewhat later came the Rancho La Brea Adobe in Los Angeles, California, c1828, Figs. 5–6. (Historic American Buildings Survey)*

4

5

6

# CHAPTER 3

# The House and the Coming of Technology

## GETTING MORE COMFORTABLE

On the banks of the Delaware downriver from Philadelphia stands the house in New Castle, Delaware, that George Read II built at the turn of the 19th century, the century that produced a revolution in technology. When the Reads moved into the house in 1803, Philadelphia was America's principal commercial city, and the river traffic gliding practically by the Reads' front door was the traffic of a rapidly growing national economy that would be the base of industrial growth ahead.

Besides being the commercial capital, Philadelphia arguably was also the capital of technology for its waterworks, completed in 1801—the first large-scale water-supply system and the first major application of steam power in America.

The age of steam in the New World, and thus of modern technology, began one day in March 1755 when an engineer named Josiah Hornblower opened a steam cock atop the boiler of a gangly-looking contraption then known as a fire engine, amidst what was almost certainly a cacophony of hissing and clanking. The site was the Schuyler copper mine in southern Bergen County, New Jersey, the largest such mine in North America, and the engine was used to pump water from its principal mine shaft. Hornblower's father had worked with Thomas Newcomen in the development of practical steam engines early in the century.

Although the Schuyler engine was successful in this first application of steam power—very successful by any measurement relative to the existing use of wind or water or draft horse or human arm to generate power—steam remained essentially experimental in America until the very end of the 18th century, when Benjamin Latrobe made it the motive force for the waterworks he designed for the city of Philadelphia. This also heralded, although not immediately, the eventual development of public water supply, which in turn had a profound impact on the evolution of the house in the century ahead.

Europe, and England in particular, had ridden the wave of innovation earlier, not only in the use of steam but in the application of technology within the house—and all for the simple purpose of making life easier, more pleasant, and more comfortable. Even before the turn of the 19th century, real estate advertisements in London were beginning to make the house seem relatively modern:

"convenient kitchen"—Highgate Hill, 1785

"breakfast parlour"—Vauxhall, 1790

"A Genteel MODERN HOUSE . . . [including] Water Closet and Cistern, supplied from the Main"—Park-street, Westminster, 1790

"numerous closets"—18 Chad's Row, St. Pancras, 1793

"water closet . . . capacious Eating Room" —Upper Harley Street, 1795

"Bed-Chambers with Closets"—Hampstead, 1795

"Dressing-room and Closets"—Woodford Essex, 1795

"Water-Closet on each floor"—Park Lane, 1795

"Dressing-room and Water-Closet"—Kensington, 1795

"powdering-room and water-closet" [on first floor]—Charlotte Street, 1800

"3 newly erected brick dwelling-houses, 2 spacious distinct cold-baths, 2 warm-baths, and a vapour bath, supplied with excellent water, flowing in constant succession together with a shower-bath, with copper and apparatus complete"—Horsemonger-Lane, Newington Grove, 1804

"airy bed-chambers"—Austin Friars, 1807

"6 bed-chambers, with closets [plus] water closet"—4 Woburn Place, 1815

In looking back at these contemporary-sounding references to powder rooms* and spacious, airy bedrooms and the like, we should remember that ads appearing in American newspapers of the time had scarcely anything as sophisticated to offer. Most American homes at the turn of the 19th century were little more advanced technologically than the Fairbanks House.

George Read II (1765–1836), living in the shadow of Philadelphia and its prominent application of technology, also had exposure to

---

* A powder (or "powdering") room c1800 was a place for powdering wigs but sometimes had a water closet attached, hence the possible derivation of the modern term.

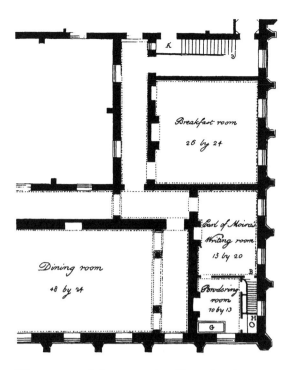

*The emergence of the more comfortable, modern house as heralded in London real estate advertisements of the 1790s and early 1800s: new concepts of space as evidenced in the more informal "breakfast room"; new concepts of convenience as expressed in the "powdering room" with bathtub, G, and water closet, H. Although powdering in this case still referred to wigs, the idea of the modern powder room was already intact. The detail shown here is of Donington Park, Leicestershire, the home of the earl of Moira, built 1790–1800. (Richardson,* New Vitruvius Britannicus)

the city's architectural prominence. There were probably more fine homes per square mile there than anywhere in America. Read, although he rarely traveled otherwise, did visit Philadelphia frequently and was clearly impressed with what he saw. When it came time to build his own home he constantly referred to houses he had seen in Philadelphia, instructing the carpenters to make lintels like this house, or windows like that, and so on.

It may well be that Read's visits to Philadelphia also provided insight into emerging domestic technology. Read undoubtedly mingled with people who were more widely traveled than he—Philadelphians who had been to England and had seen firsthand what was changing in the home there.

Read, aged twenty-one, in 1786 had married his first cousin, Mary Thompson, of Carlisle, Pennsylvania. They set up housekeeping at 10 Delaware Street in New Castle, a rented house, and began a family that eventually would number eight children. They lived in two more rented houses in the same neighborhood before buying Aunt Mary's house (Mary Read Bedford) at 6 The Strand in 1798. By now the family included sons George III, aged ten, William, six, and Gunning, one, and daughter Catherine, four. The year before, Read had also acquired property on which to build a house all his own, one that would provide space for a growing family. But that was not all he had in mind.

George Read II also lived in the shadow of a famous father. George Read I (1733–1798) had been a delegate to both the First and Second Continental Congresses and was a signer of the Declaration of Independence. It is largely a reflection of his influence in state politics that Delaware was the first state to ratify the Constitution, of which he was also a signer. He served as acting president of Delaware and was one of the state's first U.S. senators, resigning in 1793 to become chief justice of the Delaware supreme court. Despite being the most powerful force in Delaware politics in the 18th century, he was a rather humble man, clearly loved by everyone who knew him.

The son of this mover and shaker was hardly a nobody. George Read the younger was a lawyer and served for nearly thirty years as U.S. attorney for the state of Delaware. He was a captain of the Delaware Light Artillery during the War of 1812. But in his two forays into elective politics, he was unsuccessful; he lost both times that he ran for Congress.

His is nevertheless a name remembered. But whereas the elder Read is known to history for his impact on the building of a new nation, the younger is remembered for the building of a house. And it would likely not surprise him. When he set out in 1797 to build on his newly acquired lot at 42 The Strand, Read was clearly thinking in superlatives; he would build "the grandest house in Delaware," he once re-marked. And it was—at the cost of something like $2.5 million in modern dollars and of his being almost perpetually in debt.

What made the house (and makes it still) grand-looking is its obvious stateliness. Having first-floor rooms with a ceiling height of 13 feet, it is perforce so; but the effect is heightened by the great and imposing dignity of architecture: late Georgian blending into Federal. It has the simplicity of parts and resolute symmetry characteristic of Georgian. But its balustraded captain's (or widow's) walk atop the roof, functional here for the view of the Delaware thus afforded, is more an attribute of the Federal, and there is an even stronger manifestation of the new style in the front entrance, with its huge arch bordered with sidelights. The front door, although very formidable in size with a width of 4 feet 5 inches, yet looks small within the context of the entrance as a

*George Read II House, New Castle, Delaware (1804): part Georgian, part Federal, all stateliness (and inside, technologically modern).* (Historic American Buildings Survey)

whole. A high staircase of granite steps adds to the imposing formality. The overall effect is an elegant blending of old and new in architecture—or, as was probably the case, the picking and choosing of the best in Philadelphia. And indeed, Read hired a Philadelphia carpenter named Peter Crouding to supervise the early phases of construction.

The sheer size of the house was literally enough to cast a shadow over the rather modest and much smaller dwelling immediately next door—the rented home of George Read I. But the "Great Fire" that ravaged New Castle in 1824 took the home of the father and left the son with his measure of posterity intact.

The Read House took seven years to complete, from the digging of the foundation in 1797 until it was entirely finished in 1804. It was a house of twenty-two rooms, far above average. But it by no means represented a lot of space wasted for sheer effect of size. By the time they were all moved in and settled down in 1804, the family, besides George II and Mary, included George III, now fifteen, William, eleven, Catherine, nine, Gunning, six, Charles, three, and John, who was born shortly after the family moved in. (There would be two more children, Mary, born in 1805, and a girl, born in 1808, whose name is not a matter of record and who probably died in childbirth or almost immediately after.)

Besides the immediate family there were extended-family members and a sizable number of servants, all of them totaling between twenty and thirty persons making the Read House home at any one time.

Servants usually remain forever anonymous, but correspondence and personal papers of Read make identity out of anonymity. Probably the most important person outside the family was Juba Sharp, a free black man who received no salary but lived in the Reads' house and had all of his worldly needs provided for by them. Juba acted as something of a butler and valet but was also entrusted with paying bills and making purchases, and from time to time

*Father and son: George Read I* (above) *and George Read II* (below) *and their homes (the elder's* left, *the younger's* right), *as depicted in Benjamin Latrobe's "Survey of New Castle, Delaware," 1804 (detail).* (Portraits courtesy of the Historical Society of Delaware/George Read II House; Latrobe's survey courtesy of the Delaware State Archives)

was sent to Philadelphia or the state capital at Dover to attend to minor business matters for Read—no small degree of importance for a black in the early 19th century.

Another free black, Worrel Passaway, was a servant in the house and also ran errands. A slave named Sam also did servant duty, without the distinction of also doing errands. Other free blacks lived independently of the household and were paid a wage: Sylvia Rice, for example, did the cooking; Rachel Green, the laundry. A white woman named Susan Allcorn worked as a maid by similar arrangement; likewise Elizabeth Harvey as a housekeeper, and various other women as nursemaids. Indentured whites were also part of the live-in staff. At the time the Reads moved in, these included Alexander Roberts, age unknown, and children named Augusta and Joseph Reble, probably in their early teens. Augusta was perhaps a scullery maid and Joseph a stable boy. As indentured servants they received no wages, but Read paid pew rent for them at the Presbyterian church.

This was the Read House—in its concentricity of life not unlike a medieval manor. And to New Castle residents its imposing presence must have made it seem a very lordly place (although local artisans whose bills for work on its construction were rolled over month after month undoubtedly suspected the always-in-debt master of the house was not as rich as an imposing presence suggested).

## A VERY MODERN HOUSE

But New Castle residents only knew the house from the outside; it is the inside that is imposing from our point of view.

*The early 19th-century equivalent of an intercom: the bellpull system of the Read House connecting various rooms with this row of nine bells of differing pitch in the kitchen.* (Photograph by the author)

This was a *very* modern house in its day—way beyond the chimney and glass windows that had once signified modern. At a time when most people were still using only an open hearth for cooking, much the same as Grace Fairbanks, the Reads' servants (Mary Read did not need to cook) also had the absolute latest in kitchen technology—a Rumford oven and a steam kitchen. When many a weary housewife was hauling in water by the bucketful from a well out back, the Read household had water pumped into the kitchen. When most people rarely bathed beyond sponging body parts one by one in a basin, George Read could recline in a full-size tub near his bedroom on the second floor, a tub filled with *hot* running water. Or he could take a shower. Should he need the assistance of a servant, he could summon one from just about any room in the house through the equivalent of a modern intercom—a system of bellpulls connected with the kitchen. And should it be from bed that he desired a helping hand, he could unlock the door to his room without getting out from under the covers.

This was a modern household. To be sure, from the point of view of the age of computerization, a row of bells, each with a slightly different tinkle to denote the room whence rung, is pretty primitive. So too the cable and pulleys that stretched from bedside up and over the door frame to the lock on the door; we could manage the same trick electronically with nary a wire in sight. And that tub full of hot water: Existing technology only managed to *fill* it with running water; when Read finished his bath he still had to ring one of those bells for a servant to come and bail out the used bathwater with a pail, for there was yet no system for draining the tub. As to the shower: It was a painted tin box hanging from the ceiling. Once filled with water it could, when tipped with the pull of a chain, give a nice sensation of allover cleansing but only in a very genteel way.*

But what is modern is relative. For some perspective of up-to-dateness then, we have those London real estate ads.

For one thing, modern meant increasing diversity of space—a "breakfast parlour," for example, to allow for informality at some meals

(breakfast and otherwise) as opposed to formality for all meals in the dining room, even though the latter was more desirable for being more "spacious"; or the breakfast room was an alternative to taking all meals in the kitchen. Bedrooms meanwhile were becoming more airy—presumably owing to more windows for cross ventilation. There was better overall utilization of existing space with an increasing proliferation of closets, clearly a big selling point in many ads. Closets made use of space that would otherwise be wasted—adjacent to chimneys, under stairways, and so forth. But they were still generally shallow; those in bedrooms or elsewhere that were intended for hanging clothes needed only hooks. The hanger, that modern indispensable for storing clothes, had not yet been invented, and it is the length of the hanger that has dictated the depth of the modern closet.

A primitive version of the water closet had been in very limited use in England since early in the 18th century. A substantially new design was patented in 1775 and improved in 1778, increasing both its usefulness and popularity. By the 1790s the water closet was a sufficiently known convenience to make it a selling point among prospective home buyers who could afford such luxury; hence it is found with increasing frequency in London real estate ads toward the end of the century.

The kitchen had also been undergoing modernization to make it the "convenient kitchen." Notable on the Continent as well as in England were the thoroughly modern cooking appliances devised by an American emigré named Benjamin Thompson (1753–1814), a native of Woburn, Massachusetts, who was one of the most accomplished physicists of the late

---

* George Read's 7½-foot bathtub was obviously fixed in place owing to the plumbing to which it was connected; so it is distinguished for both its permanency and its size. There were also smaller, portable tubs in use at the time, as recorded in her diary by Elizabeth Drinker of Philadelphia. On July 8, 1803, she described "a new bathing Tub, which WD bought yesterday for 17 Dollars—made of wood, lined with tin and painted—with Castors under ye bottom and a brass lock to let out the water." The castors clearly made it portable, and its size may be judged accordingly; indeed, the Drinkers on occasion lent it to neighbors.

*Count Rumford: symbol of a new order of convenience in the kitchen.* (Frontispiece, Rumford, *Essays, Political, Economical, and Philosophical,* vol. 1, 1st American ed., Boston, 1798)

18th and early 19th centuries. By a circuitous route and through circumstances only briefly relatable here, he fled America early in the Revolution and in time became England's undersecretary of state under George III, then an imperial count of the Holy Roman Empire, and then minister of war and police in Bavaria. He made his home at various times in London, Paris, and Munich, becoming in the process Count Rumford, as he is known to history. Rumford did pioneering work in the science of heat and light and cooking technology, expounded in his published writings, beginning in 1796.

His contribution to the domestic kitchen was an outgrowth of his modernization of the institutional kitchen—notably the House of Correction in Munich and the Hospital of La Pietà at Verona, Italy. Rumford was perhaps the most vociferous contemporary critic of traditional means of cooking—the open fireplace or the so-called kitchen range.* "The loss of heat and waste of fuel in these kitchens is altogether incredible," he wrote in *On the Construction of Kitchen Fire-places* (1802). But there were other evils as well: "noxious exhalations," especially when charcoal was used as fuel, and currents of *cold* air occasioned by a strong draft up the chimney. There was also the efficiency of the one doing the cooking, for whom standing before the open fire was a "sweltering business."

To correct these ills and generate a new level of efficiency, Rumford designed for the kitchen of the House of Correction a large semicircular brick enclosure, roughly waist high, connected in back to a chimney. Within the enclosure were separate "boilers," each with its own firebox, all these in turn being connected to the central flue of the chimney. Into a boiler was set the pot or kettle to be heated. Depending on the meal being cooked, all ten boilers (five on each side of the semicircle in this particular installation) might be used, or only one or two.

Now, in comparison with the open hearth or old-style range, let's see what this meant. For the cook, most notably, relief from an open fire. The fire was fully contained within the enclo-

* In Rumford's time, as for centuries before, a kitchen range was "a long open grate [heated by an open fire] over which the pots and kettles are freely suspended, or placed on stands" (Rumford's own definition in his essay *On the Construction of Kitchen Fire-places,* 1802). These ranges were chiefly found in England and Ireland; the open fireplace was the usual means of cooking in America. The *modern* range is a closed apparatus with multiple heating surfaces that evolved substantially out of Rumford's work.

sure. This arrangement was also far more fuel-efficient in that all the heat of a particular fire-box was directed to the pot it was heating, so there was no loss of heat into the room or, more significantly, up the chimney. Now instead of just one large fire doing a multiplicity of chores inefficiently, there were a number of small fires, each directed to a specific need. This fulfilled Rumford's dictum that many small fires are more efficient than one large one. But there was another major advantage, one that really made this modern: Each firebox had its own damper, which meant that the cooking process could be "regulated at pleasure" (quoting Rumford).

From this brick enclosure, waist high, with its various circular openings on top, one can actually visualize what eventually came about a

*The kitchen of Baron von Lerchenfeld, Munich, 1790s. In addition to designing kitchens for institutions, Count Rumford also accepted a number of commissions from European nobility. This was the "enclosed fire-place" Rumford chose as an illustration for the first publication of his* On the Construction of Kitchen Fire-places *(1802). Each of the openings atop the brick enclosure is a boiler into which is placed a pot or kettle. Under each is a separate firebox, adjustable by its own damper. Flues from the separate fireboxes converge at the chimney (vertical structure) in back. Here was a significant predecessor of the modern kitchen range. (Rumford,* Complete Works)

century or so hence: an enclosure waist high with four or so circular openings, each separately regulated—the modern gas range. In the early 1800s there was only limited application of so modern a concept relative to the vast number of open fireplaces that remained as the mainstay of cooking for some years to come. Yet since Rumford never sought to patent any of his devices, he left it to those who wished to do so to duplicate them from descriptions and drawings in his published writings (his essay on kitchens, published in England in 1802, was reprinted in Boston in 1804). And there were those, knowing and able, who did so—like the Reads, or the James Rundlets (see pages 59–60).

These various devices that still exist are commonly known as Rumford ranges although Rumford himself never used "range" for one of his devices; it was too connotative of the ar-chaic kind, and he was satisfied just to say it was an improved kitchen fireplace.

Equally as significant was the Rumford roaster, which offered a very sophisticated means of cooking, particularly for meat. The roaster was a cylinder made of sheet iron, roughly 18 inches in diameter and 24 inches in length, set into a brickwork enclosure. It had two tubes underneath ("blowpipes," Rumford called them) and another tube atop (the "steam-tube"). Other important features in-cluded a dripping pan full of water within the oven and an ashpit door in the enclosure below the oven. These various components meant that the cook was "enabled not only to regulate

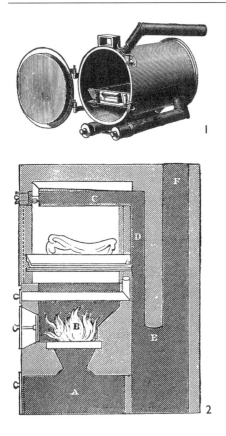

*The Rumford roaster: gourmet cooking, c1800. Out of its enclosure (Fig. 1) the roaster can be seen as a hollow cylinder of sheet metal, roughly 18 in. in diameter and 24 in. long for the average installation. Above it is the steam tube, regulated by a damper; the tube controls moistness by controlling the degree to which steam in the oven is allowed to escape. Below are the two blowpipes regulated by in-out stoppers; these control the degree of browning. The heat of the oven is adjusted by a register in the ashpit door of the firebox. When browning of the meat is desired, the stoppers in the blowpipes are partly drawn out or removed and the steam tube is opened, conducting out moist air and allowing for deep browning of the meat. If very moist rather than very browned meat is desired, the settings are reversed. Fig. 2 is a side view of the roaster within its brick enclosure. A is the ashpit and B the firebox. C is a section of an arch of brickwork surrounding the roaster. Smoke passes around the roaster, descends through D, turns through E, and rises out the chimney through F. These illustrations appeared in the original edition of Rumford's* Essays, Political, Economical, and Philosophical *in England.* On the Construction of Kitchen Fire-Places, *was first published in America in Boston in 1804. (Rumford,* Complete Works, *vol. 3)*

the degrees of heat at pleasure, but also to combine any given degree of heat with any degree of moisture or of dryness required" (Rumford, *Collected Works*).

This was gourmet cooking compared with the open hearth. Regulating the damper of the steam tube controlled the relative moisture of the meat. Adjusting the blowpipes regulated the degree to which the meat was browned. Opening and closing the ashpit doors adjusted the heat within the oven. All of this meant not only quality but quantity: "When meat is roasted in this machine," said Rumford, "its quantity, determined by weight, is considerably greater than if it were roasted upon a spit before a fire."

Rumford also experimented with redesign of the fireplace and produced a configuration that slanted the sides, moved the back wall forward, and narrowed the opening into the flue, producing greater efficiency with less use of fuel.

George Read obviously was aware of Rumford's work, either through word of mouth or through Rumford's writings on domestic technology, being published just at the time Read was building his house. The Read House had a Rumford-style oven as well as what was called a "steam table."

The Read oven was less sophisticated than the Rumford roaster, cooking with hot air only, by means of flues from the fireplace, but it was still a far cry from the traditional brick oven that was the mainstay of almost everyone else's kitchen and where the closest thing to "regulating" was the inevitable cooling down of the bricks, a process that dictated the order in which pies, breads, and other baked goods were put in and taken out. The oven of 1804 is still in

the house, although renovations over the years have left unclear exactly how it worked.

The kitchen, as was everywhere the case, had a fireplace, the source, through flues, for the hot air to the oven. But this fireplace was different, in that a 30-gallon tin drum was built in at the back. This was the water heater and also the source of steam for the steam table. Water was supplied by a pump in the "pump house" (actually a room) immediately adjacent to the kitchen and connected to the well. (This was one of the ideas Read got in Philadelphia.) The pump assured a steady supply of hot water via the tin drum. The tin drum was the source of steam for the steam table, of which nothing remains except a record of its name; there is not even a description.

In 1811 Read "modernized" still further, installing what his records show as a "steam kitchen" that superseded both the steam table and the oven. Exactly what he meant by steam kitchen we can only guess. Probably it used steam from a central fire to provide heat for cooking at an array of pot holes as well as for generating hot water. The steam kitchen was either built into the hearth or installed just in front of it.

It was also in 1811 that George Read purchased the "Bathing Tub and Shower Bathe." At the same time he got his tub and shower Read installed additional pipe to run from the new steam kitchen upstairs to the "bathing room," along with another pump to get the hot water there. But whereas there was a direct connection to the tub, it can only be assumed that the overhead shower box had to be filled by hand—the same means by which the tub was emptied.

The Read House also resembled the London

*The Read kitchen fireplace: seemingly typical of the time but with a difference. This one had a 30-gallon tin drum at the back. Filled with water supplied by a pump in an adjacent pump room, it provided hot water for kitchen purposes.* (Photograph by the author)

(Below) *Something similar to the Reads' hot-water heater is illustrated in this 1835 patent drawing. As the cooking stove came into use during the 19th century, a reservoir for hot water attached thereto became common, superseding the use of the fireplace for heating water as well as for cooking.* (U.S. Patent Collection: "J. & W. C. Bailey. Kitchen Boiler. Patented May 22, 1835")

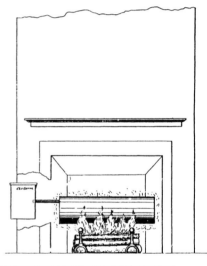

ads in its spacious dining area and its many closets; there were four closets in the master bedroom alone, at a time when most houses in America still had none.

Central heating was barely known at this time, and Read was content with wood-burning fireplaces when he moved in. By 1818, however, he had converted them all to coal-burning with the installation of grates.

An obvious Read House exception to London's evolving standard of comfort and conve-nience was the absence of a water closet or even an indoor privy. The latter were coming into occasional use in the late 18th century; there were instances in New England of prosperous families enlarging their houses with an ell and then building in a privy at the far end. An in-door privy was included as part of the original construction of the house of Bishop William White in Philadelphia (1786). Read knew White but may never have had occasion to visit his house. There were almost certainly water

*The Bishop White House, Philadelphia (1786): an early indoor privy.* (Photograph by the author)

closets in use as of 1804, but perhaps none that Read saw, or he likely would have wanted one of those too. Even so, at the turn of the century of technological revolution, this was a very modern house.

## CHANGERS AND NONCHANGERS

Innovation was not always the choice of the affluent at the turn of the 19th century. Whereas there were the George Reads who delighted in technological change, there were also the Janet Montgomerys who liked things just as they were.

Janet Livingston Montgomery, daughter of New York's Robert R. Livingston, was in her early twenties when she married Richard Montgomery in 1773, only to watch him set off for war two years later as one of the first generals appointed by the Continental Congress. She followed the course of the Revolutionary War in that most personal of ways, through the letters Richard sent back as he led a tattered band of ill-equipped, ill-trained, and sometimes obstreperous citizen-soldiers into laying siege against the British in the city of Quebec. On the last day of the last year before independence, the letters stopped as he fell mortally wounded.

Janet Montgomery never remarried; and since her brief union had produced no children, she remained childless. In 1804, the same year that George Read finished his splendid and very modern house overlooking the Delaware River, Janet Livingston Montgomery undertook construction of Montgomery Place overlooking the Hudson River near what is now Annandale-on-Hudson, New York—a house, for a widow in her fifties, suitably larger and grander than what had sufficed for a newlywed in her twenties; a house as splendid as George Read's but hardly modern at all. There would be no Rumford oven, no steam kitchen, no bathtub, no pumped-in water, no hot running water, no water closet nor even an indoor privy. Household life would retain only those traditional elements that represented home as she knew it with the man whom, until her death in her seventies, she called "my soldier."*

But elsewhere technological change was catching on; other houses at the turn of the 19th century were indeed in the forefront of a new era in household convenience and comfort.

---

* The kitchen does have a "stewing stove," so called, but whether this was installed at the time the house was built or added at a later date is not known. There is also evidence of a heating stove c1811 and perhaps an additional stove or stoves by 1816.

*Monticello, Charlottesville, Virginia.* (Historic American Buildings Survey)

Hardly surprising is it that Thomas Jefferson's Monticello was one.

We may recall from the ads that a popular new feature of houses in London was the water closet (it was called this even in America into the 20th century, the term "toilet" only coming into use roughly during the 1920s). There is no evidence that there was ever a working water closet inside Monticello, but Jefferson clearly contemplated having one: A drawing in his own hand (see illustration on page 57) shows a scheme for piping water into Monticello for both a greenhouse and what appears to be a water closet. Jefferson had knowledge of the successor to the privy from living in Paris during his tenure as U.S. minister to France from 1785 to 1789. He made as his residence the recently built Hôtel de Langeac, which was equipped with what was known there as a *lieu*

*à l'anglais,* or "English place." (The predilection of the French and English for insulting each other found fertile ground in the place of elimination; the English by at least the 1500s had taken to calling a privy a jakes, a mock of the French *Jacques,* which by modern times had evolved into john.) The *lieu à l'anglais* of the Hôtel de Langeac was undoubtedly similar to the water closets in use in England (a fuller discussion of the evolution of the water closet will be found on page 89ff).

While Jefferson apparently never followed through on his plan for constructing a working water closet at Monticello, he did do what undoubtedly the many would have liked: make unnecessary the *outdoor* necessary house. Monticello was begun in the early 1770s. In 1796 Jefferson began a major renovation that more than doubled the size of the house. Just outside one wall of the original (now an inner wall) he installed three indoor privies—one of them private, connecting only with his bedroom, and two of them for general use of the household. Each privy had a shaft descending to a brick tunnel, 160 feet long, stretching from underneath the privies out into the grounds. There were also shafts ascending from the privies through what looked like chimney flues in the roof. The idea was that air was drawn from outside through the tunnel (which Jefferson referred to as an "air tunnel"), thence to vent through a flue in a chimney. In effect this was the venting system that is a required part of every modern plumbing installation; it may have been the first of its kind in America. A contemporary reference work (A. F. M. Willich's *Domestic Encyclopedia,* first published in London in 1802 and in America in 1804) describes a similar venting

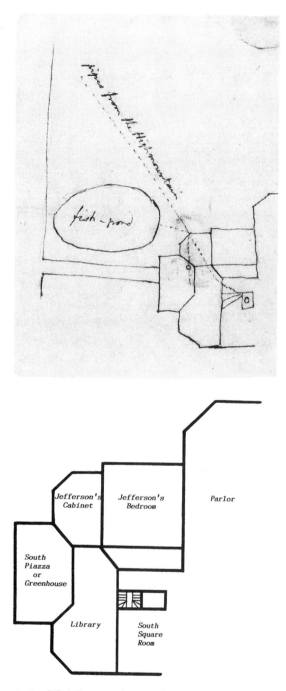

*Sketch by Thomas Jefferson (no date, probably before 1808) showing, in concept, "pipes from the High mountain" (Mt. Alto) and "fish-pond" to provide water for a water closet and greenhouse at Monticello. Jefferson did incorporate three indoor privies into Monticello but no water closet. The greenhouse was a glassed-in piazza and remained without either heat or water. Although this plan did not become a reality, Jefferson did direct installation of a water closet at the White House. And like the sketch of a central-heating system (see chapter 5), and indeed much of Monticello, we have here an example of his conceptualization of the modern house before its time. (By permission of The Huntington Library, San Marino, Calif.)*

system for outdoor privy vaults; this was the same concept extended to the house.

This much we know. What we don't know is how waste was removed. There has been conjecture that chamber pots were used and then lowered down the shafts by pulley. The only clue, from Jefferson's own records, is that he paid one of his slaves on a regular basis for "cleaning the sewers." The first payment was made in 1806.

Besides the indoor privies, there were two outdoor "necessaries." These were square structures with stepped pyramidal roofs at the corners of the dependency wings. Excavation near the privy at the north wing has uncovered a brick-lined tunnel about 20 feet long leading from the privy. It is presumably a drain. There is also a cistern adjacent to each privy. Were these used for flushing water through the privy? There is no clear evidence, but the existence of pipe, possibly replacement pipe from a later date, raises the possibility. If so, these were, in effect, primitive outdoor water closets.

The cisterns undoubtedly served as a general

*A simplified diagram showing the area of Monticello appearing in Jefferson's sketch.* (Diagram by the author) source of water for household use. Water supply at mountaintop Monticello was always a problem. The well seemed forever to be running dry. Dug in 1769, it failed in 1773, came back, failed again in 1777, again in 1789, and again in 1791, 1796, and 1797. There were also springs lower on the mountain, but these appear also not to have been entirely dependable. Finally Jefferson built cisterns, including the two adjacent to the outdoor necessaries, fed through gutters with rainwater from the roofs of the main house and the dependencies. In 1808 Jefferson calculated that this system was sufficient to furnish the household with more than a thousand gallons of water a day, given optimum rainfall.

Some of this water went to the bathing house. George Read might have enjoyed his hot tub by his bedroom, but Jefferson was content to have a bathing house in the pavilion at the end of the north dependency wing. When Monticello was restored in the 20th century, this was reconstructed as a laundry; subsequent research suggests it was the bathing house. There is no evidence there was ever a tub inside the main house.

Monticello's indoor privies were not the first. The Bishop White House in Philadelphia, built in 1786, had one of the earliest of indoor privies, located at the rear, off the kitchen. It is believed that with a sort-of flushing action of water dumped into the privy vault by servants using wooden buckets, augmented by water from the kitchen, the privy emptied into a brick-lined sewer that drained into Dock Creek. Almost, but not quite, a water closet. It was an arrangement that afforded great convenience in the age of the outdoor privy and the indoor chamber pot. But care

was taken in design of the house to minimize one's use of the privy from intruding on others: Two sets of doors shield the kitchen.

One of the earlier water closets in America was that installed by Massachusetts governor Christopher Gore (1758–1827) at his country estate, Gore Place, in Waltham, Massachusetts, completed in 1806. Gore had served in England as one of John Jay's fellow commissioners in negotiating Jay's Treaty (1794) and clearly became accustomed to the newly emerging domestic technology there. Construction records for Gore Place detail specifics of what went into the house. Among them:

May 4 [1806] paid Whitwell for a Stove

May 22 paid Fisk & Crooker, by J. Hunnewell for setting Rumford Kitchen & the copper for Bath & Laundry

July 10 John Winslow & Co. for Window Fastenings & Weights

Septr 28 C. Davis for [installing?] Bathing Tub

Octr 15 Joseph Howe [for installing?] Rumford Kitchen

Augt. 6 [1807] [Received] Water Closet 103.75 [dollars] Freight [for this and other items] 30. Dolls

So we know that Gore Place—a quintessential example of Federal architecture at its best—had a stove, either for heating or cooking; a bathtub; a Rumford kitchen, perhaps including both roaster and steam table; a laundry; and a water closet, surely imported from England. It also had windows with weights in the sashes, a commonplace of later times but a relatively remarkable innovation when most sash windows were still held open by props of various sorts. There was also a plenitude of closets, including a walk-in wardrobe adjacent to the master bedroom. Down the hall was a built-in linen closet. Inside the attic was a cistern fed with rainwater from the roof, presumably linked in some way to the kitchen, bathing room, and water closet. A cupola atop the roof provided not only a nice decorative touch but a means of venting warm air during the summer.

Like the Read House, this was a modern place in which to live—practically an American re-creation of the modern house exemplified in those London real estate ads. But do we credit Christopher Gore? Or his wife, Rebecca? It was Mrs. Gore who collaborated with architect J.-G. LeGrand of Paris in designing the house as a whole; was it she also who made it so modern technologically? We don't know; we are entitled to an intelligent guess that she was.

As a student at newly founded Phillips Exeter Academy in Exeter, New Hampshire, which he entered in 1785 at the age of twelve, James Rundlet (1772–1852) showed a clear preference for scientific and mathematical courses, including geometry and trigonometry. As an adult he set aside his scientific bent to become an epitome of the Yankee trader—a merchant (predominantly textiles) who by his mid thirties had acquired sufficient wealth to build, with his wife, Jane, one of the grand houses of Portsmouth, New Hampshire. It was here, on Middle Street, that his inclination to

science found a practical outlet. The Rundlet-May House (built between 1807 and 1811) is another paragon of developing technology in the American home: Rumford roaster, Rumford range, fireplaces designed on Rumford principles, a set kettle (see page 60), an indoor well, a ventilating system, a bellpull system, and an indoor privy. There are also ample closets and an attached carriage house.

The Reads' Rumford oven, we may recall, was a less sophisticated version; the Rundlets' was one that adhered to Rumford's specifications for a roaster, with a combination of dampers, steam tube, and blowpipes. It was built in Portsmouth and sold to Rundlet by John Badger in January 1808; Badger's bill for $37.49 was for "Rumford works" that presumably also included the range (see below). This roaster obviously was used. It has been conjectured that not all were; that the complexity of operation left many an early-1800s housewife or servant to scratch her head and go back to the hearth. The Rundlets' roaster was used to the extent it had to be repaired and reset in its brickwork enclosure in 1834, and as late as 1858, six years after Rundlet's death, there is record of another bill paid for repair work. The roaster is still in place, in its original location in the fireplace wall immediately adjacent to the hearth; it has been restored to its original appearance.

Rundlet also installed a "Rumford range" along a wall perpendicular to the fireplace. It consists of a series of three boilers set into a brickwork enclosure, each with its own firebox accessible through a cast-iron door. Into each boiler could be inserted a covered pot or kettle. The heat for each boiler could be individually regulated by a damper on its firebox. The range also remains, although the pot holes are hidden by a modern countertop (the kitchen remained in use by descendants of the Rundlets until the 1960s). Over the range Rundlet built a masonry hood that was intended to draw smoke and steam from the range and funnel it into the chimney—a forerunner of the modern range-top hood and clearly something well ahead of its time.

Elsewhere in and around the kitchen were the indoor well, housed by a small extension off the back (or summer) kitchen, and the set kettle, also in the back kitchen, a masonry enclosure housing a copper kettle heated by a firebox underneath. The set kettle provided hot water for laundry and other household purposes.

Other conveniences were included as part of a series of connecting outbuildings in the

*An adaptation of Rumford was the stewing range found in some American homes of the early 1800s. It consisted of a series of boilers set into a brickwork enclosure, each with its own firebox. Into each boiler could be inserted a pot or kettle. The heat for each boiler could be individually regulated by a damper on the firebox.* (This diagram is from Rumford, *Complete Works,* vol. 3)

shape of an ell. The most immediate is the scullery, followed by a woodshed and then two indoor privies in the corner of the ell (making any necessary trip an indoor one); around the corner from the privies, and immediately adjacent, is the pigsty and then the carriage house at the far end (also reachable without going outdoors). All in all, a modern house.

Still another house of the same period that stands to be of interest to us is the house that Joseph Priestley completed in Northumberland, Pennsylvania, in 1796, after moving to America in 1794 from Birmingham, England. Priestley the founder of modern chemistry and discoverer of oxygen; Priestley the eminent scientist; Priestley who presumably knew what was up-to-date in England—what might *his* house be like?

Alas, from our point of view here, very little was modern. There was only a simple apparatus for heating water adjacent to the kitchen hearth, apparently consisting of two open copper kettles heated by a charcoal fire underneath. There was apparently no connection to the flue of the hearth. The only means of ventilation thus would have been the kitchen door in the far wall of the back kitchen. (There were two kitchens: a larger one for cooking and a smaller one in back that was unheated and probably used for storage. The bake oven was outside.) This presents a curious paradox: Priestley, of all people, should have known the peril of inadequate ventilation; it was he who identified carbon monoxide. Somehow the system worked. Still another paradox is it that despite his close association with Benjamin Franklin, Priestley apparently had no interest in room stoves. There were only the usual fireplaces for heat. Some minor concession to a

*Joseph Priestley*

new order of convenience existed in the availability of household water inside the house; there was a well inside the back kitchen, dug to a depth of roughly 40 feet at the time the kitchen was constructed. There were also a few closets; three of the four bedrooms had them, and there was a linen closet of ample size in the upstairs hall. On the other hand, the privy was outside where it had been since time immemorial.

This eminent scientist who had seen, and indeed been a part of, the beginning of technological revolution in England thus appeared to be content with a house that reflected very little of that change. But we can understand this more readily by understanding the man. He was first a scientist, and his life largely centered around his laboratory, which was a wing of the house and was, to be sure, quite up-to-date. There was, for example, a fume hood to ventilate noxious gases; the place was also unusually well lighted for the late 18th century. Then there was Priestley the Unitarian minister, for whom the house was as much a setting for preaching and teaching as a place for living; his

drawing room was regularly the site of services for his Unitarian congregation. And then much of the early planning for the house was the work of his wife, Mary, who died before it was completed. She had taken great delight in it; had she lived, would she have impressed upon it a greater degree of domesticity in the finishing stages? Priestley himself died in 1804, and the rest of the family—never really transplanted to new soil—returned to England in 1811.

## SHAPING THE FUTURE

Selected in 1790 as site of the capital of the United States, a semiwilderness on the Potomac River began a slow metamorphosis into a city. By the mid 1790s there were unmistakable signs of life in this new "Washington," notably the sounds of construction atop a prominence known as Jenkins Hill, where they were building something known as the "Congress House." And not far away were the makings of a veritable mansion, which was to be called the "President's House." Otherwise there were a few modest dwellings, and here and there a shop or tavern, but little else to signify the singular importance of a nation's capital, although there was a magnificent plan for one—a city plan worthy of a stately city in Europe, a plan that would transform muddy lanes and open pasture into grand boulevards and spacious avenues. Its device was a gridiron pattern of evenly spaced blocks broken up with broad avenues radiating diagonally from the two principal buildings under construction, the future U.S. Capitol and the White House.

This carefully crafted geometric network promised to open up what Pierre L'Enfant called "magnificent distances," but it also created an odd assortment of spaces on which to build. As of the mid 1790s, that made little difference; not many people were buying real estate, and still fewer building in this oasis of yet suspicious opportunity. Would this be merely an enclave of legislators, with no other life of its own? No commercial prospects beyond supplying the needs of a handful of fledgling congressmen? No culture beyond that offered by a fiddler at a neighborhood tavern?

There were those to take up the challenge of this veritable frontier city. Among Washington's early settlers was a country gentleman from near Richmond, Virginia, whose estate there, named Mount Airy, rambled over some 3,000 acres and included a private racetrack. Convinced of Washington's future, Col. John Tayloe III sought out property and an architect to build on it a winter town house.

His choice of architect was the distinguished Benjamin Latrobe, who sometime soon after 1796 designed for Tayloe a grand home that would rival the President's House ("White House" came later). It was nearly the same size and probably something of the same magnitude in cost. Tayloe, though wealthy, found Latrobe's plan costly beyond what he thought fit for this still largely wilderness setting. He turned to another architect of equal stature, Dr. William Thornton, whose chief project of the moment was the U.S. Capitol, a-building on Jenkins Hill. By the time Tayloe enlisted Thornton, he had settled on a piece of property at the intersection of New York Avenue and Eighteenth Street—one of those

strategically located but odd-shaped lots created by radiating diagonals. As for location, the site was two blocks from the President's House, more or less assuring that, until other pioneers chose this same frontier, this house would be within the sheltering arms of a legitimate semblance of civilization. There was also a fine view of the Potomac River; and from it, a fine view of the house.

Thornton worked up an entirely new proposal, taking into account the odd-shaped lot. It was a house of somewhat smaller size, and lesser cost, on which construction began in 1799 and was completed in 1801. The house is irregular in shape to fit this lot most easily described as keystone in configuration, with the narrower end representing the front of the house. The house nevertheless has come to be known as The Octagon, despite its not being even vaguely octagonal in shape. The name came into use with Tayloe's children after they inherited the house and most likely derives from what is perhaps the house's most striking feature: the grandly scaled round room that is its entrance hall. At the time of construction, such round rooms were typically constructed of eight angled walls plastered so as to be circular. In deference to their construction, they were known as octagon salons. Hence, apparently, the name by which the house has come to be known.

Technicalities of shape aside, it is easily one of Washington's most historic houses (it served as the President's House after the latter was burned during the War of 1812 and was the site of ratification of the Treaty of Ghent, which ended the war). Yet though this structure is historic from the point of view of national affairs, it is history from a closer

*The Octagon, Washington, D.C. (1801). An irregularly shaped building lot in the nation's capital produced a dwelling that has come to be known as The Octagon even though it is not octagonal in shape. Significant features are its circular entrance hall and its flat roof, which leaked almost from the start and was replaced by a low hipped roof that, from the street, maintains the original appearance of the roof line.* (Historic American Buildings Survey)

*The Octagon, entrance hall: one of two coal-fired heating stoves. Coal was also used in all the fireplaces; an underground storage vault adjacent to the basement kitchen was filled through a hatch accessible from the street.* (Historic American Buildings Survey)

perspective that invites us to look about The Octagon: This pioneer settler of a wilderness on the Potomac was also a pioneer of technology in the American home.

Latrobe's plan included such features as a water closet that might well have been Washington's first (when John Adams moved into the White House in November 1800, the president had only an outhouse for his needs). Thornton's somewhat more modest plan was nevertheless also a model of the modern house. Water supply was a sophisticated system for capturing water from the roof and window wells using conduits in the cellar floor to fill or supplement a cistern/well in the basement (as of this writing, archaeological digging had not proceeded far enough to determine whether there was a masonry bottom, establishing it as a cistern, or no bottom, making it a well). In either case, the cistern/well was a remarkably convenient source of water for the kitchen, which was in the basement—an unusual place at this time. The kitchen appears to have had a Rumford-like range for cooking as well as a separate stewing range, both coal-burning. Over the stewing range was an exhaust hood and flue connecting to the main chimney flue. Since The Octagon was originally a winter home, refrigeration was not a major concern. By the time it became a year-round home, about 1817, there was an icehouse, 15 feet square, in back.

Although drawings of Latrobe's earlier proposal show that a water closet was to have been included, no clear evidence survives of one in this house. There is a strong probability, however, since design studies by Thornton for Tayloe's home included water closets adjacent to or beneath the stairs. The house certainly had a sophisticated enough water supply system (there was also a stable-yard well out back), and archaeological evidence points to a likely basement location easily accessible to the well/cistern. Furthermore, since Tayloe had a water closet in Latrobe's plan, he may well have instructed Thornton to follow suit.

Heating was by coal from the start. All the fireplaces had grates, one of which, in the first-floor drawing room, remains practically intact. There were also two coal stoves in the entrance hall. Coal was stored in an underground vault adjacent to the kitchen; the vault was filled through a hatch accessible from the street.

Built-in chandeliers using either candles or oil furnished light in the stair hall and drawing room, and perhaps somewhat later in the dining room. There was a bellpull system connecting most of the rooms with the servants' hall, and there was a relative profusion of closets, resulting in part from the house's unusual design: Triangular spaces at the corners of each floor were ready-made. Altogether, over four floors, there are today seventeen closets, most if not all of them part of the original construction.

Perhaps the house's most unusual feature was the flat roof that originally capped it. It was made of layers of tar-soaked canvas laid on wooden planking and was just slightly sloped from front to back to drain rainwater into scuppers that funneled it into two downspouts attached to the exterior rear wall. It was one of these that channeled water through the cellar floor conduits to the cistern (or well). Clearly an innovation, the flat roof was also a major problem; it began leaking almost from the start. Sometime between 1815 and 1817 it was replaced by a hipped roof that remains in place today. Owing to a careful design and a wooden balustrade that replaced the original brick parapet, there was no noticeable difference from ground level.

After the burning of the White House during the War of 1812, President James Madison made this the temporary Executive Mansion while John and Ann Tayloe and their substantial family (there would be fifteen children altogether) returned to Mount Airy. The Treaty of Ghent, signed in Belgium on Christmas Eve, 1814, and ratified by Madison here in February 1815, marked both the end of a war and the beginning of a new phase of transformation of a still sparsely settled frontier town into a thriving city. Among those leading the way were the Tayloes, who in December 1817 moved from Mount Airy to make The Octagon, and Washington, their permanent home.

As for that most symbolic of all American residences, the White House: While it was not always in the forefront of technological innovation, compared with other houses we have seen, neither was it far behind in trying out what was new in the way of comfort and convenience.

When Andrew Jackson arrived in 1829, water still had to be pumped into the house from two wells that were there when it was first occupied in 1800. In 1833 a system was devised for tapping a spring at nearby Franklin Square. Water from the spring flowed to a pondlike reservoir on the White House grounds; from there it was pumped through pipes into the house itself, primarily for use in a bathing room in the basement of the East Colonnade. Now the White House had a hot bath with running water, supplementing portable tubs that had been used in the upstairs bedrooms and dressing rooms since the earliest days. A coal fire under a copper boiler furnished the hot water. During the term of Franklin Pierce (1853–1857) a bathtub with both hot and cold running water was added on the second floor. The bathing room had wallpaper that looked like oak paneling and an oilcloth floor that resembled tile. A ground-floor bathroom included a porcelain sink and a water closet in a mahogany enclosure. In the spring of 1861, shortly after the inauguration of Abraham Lincoln, the Potomac River supplanted the Franklin Square spring as the source of White House water.

There was a water closet during the Jefferson administration, and indeed evidence exists that one or more were intended at the time of construction. After moving into the still uncompleted mansion in March 1801, Jefferson complained about the wooden privy that was all the Adamses had had since arriving in November 1800, and directed the federal commissioners overseeing the White House to arrange for purchase and installation of a water closet. It was in place by late 1804. That the mansion was intended to be so equipped from the start is evident in a letter from James Hoban, the original architect, to the commissioner of public buildings on January 4, 1816,

during reconstruction of the White House following its burning. Hoban observed that "one [water closet] in each story . . . was contemplated in the original plan," and he recommended "having them again in the Building." He placed the cost at about a hundred dollars each—almost exactly what the Christopher Gores had paid ($103.75) in 1807.

A very early version of central heating—a furnace in the basement, but one that heated only the state dining room above it—came during the Madison administration (1809–1817). It was a simple gravity-feed, hot-air system using registers in the floor of the dining room. Otherwise, coal-burning fireplaces sufficed for heat. Martin Van Buren (see "The Modern House: 1850," page 104) saw to a number of improvements to the White House in advance of the modernization of his own home, including a more comprehensive version of central heat. This one warmed the state rooms beyond just the dining room as well as some of the halls; coal- and wood-burning fireplaces took care of all other rooms. This heating system, which went into use in the autumn of 1840, used a coal-burning furnace in a masonry enclosure apparently similar to what Van Buren would have at Lindenwald after returning to private life.

Gaslight came to the White House in 1848 as an offshoot of the installation of gas lighting at the Capitol. It was undertaken there in 1847 with the construction of a coal-gas generating plant on the Capitol grounds. Since gas was now available only a short distance away, it was thought advisable to pipe it also to the White House, making the James K. Polks the first First Family of the post-candles-and-oil-lamps age.

In these various homes we have a composite of the house of the future—the future from the perspective of the turn of the 19th century. But the Reads and Jeffersons and others like them, who were cognizant of technical innovation and had the means to acquire it, were a small minority. The vast number of houses of 1800, though outwardly beginning to reflect changing architectural styles, were inwardly little more advanced technologically than the Fairbanks's home. The all-purpose hall of the 17th century had largely disappeared in favor of a separate kitchen, but it was little different from the point of view of the housewife. She was still hauling in water from outside, still using a cold cellar for refrigeration, still cooking (and keeping warm) at an open hearth, though its design had changed in subtle ways to make it a little more efficient. By 1900 there would be a stove, probably coal-burning; there would be piped-in water, perhaps hot as well as cold, perhaps even flowing into a sink that was built into a continuous countertop; and there would be an icebox, maybe even an electric refrigerator (one was available but at a price that ruled it out for all but the wealthiest).

Though the Christopher Gores and a few others might have their water closet, almost everyone else at the turn of the 19th century was using the chamber pot and the privy. Where such a novelty as a "bath room" even existed, it was literally just that. By 1900 the bathroom as we know it today—with tub, toilet, and sink—was common.

This was a century of profound change that saw the average house go from virtually postmedieval to virtually modern. Obviously, industrial capacity played a part—that is, the capacity of society to invent, produce, and

market a wider and wider variety of devices and appliances of ever greater sophistication, all made continually more affordable to the average householder through force of competition. It is not necessary to examine that aspect of technological evolution here. Rather we should look at significant factors inside and outside the home that influenced the development and adoption of domestic technology and thus shaped the modern house.

## TECHNOLOGY IN AND AROUND THE KITCHEN

Were an inhabitant of the early 17th century to return and visit today's house, he or she would find it, while changed, fully recognizable . . . until reaching the kitchen. Here any sense of logical continuity would vanish in a gasp of astonishment. Indeed, our visitor would have to be convinced that this *was* the kitchen; that all those dazzling contraptions of various sizes and shapes—some with knobs and dials, some with little windows, some making strange whirring and beeping sounds—actually could make dinner, let alone a dinner as substantial and wholesome as that hearty fireplace of old had produced with its array of iron pots and ladles and spoons hanging about, softly glittering in the glow of reassuring warmth within.

Two centuries of technological change have impacted upon the kitchen most of all. It is here that the full thrust is most clearly to be seen. Even before the first use of steam power in America, there was an awakening to the potential use of technology in the house, and especially in the kitchen, with the hypothesizing that:

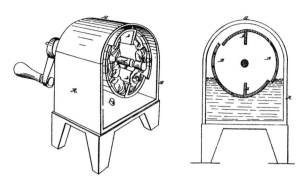
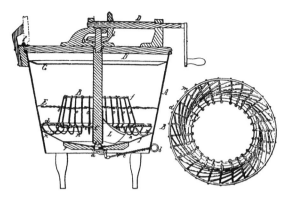

*Technology's assault on drudgery focused early on the washing machine; the first was patented in 1797, and by 1873 there were some two thousand patents for these and related devices. The one above, looking remarkably ahead of its time, dates to 1828. Inventors also sought to minimize the chore of dish washing with this "Dish Cleaner" (above right) patented in 1863 and similar devices. Most of these never got beyond the drawing board, and all suffered from one principal shortcoming: While labor-saving in intent, all required the human arm for power, and it was easier just to go on doing things the way they had been done. It was not until development of the compact electric motor that real labor saving was possible in machines of this kind. (U.S. Patent Collection: "Washing Machine," Mar. 28, 1828; "Dish Cleaner," Oct. 13, 1863)*

a turkey be killed for our dinner by the *electrical shock,* and roasted by the *electrical jack* [a rotating spit, the equivalent of a modern rotisserie], before a fire kindled by the *electrified bottle* [a Leyden jar]. (Benjamin Franklin, 1749)

Franklin never actually made dinner using electricity, but he was pointing the way to the use of technology for easing the burden of many of life's most basic tasks. In the century ahead, as the industrial revolution gathered momentum, inventors and would-be inventors took up the cause.

If numbers of early patents are indicative, the most onerous of household tasks—or at least the one seemingly most suited to being accomplished by a machine—was the laundry. Doing the laundry was a species of drudgery all its own. In early colonial society clothing was washed in a stream and then spread out on grass or bushes to dry. Even in the early 19th century, with a tub in the kitchen or just outside the back door, doing the laundry was an unwelcome ritual. Done right, it meant separating clothes by color and fabric and soaking them overnight. Next morning they were sudsed, wrung out, boiled or scalded, then rinsed in plain water (after rubbing the particularly dirty spots), and wrung out again; then the clothes were rinsed in bluing, wrung out again, starched, wrung out again, and finally hung out to dry.

No wonder inventors were quick to seize on the possibilities of a machine to take over most of this work. The first patent in America for a "washing machine" was issued in 1797, even before a formal patent office was established. Other patents for washers of assorted designs followed [see an example from 1828 above]. By

1873 there were some two thousand patents for clothes washers and related equipment (wringers, for example). Most never got beyond the drawing board, and none revolutionized laundry day. Generally speaking, these devices worked by simulating the motion of the human arm; unfortunately, that is also what powered them. By 1869 the concept had essentially been refined to what it is today (a big tub with a gyrator), but the machinery was still hand-operated. Until the age of electric power, the washing machine (like countless other labor-saving devices) remained relegated to the drawing board.

So too the dishwasher. Here also the principle was established long before the commercial practicality. A dishwasher that had all the essential elements of its modern counterpart, save an electric engine to run it, existed in 1865. It consisted of a tub with a slotted wire basket inside. The dishes were placed in the slots, the tub was filled with hot water, soap was added, and then a crank was turned. With step-up gearing, the effect was centrifugal motion to impel the soapy water over the dishes, presumably with sufficient force to clean them. But the energy behind the crank, of course, was one's arm; and given all the other requirements—heating the water, loading it into the washer and then unloading it, stacking the dishes, taking them out, and so on—that arm might better be used just to wash the same dishes in a basin. The electric household dishwasher did not begin to appear until shortly before World War II; it was only after the war that its use became widespread.

Other early inventions included a mechanized churn (1807), a vegetable cutter (1831), a vegetable washer (1835), and a coffee cleaner

(1836). But it was the major appliances that would revolutionize the kitchen—the stove (see "Concentrating the Heat Source," page 73) and the refrigerator.

With the possible exception of running water, refrigeration was perhaps the most significant addition to the modern kitchen. A heat source had been a component of the kitchen all along; means of refrigeration in or adjacent to the kitchen was new to the 19th century. Before refrigeration the household was at the mercy of food-preservation techniques dating back to antiquity. The most common of preservation methods were smoking, drying, salting, fermenting, pickling, spicing, and even freezing (but only during the winter in colder climates, as the Native Americans were known to do with poultry and fish). In some form or another, all these methods continue to the present time—in many instances being doubled, as when smoked meat comes to the consumer refrigerated as well.

Despite the usefulness of smoked, dried, salted, fermented, pickled, and spiced foods, variety was limited to what was available for preservation in the household. A great milestone therefore was the development of canning in the early 19th century. Now for the first time there was a prospect of local products reaching other regions. Yet it was not the needs of the household that gave impetus to the breakthrough. An army, as oft stated, marches on its stomach; and in 1795 it was all over Europe that the French army was marching, with indications that it might have to march on to Egypt or even India. The French directorate offered a prize for a method of preserving foods in containers that could conveniently be taken along. After considerable experimentation a chef named Nicolas-François Appert finally claimed the prize in 1809 by demonstrating a way of sealing cooked vegetables and meats in airtight bottles and then immersing them in boiling water to kill bacteria. In a book titled *The Art of Preserving* (Paris, 1810) he described the method in detail and claimed it worked for everything from meat and truffles to eggs, jelly, and asparagus. In the case of *pot-au-feu de ménage* (boiled meat), he said, "At the end of a year, and a year and a half, the broth and boiled meat were found as good as if made the day they were eaten." The shortcoming of Appert's method was the use of glass bottles, which were subject to breakage. An Englishman named Peter Durand then patented a similar process using metal cannisters coated with tin; hence, the tin can.

The can did not become commonplace until the Civil War; and even then, not everyone trusted canned goods. And for sound reason: There was no way to be sure a product was not adulterated to start with (as, for example, by the dyes that were used to make unwholesome foods look good) or had not become unsafe while in the can (it was feared that acid foods could dissolve the tin plating). The federal Food and Drug Act of 1906 and the resulting Food and Drug Administration sought to assure the public, and canned goods proliferated to become a staple of daily life.

Meanwhile refrigeration, the now standard form of preservation, had been slow in developing. Although mechanical refrigeration awaited the age of modern technology, natural refrigeration using ice or snow was always available. Ice cellars or icehouses in some form or another went back to antiquity and certainly existed in colonial America. But they became more prevalent in the late 18th–early 19th century. John F. Watson in his *Annals of Philadelphia* (1830) observed that "these [icehouses] have all come into use among us since the war of Independence. After them came the use of ice creams. . . . The winter of 1828, from its unusual mildness, they failed to fill their ice houses for the first time."

But the icehouse was hardly a convenience of the kitchen, or even the pantry. It was also about the turn of the 19th century that the icebox made its appearance, the first known reference being *An Essay on the Most Eligible Construction of Ice-Houses. Also, a Description of the Newly Invented Machine Called the Refrigerator*, written by Thomas Moore, a Maryland farmer, and published in Baltimore in 1803. Moore claimed to have thought of the term

*While larger than most, this icehouse at Belair, in Bowie, Maryland, was especially efficient, with its storage area almost entirely below grade.* (Historic American Buildings Survey)

"refrigerator" for the device, although not necessarily to having invented it. (This machine, of course, was what came to be known as the icebox, as distinguished from the modern mechanical refrigerator.) The device Moore described was basically a box with a "coat" around it—in other words, a covering such as one might put on for going out into the cold, except that this coat kept the cold in. The analogy even extended to the contents of the insulation—cloth and rabbit fur.

Obviously it was a rather primitive apparatus. Moore said he built an experimental version that was used quite successfully for carrying butter a distance of some twenty miles (taking several hours then) to market on a hot day. The next known account of the refrigerator appeared only a few years later but showed a quantum leap. This was a description included in perhaps the most popular and influential cookbook of the 19th century, Mary Randolph's *The Virginia House-Wife*, first published in Washington in 1824 and reprinted many times thereafter; but the refrigerator appeared only in the 1825 edition. The device was 4 feet long and 3 feet high and was actually a box within a box. The 4-inch space between the two boxes was filled with powdered charcoal that served as insulation. In the center of the inner box was a cannister that was filled with chunks of ice. The cannister rested in a tub that received the melting ice. All in all, in every essential respect, the modern icebox.

Randolph does not say whether the device was intended specifically for the kitchen (or at least the pantry), but that is the implication of her observation that "the refrigerator is more convenient than an ice house." As for use, she lists "both raw and cooked provisions, water

melons, milk, butter, etc. etc." as appropriate for storage.

The limiting factor was the availability of ice. It was not until the 1850s that ice harvested from ponds and lakes could readily be obtained in cities (owing in large part to the recent invention of an improved ice cutter); and it was late in the century when artificially produced ice became common.

On the other hand, cities had their markets and plenty of fresh food; indeed, a big market in a big city could be a veritable encyclopedia of good eating. Moreau de Saint-Méry, visiting from France, told of a mouth-watering visit to a market in New York City in 1794. There were, he said, sixty-three kinds of fish *plus* oysters, lobsters, crabs, crawfish, shrimp and other shellfish, and turtles. In another part of the market he found fifty-two varieties of meat, including game, kid, bear, opossum, hare, and rabbit. Adjacent to the meat and fish market were the vegetable dealers. Even if his account is greatly exaggerated, there was considerable variety; and if one went to the market each day, one did not have to worry about refrigeration at home. However, the lack of refrigeration at the market was probably best not thought about.

Once the use of iceboxes became widespread as a result of the mechanical production of ice, they remained popular well past the coming of the mechanical refrigerator. Many people were still using them midway through the 20th century.

When mechanical refrigeration did appear, it was not intended for the kitchen. The pioneer was a medical doctor named John Gorrie, a native of Charleston, South Carolina, who, after graduation from the College of Physicians and Surgeons in New York City (now part of

Columbia University), settled in the cotton port of Apalachicola, Florida. Gorrie's practice confronted him with many cases of tropical fever, and his intent was to provide artificial cooling for the sickrooms of his fever-wracked patients. While never accomplishing the equivalent of modern air conditioning, by 1844 he did develop, on a smaller scale, a machine that could make ice as well as provide a certain degree of cooling effect. Gorrie's "ice machine" (U.S. Patent No. 8,080, May 1851) used a force pump to compress air, thus creating heat (compression equals warming); the machine then allowed the air to expand (expansion equals cooling) and pass around a vessel containing water. As a result the water inside froze, thus forming ice; or, if the air was allowed instead to pass through a tube, a certain amount of cool air was dispersed to the immediate environment.

Experimentation with refrigeration had been going on in Europe as well, notably in France with Ferdinand Carré, who produced the first successful commercial freezing machine in 1860. This and its immediate successors both in Europe and America were too large to be practical in the kitchen, however, and it was not until after World War I that a compact enough unit would be mass-produced.

Meanwhile, technology was readying still another major contribution to the modern kitchen—frozen food. That, of course, is not to say that food was never frozen before the coming of modern technology. Native Americans were known to use holes in the ice on ponds and lakes to preserve food. In early American homes, where there was heat only in rooms with fireplaces, fairly efficient freezers were often to be made of unheated rooms, especially if

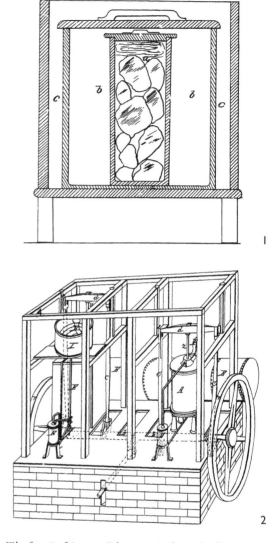

*The first "refrigerator" by name is claimed to have been invented in 1803, using a box with a coat of insulation around it. An improved version was this so-called refrigerator (Fig. 1) patented in 1835; but the icebox did not become common until the second half of the 19th century, when commercial ice became increasingly available. Modern refrigeration, of course, is mechanical. A leading pioneer was Dr. John Gorrie, whose "ice machine" of 1851 looked like this (Fig. 2). (U.S. Patent Collection: "Refrigerator," June 12, 1835; J. Gorrie "Ice Machine," May 6, 1851)*

drafty and on the north side of the house. Such a room was described by Harriet Beecher Stowe in *Oldtown Folks,* where pies stored after baking for Thanksgiving "often came out fresh and good with the violets of April."

But clearly this was not modern "frozen food"—food technologically processed and preserved for modern forms of preparation. Experimentation had begun in the wake of the patent for the first commercial ice-making machinery. In 1876 frozen meat packed in ice and salt was shipped from the United States to England. But a half century would go by before frozen foods reached the marketplace. The first commercial freezing plant went into operation in 1929 in Hillsboro, Oregon (a plant that would later become a part of General Foods). Birds Eye products first appeared in March 1930 in stores in Springfield, Massachusetts. Selections included peas, spinach, raspberries, loganberries, cherries, and various meats and fish. A package of frozen peas cost thirty-five cents, more than twice the price of the fresh. Precooked foods (beginning with chicken fricassee, creamed chicken, beef stew, roast turkey, and soups) went on the market just before World War II.

About this same time, Borden's and National Dairies unsuccessfully tried marketing frozen orange juice in small paper containers distributed by milkmen. But it was only after concentrate was perfected in the postwar period that frozen orange juice became popular. Along the way thought was given (and given up) to marketing the juice in the form of a frozen ball that could be dropped in a glass like a tea bag. Complete meals finally arrived on the market in the form of the TV dinner, as it was called, in the spring of 1954. A product

of C. A. Swanson and Sons, of Omaha, Nebraska, the first was a dinner of sliced turkey and gravy on corn bread with sweet potatoes and peas. The dinner was heated in the oven; its tray was disposable. Other convenience innovations of the time included boilable bags (late 1950s) for heating such precooked or prepared foods as meat and gravy, beef and sauce, stews, seafood, poultry, and vegetables with sauces. Another late 1950s innovation was "pour and store" plastic bags permitting storage of larger quantities of frozen foods than had been possible with the usual 9- or 10-ounce packages.

Except for orange juice and the like, these frozen foods were for preparation in the oven or, in the case of boilable bags, on the stove top. But changing technology would substantially alter food preparation with still another mainstay of the modern kitchen. Derived as it was from radar, one of the most significant weapons of World War II, it is fitting that its sighting be detected during wartime. Hence, in October 1944 *Science Digest* reported:

A post-war innovation of the frozen food processors will be the completely prepared dinner. The shopper will choose between menus offered by competing companies. . . . Then, one minute before dinnertime, she will place the pre-cooked frozen meal, in its sectioned, plastic container, into a special electronic oven. This oven will employ high frequency radio waves which penetrate all foods equally, warming a whole chicken as fast as a portion of peas. In a few seconds a bell will ring and the whole dinner will pop up like a piece of toast—ready to serve and eat. Best of all, there will be no pots to scrape for the plastic container will be discarded after use.

*Science Digest's* incredibly accurate prediction was a little premature as far as the household was concerned. Its 1944 report was apparently a reference to a partially cooked dinner developed by the W. L. Maxson Company of New York, the entire output of which was bought up by the armed forces.

The electronic oven is what became known as the microwave. Plans for producing one for the home were first announced in 1949, but it was not until the mid 1950s that the microwave oven became commercially viable for household use.

With the microwave, preparation time was practically reduced to that magical "minute before dinnertime" prophesied by *Science Digest,* while clean-up time dropped almost to zero with a plastic container that could be discarded after use. The combined effect of prepared frozen foods and the microwave was to accentuate a century-long trend toward compactness of the kitchen and, more than that, to reduce the time that must be spent there.

A further instance of technological progress has occurred in . . .

## CONCENTRATING THE HEAT SOURCE

Let us think back to the medieval great hall and its open hearth—that great indoor bonfire open on all sides, the smoke from which spiraled upward through darkened rafters to find release through an opening in the roof. By the early 17th century the bonfire had been halfway tamed—halfway boxed in by a fireplace often 8 feet wide and 3 or 4 feet deep. This fireplace was very nearly a small room, about like a modern walk-in closet. To reach the oven in the back wall, the housewife actually did walk in, aside the fire, taking care that her billowing woolen skirt did not catch. There was sometimes even a small bench at the side, within the opening, on which to sit and keep warm.

Essentially this was the medieval open hearth, half-contained. Nor was it more than half-tamed. Although the fireplace itself was of brick or stone, the lintel across the top in front was usually wood and not immune to catching fire. The trammel bar inside, from which hung pots and kettles, was likewise also often of wood and even more hazardous, especially when the logs were piled high and there was a roaring fire. Children often curled up to nap on the hearth and there were probably many instances of the sort related of a Captain Denney, whose four children were sitting or lying on the hearth when a trammel bar gave way and a pot of boiling liquid spilled, "which scalded them in so terrible a manner, that one died presently after, and another's life is despaired of." By the late 17th century the wooden trammel bar was being replaced with an iron crane that pivoted out.

Nor was this huge, 17th-century fireplace anything of great convenience. Stooping, bending, lifting, holding, reaching, pushing, stretching, leaning . . . the poor housewife went through a back-breaking ritual to get her pots and kettles (usually wrought iron) into and out of that flaming cavern. The oven had a separate ritual all its own. A fire had to be built within the oven cavity at the back of the fireplace (later to the side, in front) and allowed to

*The basement kitchen of the William Brinton House (1704), Delaware County, Pennsylvania: The hearth is still virtually a half-enclosed bonfire, modernized with a pivoting iron crane succeeding the inside trammel bar of earlier fireplaces.* (Historic American Buildings Survey)

get its hottest. When the bricks were suitably bright in color, it was time to remove the fire and its ashes using a long, flat-bladed shovel. The brick bottom of the oven was then brushed clean with a broom of hemlock twigs, and in went the brown bread, beans, pudding, pie, or cake to bake directly on the hot bottom bricks. When it became customary in the 18th century to situate the oven in front, this was then a "modern" fireplace.

Modern, of course, is relative. In the 19th century, modern meant a stove—burning wood at first, coal later in the century. The first satisfactory cooking model was patented in 1815, and by the 1840s stoves were becoming common. The mass-produced kitchen stove was one of the first great accomplishments of the industrial revolution and a fixture of most new homes built from the Civil War on. The advantages of stoves: Safer, easier to use, they required less bending and stooping and they provided more efficient heating of the kitchen.

It would seem everyone would have wanted one, but progress takes its own course. Harriet Connor Brown, getting married at roughly the time of transition from fireplace to stove, recalled that the fireplace at her childhood home in Athens, Ohio, had an oven that was still the same as in colonial times. She and her sisters helped their mother fire it twice a week and do all the baking at once. They built a fire, waited for the oven to get thoroughly hot, then took out the coals with a scraper and put in roasts and fowls and pies and bread. At other times they simply used the open fireplace. "It was'nt [*sic*] nearly so difficult to work as people think," she insisted. Then she got married . . .

When we went to keeping house in 1845, Dan'l and I, he bought me a little iron stove, a new thing in those days. It was no good, and would only bake things on one side. I soon went back to cooking at an open fireplace.

There were undoubtedly other Harriet Connor Browns who had their doubts about "progress," but for the majority of housewives the stove quickly became the standard of the modern American kitchen.

Convenience and efficiency aside, the stove was of its greatest long-range significance as the first major reduction in the size of the heat source and thus in the layout of the kitchen. The early colonial fireplace was often 8 feet wide. Even the somewhat smaller 18th century fireplace still dominated the room. The stove could be measured in so many inches. And yet this was not the so many inches of a 20th-century gas range. The cast-iron stove demanded its own space. It was, wrote Charles Dickens, a "red-hot monster." It could not abut a wall, and certainly it could not form part of a continuous working space, as is the case with the modern range. Its effective size necessarily included a protective zone on all sides.

The stove or range (the names are basically interchangeable today) became more elaborate and sophisticated over the years, with draft controls, grates to take either coal or wood, and a reservoir to keep water hot. Before this last came into use, a kettle on top of the stove had to suffice. A well-equipped model of the kitchen range was a family possession not quite but nearly as much a source of pride as would be the family car of the next century.

Gas as fuel came into use by roughly the mid 19th century but was slow in gaining acceptance and did not begin to become popular until roughly the turn of the century. By 1910, it was in fairly general use. Gas meant no hauling buckets of coal, or chopping and stocking wood. With gas it was far easier to start the fire—just turn a valve and light a match. Gas was clean-burning and efficient, and a gas stove looked the same as a coal or wood stove, making for a comfortable transition to the new era of cooking. Some ranges used gas for the burners and had a separate oven, fired by either coal or wood. Gas ovens profited immeasurably from the oven regulator, first offered in 1915 by the American Stove Company. Prior to the regulator, there was no way of controlling oven temperature. At first the regulator wheel had numbers from 1 to 11 to identify temperature settings; by the late 1920s the wheel was marked with actual degree settings (300, 350, and so on).

Electricity for cooking was tried in the late 1880s but was slow to catch on. The stove was high-priced, current was expensive, and use was limited for many years only to urban areas with electric service. On the part of the public, there was also concern about safety; and, perhaps more important, there was an innate distrust that it was actually possible to cook without an open flame, as humankind had been doing since the beginning of history.

The public's first good look at cooking with electricity came at the Chicago World's Fair of 1893, which exhibited a model electric kitchen featuring a small range, a broiler, kettles, and even a saucepan, all of them electrical. Even so, the first commercial electric range did not go on the market until 1910, and widespread use did come until the 1940s.

Thus had the kitchen heat source been reduced in size from a half-enclosed bonfire perhaps 8 feet in size to (in architectural historian Siegfried Giedion's phrase) a "mere spiral of wire"—the ultimate condensation of the heating medium, although the apparatus in

A different view: the kitchen of the Buttolph-Williams House, Wethersfield, Connecticut (c1710–1720). (Antiquarian and Landmarks Society, Hartford, Conn.)

The kitchen of the General Lyman Mower House, Woodstock, Vermont (1823): The oven adheres to Rumford principles with its smaller opening, slanted sides, and narrow throat; the bake oven (upper left) is in front, the "modern" location that has prevailed for more than a century. Below the oven is a bin for wood storage. Here is the kitchen fireplace at essentially its highest state of technological development. Stoves for cooking have already come into use and will soon eclipse the open hearth. (Historic American Buildings Survey)

(Left) *The modern kitchen, 1872: The David Davis Mansion, Bloomington, Illinois. Notable here are the coal-fired cast-iron stove, copper water heater, and soapstone sink with hot and cold running water. Out of view are the "refrigerator" (or icebox, by later nomenclature) and a gaslit wall sconce that could be adjusted for position over a work area. That the sink is by a window may not be coincidental: Sarah Davis had been a student of Catharine Beecher and was familiar with her* American Woman's Home, *whose model kitchen has windows at the main work area.* (Photograph by the author)

(Right) *Recognizably modern now is the kitchen, c1930, of the Browne-Wagner House, Brownsville, Texas, part of a renovation of an older dwelling. The primary working space, including sink and window above it, reflects even more the concept of the kitchen as illustrated in* The American Woman's Home. *By now the kitchen stove is a compact unit that matches the general decor. The tiers of shallow shelves in* The American Woman's Home *now are glass-front cabinets.* (Historic American Buildings Survey)

(Left) *Even though the stove is not seen here, the effect of concentration of the heat source is evident in the compact and efficient kitchen of Frank Lloyd Wright's Fallingwater (1938). Modern as it was for the mid 20th century—and still for the late 20th—there is a curious echo of the Brinton hearth of 1710 in the texture of the walls. Here it is coincidental; elsewhere in Fallingwater evocation of the centrality of the hearth is very much intentional.* (Historic American Buildings Survey)

which the cooking takes place still must be roughly the same size as a gas range, or a large wood stove for that matter. But unlike the "hot monster" radiating heat from all of its cast-iron sides, the modern range, with its concentrated heat source, gas or electric, can be insulated and thus able to be located immediately adjacent to other components of the kitchen. The net effect is to make possible the compact and continuous working space that is the essence of the modern kitchen.

Nerve center . . . nucleus of domestic technology . . . hub of family communications . . . all this and still the family hearth as well. The modern kitchen is the heart of the modern house and the most dramatic evidence as well of the social and technological change that has swept over the house since the days of Mary Read's very modern kitchen. It is the most changed room. It has undergone a degree of transformation that would make it unrecognizable to the housewife of the colonial period and nearly so to one of even a hundred years ago. While most of the house has remained more or less traditional, the once medieval kitchen is space-age. Although there may be period accents (an old-fashioned clock, a colonial spice shelf) or even an overall decor evoking the warmth and homeyness of kitchens of old, there is inevitably an array of knobs and dials and flashing lights and little tinted windows; an ensemble of soft colors, softly lighted; a little orchestra of gentle whirring sounds with an occasional percussion of clicks and beeps.

From here the housewife conducts, be it meal planning, meal making, family scheduling, household financing, bill paying, or checkbook balancing. This is the communications center of the house, signified by the re-frigerator door that is the family bulletin board. This is the house's loading platform. If there is a back door or side door leading into the kitchen, it is the entry point for most of what goes into the house, whether groceries for the kitchen or new curtains for a bedroom. And this is where what goes out goes out.

This is usually the communications hub, home base of the cordless telephone and of increasingly sophisticated household computerization that can oversee electronic systems for security, lighting, audiovisual devices, and heating and air conditioning. The latest computer technology can take a spoken command like "Going out" and respond with simultaneous activation of alarms, outdoor floodlights, appliance timers, and thermostat resettings; or a command like "Going to bed," in which case the ever wakeful computer, knowing the family's rising time, will be on duty first, turning up the heat, switching on the lights, tuning in the radio, and starting the morning coffee perking.

Yet here is also the traditional kitchen—the family hearth, the place for coming together for that most fundamental of all social activity, breaking bread together. And, except that that bread is now 95 percent bakery-made instead of family-hearth-made, this kitchen, even with its microwave and self-defrosting refrigerator, fills the same sustaining role in family life as the hall-kitchen of Grace Fairbanks.

## THE BATHROOM AND ITS CONNECTIONS

It may seem axiomatic to call the bathroom the most private room of the house. Private, indeed. It is a sanctum of solitude. No other room—indeed no other place anywhere—is quite the refuge that is the modern bathroom. The bedroom also has privacy, but not on the same order; for the bedroom is commonly shared, as by a spouse or a sibling. The bathroom, on the other hand, is all one's own, for as long as one keeps the door locked.

This point about privacy is made for good reason. It brings us to a paradox. In the history of the house, the very private bathroom is also the most connected room of the house, in the sense of its evolution's intertwining with technological and social evolution outside the home. Notable is the impact of a growing awareness of public health.

Had he not been a prince, once remarked Prince Albert, consort of Britain's Queen Victoria, he would like to have been a plumber. By this he meant he would have been able to do something—really do something, like actually take a wrench to a pipe—to help alleviate the spread of disease caused by lack of sanitation. Ironically, Prince Albert's premature death in 1861 at the age of forty-two—nearly as much a shock in America as in Britain—was primarily attributable to typhoid fever, one of the afflictions most eradicable by sanitation.

Regularly, year after year, Buckingham Palace had been sending Parliament a plea for "a comprehensive scheme of drains and sewers in order to clean up the river [the Thames]," and regularly Parliament set it aside. Shortly before his death Albert managed to prevail upon a new prime minister, Lord Derby, to move forward with legislation. The result, chiefly engineered by Sir Joseph Bazalgette, was a network of sewers totaling 83 miles.

Opened partly in 1865 and completed in 1875, it was the first major sewer system of modern times and a model for sewer systems elsewhere.

Awareness of the need for public sanitation did not come easily. What generated it as never before was widespread dread of cholera. William IV of England had opened Parliament in June 1831 with the ominous warning, "I have directed that . . . precautions should be taken . . . against the introduction of so dangerous a malady in this country." Yet despite precautions, cholera had taken hold in England within the year. In the United States there were also precautions, aimed chiefly at preventing the disease from entering the country. Immigrants arriving on suspected ships were often not allowed to land or, if admitted, were relegated to a quarantine area of makeshift tents. As in England, such safeguards fell short, and by June 1832 America had buried its first victims. Hardest hit were New York and Philadelphia; in New York alone, more than three thousand died during July and August. New Orleans recorded forty-three hundred deaths in three weeks when the epidemic reached there in October.

One who lived through it all was William C. King, of Detroit. His diary account is particularly poignant because of his occupation. He was a carpenter.

Tuesday, 25th [June 1832]. News arrived of cholera raging in Quebec and Montreal to dreadful degree, 100 deaths out of 120 cases.

Wednesday, 26th. Alarming reports of cholera.

Sunday, [July] 8th. Morning, all hands called to make boxes for soldiers dead and dying of cholera. Made 6, used 4.

Wednesday, 11th. . . . made 3 rough coffins for hospital.

Thursday, 12th. Called up early to make a coffin, young woman, died of cholera.

Saturday, 14th. . . . made 6 rough coffins.

Monday, 16th. . . . made rough coffin for boy, died of cholera.

Wednesday, August 8th. Made rough coffin for Swiss woman, cholera.

Monday, 20th. Morning, made rough coffin for cholera.

September 2. Took long walk through the fields by the side of the graveyard, the city of the dead, which by the aid of the cholera is becoming populous. Evening made coffin, cholera.

The disease then seemed to disappear; but as it had in its earlier manifestations in Asia and Europe, it rebounded periodically. New York had more than five thousand casualties in 1848–1849. From the eastern seaboard the epidemic moved west. In St. Louis, one of every twelve died. As the disease spread, it created havoc among the Native Americans, whose close-knit encampments were particularly prone to contagion. The Indians concluded they were purposely being poisoned by

A PERIL OF THE YEAR.—In congratulating the country at the close of the year over the happy stoppage of the scourge of war which took place in its earlier months, we must not lose sight of the fact that there is danger of our suffering in the present year from the scourge of pestilence. If it be true that cholera is in the West Indies, it may touch our Southern seacoast cities before the first on the new year passes away.

The Legislature me

*In looking ahead to the first full year of peace since the beginning of the Civil War, the* New York Times *on January 1, 1866, warned that a war of comparable magnitude was still to be won—the war against cholera. The* Times *urged energetic measures to build sewers and a safe public water supply as the only way of winning the battle.*

the white man and retaliated against the forty-niners trekking west by covered wagon.

In the wake of a world pandemic that broke out in 1863, cholera spread rapidly in America in 1866, especially as Civil War armies demobilized and newly freed slaves scattered. In this age of improved rail and steamship travel, the technological capacity that had greatly increased personal mobility also increased the mobility of infection. That same technological capacity also had the power to control if not someday eliminate cholera, but it would take an awakening on the part of public institutions.

On New Year's Day 1866, the *New York Times* noted the irony of marking the end of one peril with the threat of another:

In congratulating the country at the close of the year over the happy stoppage of the scourge of war which took place in its earlier months, we must not lose sight of the fact that there is danger of our suffering in the present year from the scourge of pestilence. . . . the cholera; but it is as certain as statistics and science that its ravages may be greatly abated by the adoption of energetic sanitary measures.

"Energetic sanitary measures." The connection between sanitation and disease was hardly new. Even in antiquity there was at least some primitive understanding of it. Underground conduits for removal of waste existed as early as 2500 B.C. in the ancient Indus civilization at Mohenjo-Daro; similarly, crude drainage systems at Knossos in Crete. Rome's sewer system, the likes of which would not be seen again until the mid 19th century, consisted of a network of small sewers feeding into a main trunk line, the Cloaca Maxima.

The Middle Ages produced no such public works but at least allowed for recognition of the link between disease and sanitation, as is evident in this proclamation by Richard II in 1388:

> For that so much Dung and Filth . . . be cast and put into Ditches, Rivers and other Waters . . . that the air there is greatly corrupt and infect, and many Maladies and other intolerable Diseases do daily happen . . . [he] that do cast or throw any such annoyances, issues, dung, intrails or other ordure in Ditches, Rivers and Waters, shall cause them to be removed . . . upon pain to lose and forfeit to our Lord the King £20.

Such proclamations had only limited impact, as was so also in colonial America. An echo of King Richard can be heard in an edict issued in New Amsterdam in 1644 forbidding residents from relieving themselves or dumping their chamber pots within the fort itself (there being ample place outside the walls). In late 17th-century Newport, Rhode Island, there were "several Privy houses sett against ye Streets" and emptying therein, with the result that passersby were in constant risk of "Spoiling & Damnifying" their clothes.

In New York a partial solution was presumably achieved in 1691 with construction of a "Necessary House for the Use of the publicq," built on a wharf near City Hall. Half a century later the effects of an increasing concentration of population were manifest as yellow fever threatened New York. A New York physician and scientist named Cadwallader Colden, who had trained in London, in 1743 warned that unsanitary conditions were the root of the threat and urged that the municipality take responsibility for sewers:

> What has been before observed, naturally leads us to the preventive remedies of the annual epidemical diseases of New-York; that is, faithfully . . . to take care that all the filth and nastiness of the town be emptied into the stream of the river. . . . I am of opinion this cannot be done effectually, but by the drains [a few, now private] being put entirely into the hands of the [municipal] corporation [and] managed by a public tax. . . .

The substance of Dr. Colden's warnings about sanitation was obviously valid, even if also ahead of its time for all practical purposes. Today all sewers are "managed by a public tax."

What finally had dramatic impact on establishing sewers was the realization that cholera put the entire population at risk, not merely those living in congested, unsanitary neighborhoods. The cause of the spread of cholera was pinpointed in 1849 by the English physician Dr. John Snow after investigating various outbreaks in England.* Dr. Snow turned his attention to cholera because he was an authority on respiratory illness, and it was still assumed that cholera was spread through the air. But Dr. Snow suspected that since this was a disease of the alimentary system, it might be attributed to something swallowed. His investigations pointed to drinking-water, and his most dramatic evidence was the account of a Broad Street, London, neighborhood whose residents used a common pump. The incidence of cholera among these residents was high, yet several who worked outside the area and took no water at home were untouched. On the other hand, seven workmen employed in the district but living elsewhere who drank from the pump during working hours were afflicted. There was also the case of a neighborhood brewery that employed some seventy men. Not one came down with cholera; instead of partaking of water, they drank only the free beer the brewery provided. Dr. Snow's *On the mode of communication of cholera* as revised in 1855 (it was first published in 1849), made quite clear the significance of his findings:

If the cholera had no other means of communication . . . it would confine itself chiefly to the crowded dwellings of the poor. . . . But there is often a way open for it to extend itself more widely and to reach the well-to-do classes of the community; I allude to the mixture of the cholera evacuations with the water used for drinking and culinary purposes, either by permeating the ground, and getting into wells, or by running along channels and sewers into the rivers from which entire towns are sometimes supplied with water.

A few years before Dr. Snow's observation, the need for modern sanitation generally was emphasized in the highly regarded *General Report on the Sanitary Conditions of the Labouring Classes in Great Britain,* published in 1842 and better known as the Chadwick Report, for Edwin Chadwick, who drafted it. The report, quite ahead of its time, proposed that every dwelling unit have a water closet. It was a wholly unrealistic goal in 1842; but in due time a water closet in every dwelling would become a taken-for-granted provision of building codes not only in Britain but America.

In America, even before Cadwallader Colden's time, there had been primitive attempts at constructing sewers, usually in the form of covered ditches. One such was dug in 1703 alongside New York's Broad Street for a length of roughly a quarter mile. But at best any such sewers (and there were very few until the 19th century) simply took away whatever was dumped into them, as opposed to modern sewers connected house to house; and they emptied into rivers and streams, thus taking pollution from one place to a different place, which even Dr. Colden seemed not to mind. Philadelphia, in an 1809 survey of the city,

*The etiology of yellow fever is entirely different, but it was not until the late 1890s that its transmittal by mosquito was established. See pages 194–195.

showed only a few sewers for a population of fifty thousand, and some of these were private, the owners charging fees for their use. Even in 1857 little more had been accomplished; the chief engineer of Philadelphia's department of sewage was still urging a culvert on every street, into which waste would be discharged instead of using the gutters.

Meanwhile, for the most part, disposal of human waste remained about as primitive as it had been over past centuries: by either an outdoor privy (the colonial "necessary" or "necessary house") or a chamber pot (sometimes given the convenience and fashion of a close-stool) that was kept in one's bedroom or some other suitable place inside the house. In either case the waste went (or was supposed to go) into a privy pit—one of those "magazines of putrefaction" known to Benjamin Franklin. The privy, for example, was simply built over the pit; if there was no privy, there was presumed to be at least a pit for the dumping of the chamber pots. But as was so notoriously the case in the Middle Ages, the streets were often the recourse of choice of lazy householders in towns or cities. The rural resident was less constrained about where he dumped.

It was a matter of common understanding that the pits should be emptied from time to time. In between, a heap of lime was useful. As a practical matter, poorer people could not afford the expense of having this done, and even the wealthier rarely bothered. The relatively well-to-do Drinker family of Philadelphia, for example, went from 1735 to 1779 without bothering, and when the time came it was an occasion worth recording in Elizabeth Drinker's diary. The work was done overnight and took two nights. The family purposely scheduled it

for March in hopes the cold weather would cut down on the smell, though the Drinker children took the precaution of burning incense anyway. Wrote Elizabeth on March 7:

> The jobb in our Yard is finish'd except what the Carpenters are to do—It has been nothing to what we expected—I dreaded it before commencement, and am pleased 'tis over—ther [they] were at work two night . . .

When the carpenters had finished up, probably rebuilding the privy seat, the pit was 16 feet deep measured from the seat—"a dreadfull gulph it look[ed] like" to Elizabeth.

The workers might have dug it deeper, but Mr. Drinker refused. Such conscientiousness was not universal. One way people got around ever having to empty their cesspits was to dig them down to ground water. In this way the fecal material steadily dissolved and washed away . . . eventually into someone's well. The result was what has sometimes been known as the circular system of water supply. In fact, a constant danger to health lurked wherever there was a concentration of population. Recurring epidemics of fever of otherwise unexplained origin were undoubtedly the result of polluted drinking water. Sometimes there was no way of knowing; in other cases suspicions should easily have been raised. Dr. Benjamin Rush, physician and signer of the Declaration of Independence, wrote in 1773 of a sample of Philadelphia water that

> when it first comes from the pump, has a slight faetid smell, is somewhat turbid, and after standing a few hours exposed to the air,

*Until the combined effect of cholera and the increasing concentration of population was felt in the 19th century, the danger of the proximity of water supply to human waste disposal was largely not understood or, if understood, usually overlooked. That proximity is graphically illustrated in this photograph at the National Park Service restoration of Franklin Court in Philadelphia. The nearest circle marks the site of a 1700s water well serving 318 Market Street; the other circle a few feet away was No. 318's privy pit.* (Photograph by the author)

deposits a yellow sediment. The smell of the water is increased by rest.

From time to time, governing bodies attempted to regulate cesspits and privies, but circumvention had the weight of centuries behind it. A court in England in 1328, for example, heard the case of one William Sprot, who complained that his neighbors had filled their "cloaca" to the point that it had overflowed and seeped through his wall. The pit was closer to his house than regulations allowed. In 1347 two men were accused of actually piping their "ordure" into a neighbor's cellar. A Philadelphian of the late 18th century noted in his diary that a man, after dutifully cleaning out his cesspit, simply dumped the contents into the street in the middle of the night.

Awareness of public health became more acute in the 19th century, especially the second half. A series of national sanitary conventions at about this same time showed the beginning of a formalized effort at public sanitation—the so-called sanitary movement—a process briefly interrupted by the Civil War that, in the postwar years, gathered momentum and carried into the early 20th century. Finally there began the systematic construction of sewers to replace patchwork systems of conduits, some open and some covered, many privately owned. As in England, the predominant material at first was brick, often constructed with a pear-shaped cross section, the narrower end at the bottom facilitating flow even when the level was low. But construction was often piecemeal, with the result that sewage now systematically collected in one neighborhood actually increased groundwater pollution in another because of inadequate means of disposal after collection.

Although Boston had some sanitary sewer lines by 1833, perhaps the first comprehensive underground sewer system in America was that constructed in pre-Fire Chicago in 1856–1860 (population 112,172 in 1860 and growing rapidly). The main sewers were of brick, 3 to 6 feet across, with branch lines 2 feet in diameter fed from laterals of pipe or wood plank. By 1860 some forty-six miles had been completed. The sewer system followed a grid pattern. Now instead of uncoordinated sewers sometimes working literally at cross purposes, there was a consolidated system serving an entire municipality.

But in such systems over the coming years, the "stream of the river" advocated by Dr. Colden in 1743 continued to be the usual method for disposal even after it was growing clear that this action only moved the problem from one place to another. The dilemma was eventually resolved with the development of sewage treatment plants in the late 19th and early 20th centuries. An early model was that of Worcester, Massachusetts, built in 1890, which used six 60- by 100-foot settling tanks to treat raw sewage with lime. The effluent, after settling, was pumped into lagoons. By the early 20th century bacterial decomposition was being used; the first major treatment plant was opened in Manchester, England, in 1914. From then to the present day the process has been essentially one of refinement.

## "AND THEN THROUGH PIPES . . ."

Stimulated by a far deeper understanding of the nature of the transmission of disease, especially the dreaded cholera, and facilitated by expanding technological capacity, the development of public sewerage systems in the second half of the 19th century came just in time to cope with a rapid expansion of population, particularly in the cities. The sharp increase in both population size and concentration is evident in census figures for these cities:

|              | 1850    | 1900      |
|--------------|---------|-----------|
| New York     | 696,115 | 3,437,202 |
| Philadelphia | 121,376 | 1,293,697 |
| St. Louis    | 77,860  | 575,238   |
| Buffalo      | 42,261  | 352,387   |
| Chicago      | 29,963  | 1,698,575 |
| Memphis      | 8,841   | 102,320   |
| Los Angeles  | 1,610   | 102,479   |

Failure of public sewerage systems more or less to keep up with such growth would have had dire consequences, as would the lack of development of water supply.

Grace Fairbanks had a small brook about a hundred yards in back of her house, and she may have used it for nondrinking purposes. For drinking water, like other of Dedham's earliest householders, she (or Jonathan, or one of the children) probably trekked several times a day to a spring somewhere in or near the village. We may recall here that the Fairbankses were among those becoming town residents in Dedham's second year. The first signers of the town covenant got the first choice of lots, probably nearest whatever springs there were. In time, wells were sunk, and these supplied Dedham's needs until the Dedham Water Company came into being in 1881. (Nothing in the way of sewerage existed in Dedham until an act of the state legislature in 1897 resulted in construction of a seventeen-mile sewer system, approved at a town meeting in November 1900.)

Siting of colonial houses, indeed of the towns and villages themselves, kept proximity to water in mind. And for roughly the duration of the colonial period, wells and nearby streams were sufficient for water supply everywhere, and in rural areas into modern times. In towns there were public pumps in addition to wells at many private homes. Public wells not only provided water for households but for fire fighting as well. Hence the Union Fire Company of Philadelphia in 1744 announced a reward of £5 "for apprehending the persons who stole the nozles from High street, and other streets." The Swedish scientist Peter Kalm, after visiting the city in 1748, wrote that there was a well in every house and several in the streets; but "every house" was clearly an overstatement. Still another visitor from Europe later in the century was Moreau de Saint-Méry. In New York in 1794 he recorded in his journal that a few households were served by piped-in water from a small reservoir supplied from a spring. The pipes, he said, were lead. Considerably more home owners took advantage of water delivered by horse-drawn carts. In Philadelphia, which he visited the following year, wooden pumps at intervals along the sidewalk provided "not particularly good" water from the Schuylkill River.

Even long before urbanization, it was obvious a time would come, sooner or later, when there would be too many people for a well at every house; private wells and individual pumps would not suffice. Ancient Rome, with its million people, gave public water supply high priority. Its fourteen aqueducts spanning a distance of 359 miles conveyed to the city as much as three hundred million gallons a day

(though this gallonage was probably only rarely reached, one or more aqueducts at any given time usually being under repair).

The first primitive attempt at a mass water supply in the American colonies was at Boston in 1652, when the Water Works Company constructed a series of wooden pipes to carry water from springs to a central reservoir; this, being only 12 feet square, made the system of limited usefulness.

Nor did Boston's system really constitute a waterworks, in the sense of a works being comprised of pumps as well as pipes and a reservoir. The honor of first would appear to go to the town of Bethlehem, Pennsylvania, whose ambitious scheme to tap the Monocacy Creek, a tributary of the Lehigh River, was described just prior to going into operation by the Reverend Israel Acrelius, of Sweden, visiting Bethlehem on June 18, 1754:

> In the same house [a mill using a waterwheel] they were now arranging waterworks, which were to drive the water up the steep hill, and then through pipes distribute it to every house, which work a Jutlander [millwright Hans Christiansen] had undertaken to accomplish. . . . This will be a very useful work . . . for hitherto it has kept a man busy from morning till night to carry the water up the hill to the houses.

Bethlehem's waterworks used the power of water itself—the waterwheel in the mill house—to operate a pump that forced water up a steep hill to a water tower at the grade level of the town itself. The pipe through which the water was pumped was made of hollowed-out hemlock trunks. The system had been given a trial run prior to Acrelius's visit and went into regular operation on June 27, 1754. Apparently there were some connections, using wood pipe, to nearby houses, but how many is not a matter of record. It is probably safe to assume most residents carried water home from the tower in buckets.

New York in 1774 commissioned Christopher Colles, an engineer and cartographer, to construct a waterworks using steam power. Interrupted by the Revolutionary War, the project came to naught. In 1796 Salem, Massachusetts, built a gravity-flow system supplying water from a nearby pond. Portsmouth, New Hampshire, began construction of an aqueduct the following year.

By the turn of the 19th century, at least seventeen American cities and towns had experimented with water-supply systems, but clearly the most important of these was Philadelphia, then the nation's largest city with seventy thousand in population. The city in 1799 commissioned English-born architect and engineer Benjamin Latrobe to build a steam-powered waterworks, and this one succeeded—at least for a while. It was opened on January 27, 1801. Water from the Schuylkill River, pumped out at Chestnut Street, was conveyed by a water main along Chestnut and Broad Streets to Centre Square, where a second pump raised it to a wooden reservoir. From there wooden pipes carried water to various parts of the city. But the system was plagued with frequent breakdowns of the engines and never managed to keep up with the needs of an increasing population. The works was abandoned in 1815 and a new system subsequently opened with a reservoir on Fairmount Hill. The wooden mains of the old were replaced with iron.

Not all cities followed immediately. As of 1834, Boston was still using wells. With a

*The Philadelphia waterworks: in operation in 1801, the first major water-supply system in America. This was the heart of the system, a steam-powered facility in Centre Square that pumped water from the Schuylkill River into a wooden reservoir, from which wooden pipes conveyed it to various parts of the city.* (Library of Congress, Prints and Photographs)

population of some seventy-four thousand, it had 2,767 wells, of which 2,085 were producing drinkable water. But in 1837 the city began exploring mass supply and in 1846, with special enabling legislation, embarked on a water-supply system that would include a reservoir in Brookline supplied by water from Lake Cochituate. By 1850 the Boston water system, which included a reservoir on Beacon Hill, supplied 11,383 households with piped-in water. The average water bill was eight dollars a year, and this, according to a description written at the time (*American Almanac*, 1850), was "for water for all domestic purposes, including private baths, water-closets, &c. No public hydrants, for the gratuitous supply of [free] water for domestic uses are provided." In other words, homes that were not connected to the municipal system had to cope for themselves by digging wells or buying from vendors. On the other hand, for those connected, there was no extra charge for having tubs and/or water closets. This was not always the case, and even in Boston, in the years immediately ahead, separate charges were made for these modern conveniences. Hence, it is known that in 1860 Boston had 3,910 bathtubs and 9,864 water closets—for a population of some 178,000.

New York in 1856 had only 10,384 water closets and 1,361 tubs for a population more than three times as large—and this despite the fact that New York City had recently completed perhaps the most significant water-supply project of the century, the Croton Aqueduct. Opened in 1842, it conveyed water from the Croton River, forty miles north of the city, to a reservoir at what is now the site of the New York Public Library, and from there

through mains and pipes to customers throughout the city. Its total cost, including laying pipe, came to $12.5 million, almost exactly half the entire federal budget of $25.2 million in 1842. By 1856 there were 53,745 customers hooked up.

During this same period, the years immediately preceding the Civil War, municipal water systems were also established in Cleveland, Detroit, Hartford, Brooklyn, Jersey City, Louisville, and Cincinnati. By the 1860s all but four of the sixteen largest U.S. cities had municipal water supplies. Meanwhile, in the still developing West, water supply was somewhat more primitive. Salt Lake City in 1860 ran water in open ditches along streets; San Francisco pumped water from wells and brooks, but had it delivered to homes in carts.

It is now long forgotten that public water supply did not necessarily mean running water in the house. For example: Hartford in 1862 supplied 4,246 households; of these, 857 still without indoor plumbing had to make do with hydrants in their yards. It was hardly the same as having running water in the sink, but it was a dependable source of water presumably safe from pollution by some neighbor's privy. Eliza Ripley, however, had less than pleasant recollections of New Orleans in the mid 1800s:

> . . . The only running water was a hydrant, the only sink was a gutter in the yard. . . . To be sure there was a cistern for rainwater, and jars like those Ali Baba's forty thieves hid themselves in. Those earthen jars were replenished from the hydrant and muddy river water "settled" by the aid of almond hulls or alum.

Today's water-supply systems, virtually universal in urban and suburban areas, go vastly beyond almond hulls and alum to assure not only quality (taste, color, odor) but safety (absence of harmful bacteria, pathogens, and other disease-causing organisms). Most rural homes continue to make use of wells and pumps, although modern environmental regulations and testing procedures largely guarantee that the water is safe and, if anything, better-tasting than chlorinated public water supplies.

Now that we have water being supplied to the bathroom, let us see where most of it goes.

## FROM OUTHOUSE TO IN-HOUSE

Of all the standard conveniences of modern life, perhaps none that is so simple took so long coming into use as the toilet (or water closet).* After all, it is no more than a few uncomplicated parts requiring as a source of power nothing even as sophisticated as electricity—just a few gallons of the most prevalent stuff on earth, water. Yet its common use has come only in the 20th century.

There were probably some water closets in use in America by the beginning of the 19th century—almost certainly all imported, perhaps all from England. And the earliest can be traced as far back as c1765. It was a very primitive form of apparatus (see Appendix, page 253) incorporated into Whitehall, the home built by Governor Horatio Sharpe at Annapolis, Maryland. An early documented instance is the White House, which had a water closet (most likely of more advanced design than Whitehall's) in place by late 1804; another is Gore Place in Waltham, Massachusetts, where a water closet was installed in 1807. In 1808 Benjamin Latrobe designed for John Markoe of Philadelphia a house with a water closet and bathtub with heated cistern on the chamber floor. Latrobe's original plan (c1796–99) for Colonel John Tayloe III in Washington included a water closet; turning instead to William Thornton as architect, Tayloe built what has come to be known as The Octagon (1799–1801). There is no clear evidence of a water closet, but since Thornton's design studies included one and since the house had a sophisticated enough water-supply system, there is a strong probability. In that case it most likely would have been Washington's first; and if so, there would surely have been water closets in use in Philadelphia by the late 1790s, and likely in New York and Boston as well.

But very, very few. Even by the mid 19th century the water closet was still relatively

---

* "Water closet," meaning the apparatus, was the term in use in America from its first appearance c1765 until well into the 20th century. Since the earliest fixtures were the only ones in whatever small enclosure they occupied, the name of the place was presumably the same. From roughly 1850 on, when a water closet and tub were located together, the place took on the name of "bathroom," as it is still known today. "Toilet" as the name of the fixture had only very occasional use in the early 20th century ("toilette," for example, in *House and Garden,* July 1911) and did not start to gain currency until the late 1920s. *Domestic Engineering Catalog* was still using "water closet" in the mid 1920s, and there was occasional use of other terms (as, for example, "flush closet," *House Beautiful,* 1925). There is evidence that "toilet" came into use first for the room. From an insurance survey of the Philadelphia Contributionship dated July 12, 1900: "2 Enclosures . . . for toilet rooms [with] 2 water closets [and] one Enamel iron wash basin . . ." Of course, both water closet and toilet are euphemistic; there has never really been a word specific to function for this now universal fixture of the house. Slang terms, on the other hand, have abounded. The choice between "water closet" and "toilet" in this book is according to its contemporaneous usage.

rarely to be found, and usually only in the homes of the wealthy. New York in 1850, with a population of roughly 700,000, had fewer than 10,000 water closets; Baltimore in 1859 had 698 for a population of 212,418. A. J. Downing's influential *Architecture of Country Houses* (1850) had plans for thirty-four model homes, ranging in cost from moderate to expensive; only eight of the plans included water closets. Why not all? These were after all model homes, presupposing that they were indicative of what was modern. The fact that they were country as opposed to city homes did not make them less amenable to having piped-in water. Public water supply in 1850 accommodated only a handful of major cities (notably New York and Philadelphia), and in the country it was easier to improvise supply, as for example by piping water from a nearby stream into a cistern adjacent to the house or even one on the roof. More important, since many cities still lacked sewerage, disposal of waste water was easier in the country. Yet the fact that these were model homes should have tended to override such technicalities, since both public water supply and sewerage were clearly part of the "model" future.

Cost of installation was certainly a factor. The Gores' water closet as installed in 1807 came to $103.75 plus freight, a considerable sum. For comparison, they bought a copper-lined bathtub for $27 and a stove for $22.50 at the same time. By late in the 19th century, when the water closet was becoming relatively common, mass production had driven down the price significantly.

But what gave pause, whether or not one could afford a water closet and arrange for the necessary water supply and waste disposal, was

that the water closet needed time to gain acceptance. From time immemorial, human waste was associated with the out-of-doors; using either a privy or, in more primitive times, a pit, one went outside to relieve oneself. If one used a chamber pot inside because of the weather or the hour of day, one took it outside to dump at the earliest opportunity. Now with the water closet, one was being asked to defy tradition and complete the process inside the house.

Besides the matter of habit, there was concern about having offensive odors within the house—odors that traditionally belonged outside. An offensive chamber pot could be removed; the water closet was fixed in place. Furthermore, there was a gnawing suspicion that the water closet wouldn't always work and that one's very private offerings would remain unaccepted instead of being flushed discreetly away. Some sense of this resistance to change is evident here:

> A fashion prevails of thrusting these noisome things into the midst of sleeping chambers and living rooms—pandering to effeminacy, and, at times, surcharging the house—for they cannot, at *all* times, and under *all* circumstances, be kept perfectly close—with their offensive odor. *Out* of the house they belong, and if they, by any means, find their way within its walls proper, the fault will not be laid at our door. (Lewis F. Allen, *Rural Architecture,* 1854)

On the other hand, a few years (and not many water closets) later, there was this rather down-to-earth explanation of why water closets were needed *in* the home:

In dry summer weather, they [privies] answer the purpose well enough, perhaps; but in wet weather, and especially in winter, their use involves an exposure which few constitutions are strong enough to bear with impunity. Women are especial sufferers from this cause; hence we find that in wet or cold weather they defer their visits to the privy until compelled by unbearable physical discomfort to brave the dangers and annoyances of a dash out of doors. . . . It is not an uncommon thing for women in the country to allow themselves to become so constipated that days and sometimes weeks will pass between stools. . . . A visit to an outdoor privy in a cold storm or when the ground is covered with snow and the air frosty is attended with a physical shock which even strong men dread. (James C. Bayles, 1880)

At midcentury the water closet was not yet perfected, but it was certainly a usable device within the house; and its level of development was advancing in pace with the development of water supply and sewers. For a time, however, the general lack of sewers meant that many early indoor water closets had to be drained into the pit serving the outdoor privy. This meant the pit had to handle a flow of waste water far in excess of what it was built to accommodate, often resulting in overflow. Or where sewers existed, they were often too primitive to cope with the high gallonage that early water closets required. The result, for a time, was often a greater threat to public health than was posed by the privy and chamber pot of old. Still another danger was improper plumbing that allowed sewer gas to escape into the house.

"*A visit to an outdoor privy . . . when the ground is covered with snow and the air frosty is attended with a physical shock which even strong men dread.*"—*James C. Bayles, 1880. A privy in Oswego County, New York, 1937.* (Library of Congress, Farm Security Administration Collection)

Writing in 1876, pioneer sanitary engineer George E. Waring pointed to experience in Edinburgh as an example of the inherent dangers of water closets where there was not yet safe and adequate means of drainage:

In 1872 the Medical Officer for Edinburgh reported that wherever water-closets were introduced, in the course of one year there were double the number of deaths from typhoid and scarlet fever, and any epidemic fever occurring in these houses assumed a character of malignant mortality. In our own cities [in America] it is known that the fatal prevalence of typhoid, and it is believed that frequent epidemics of diphtheria and cerebro-spinal meningitis, are due to faulty drainage alone.

Sewer systems of adequate capacity to accommodate water closets, coupled with sewage treatment, would effectively solve that. And meanwhile, at the time of Waring's comment, most Americans did not have water closets anyway; they were doing what their forebears had done before them: They went outside to the privy or used a chamber pot or closestool inside.

It had been so in the Middle Ages, a lingering bit of which the earliest colonists brought with them. In medieval towns and cities, where space was insufficient for privies, the chamber pot was basically the only recourse, and there was a notorious tradition of dumping these in the gutter or simply emptying them from an upper window, the contents falling where they might. There is no indication that window dumping was prevalent in the American colonies, but gutters continued to serve this unintended purpose. In the earliest and most primitive colonial settlements, where privies had not yet been constructed, the recourse was often a muck heap in back of the house.

 Primitive apparatus for disposing of human waste in fact goes back to antiquity—even including the use of water for flushing. A slab with "a groove for a seat" coupled with signs of "some vessel used for flushing," as described by British archaeologist Sir Arthur Evans, suggests that a primitive water closet was in use at the Bronze Age palace of Knossos in Crete. And indeed there is evidence of similar apparatus elsewhere in the ancient world. But the first water closet of essentially modern design was probably the one that Sir John Harington built sometime around 1596 for the residence he used as high sheriff of Somerset and that, by royal request, he is said to have duplicated shortly thereafter for his godmother, Elizabeth I, at Richmond Palace (see illustration on page 94 for an ampler description). Harington recorded details in his satirical work *The Metamorphosis of Ajax* (London, 1596). Both closets, obviously too imperfect to depend on, disappeared in time, and the queen when at Richmond returned to using a closestool as she had at her other royal domiciles. The closestool, common among better-off colonial American families, could be as simple as a ladder-back chair with a cloth hanging around the bottom to hide the pot that set it apart from other furniture; or it could be fit for a king, as was a favorite closestool of Henry VIII, a magnificent piece of furniture decorated with black velvet and ribbons and fringes and studded with two thousand gilt nails.

It was nearly two hundred years later that a watchmaker named Alexander Cumming received the first English patent for a water closet, in 1775. This does not mean that no water closet had been devised since the patent office opened in 1617; and indeed there are documentary references to a few, probably very primitive ones, in use in England in the early 1700s, but none, it would seem, that had sufficient distinction to deserve a patent. Cumming's was sold with the promise of being "perfectly sweet" to use; and while this was obviously so much hyberbole, his device could legitimately claim to work. It used an overhead cistern to supply water to the bowl, which emptied by means of a sliding valve at its base; odor was ostensibly prevented by means of an S-trap in the outflow pipe (water remaining in the bottom of the S closed off the passage of air through the S).

Suffice it to say that Cumming's invention effectively began the evolution of the modern water closet. It was improved upon by inventor Joseph Bramah, whose firm, J. Bramah and Sons, manufactured some six thousand water closets by 1797 and continued making them until the late 19th century. It was the Bramah firm that exported some, if not most, of the early water closets used in America. Bramah's closet followed the basic form of Cumming's but substituted a more dependable flap valve for the sliding valve of its predecessor.

The valve closet, essentially as designed by Bramah, remained in use until the late 1800s. By about midcentury, however, another kind, the relatively simple "pan" type, had come into use. The bowl contained a pan. After use, actuation of a mechanism caused the pan to tilt, emptying its contents down a drain; simulta-neously, a flow of water from an overhead cistern washed out the pan. In fact, the pan was not always efficient in voiding its contents, and there was not sufficient flow of water to make up the difference.

Successive improvements to the water closet dispensed with the tipable pan in favor of a fixed earthenware bowl and increased the flow of water (hence a new model in 1883 designated the Niagara). Variations known as

---

*1890s: Although most modern toilets make use of siphonic action in the tank, early siphon closets generated a siphon in the bowl. A good example (and one perhaps more easily observed than siphon action in the tank) is this water closet patented in 1890. The bowl is a one-piece earthenware shell. At left is the basic configuration. C is the intake from the tank, or cistern, as it was still called. When flushed, some of the water is discharged through a "jet-forming orifice," c, forcing out some of the air in B and producing a partial vacuum that starts the siphon action, shown as the heavy black area at right. With siphonic action the water closet entered the 20th century as a practical and efficient component of household technology. (Artwork using patent drawing No. 441,268, Nov. 15, 1890)*

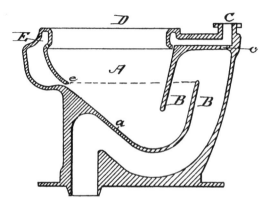
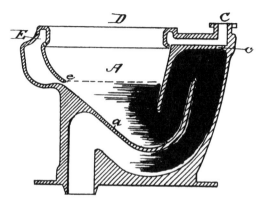

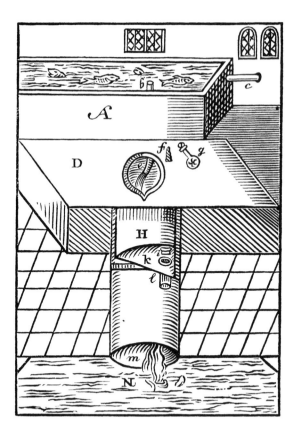

1596 (left): *Sir John Harington's water closet, as illustrated in his* Metamorphosis of Ajax (1596), *the first documented attempt at a water closet reflecting modern principles. Only two are believed to have been built: one for Harington and one for his godmother, Queen Elizabeth I. The fish in the cistern are presumed to be a whimsical touch on the part of the artist.*

1775 (below): *The water closet developed by clock maker Alexander Cumming, the first such invention patented in England. An overhead cistern (not shown) supplied water. When the handle was pulled, a sliding valve,* b, *opened, emptying lead bowl* a *into the drain. The diagram shows mechanics only. When installed, a wooden cabinet with seat would enclose what is shown here. The S-trap, a mainstay of plumbing ever since, is believed to have been used here for the first time.* (Brown, Water-Closets, p. 21)

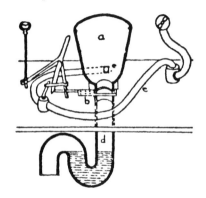

1778–Mid 1800s (above): *The Bramah, as it was commonly known, was an improvement by cabinetmaker Joseph Bramah on Alexander Cumming's design. With minor modification, it remained in production in England until nearly the end of the 19th century. This was probably the most common of the early water closets in use in America. The illustration is from the set of instructions used for installation of a Bramah closet at Hyde Hall, near Cooperstown, New York, in 1827.* (Courtesy of Friends of Hyde Hall)

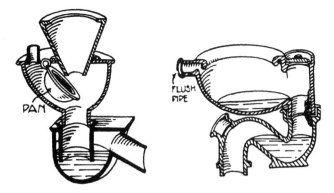

Mid to Late 1800s (left): *Two of the most common types of water closet before the modern siphonic-action toilet were the pan closet (left)* and *washout closet (right). The pan type was literally that, having a hinged copper pan that tipped when flushed. Neither type was really satisfactory.* (Fletcher, *English Home,* pp. 140–141)

1884 (below left): *J. L. Mott: The "Purita." The external levers and springs dating back to Alexander Cumming's time have given way to an improved flushing mechanism incorporated into the bowl itself.* (J. L. Mott Iron Works, Catalogue "D," *The Bath Room Illustrated* [1884], p. 37. Science, Industry and Business Library/New York Public Library/Astor, Lenox and Tilden Foundations)

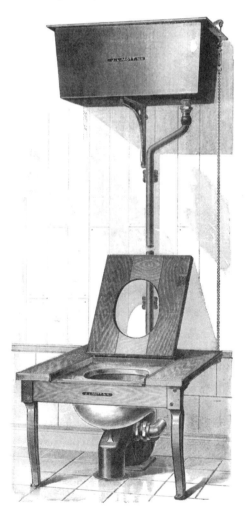

1909 (above): *N. O. Nelson Manufacturing Company: "New Dominion Low Down Syphon Jet Closet." Though still called a water closet, here was essentially the modern toilet as it would look with only minor variations throughout the 20th century.* (N. O. Nelson Manufacturing Co., *Nelson Blue Book* [1909], (Catalog N). Science, Industry and Business Library/New York Public Library/Astor, Lenox and Tilden Foundations)

"washout" and "wash-down" closets solved the shortcomings of the pan type but required a large volume of water to be effective. They also tended to splash, and made a noise like Niagara Falls that could be heard all over the house.

The next improvement, which began commanding attention about 1895, was the siphon-action water closet. The key to its development was the realization that the principle of the siphon contributed greatly to the effectiveness of flushing action. There was nothing new about the principle—an inverted U-shaped tube or pipe, its sides unequal in length, set up so that atmospheric pressure forces liquid to flow from one level to another. The ancient Greeks used siphons in their water-supply systems wherever obstacles existed en route; the siphon provided an up and over. (The Romans, being Romans, built massive aqueducts instead.)

In the modern toilet a bell-shaped part—actually tubing in the form of an inverted U—is raised when the flush lever is pulled; as it goes up, it creates a partial vacuum. This begins a siphon through the tubing, resulting in an effective flushing of the bowl without causing splashing, without sounding like Niagara Falls, and without using a large volume of water (the average today is about two gallons).

Siphonic action is the basic principle of most modern toilets. Another basic change came in the shape of the bowl itself. It was originally circular, a logical design until it was found that an oval bowl—the standard shape today—added to the effectiveness of the flushing action by increasing centrifugal force. The oval bowl was patented in 1877; siphonic action became common by the turn of the 20th century, and by the end of the first decade the toilet looked, and worked, basically as it does today. The only other essential changes have been refinement of design and the use of color to match the other standard fixtures of the modern bathroom.

## SCRUBBING AWAY OLD ATTITUDES

Meanwhile, there had been a transformation of the "bath" side of the bathroom, beginning roughly at the turn of the 19th century.

> . . . went into the Shower bath. I bore it better than I expected, not having been wett all over att once, for 28 years past. (Elizabeth Drinker, Philadelphia, July 1799)

> It may shock the feelings of a young lady, to be told that . . . perspiration, which is constantly passing off through the skin, has an individual odor, more or less disagreeable in different persons; but it is nevertheless true. . . . Once at least, in twenty-four hours, the whole surface of the body should be washed in soap and water. . . . (Eliza Farrar, *The Young Lady's Friend,* 1836)

What is remarkable about Elizabeth and Eliza is that so thoroughly divergent outlooks on personal bathing came so close together in time. For her part there was nothing extraordinary about Elizabeth; the past centuries had not held bathing in high esteem. A little dabbing with a sponge dipped in a washbasin in the privacy of one's bedroom was usually bathing enough. Men and boys often splashed in the river or even the ocean, but more for the fun of it than for cleanliness; women, needing to remain fully dressed, more readily contented themselves with the ablutions of the chamber. Reluctance to bathe, really bathe, was general. Vast in number were the "M's" of this world, as recorded by Henry David Thoreau in 1852:

> M——[a farmer] was telling me last night that he had thought of bathing when he had done his hoeing—of taking some soap and going down to Walden and giving himself a good scrubbing—but something had occurred to prevent it, and now he will go unwashed to the harvesting, aye, even till the next hoeing is over.

This does not mean no one ever got wet bodily. There was sea bathing, and there were spas. Indeed, Elizabeth Drinker's last immersion had been in 1771 at Bristol Springs, on the Delaware River north of Philadelphia, which in the latter 18th and early 19th centuries was a popular resort for Philadelphians. But here taking the waters was social and restorative rather than hygienic. The Drinkers also went to the seashore from time to time. Of a visit in 1776 Elizabeth recalled that her husband went sea bathing while she, not venturing in, took the waters in another way that was somewhat in vogue at the time. She drank a pint of seawater that, as expected, "Operated largely & speedily" on her system.

For the Drinkers, bathing for cleanliness was, as it had been over the years, primarily a matter of sponge and washbasin in the bedchamber. Whether it was done once a day or once a week, or only for special occasions, was a

*Curiously resistant to the scrubbing of wind and rain is this ancient ad for Ivory Soap in an alley off The Strand in New Castle, Delaware, photographed in the mid 1990s. Yet its time-etched surface may be less obdurate than age-old notions of personal cleanliness that prevailed when Ivory first floated to public attention.* (Photograph by the author)

matter of personal choice, as was how much of the body got cleansed at any given time. Furthermore, soap was still for doing the laundry; soap for personal use did not become common until after the middle of the 19th century.

But a hint of changing times was the shower bath that the Drinker family rigged up in the backyard of their Philadelphia home in the summer of 1798 (it obviously took a year for Elizabeth to "bear it" while her husband and children apparently got wet right away). The idea of taking a shower was relatively new. To be sure, it's not that no one had ever done it before. When attendants poured water over the head of their mistress in ancient Egypt, as is known from depictions, was this a shower? Or the bathers painted on an Etruscan vase, cavorting under a spray of water from an overhead cistern, were they taking a shower? Of course, but until the development of a modern public water supply, the shower bath remained little more than a genteel spray, and even then only for those whose means made their likenesses worthy of vases.

Modern public water supply was just around the corner in Philadelphia in 1798 (recalling here the Latrobe project begun in 1799), and notions of cleanliness had begun to change since Elizabeth Drinker last got wet all over. Although in her diary she provided no details about the construction of the shower bath except that one "pulled the string of ye shower" to use it, there was obviously a container of some sort above head level that held the water—an arrangement similar to that at the Read House. An account of another such device of the time notes that the receptacle was tin, and when ready, the shower taker "pulls at a cord and the water falls upon her through a cullender." The usual practice at the Drinkers' was to let the water stand "some hours" to let it warm up to body temperature. A female using the Drinkers' shower wore a thin gown and "an Oyl cloath cap," which meant that her whole body except her hair got wet—but not soaped up.

Why did it take Elizabeth twenty-eight years to break her drought? Simply stated, she didn't think bathing was important, let alone necessary, and she was hardly atypical. For the past two centuries in America, and since the Middle Ages in Europe, bathing was thought perhaps to be even deleterious. Doctors and religious authorities generally frowned on it. The Puritans looked particularly askance at it; after all, whatever was washed had to be exposed. Even into the 19th century there were municipal ordinances prohibiting bathing except on medical advice or for certain months of the year. As late as 1860 *Godey's Lady's Book* still advised readers that bathing at night was definitely ill-advised, while bathing in the morning, *briefly,* was probably all right if not done oftener than once a week.

Now to Eliza Farrar. Middle-class attitudes toward cleanliness were beginning to change, particularly in England, by the mid 18th century—as exemplified by evangelist John Wesley's admonition that "cleanliness is next to godliness." On the medical side there was Edinburgh's Dr. William Buchan, whose remarkably durable how-to-stay-well book, *Domestic Medicine* (1769), first appeared in America in 1772 (and itself stayed well, through one revised edition after another on both sides of the Atlantic, into the middle of the 19th century). Dr. Buchan preached that perspiration was of such great importance to health "that few diseases attack us while it goes properly on," which is to say, when the skin is regularly washed.

By the last decade of the 18th century, public baths were beginning to appear in American cities, reviving, in America as elsewhere, a custom that had declined with the Roman Empire; Rome's public baths were among its noblest accomplishments. Baths continued as a public institution into the early 20th century. But for many there was not even the luxury of a public bath, let alone a bathroom in one's own home. Hence, as was observed at mid 19th century of the poor in New York City:

> The wealthy can introduce water into their chambers . . . but for the innumerable poor, this is a luxury that can seldom, if ever, be enjoyed. Open bathing around the wharves is of course prohibited; and the labouring man has to walk three or four miles [to the ocean] to obtain a privilege so necessary to health. (author Lydia Maria Child, 1845)

The first household bathtubs in America began appearing at roughly the turn of the 19th century—in the Read House and Gore Place, as we have seen. But these were rare examples and usually not yet connected to any form of plumbing. With an exception like that in the Read House, tubs of the period normally had to be filled with pails of water and emptied the same way.

Proliferation of bathtubs, not surprisingly, coincided with the development of piped-in public water supply. Hence, by 1860 we find 3,910 tubs in Boston, a significant number relative to their near absence earlier in the century, but not a great many given that Boston at the time had 177,902 bodies to be bathed. (There were also 9,864 water closets and 31,098 sinks, the latter figure presumably including those in kitchens.) Bostonians, with a ratio of one tub for every 45 people, nevertheless were statistically better scrubbed than Baltimoreans, who had a ratio of one for every 84 people; and heads-and-shoulders cleaner than New Yorkers, with one bathtub for every 463 residents. Albany, meanwhile, with a head-to-tub ratio of one to 3,282 (the population was 62,367 and there were only nineteen tubs in

town) was probably closer to reflecting the country as a whole in 1860. We must recall that it was not until late in the 19th century, and indeed in many areas into the 20th, that public water supplies became common. In the absence of piped-in water, the usual recourse continued to be the portable tub, more often than not placed in the kitchen and filled with water heated by the kitchen stove.

Another factor encouraging bathing was the increasing availability of soap. Soap was relatively rare for personal use until after the middle of the 19th century, when developing technology made mass production of soap practical. Boston's Tremont Hotel, the first to have bathtubs (and water closets) when it opened in 1829, also set a precedent by providing a complimentary cake of soap in each room. Procter & Gamble's Ivory Soap appeared in 1882 and was advertised as suitable for washing fine laundry (silk hose, gloves, laces, and so forth) and as being "purer and much more pleasant" than the run of toilet soaps. To emphasize its dual nature, the bar came with a notch across the middle. The bar could be used full size for laundry, or, by pulling a stout thread tightly around the notch, one could easily break the bar into two pieces convenient for personal use.

But the underlying impetus to washing and bathing was essentially the same as what spurred development of sewers and public water supply—increasing awareness of how disease was spread and hence of the value of personal cleanliness. With exceptions (yellow fever, for example, which is spread by mosquitoes) disease was correctly understood to be transmittable by germs, and germs could be combated through personal hygiene. On the eve of America's entry into world war, mortal conflict was no less to be faced at home than abroad; writing in *Collier's* magazine on September 23, 1916, William J. Cromie warned that the

> war of the body against invading germs [is] a great battle that one is called upon to fight . . . continually throughout life.

The two principal bathroom appliances for bathing are, of course, the sink (also known as the lavatory, a confusing term since lavatory also signifies a room with toilet facilities) and the bathtub/shower.

The sink is a relatively direct descendant of the bedroom washstand of old. Prebathroom personal bathing, usually done in the bedroom, used either a basin or stand, the latter being simply a standing adaptation of the basin, which was commonly of metal or china. A jug of water and some towels completed the ensemble. The modern sink keeps the same essential configuration, makes the basin larger for convenience, and uses piped-in hot and cold running water.

The modern bathtub likewise is simply a refinement of the portable tub that goes back to colonial times, the most obvious difference being its length, which, because the modern version is a fixed rather than portable appliance, allows for full-body immersion. Otherwise, the principal advances have been the use of color and of materials like porcelain enamel and fiberglass that are vastly easier to keep clean and sanitary than the lead, copper, or zinc with which early- to mid-19th century tubs were lined. Indeed, there is hardly a feature of the house that shows so simple a degree of lineage

as the sink or the tub. The most significant difference is that these once portable items are now fixed in place.

By the mid 20th century, America was the world's best-bathroomed nation. Roughly ninety-five of every one hundred homes had running water, eighty-five had indoor toilets, and eighty had bathtubs or showers. By the 1990s, the U.S. census bureau reported that complete plumbing facilities existed in 98 percent of American homes.

## THE MODERN BATHROOM

Since it is now so fixed in configuration—its basic layout, its relatively compact space, its primary components—we lose sight of the fact that the bathroom is quite modern in concept.

Let us reflect for a moment. The bathroom actually accommodates very disparate functions. Until the latter 19th century (in a few instances earlier), bathing and elimination, from time immemorial, had had no connection. One bathed here and eliminated there. One normally went outside and used a privy or pit to eliminate; at night or in bad weather, one used a chamber pot or closestool inside, usually in the bedroom, but dumped the pot outside as soon as possible. Taking a bath, or bathing in whatever manner, was an entirely separate matter; it had nothing to do with elimination. When one bathed in the house, using a portable tub, it was commonly in the kitchen; or one found a stream or a river. As for the kind of washing one does in a bathroom sink, one used a washbasin, most likely in the bedroom.

Various places constituted the "bathroom" of the Fairbanks House—which is to say there

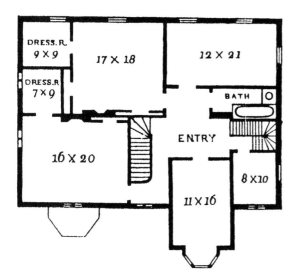

*By the mid 19th century, the place of both ablution and elimination was, for either purpose, coming to be known by the euphemistic "bath" room. Here in A. J. Downing's* Architecture of Country Houses *(1850), for example, the room marked "bath" has both a tub and a water closet. The sink did not become a common part of the grouping until later in the 19th century. (*Architecture of Country Houses, *p. 326)*

was no single place that served either for elimination or bathing within the house. Whether there was a privy at the outset is not known. Most of the early houses at the Plymouth Colony had none; a muck heap in back of the house served the purpose if weather permitted, and periodically this had to be cleaned out. Inside the house, one used a chamber pot. And here we may recall that some of the Plymouth houses consisted of only one room and were occupied in some cases by relatives outside the immediate family. In other words, there might be six or eight people in this single room when one felt nature's call, and let's say it was night or it was raining. What did one do for privacy? Apparently one didn't. It can only be assumed

that one simply picked up one's chamber pot and went to the farthest corner of the room and that the others present, by custom, made certain they kept busy with whatever they were doing and paid no notice. After all, their turn in the corner would come.

The Fairbanks House had four rooms, so there was a degree of privacy possible when a chamber pot was used inside. An outdoor privy, if it was not part of the original construction, was built sometime after and, whether at the same site or whether reconstructed a number of times, served throughout the years the house was occupied. There never was (and is not today) indoor plumbing. The Fairbanks House ceased to be occupied about 1906 and is a museum today.

Bathing was typically a function of the kitchen, for good reason. The kitchen had the best facilities for heating water, at first simply in a kettle in the fireplace. Beginning about 1840 a water heater was commonly installed within the fireplace, and this was superseded by a hot-water reservoir that became virtually a standard part of the kitchen range. Furthermore, the kitchen was normally the warmest room of the house, making it the most suitable for taking a bath. The tub was portable and, often without change of water, took care of all the family's bathing (thought was sometimes given to the order, the dirtiest waiting until last). So much taken for granted was the kitchen as the "bath room" that when in 1846 a Boston merchant named Nathaniel Waterman advertised for sale "every thing appertaining to the kitchen," he perforce included bathtubs.

The earliest applications of indoor plumbing actually kept bathing and elimination separate. We have seen, and will see further, that the evolution of the house was previewed in the hotel, which is to say that many an American got his or her first look at some new convenience while staying in a hotel—central heating, air conditioning, electric lights, television, and on and on. It was notably so for the basics of the modern bathroom, and the classic case is the Tremont Hotel in Boston, which, as already noted, opened in 1829 with the first hotel bathtubs and the first hotel water closets. They were separate. There were eight of each in the basement, serving any and all guests (the hotel had 170 rooms) who wanted to indulge in such modern conveniences; but tubs were in one section and water closets in another.

Hotels of the 19th century were modernizing at a prodigious rate. When the luxurious New York Hotel opened in 1844, it had baths on each floor and a few private baths in rooms as well. Other hotels followed with similar accommodations. The first to claim a private bath with each room was the Victoria Hotel in Kansas City, Missouri (1888), but this hotel was primarily residential. Ellsworth Statler's original Hotel Statler in Buffalo (1907) was the first night-to-night hotel to claim "every room with bath," which now meant water closet, tub, and sink.

The integration of the disparate functions of bathing and elimination actually came sooner in the house than the hotel. The principal reasons were practicality and economy—the installation of plumbing within the house almost demanded consolidation (as it would in the hotel, but constraints of economy were more immediately felt in building a house than in building a conspicuously luxurious hotel). It wasn't feasible in the house to have pipes here for a tub and there for a washbasin and there for a water closet. All that piping had to be interlinked; this necessity interlinked functions as well.

Before public water supply and public sewerage made possible the near universality of indoor plumbing in the 20th century, a simple change in technology was already furthering the process, even early in the 19th century in some cases—a cistern in the attic. The cistern was fed with rainwater or with water pumped up from a well or nearby spring. Gravity flow then made water available within the house for a variety of uses. In his book *A Home for All* (1854), Orson S. Fowler observed that "cisterns in the tops of houses are most desirable . . . because they save carrying wash-water up to chambers. . . . One of these cisterns [in my house] also connects with the copper boiler attached to the kitchen range."

The proximity of an attic cistern (along with the traditional use of the bedroom for daily washing and for the chamber pot) made it expedient for the bathroom to have the second floor as its most common location. A. J. Downing's *Architecture of Country Houses* (1850) confirmed both the location and the terminology: What is called the "bath room" has both a tub and water closet and may be cited as early evidence of the coming prevalence of the euphemism "bathroom" for what was used more commonly for elimination than bathing.

The early location of the "bath room" on the second, or sleeping, floor—rather than on the first, or living, floor—owes in part to the early appreciation that "cisterns in the tops of houses are most desirable." But the second floor had other advantages. As the bedroom floor of the typical 19th-century home, it provided continuity: The bedroom was the primary place for using a chamber pot or closestool as well as a washbasin. If one didn't want to, or couldn't, use the outdoor privy, the bedroom was the place of choice. So it was logical to make this new bathroom almost an extension of the bedroom. The second floor as opposed to the living floor also accorded a greater degree of privacy.

And another factor: Including a bathroom as part of the original design of a house still reflected relative affluence until the beginning of the 20th century. Most homes of the latter 19th did not yet have bathrooms, owing to lack of water supply or sewerage or for reasons of economy. As changing technology made tubs and sinks and, in particular, water closets more practical and economical, more and more people began adding bathrooms to their homes. Wherever the conversion was made to an existing home, it was necessary to find space. Far more often than not it was a small bedroom that could be spared, and this of course would have been on the second floor. So for these various reasons, the typical bathroom of the typical house—until single-floor houses became common in the mid 20th century—

was on the second floor. And for reasons of practicality and economy in the installation of plumbing, it was a single room serving the whole house.

By the latter 20th century, that single room has become two or three (or even more) bathrooms, one commonly being a half bath (no tub or shower) adjacent to the living area and intended for guests or for the incidental use of the occupants.

The modern bathroom, in comparison to its size—which is to say, it is almost inevitably the smallest room of the house—has a disproportionately wide range of uses. This is worth pausing to think about. Of course this room is used as one of those prototypical "bath rooms" of 1850, for bathing and for the basic needs of nature, but there are so many other assorted daily routines—brushing teeth, putting on makeup, shaving, shampooing, cutting one's nails, inserting contact lenses, taking medicine, cleaning and treating cuts and scrapes, weighing oneself, using a sunlamp, even working out (some new master baths are part fitness center)—that if the modern bathroom didn't exist, it would have to be invented.

# The Modern House: 1850

In public life, which is to say politics, Martin Van Buren was Jeffersonian; so too in private life. His home in Kinderhook, New York, is curiously similar to Monticello in its fondness for modern convenience. Van Buren's Lindenwald, in a sense, is a realization of what Jefferson had been contemplating a half century earlier, before technology had quite caught up with expectations. The house, a relatively simple Georgian structure, was built in 1797 by Judge Peter Van Ness; it became Van Buren's home in 1841. It was extensively remodeled by architect Richard Upjohn in 1849–1850, and this occasioned the installation of the technology that made it the quintessential modern home in its time. Even more remarkable, most of that technology remains intact, even if long since taken out of service (except for the ductwork for the modern hot-air furnace, which is still the original). Midway through the century that produced the most dramatic change in the American house, this is how the modern house looked. As an example of mid-19th-century domestic technology preserved in situ, Lindenwald is perhaps one of a kind. (Unless otherwise noted, photographs by the author by permission of the National Park Service)

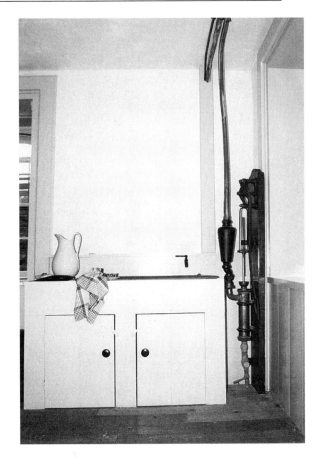

(*Bottom right*) The bathroom was actually two rooms: a "bath room" proper, comprised of a bathtub and sink, and a smaller, adjacent room with a water closet. The bathtub is made of copper alloy built into a wooden case. It has one faucet supplying cold water from an overhead cistern that also supplied the sink and water closet. Hot water was added from a separate source, probably a combination heating stove and water heater built into the fireplace just across the room; the stove is no longer there. The tub drained to the outdoors.

(*Left*) The water closet is original to 1849–1850 and remains intact and unchanged because, when a modern bathroom was installed elsewhere, this tiny space became a linen closet. With the shelves removed, everything looks as it did in 1850. Except for connections to a water source and sewer, the water closet remains virtually operable. An overhead cistern provided the source of water. After use, the handle on the left was pulled, simultaneously admitting a flow of water and moving to one side (it still works) a copper pan at the bottom of the bowl. The bowl rests atop a cast-iron pipe that drained into a cesspool. The small object at the right is the seat cover.

(*Facing page, top*) The source of water for the bathroom—water closet, tub, and sink—was a 90-gallon cistern above the ceiling of the water closet. It was filled by means of this pump adjacent to the kitchen sink in the basement. A small overflow pipe leads back from the cistern to the sink; when water began flowing through the overflow, the servant doing the pumping knew the cistern was full and it was time to stop.

(*Left*) The original furnace of c1854 remains in place in the cellar; in fact, it was the primary source of heat until 1937. Its 10-in.-diameter ductwork is still in use, coupled to a modern forced hot-air furnace that is immediately adjacent. The original furnace itself is not visible here; this is the brick enclosure that surrounds it. The cast-iron door is the fuel-feeder door; at the bottom is the ashpit, which also had a door. All in all, this is a remarkable example of evolution in house heating. The early colonial house had an immense fireplace that was, in effect, an open bonfire, half enclosed. Gradually the enclosure shrank. Here the closure is complete. Unlike a modern hot-air furnace that heats the air within the furnace, here the furnace heats the air within what is still, in effect, a big brick fireplace, fully closed. Cold air enters an intake on the side of the enclosure and passes at the bottom into an inner brick chamber; as it is heated, it rises and passes through ducts leading out of the top of the chamber, then to various rooms (on the north side of the house only). Rooms not connected to the furnace relied on fireplaces or, in the case of the kitchen, a cook stove.

PATENTED AUGUST 22, 1854.

(*Left*) This is the original furnace, patented by Nathaniel A. Boynton, of New York, in 1854, inside its brick enclosure. The illustration here is from the billhead of Cox, Richardson and Boynton of New York for the installation of a furnace identical to Van Buren's at the home of William Reynolds in Meadville, Pennsylvania, in 1857 (see chapter 5).

(*Above*) Hot air reached the rooms of Lindenwald through floor or baseboard registers. One of them is virtually identical to this register, also patented in 1854. (U.S. Patent Collection: "Hot-Air Register," Jan. 3, 1854)

A double-oven cook stove installed c1850 was the centerpiece of the kitchen. The firebox (which was presumably coal-burning from the outset) heated both the ovens and a cooking surface over the top. It is believed that this surface originally had six holes for pots; only the framework remains. The lower oven was for cooking and the upper one for warming.

CHAPTER 4

# The House as a Reflection of
# a Changing Society

## THE HOUSE A CABIN BUILT

The neighborhood in Hartford, Connecticut, has changed, but the picturesque, two-story house at 73 Forest Street is as much a quintessence of the comfy and cozy as it was a century ago. One enters to find

an air of hospitality and welcome about it which is difficult to describe, but always pleasant to witness. A door leads to the family-room which has books, pictures, easy chairs, and everything necessary for comfort and repose. The drawing-room opens from this room. The carpets and hangings are a pretty shade of blue; there are some fine paintings on the wall, one or two bits of statuary, and a piano, with plenty of music-books which show constant use. Near a large

bay window, from which a good view of the garden is obtained, stands a small table set out with a pretty tete-a-tete tea set, and one can hardly imagine a cosier corner for taking a cup of afternoon tea.

This description, essentially as it appeared in *Drake's Magazine* in 1889, is as much applicable to the house today as it was then, except that no one lives here now. It is a museum of a house . . . a place preserved, a changeless place, this house on Forest Street; and yet, given whom it is we visit with in spirit, a veritable monument to change.

The house was built in 1871 by a real estate speculator named Franklin Chamberlain and was one of two nearly identical dwellings that he erected on a large plot he had recently bought. Both houses were built for speculation, but Chamberlain himself took 73 Forest

*Harriet and Calvin, 1853.* (Original daguerreotype portrait of Harriet Beecher Stowe and Calvin Ellis Stowe in the Beecher Stowe family papers, Schlesinger Library, Radcliffe College. As frontispiece, Harriet Beecher Stowe, *Oldtown Folks* [Boston and New York, 1900], reproduced by permission of the New York Public Library/Astor, Lenox and Tilden Foundations)

as his residence; by 1873, still speculating, he took another house for himself and sold this one to a Hartford family by the name of Stowe—Calvin, Harriet, and their twin daughters, Eliza and Hatty.*

It is Harriet Beecher Stowe (1811–1896) we principally visit with in spirit here, for it is she, along with her sister Catharine Beecher, who symbolizes so much of the change in society that we now look at as manifested in the house and household.

This was a modern house, as up-to-date for

its time as Jonathan Fairbanks's was relatively so for his time or George Read's definitely so for his. But Harriet Stowe was a new kind of woman. We might think back to Grace Fairbanks, whose essential function in life was the bearing of children and the tending of the house in accordance with her husband's wishes; or to Mary Read, who had considerably more say in daily life but whose primary influence on the shape of the house was in necessitating that her bedroom be finished first because she was bearing a child.

Ah, now Harriet Stowe: literally the family breadwinner . . . the luminary by whom the husband is remembered . . . with an impress on the house so far-reaching that she very nearly played the role of architect.

The latter description requires a brief explanation. It was not this house on Forest Street in which Harriet had so fine an architectural hand. Prior to their move here, the Stowes had resided at a considerably more spacious dwelling, which Harriet called Oakholm, on the Park River, about a mile from Forest Street. This was the house that a cabin built. Harriet's fame, and a measure of fortune, derived of course from *Uncle Tom's Cabin,* first published in 1852. The novel made her one of America's best-paid writers and brought her international renown; it was eventually translated into more than sixty-two languages and dialects

---

* There were seven children altogether, including the twins. Frederick, Georgiana, and Charles had married or otherwise gone out into the world when the family moved to 73 Forest Street. Henry drowned in 1857 while swimming with classmates from Dartmouth. An infant son, Samuel Charles, "Charley," fell victim to cholera when the family was living in Cincinnati in 1849 while Calvin taught at Lane Theological Seminary. Harriet herself had cholera and only barely survived.

and published as far away as the island of Java. She was in demand as a speaker, in Europe as well as America, touring frequently. With renown went profits and with profits the wherewithal to build a dream house.

It was almost entirely Harriet who determined the form and substance of Oakholm. Begun in 1863, this was a very spacious Victorian Gothic structure, its charm accentuated by its eight gables. During its construction the *Hartford Times* informed a curious public that

[the] entrance hall will be 24 × 48 feet [with] winding stairs to upper floors. In rear of hall will be a conservatory of glass two stories high on the south side; an ornamental gallery around it on the inside. The house is planned for convenience and comfort with bathroom and closets, which lovers of homes value. The first floor parlor is lighted by a large bay window. Upper windows open on ornamental balconies.

Besides being an expression of what was modern, Oakholm also reflected Harriet's personal philosophy as to what constituted the essentials of a comfortable, healthy, "Christian home." There were four basic elements, she wrote—air, fire, earth, and water—that needed

*Oakholm, c1865: the dream house that became a nightmare.* (Harriet Beecher Stowe Center, Hartford, Conn.)

to be incorporated into the house. Air was expressed in the number of large, interconnecting rooms; fire (heavenly light), in the extensive use of glass unencumbered by the usual heavy draperies then in vogue; earth, by the presence of house plants and ivy as window decoration; and water, by indoor plumbing. As a further instance of the house's Christian spirit, the gables had finials in the shape of crosses, and of course the architecture was Gothic, which was associated with Christianity.

The house had a bathroom. Hartford by this time had public water supply, and Harriet took advantage of it. She insisted that "the power to command a warm bath in a house at any hour of day or night is better in bringing up a family of children than any amount of ready medicine." There was almost certainly also a water closet connected to a sewer that presumably drained into the Park River; there was not yet a municipal sewer system.

This house that was modern over and above its Christian symbols was Harriet's vision. The official architect is not a matter of record; she was the unofficial, and as that had more to do with the outcome. It was *her* House of the Eight Gables—one better than Nathaniel Hawthorne's—and she watched it "growing wonderfully . . . I go every day to see it—I am busy with drains, sewers, sinks. . . ." While overseeing the final stages of construction in April 1864, she wrote that "the confusion at present grows wilder every day, but it is the confusion of activity & I am driving at everybody's heels." Along the way she found, as have many since in regard to the trials of house building or house renovating, that the heels, and the rest of the anatomy, don't always move

to one's expectations. She complained about being dependent

> on a carpenter, a plumber, a mason, a tile hanger who come & go at their own sweet will breaking in, making all sorts of chips, dust, dirt—going off in the midst leaving all standing—reappearing at uncertain intervals & making more dust, chips & dirt . . .

In due time, having finally been able to "get my brains right side up," she saw the last of the dust and chips cleared away and a dream appear as reality. But as with dreams, morning comes—and with it came a new reality, a cost of running the place that was completely undreamed of. Despite Harriet's continually looking over the shoulder of the contractor, shortcuts had perhaps been taken in construction or the quality of materials. Pipes burst, the cellar flooded, windows jammed. The cost of these repairs, coupled with the normal maintenance of a grand mansion complete with two-story conservatory, became staggering. Calvin turned out to be right. He had predicted from the start that the house would be too much for them. Had Calvin alone been the breadwinner, there never would have been anything but the simplest of quarters. As a professor, he had only a very modest income; and before Harriet's success with *Uncle Tom,* he had fretted about ending his days in a poorhouse.

Since Harriet was also going through a time of thinner royalties and other fees, the decision was made to sell the house (at a loss). The Stowes left Oakholm in 1870 and spent the next few years living at a home they had in Mandarin, Florida, or sojourning with friends

*73 Forest Street, Hartford: a house more practical.*
(Photograph by the author)

or family, or making do with a hotel room. It was a nomadic life that left Harriet to complain in December 1872, writing from Framingham, Massachusetts, that "if it please God this shall be the last season that my family shall be scattered wanderers sick in hotels & boarding houses & other people's families—it is not respectable & there must be an end to this." Hearing that it was on the market, Harriet decided to buy Franklin Chamberlain's house, back in more or less the old neighborhood, and the Stowes had moved into it by 1874. Oakholm was eventually demolished; only a photograph and an engraving remain of its romantic splendor.

## A HOUSE MORE PRACTICAL

Now we shall take advantage of its "air of hospitality" and look further at the more practical

house that Harriet Beecher Stowe made her primary home until her death in 1896. This house on Forest Street looks for all the world like a page out of A. J. Downing or Calvert Vaux, something they might have called a "cottage in the Gothic style." It is a two-story house, plus attic and cellar. The attic has rooms that were originally intended for servants, although it appears the Stowes never had more than live-in nurses. They probably had day servants, most likely free blacks, at the time they moved in and at least off and on after that, as financial means allowed. (Certainly Harriet had help when she could afford it. She hated housekeeping.) The cellar had a furnace in early times, although whether there was one when the Stowes moved in or one was added later is not clear. Otherwise the cellar was chiefly for storage.

The first floor has two parlors aside a central hall—the front for formal entertaining, the back for family use or meeting friends

*The Stowe House: Kitchen* (right) *and bathroom* (facing page) *are 20th-century restorations. The photograph of Harriet in the front parlor* (above) *was taken in 1886.* (All: Harriet Beecher Stowe Center, Hartford, Conn.)

vice that is authentic to the times, although whether something like this was here during the Stowes' time can only be conjectured. The bathroom also includes a vintage water closet; whether there was one when Chamberlain built the house, no one knows; if not, Harriet, having had indoor plumbing at Oakholm, certainly added one. The bathroom, or bathing room as it was known to the Stowes, was there at least by 1876 (a letter written by Harriet that year observed that "we have had a thorough repair of the plumbing in the bathing room and kitchen sink where the smell was unpleasant").

With the bathroom, as with the house in general, restoration has had to be conjectural to a large extent. Subsequent owners of the house made drastic changes; painstaking research was needed to restore the house at least to what it might have looked like and in some instances (with the benefit of old photos) to the exact appearance it did have. Many of the furnishings are Stowe family pieces.

The kitchen at 73 Forest is also a conjectural reconstruction. There are virtually no original kitchens of the period. Housewives then, as now, usually wanted the latest in kitchen appliances, and the old were quickly discarded. In the case of this house, however, there was something exceedingly useful to draw upon in reconstructing the kitchen—the detailed accounts, including illustrations, that appear in the Beecher sisters' *The American Woman's Home* (1869).

One wall of the Stowe kitchen is dominated by a huge cast-iron stove (no need for a fireplace here, or even central heat); another wall, by a sink built into a wooden countertop—a forerunner of the continuous counter of

informally. To the other side of the hall, in the front, is the dining room; in back of it the kitchen, with a pantry to the side. Upstairs are three large bedrooms, a smaller room Harriet used as her study, and the bathroom. The two parlors, Calvin's bedroom, and Harriet's room have fireplaces that supplemented the central heat. These four rooms are all on the north side of the house; it was a common pattern in the early years of central heating to heat only the rooms on the colder side of the house.

The bathroom has a tin-clad bathtub with a combination sink and water heater built in above it. The heater is intended to use kerosene. Water from it can be used in the sink, or the sink can be retracted so that hot water runs into the tub. It is an ingenious de-modern times. There is cold running water only at the sink; hot water was provided by the stove. Along another wall is a work center that includes bins for flour and the like, drawers for this and that, and rows of shelving for glassware, pots and pans, utensils, and so on. The shelves are shallow by later standards, but intentionally so. There is generally room for only one item per spot, and this arrangement was thought to avoid clutter. There was no icebox in the kitchen itself; the pantry, unheated, was immediately adjacent, and it was considered the preferable spot for the icebox here and in most houses of the time—although *The American Woman's Home* has its "ice closet" in the cellar, also a familiar place.

Iceboxes were rather efficient for their purpose by this time, but they had the double deficit of needing to be both filled and unfilled. The filling was done by the iceman, but the unfilling of the melted ice was the responsibility of the housewife, using a pan. Harriet, her aversion to housework matching her practicality, got around this necessity by having a pipe inserted to carry the accumulating water out through the wall of the pantry and into the garden. All in all, this was not a typical kitchen of the 1870s; it was ahead of its time.

Outside, running the perimeter of the house, are four porches. Calvin was the most avid porch sitter and liked to follow the sun, running his own course from porch to porch to keep up not with its shade but with its warmth.

This was the house to which the Stowes settled down; and although it was not a dream house, neither was it the specter that Oakholm turned out to be. Here was comfort and an air of hospitality, a place always pleasant to wit-

ness. And besides, Harriet's sister Isabella Hooker lived just up the street, and nearby was the home of William Gillette, playwright and actor; about the time the Stowes moved in, work began on an extravagant red brick mansion just around the corner that, like the Stowe house, is still there—the new home of Samuel and Olivia Clemens. It was a nice neighborhood, and here Harriet would live for the rest of her life.

## THE HOUSE AND THE STATUS OF WOMEN

It was not entirely by chance that there were literary people around. The larger neighborhood in what was then the rural fringe of Hartford had taken the name of Nook Farm and become a colony for many figures in the arts and social reform. Nor was it a coincidence that Harriet, who as a woman couldn't even vote, was so easily accepted into the milieu. Literature provided a significant opening to women in the 19th century—perhaps the first major pursuit through which they could compete with men on just about an even footing. Harriet's *Uncle Tom's Cabin* was a best-seller, and there was no qualification about its being the work of a woman. Only a year earlier had come the first book by an American author believed to have sold a million copies—*The Wide, Wide World,* by Susan Warner. One of the preeminent literary figures of the age, Sarah Josepha Hale, editor of *Godey's Lady's Book,* observed the significance of it all at midcentury: "Within the last fifty years more books have been written by women and about women than

*Symbolizing the prevailing role of woman before the age of the Beechers is this* tableau vivant *at the Pieter Claesen Wyckoff House (c1652), Brooklyn, New York.* (Courtesy of the Historic House Trust of New York City)

all that had been issued during the preceding five thousand years."

One thing about writing is its ready adaptability to working space. Harriet began her career in the parlor; and whether she used the parlor, or a room upstairs at Forest Street, or tabletops here and there on her travels, writing was a uniquely good household industry for her, as for others. It was within the grasp of any woman who wanted to have a shot at writing the great American book—be it a novel, or poetry, or tips on housekeeping. Equally ap-

propriate to the parlor was the reading of a book. With the development of printing technology during the 19th century—inexpensive sulfite papers, steam-powered presses, mass-production binding—books became cheap enough to be accessible to nearly everyone. It is hardly surprising then that women took to reading as never before; so much that, in the judgment of contemporary editor-journalist Nathaniel Willis, "it is women who read. It is women who give or withhold a literary reputation. It is the women who regulate the style of living."

Many of these proliferating tomes took the house and household as their subject matter. Particularly notable books on domestic economy in the early 19th century included Lydia Maria Child's *The American Frugal Housewife* (1832), Theodore Dwight's *The Father's Book* (1834), William Alcott's *The Young Housekeeper* (1838), and Herman Humphrey's *Domestic Education* (1840). By far the most significant work of this period, however, was *A Treatise on Domestic Economy,* by Catharine Beecher (1800–1878), Harriet's older sister. Catharine had learned the ins and outs of running a household through sheer necessity. The oldest of nine children, she was herself only sixteen when her mother died, making her a surrogate mother hen until Lyman Beecher remarried two years later. Freed of family responsibilities, she went off to study at a private school and by the age of twenty-three had become engaged to a professor at Yale. His sudden death, before they could be married, left her shattered. She never did marry but, as she explained, tried "to find happiness in living to do good."

Doing good in part took the form of encouraging higher education for women, beginning with the establishing of her Female Seminary in Hartford, Connecticut, in 1823. The goal, as later expressed, was "securing professional advantages of education for my sex equal to those bestowed on men." Beyond that there was the setting down of some of those lessons Catharine had learned in her own household classroom. Her *Treatise on Domestic Economy,* first published in 1841 and reprinted nearly every year through 1856, was a combination of advice on housekeeping and basic instruction in such matters as biology and family health, about which most readers, less well educated, were less well informed than she. Hence, there were lessons in such fundamentals of biology as the difference between arteries and veins and in such practical knowledge as the rudiments of modern first aid. Advice on housekeeping provided a forum for encouraging changes that would make the house more housewife-oriented:

> With half the expense usually devoted to a sideboard or sofa, the water used from a well or cistern can be so conducted, as that, by simply turning a cock, it will flow to the place where it is to be used. . . . Money spent on handsome parlors and chambers, for company, [should be] devoted to providing a comfortable kitchen.

Advocating a kitchen sink with running water was woman-to-woman advice of a new order. There was also some warmed-over wisdom that Catharine presumed might be new knowledge to some readers:

> The position of fireplaces has much to do with economy of expense in warming a

house. Where the fireplace is in an outer wall, one third of the heat passes out of doors, which would be retained in the house, if the chimney were within the rooms.

Here we have a configuration that was known to early colonists; an example is found in the Adam Thoroughgood House just outside Norfolk, Virginia (c1680), one of the oldest brick structures still standing in America. The chimney on the north (cold) side is within the house to contain heat; that on the south (warmer side), outside the structure to dissipate heat. Nevertheless, in addressing something so basic to the design of the house, Catharine was suggesting that the housewife, not merely the husband, be part of a most fundamental decision-making process—planning the house right from the start.

Catharine's *Treatise* offered floor plans for modern houses that included kitchens with sinks with pumped-in water, bathing rooms with heated bathwater, indoor privies, central heating, and plenty of closets. Some of her ideas were one and the same with what eventually became the standard house—the many closets, for example, and the indoor privies that became bathrooms. Other ideas didn't catch on. She extolled the virtues of "bed-presses"—essentially folding beds in alcoves off major rooms of the house. In one of her plans, there were bedpress alcoves off the parlor, dining room, and kitchen. Of the first of these she noted: "This will make it a handsome parlor, by day, and yet allow it to be used as a bedroom, at night. . . . A window is put in each bedpress, to secure proper ventilation." But the traditional bedroom remained intact.

Overall, Catharine Beecher's *Treatise* was a work of major importance. She sought to redefine the role of the woman in the household by systematizing the job of housewife in such a way that what was expected of the housewife was sufficiently within her grasp. That accomplished, the woman might find a little free time for other things besides housework—reading, for example. Or in times to come, an active role in the suffragist movement—paradoxically, since Catharine was not in favor of woman suffrage. Yet as she herself explained, "Every thing is moving and changing."

## WOMEN AS THEIR OWN ARCHITECTS

Catharine Beecher had offered suggestions—floor plans, detailed descriptions, and the like—for the more efficient, more modern home. Harriet Beecher Stowe built one. She had taken a direct role, very nearly acting as architect, in the design and construction of Oakholm, which she began building in 1862. Appropriate, therefore, to a look at the changing status of women in the context of the evolving American house is the question of whether Harriet's role was unique for her time. Or were other women also more or less the architects of their own houses?

In Harriet's own day there was Sarah Davis, a native of Lenox, Massachusetts, who was literally a product of Beecher philosophy, having been educated at Catharine Beecher's Female Seminary in Hartford. In 1838, at the age of twenty-four, she married a young lawyer named David Davis, who, after knowing Sarah in Lenox, where he was a law student, had gone west to establish a law practice in Illinois. He came back east to take her hand. They then set up home in Illinois, and Davis, prospering in both law and real estate, made a modest fortune. He became a close friend of fellow Illinois lawyer Abraham Lincoln and largely engineered Lincoln's nomination at the Republican convention of 1860. Once elected, Lincoln rewarded his friend with appointment to the U.S. Supreme Court. Davis went off to Washington; Sarah remained in Bloomington, Illinois, where in 1870 she took on the primary responsibility for the modern home they both wanted. Working with Alfred H. Piquenard (architect of both the Illinois and Iowa state capitols), Sarah made the day-to-day decisions for both husband and wife, writing regularly to David in Washington to keep him advised as to how work on *their* house was going. For example:

> [November 19, 1871] The cellar is in part cemented and work there going on—I went down to reconnoiter . . . and asked **Mr Moffatt** to have a door made [and he] promised to have it done. . . .

> [February 4, 1872] I found a carpenter at work in the Linen Closet and told him I intended . . . to go in the house the last of May—& hoped I should not be disappointed by not finding the house ready for me.

> [February 11, 1872] I decided to have the four chambers painted—that is the *walls* and the ceiling to the best room over the parlor—I shall have Sallie's a light shade of blue which you know is her favorite color. I hope you will not think me too extravagant.

(Top) *Rebecca Gore, portrait by John Trumbull, London, 1802.* (Photograph by K. Jenness. Courtesy of Gore Place)

(Bottom) *Sarah Davis, photographed c1872.* (Illinois State Historical Library)

---

The house is so nice, it seemed best to have the upper part in keeping with the lower.

[April 18, 1872] George has got men to work on the yard owing to my persistency. . . . So today they are carrying off brick bats etc. preparatory to filling in the yard—As a general thing men don't fancy *persistent women*—but sometimes one is forced to do so.

While not quite the architect, Sarah Davis nonetheless had a hand in planning the house to a degree that was customarily the husband's and filled certain of those duties that fall upon the architect; for example, keeping after the workmen. (Harriet, as we have seen, had made a specialty of this, too.) Persistence was likewise useful to Mrs. James Moore Wayne, who collaborated with her husband, the mayor of Savannah, Georgia, in planning and building their new home in 1821.* Beyond sharing with Mr. Wayne the overall concept of what kind of house they would have, letters indicate that Mrs. Wayne was constantly at the construction site, to the extent of sitting in the parlor and "instructing" the plasterers as to various decorative details.

* It is now known as the Wayne-Gordon House, the birthplace of Juliette Gordon Low, founder of the Girl Scouts.

We have already seen at Gore Place, Waltham, Massachusetts (chapter 3), the influence of Rebecca Gore. While the Gores were in England during the 1790s, they became acquainted with the new household technology developing there and, largely at Rebecca's initiative, incorporated much of it in Gore Place, which was completed in 1806. But it was also Mrs. Gore who contributed essential features of the design of their new home. The Gores had visited Paris frequently during their London tenure and had made friends with architect J.-G. LeGrand, and it was to him that they turned for the technical help. LeGrand drew up the architectural plans based on Rebecca's sketches. The process began during a visit to Paris in 1801, as recorded in a letter from Christopher Gore to Rufus King, the U.S. minister to Great Britain:

[July 3, 1801] Mrs. G. is now with Monsieur LeGrand in the adjoining parlour[,] building houses. . . .

This was a preliminary discussion—presumably about such overall considerations as how big a house, how many rooms, what architectural style, and so forth. A year later, her consultation with LeGrand in mind, Rebecca completed the details of the kind of house she wanted. Christopher Gore, obviously happy with his wife's ideas, sent the plans to Rufus King, then in Paris, for transmittal to LeGrand:

[October 20, 1802] Mrs. Gore has sent the plan of our intended house, with a wish that you should explain it to LeGrand, & request him to make a compleat and perfect plan according to her sketch. . . .

Even a few years before this, we can find collaboration that extends to the wife's actually drawing up specifications usually left to the architect. Prestwould in Mecklenburg County, Virginia (1795), was the joint effort of Sir Peyton Skipwith and Lady Jean Skipwith. The former Jean Miller and the second wife of Sir Peyton, Lady Skipwith is credited with much of the interior design, notably a carefully devised allotment of space as to family life, entertaining, and service areas. She saw to it that there was ample storage space, including assorted closets (those in the cellar having multiple tiers of shelves and iron hooks); and it was she also who sent off to James Maury, the family's agent in London, such specs for hardware as

12 pairs of the best sort of hinges for hanging doors to rise over carpets.

12 pairs of the New patent hinges for the doors of the Bedchambers.

2 pairs of hinges for hanging two large Front Doors. . . .

50 pairs of Brass pulleys for window sashes; Cords for Do [ditto]. The leads can be got in this Country.

2 Handsome Brass knockers for Front Doors.

1 strong Iron knocker for a Back door. . . .

6 Large Japan Locks of the very best quality, made in the form of Closet door locks; that is, without more than one hole—no one key to open more than its own lock.

N.B. I could wish all the Chamber door Locks to have Brass Handles to fall down against the doors, in preference to larger Brass Knobs. (From a letter with "Invoice of sundry articles" signed Jean Skipwith and dated August 27, 1795)

## THE QUEST FOR EFFICIENCY

Meanwhile, the industrial revolution was changing life beyond the household. It was re-organizing the process of production on a mass scale. Various products that had been the produce of the home were now the output of factories. The blanket that had been woven by the woman of the house, no doubt with considerable pride, was coming to be store-bought instead. Her husband's shirt, heretofore her work, was coming to him ready-made from some anonymous seamstress. These and other chores, while tedious, at least allowed some sense of creativity and could even be done while socializing. The same could not be said of the drudgery of laundry or the tediousness of doing dishes before the days of piped-in water.

At the same time, the husband who had been part of the daily life of the household by virtue of working within it, as a farmer perhaps or as an artisan, was increasingly being drawn away from the daytime scene to a factory or office. This alteration produced a certain degree of isolation for the housewife to go along with an increasing sense of drudgery in activities that left less and less of a sense of creativity to offset their tediousness. This was potent stuff for reformers. And in the application of latent dissatisfaction we have both a dynamic in the change of the role of women in

By the mid 19th century, a seemingly never-ending round of household chores continued to be the responsibility of the housewife. Here: butter making. (Library of Congress, Prints and Photographs)

the period of roughly 1850 to 1920, the period leading up to and resulting in woman suffrage, and a dynamic in the evolution of the house, particularly the kitchen. Indeed 1850–1920 is almost precisely the same period that the kitchen went from essentially archaic (mostly cooking at the fireplace, hauling in water from a pump out back) to essentially modern (gas range, refrigerator, hot and cold running water).

Except for literary figures and a few others, the perceived role of women in the mid 19th century was as allegorized in the frontispiece of *The Housekeeper's Annual and Lady's Register* of 1844: a sevenfold ritual of raising children, reading the Bible, sewing, cooking, keeping up with chores like churning butter, doing the wash, and tending to the garden. It was a role not greatly changed from the early colonial period except in the woman's legal status. When Jonathan Fairbanks sat down with a local carpenter to work out details of his house of 1637, he presumably did not consult with Mrs. Fairbanks as to its design. Certainly he did not have to. Under English common law, she was legally subordinate to her husband. She had no legal existence of her own. She owned nothing. Whatever she brought as dowry was his. "Her" children were legally *his* children, which is to say, he was the legal guardian, not *they*. She could neither sue nor be sued. At the time of the Fairbankses' arrival in Massachusetts, she was even subject to corporal punishment. It was in 1641, four years after their arrival in Dedham, that Massachusetts liberalized women's rights by providing that "Everie marryd woeman shall be free from bodilie correction or stripes by her husband, unless it be in his owne defence upon her assalt."

For dramatic contrast, we need only reach the midpoint of the reign of Queen Victoria to find the everyday housewife being likened to the world's most powerful woman:

She who is the mother and housekeeper in a large family is the sovereign of an empire, demanding more varied cares, and involving more difficult duties, than are really exacted of her who wears a crown and professedly regulates the interests of the greatest nation on earth. (*The American Woman's Home,* 1869)

That was pretty heady stuff. Of course, the right even to vote in a federal election was still half a century away, but the current was running and one of the currents in that flow was *The American Woman's Home (AWH)*, the collaborative effort of Catharine Beecher and Harriet Beecher Stowe. Although it was a collaboration, the book was in large measure an update of Catharine's *Treatise on Domestic Economy,* first published in 1841. So most of the 1869 work is Catharine's and some is Harriet's. There is no distinction as to credit in the book. Scholars have often taken delight in trying to decipher whose writing is whose, but that is not important here.

Over and above its sensing of social change in espousing not only a stronger role for the woman in the household but indeed a "sovereign" one, *AWH* also reflected changing technology as applicable to the house. For example, by 1869 travel had entered a new age of comfort and convenience not even imagined just thirty years earlier. Hence, *AWH* found analogy for comparable modernization of the kitchen:

*The model kitchen, 1869: from* The American Woman's Home. *It foresees the more modern kitchen in its emphasis on efficiency, its use of a continuous working space, and its placement of the working area adjacent to windows, both for better light and for a sense of respite from the chores at hand. Placement of the sink by a window was not entirely new, however. It was the case at Schifferstadt a century earlier (see photograph, page 36), owing to the sheer practicality of having a convenient drain for the sink. The Silas Deane House, Wethersfield, Connecticut (1766), has a sink with a drain hole just below a window; and Homewood in Baltimore (1803) also has evidence of an under-the-window sink in the original kitchen. The very narrow shelves are a Beecher trademark (for example, in the kitchen of the Stowe House) for their virtue of accommodating essential implements and cookware while presumably minimizing clutter.*

The cook's galley in a steamship has every article and utensil used in cooking for two hundred persons, in a space not larger than a stove-room, and so arranged that with one or two steps the cook can reach all he uses. In contrast to this, in most large houses, the table furniture, the cooking materials and utensils, the sink, and the eating-room, are at such great distances apart, that half the time and strength is employed in walking back and forth.

*AWH* thus foresaw time-and-motion study as a factor in modern life and was perhaps the first to try to apply it to the home—specifically the kitchen—by promoting the use of a continuous working space. Its 1869 model kitchen gathered along one wall all the essential functions that could be consolidated as of then. The stove was separate, owing to its need for proximity to the chimney and for a protective safety zone around its hot cast iron. And the icebox, or ice closet, was not yet a part of the essential kitchen grouping; it was in the cellar. The working area included a sink, a dish drainer, a molding and meat board, bins for flour and cornmeal, a storage area for pails of sugar and molasses, and drawers for towels and other supplies. There were shelves surrounding the work area, with utensils hanging from hooks on the lowest shelf. Particularly noteworthy were the windows (presumably overlooking a garden) incorporated into the layout. These provided ventilation but, perhaps more important, some degree of diversion from the tasks at hand. This was a very innovative touch. While taken for granted in the 20th century, such a degree of accommodation was significant in 1869.

This emphasis on convenience, first and foremost, was the expression of a natural desire to avoid drudgery. Technology was doing its

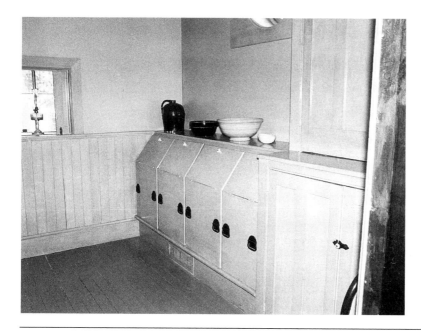

*The model kitchen: a practical application, 1872. That these bins—forming a continuous storage, if not necessarily working, space—are inspired by* The American Woman's Home *is almost surely beyond coincidence. This is the pantry of the home of Sarah Davis (see also page 153) in Bloomington, Illinois. As a teenager, Sarah was a student of Catharine Beecher at her Female Seminary in Hartford.* (Photograph by the author)

part, but there was another factor, one about which Catharine Beecher had already warned, even if prematurely, in 1841:

> Every year, as the prosperity of this Nation increases, good domestics will decrease, and young mothers are hereafter to be called to superintend and perform all branches of domestic business. . . . Every man, therefore, in forming plans for a future residence, and every woman who has any influence in deciding such matters, ought to make these probabilities the chief basis of their calculations.

In fact, the number of female domestic servants increased in the second half of the 19th century, through the influx of immigrants and the northward migration of blacks, for all of whom employment opportunities would otherwise range from scarce to nonexistent. Domestic positions were plentiful, and no basic skills were

needed. But Catharine's warning was only too early. The gathering magnitude of industrialization began opening up factory jobs for women, especially in the apparel industries—jobs that paid better than domestic service.

There is no accurate account of how many homes had domestic help. Countless houses of the Victorian period, mostly larger ones, were built with domestic quarters, frequently in the attic. The prevalence of such homes suggests a prevalence of domestic servants; but that is not necessarily so. A vast number of households could not afford more than the occasional services of a cleaning woman, if that. The Stowes apparently relied only on day help. Even so, it is something of an irony that many of these former domestics who went off to factories helped build the labor-saving devices that replaced them in the household. It is also interesting to note that, as opposed to Europe, where vestiges of feudalism remained tenacious even into the

*The efficient kitchen: changing conceptions, exactly a half century apart.* (Right) The American Woman's Home, *1869;* (below) *Christine Frederick,* Household Engineering, *1919.*

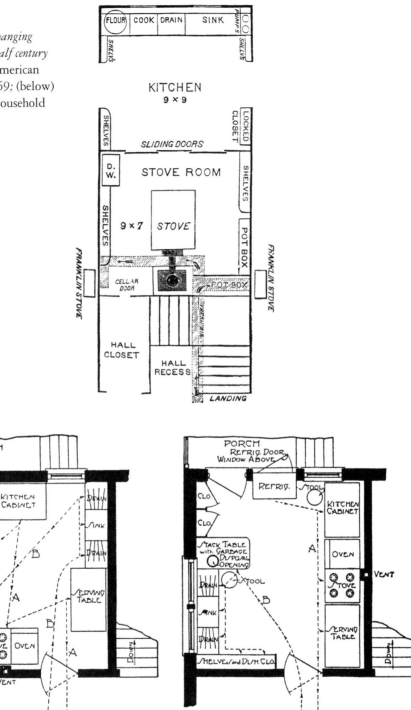

KITCHEN
9 × 9

STOVE ROOM

9 × 7 STOVE

BADLY GROUPED KITCHEN EQUIPMENT

EFFICIENT GROUPING OF KITCHEN EQUIPMENT
A. Preparing route. B. Clearing away route.

20th century, in America the freeing of domestic servants went much more quickly; and the modern house, and especially the modern kitchen, also came much faster.

The Beecher sisters personified the changing role of women as it is applicable to the house. Whether they were also significant to the women's movement was not important from their point of view. As Harriet herself explained in her *House and Home Papers:*

> We have been told how many spirits among women are of a wider, stronger, more heroic mould than befits the mere routine of housekeeping. It may be true that there are many women far too great, too wise, too high, for mere housekeeping. But where is the woman in any way too great, or too high, or too wise, to spend herself in creating a home?

The essentials of the modern household had taken root. At the other end of the great wave of change that culminated in the woman suffrage amendment, a latter-day Beecher in a latter-day *American Woman's Home* was echoing the virtues of efficiency in the household. Here we have Christine Frederick (1883–1970), whose husband was a corporate executive:

> My husband came home only to find me all tired out, with no energy left to play over a song, or listen to a thoughtful article. About this time I became acquainted, through my husband's interests, with several men in close touch with the new movement of industrial efficiency. At first it did not occur to me that methods which were applicable to organized industries, like shoe factories and iron foundries, could be applied to my group of very unorganized industries—the home. Yet the more I studied it, the more possible it seemed . . . bringing the science of efficiency into the home. (*The New Housekeeping,* 1913)

How perspicacious was this, this application of movement and efficiency to simple tasks? As it happened, it was in this same year of 1913 that the Ford Motor Company, applying in the workplace the same principles Christine Frederick was trying out in her home, forever changed the course of manufacturing by instituting the first industrial assembly line for the production of Model T Fords.

## FROM PRODUCER TO CONSUMER

A fundamental but largely forgotten change in the American home is its transition from producer to consumer. The average family today relies so overwhelmingly on commercially produced goods that it is difficult to realize how substantial a change this is. In earliest colonial times, virtually everything was homemade except for finery and furnishings that the more affluent imported from Europe.

Throughout the colonial period and into the 19th century, countless families, if not bartering, were spinning, weaving, knitting, and sewing most of their own clothing; tanning hides to make their own boots, shoes, and breeches; turning out their own hats, gloves, collars, and cuffs; producing their own soap, starch, candles, perfumes, medicines, and liniments; weaving their own carpets; baking their own bread, crackers, cakes, and pies; making their own cheese; growing and preserving their own fruits and vegetables; smoking, salting, and pickling their own meat; and making their own wine and brewing their own beer. By 1900, almost everything itemized here was routinely purchased at the store by most American families.

So great an output of production required space; the kitchen provided much of it, along with the cellar, the back porch, and an outbuilding perhaps, as well as nooks and corners of other rooms about the house or even entire rooms when possible (as for weaving). And it necessitated everyone's lending a hand. In rural Ohio, in the 1820s and 1830s, recalled William Cooper Howells, "There was hardly a family of girls where one of them did not have a loom and weave all the plainer kinds of stuff for themselves and for others." The other girls might be churning butter or doing any of a seemingly endless number of household tasks.

Recalling her childhood in Athens, Ohio, about this same time, Harriet Connor Brown had only pleasant thoughts:

> I used to love to watch my mother weaving, her shuttle holding the spool with yarn shooting through the warp, then back the other way. When she had woven as far as she could reach, she would bend below the loom and wind the woven cloth into a roll beneath. Blankets made at home used to last a long, long time. Homespun things were good.

Harriet Brown also noted that not every family made all its own necessities. There was a certain division of labor in this respect:

We did not make our candles at home, but got them usually from Uncle Dean, who made candles for the town. . . .

There were many Uncle Deans and an assortment of goods beyond candles that were made in the home for outside consumption. Household manufactures of this sort in Connecticut in the 1790s, according to Tench Coxe, assistant secretary of the treasury under Alexander Hamilton, included "woolen and linen cloth, sail cloth, bed-ticks, some cotton goods, hosiery, nails and spikes, some silk buttons, handkerchiefs, ribands and stuffs, sewing-silk, threads, fringes, and pot and pearl ashes."

The extent of household manufactures in the early 19th century was reported by an Englishman named Isaac Holmes in his account of travels around the United States in 1822:

> It is proper to state, that household, or domestic manufactures of woolen, linen, &c. are carried on to a great extent: many thousands of families spin and make up their own clothing, sheets, table linen, &c. They purchase cotton yarn, and have it frequently mixed with their linen and woolen. Blankets, quilts, or coverlets, in short, nearly every article of domestic use, is made, or a great part made, in the family. It is supposed that nearly two-thirds [apparently using an 1810 estimate by secretary of the treasury Albert Gallatin] of all the clothing, linen, blankets, &c. of those inhabitants who reside in the interior of the country, are of home or household manufacture. It is the same in the interior with both soap and candles for they have no excisemen to prevent their making those articles in the family.

The period encompassed by Holmes's visit represents roughly the high-water mark of home industry. The trend away from the "family factory" had begun even before this and accelerated in the decades ahead, although on the frontier the household necessarily remained self-sufficient. The impetus was specialization. At first came a proliferation of trades and crafts, including the hat maker, the tanner, the shoemaker, and the barber, now independent tradesmen outside the household who provided services that could be, and had been, performed in the home. But the real impact came with mechanization. Among the first examples are the gristmill and the fulling mill, both of which became common during the 18th century.

To take fulling as an example: Woolen cloth, when woven, is stiff; to be made supple and comfortable, it must be fulled, a process entailing washing, beating, and lifting of the nap. This can be done by hand; it can also be done with relatively simple machinery that can be operated efficiently with waterpower. Fulling was one of the first textile processes to be specialized. New Jersey alone had forty-one fulling mills in 1784. Similarly with carding of wool or flax before weaving. Howells recalled that "the wool was sometimes carded at home, but usually it was sent off to one of the carding machines that would be put up in a mill." The more that households came to rely on such specialized operations, the better the commercial potential and thus the more specialization. As towns grew into cities, the process was accelerated because the complexity of urban life demands a high degree of division of labor.

Meanwhile, the industrial revolution was gathering steam, with profound impact on household manufactures. During the period 1840–1860—a time of unprecedented prosperity and industrial expansion—household industry as a way of life effectively ended in the Northeast and Midwest.

Advances in transportation added to the process. Canals and then railroads cheapened the cost and sped the time of moving raw materials to factories and goods from factories to homes. Except for remnants of the frontier, by the late 19th century the household that had been producer was now almost entirely consumer.

## THE KITCHENLESS HOUSE

Almost, but not entirely. The household still produced all its own meals, made most of its own baked goods, and did its own laundry. Suppose these essential tasks, and perhaps even child care as well, also were to transcend the household? A kitchenless house? A nurseryless house? The changing social climate of the late 19th and early 20th centuries produced a number of experiments in taking essential functions of the kitchen not only out of the kitchen but out of the house; none had more than brief and limited impact. In some cases, these experiments took the form of meal delivery services; in others, cooperative kitchens. The housewife thus might be freed of cooking for her family by having entire meals delivered to the home; or the family, instead of gathering for dinner in its own dining room (and having to clean up afterward), might join with others in a community dining room conveniently located nearby, where hired staff would do all the work, before and after.

Sometimes the absence of a maid compelled a family to take its meals out. Such was the case recorded by seventeen-year-old Harry Lewis of Sauk Centre, Minnesota, in his diary:

> [July 5, 1902] We have no servant pro tempore (as servants are very "hard to get" at the present time) . . . and are taking dinner at the Palmer House [a hotel a short distance away].

The concept of cooperative services extended to baking, laundering, and even the caring of children. The first such experiment of record was the Cambridge (Massachusetts) Cooperative Housekeeping Society, established in 1869 by Melusina Fay Peirce and Mary P. Mann, which drew the attention of the press as far as New York and London. The Cambridge cooperative got as far as providing bakery and laundry services for forty families, but owing to lack of sufficient use by its members it disbanded after two years without ever actually getting to deliver meals. At least nineteen similar organizations came into being through the 1920s. Some offered only laundry, house cleaning, or child care services; others did provide meals, delivered by horse and wagon and later automobile. (Peirce had suggested that Yankee ingenuity be employed to devise a "Universal Heat-generating Air-tight Family Dinner-Box" for the delivery of meals "hot and on time"; a century later, there was pizza delivery with the same promise.) Perhaps the longest-running service was the Evanston (Illinois) Community Kitchen, which lasted from 1918 to 1951 and offered both a cooked-food shop and home-delivered dinners.

Directly analogous were cooperative dining clubs that were popular around the turn of the 20th century. Organizations ranging in size from as few as five or ten families to as many as fifty or sixty maintained dining rooms and employed chefs and auxiliary personnel to provide them with well-prepared meals. One such was The Roby in Decatur, Illinois, a former boardinghouse that in 1890 was converted to an eating club for fifty-four member families. It served three meals a day.

In retrospect, these were all experiments, since they represented no lasting change in way of life. Yet the lure of convenience persists. In recent years, in a very real sense, The Roby and the Evanston Community Kitchen have returned . . . as McDonald's, Kentucky Fried Chicken, and an assortment of other fast-food substitutes for the family kitchen.

## FROM CONSUMER TO DISPOSER

An increasingly significant aspect of the relationship between house and society is what to do with what goes back to society from this increasingly consumerized house.

The contents of today's household waste compared with early colonial times reveal, in a unique way, the great advances in comfort, convenience, and standard of living reflected in the house of today. The few bones and bits of broken pottery that were the typical family refuse of the 17th century would be unnoticeable beside the heap of waste generated by the average family of the late 20th century—a heap abounding in plastics, polyurethane foam, and other new synthetic materials that may have a half-life vastly greater (no one yet knows) than the centuries that have elapsed since a fallen ceramic cup or a discarded bone generated the meager garbage of the 17th century.

Archaeological evidence provides some idea of the refuse of early colonial times. There remain abundant assortments of broken bits of bottles and pottery as well as larger bones that were once part of roasts of mutton or beef. Other forms of food scraps were readily eaten by pigs or chickens; the remains of uneaten food and smaller bones were fragmentized by the footsteps of both humans and animals and were gradually assimilated into the ground.

The general practice throughout the 17th and early 18th centuries was to scatter garbage, usually in the backyard. Archaeological digs show that this was usually done from the back door. The result was a pattern known as sheet refuse—a random distribution characteristic of the way objects would be scattered by the fling of an arm, which was precisely the case. In early towns the flinging was often also to the front—into the street, as had been so common in the towns and cities of postmedieval Europe.

Artifacts that were once household waste usually can be dated. Pottery known to be from the 17th century usually follows the scatter pattern; fragments from a later period are more often found in compact sites, clearly indicating burying, which, by the mid 18th century, was the more common practice. Backyard trash pits of the 18th century were usually square, frequently 5 feet to a side and sometimes as deep as 7 feet.

In towns, as they developed, the burying of garbage became less and less possible because of dwindling space. Thus the need for town government to assume responsibility for the collecting and disposing of household garbage.

As a concept, it was something the settlers had brought with them, even though it was hardly yet commonplace. London had scavengers going back to the 1400s—men paid to keep the streets clean and pick up "tubs, boxes, baskets or other vessels" left outside houses.

New England's early chronicler, Edward Johnson, in his *Wonder-Working Providence,* found Boston at mid 17th century already a "City-like Towne . . . whose continuall inlargement presages some sumptuous City." With increasing sumptuousness went increasing garbage. In 1652 the town's selectmen sought to apply some measure of control by forbidding anyone to throw "garbidg or Carion or dead dogs or Catts or any other dead beast or stinkeing thing, in any hie way or dich or Common . . . but are injoyned to bury all such things." In spite of these and other regulations, public dumping continued, accompanied by increasing concern for its impact on public health.

By the 1870s garbage removal at homes in Boston had been systematized to include two collections a week in winter and three in summer, as described in a paper read at the 1879 annual meeting of the American Public Health Association:

At about four o'clock A.M., men leave the department yards, of which there are four in different sections of the city. Each gang consists of a horse, wagon, driver, and helper. The wagons are perfectly water-tight. Hanging below them are two large wooden buckets to be used by the men. Shortly after seven o'clock [after the markets, restaurants, hotels, and boardinghouses] the dwelling houses are visited. The driver or his helper

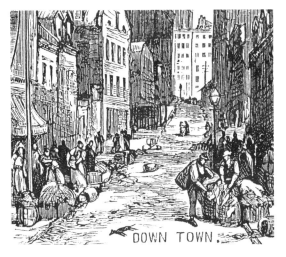

*Garbage collection day in New York, the 1870s.*
(*Harper's Weekly,* Nov. 24, 1877)

rings the bell at the yard gate, or at the basement door if there be no yard, and on being admitted quietly goes to the swill tub, empties its contents into the bucket, replaces the tub and leaving the house passes to the next one, and so on until his bucket is filled.

New York had regular garbage collection by the mid 1800s, although its contribution to quality of life was somewhat debatable, as recorded by British author George Sala in *America Revisited* (1882):

The garbage-boxes or ash-barrels on the sidewalks [of New York City], in which receptacles the inhabitants deposit their household refuse, are still the same unsightly and unsavoury nuisances that I remember them [the last time I saw them, in 1865]; and in windy weather the miscellaneous contents of these 'hopeless Pandoras' are distributed by the bounteous blast in unstinted profusion over the garments and into the eyes of passers-by.

Out in the countryside, and even in the incipient suburbs, no one yet thought about collecting garbage. But householders had time-honored ways of disposing of it: Use meat refuse and other swill as feed for domestic animals; save fat, lard, tallow, and grease for making soap; set aside whatever content might be dried out and burn it in the kitchen range; and take whatever is left and store it away until some itinerant junk dealer comes by, knowing he will be glad to cart it off and try to salvage some value out of it.

If the last has the ring of a recycling message of the later 20th century, it is worth taking as an example of how the approach to garbage disposal has tended to run somewhat in circles. For recycling has itself been recycled over the years, not only to combat the increasing wastefulness of a throwaway society but simply to make money out of the still usable. Whereas London's first scavengers were paid for their work, by the early 1800s they were paying the city for a permit to scavenge, so as to sell what they could salvage: coal cinders to make bricks, rags for the manufacture of paper, bones for pigment in paint and dye, other residue for use in repairing the roads.

This process, of course, meant separation of waste at the city dump. Yet "source separation"—requiring the householder to separate various recyclables before collection—was also tried on a limited scale more than a century ago. When George E. Waring became New York City's street-cleaning commissioner in 1895, the city's garbage disposal was of a sort that "would have done credit to a medieval town." Garbage and ashes were indiscriminately piled on scows and either towed out to sea or to tidal lands in need of fill. Court decisions and legislation halted the tidal filling, but the dumping at sea continued. Waring, in one of his first acts, ordered householders throughout the city henceforth to separate their refuse into two containers—one for the garbage, the other for ashes. Rubbish and wastepaper that heretofore had been mingled in with the garbage were to be tied up and placed separately at the curb. But Waring's term in office came to an abrupt end in 1898 when Tammany Hall regained city hall and undid his reforms. By 1903, however, administrations had changed again, and recycling of refuse, at the dump site, was resumed. World War I shortages helped to popularize recycling. In 1918 many cities had pick-and-sort programs. Camden, New Jersey, used prisoners from the city jail. Passaic, New Jersey, opened its dump to junk dealers and gave them carte blanche. Cleveland estimated its revenue from the sale of recyclables at $30,000 a year (as against the $230,000 it cost to collect the rubbish and ash in the first place).

In coming years the use of incineration as well as open dumping on land made cheap by the Depression resulted in a sharp drop-off of even these modest attempts at resource recovery, although World War II, with its shortages and unprecedented demand for metallic raw material, gave recycling a brief revival.

In postwar years an increasing concern for the environment turned the tide against pollution-spewing incinerators and toward air-friendly sanitary landfills. But the latter had two serious shortcomings: There was only so much available land, especially in urban areas,

and the landfills were in effect giant replicas of the trash pits of colonial times, preserving part of every household's refuse for posterity. On the other hand, modern technology has not been a one-sided creator of garbage. Frozen foods have substantially reduced the potential waste generated by the household. For example: Those fresh carrots that would require discarding of greens and surface residue are, in frozen form, ready for cooking. Similarly, a wide range of food products come to the consumer devoid of greens, residue, shells, husks, and leaves. All this inedible matter, which would become garbage, is either recycled by the food processor as, for example, animal feed or at least disposed of in a more efficient way than is feasible for the householder.

Nevertheless, recognition of the overall wastefulness of throwaway consumerism, spurred by the federal Resource Recovery Act of 1970, has made recycling at the household level a way of life for most Americans in the late 20th century.

That is not to say that recycling is something new. Above and beyond the examples cited, there was once a house in Boston, at the corner of Ann Street and Market Square, with a roughcast plaster finish of a sort usually utilizing pebbles as part of its mixture. This house, built in 1680, made use of "recycled" junk bottles pounded into pebble-size bits and pieces.

## RECYCLING THE LIFE CYCLE

The interaction of house and society is further to be seen in the locus of the most significant points in the life cycle: being born, getting

*The cycle of life:* (above left) *a Pennsylvania Dutch birth and baptismal certificate, Berks County, Pennsylvania, 1806;* (above right) *a marriage certificate, Burlington County, New Jersey, 1855;* (below) *a lithograph, 1877, showing what appear to be the last hours of a beloved one. All that these represent—birth, marriage, death, and the funeral—were events in the life cycle that routinely took place within the home until the 20th century.* (Library of Congress, Prints and Photographs)

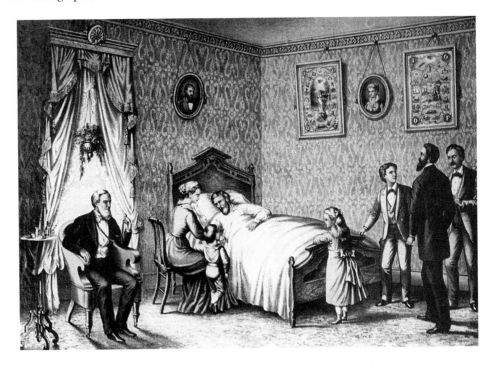

married, dying, and being buried. Here we have a clearly discernible reorientation from house to institution.

As for being born: Until the 20th century, nearly all mothers in America gave birth in their own bedrooms, most often with the help of a midwife (even as late as 1910, half of all births were attended by midwives). A very good example of one is Martha Moore Ballard, of Augusta, Maine, who practiced between 1785 and 1812, attending at a total of 996 births. She charged a uniform fee of nine shillings regardless of the distance traveled, and besides helping at birth, she functioned as something of a nurse and physician, as recorded in her diary:

10 [September 1789]. I was called to see Capt. Pinkham's wife. I left home at the 12th hour; walked under shore; had a faint turn after I arived there. My patient was safe delivered of a daughter at the 9th h. evening. It was dead born.

20. Sunday. I was called by Mr. Medcalf to see Mrs. Sherburn who is in travail. Shee was siezed with her illness at the 3rd h. morn.

22. Mrs. Sherburn was safe delivered at 3h. and 30m. morn, of a daughter. I took a nap of sleep which was the first since Satterday night.

28. I was called up at the 4th hour to go to Shaw's at the Hook; walked as far as Mr. Weston's, from there by water; was very wet indeed. Found the woman safe delivered of her 2d daughter by the help of Mrs. Clark.

2 [October 1789]. I was called at the 4th h. morn, to Mrs. Goff, who is in travail. I walkt to Davis, store; crost the river and went by land on horseback. Arived at the 6th h. I tarried there this night.

3. Mrs. Goff's illness increast, and shee was safe delivered at 11h. and 30 m. morn, of a daughter.

9. Mrs. Daw was safe delivered at the 6th hour this morn of a fine son, which weighed 11 lbs. Mrs. Daw is the 32d woman I have putt to bed since Feb'y 5th.

Throughout the colonial period and into the 19th century there was usually no alternative to one's bedroom for giving birth. The first general hospital in America was Pennsylvania Hospital in Philadelphia, opened in 1751. New York's Bellevue Hospital had begun as an infirmary for the city's almshouse in 1735 and only became a separate institution in 1825. They were a few of a kind and at that were definitively for people who were sick or injured; if these hospitals ever handled a maternity case it was only for some singular and exigent reason. Even when hospitals became more common in the 19th century, they were not places in which to give birth; childbirth was neither illness nor injury.

While tradition was perpetuating the home as the place for giving birth, there was also good medical reason: Hospitals were full of germs. In cases where maternity patients needed hospital assistance, the connection of hospitals with germs was not understood until Ignaz Semmelweis deduced it in 1847 at Vienna's general hospital and mandated the washing of hands with chloride of lime by any practitioner having contact with an expectant mother. But few hospitals took heed. By the time specialty hospitals for obstetrics began to appear, antisepsis was also being accepted and practiced. New England Hospital for Women began using carbolic acid in 1877; New York Maternity Hospital, bichloride of mercury in 1880.

With some use of the hospital for childbirth came an increasing degree of safety. In the 20th century the hospital not only learned to safeguard against the spread of germs but also began to acquire equipment and technology to protect the woman and her child in the event of difficulty (the need for a cesarean, for example). And with this technological advance, especially during the 20th century, came dependency on the hospital as the place of choice for giving birth. Whereas in Chicago in 1920 fewer than ten percent of births occurred in the hospital, by midcentury it was nearly all. Hospital births in Detroit in 1908 were about 5 percent; in 1945, 94 percent. In 1944 the American Obstetrical Society advised that "all maternity patients" have hospital care. By the late 20th century a mother's bedroom was so rarely the place for giving birth that virtually the only reason was unexpected early labor.

In its day as the delivery room of choice, the bedroom became for two months or more almost the entire world of the mother. The latter period of pregnancy was not a time to be seen in public, and the expectant mother took to her room for the period of her confinement. When the Reads moved into their new house in 1803, there was still much work to be done. Priority was given to Mrs. Read's bedroom, in particular to finishing off the fireplace, for she

was getting late into her pregnancy and wanted the room ready for her confinement.

Once a child was born, often another month was spent in the bedroom, nursing the infant and convalescing. The tradition of not appearing in public during the time of obvious pregnancy probably owed to ideas about risking health or even to old wives' tales in earlier times and primarily to notions of modesty by the Victorian period. The trend away from the bedroom and to the hospital as the place for giving birth also broke down social sensitivity about a woman's being seen pregnant.

As for getting married: In assessing this reorientation from house to institution, the transfer is less complete. There are probably more home weddings than there are home births, but as a generality the home wedding is also largely a thing of the past. The institution, be it religious or commercial (catering hall, restaurant, country club), is now the most common place of choice.

That is not to say there was ever as clear-cut an emphasis on the home for marriages as was the case for giving birth. Colonial New England did unquestionably favor the home. During the Puritan period the wedding was invariably performed in the house by a magistrate in a simple civil ceremony, followed by a usually modest celebration. A Quaker wedding, on the other hand, took place in the meetinghouse with a simple exchange of vows preceded and followed by periods of solemn silence. The bride and groom then took up residence in the bride's father's house for a fortnight to receive well-wishers.

In the colonial South, with its stronger Church of England tradition, marriage vows were professed with liturgical ritual, but the ceremony might be performed in either the church or the bride's home, and the latter was more common.

There was something practical about getting married at home, whatever the faith. The fuss could be minimized and the enjoyment maximized, as was clearly the case for Caesar Rodeney (?–1745), father of Delaware's Caesar Rodney, signer of the Declaration of Independence. The elder Rodeney was married on Wednesday, October 18, 1727, to Elizabeth Crawford, whose father, the Reverend Thomas Crawford, presided over what was apparently a brief ceremony. The setting was the Crawford home on a farm in Jones Neck, near Dover, Rodeney's journal recounts:

October 18. A.M. I Drest In Order to be Married Got brakt [breakfast] Went to Mr. C[rawfor]d & Got him to Christin Me about Noon I wass Married by my father In-Law Mr. Cd about 2 a clock Got Diner and Did not finish tell Just Night for we had a Grate Company So We Past the Day and Night with a Deal of Plesher

October 19. A.M. My Bride and I Got up Still holding the Weding with a Grate Company which wass fidling Danceing & verry merry We Got brakt after which Mr. Cd was Marrid to Kathean french [Katherine French, his third wife] then we Went to Bro Danils We Led our Brides & the Brides Men & Brid Maids followed us after them all the Company Cam hand In hand with the Drum and two Viol Ends Playing before us but Did not Stay Long there all Came Back We sent for more Rum and Syder and Past the night away with the Same Plesher as before

Or a wedding at home could be an occasion for fuss. The home of prosperous merchant Joshua Carter in Newburyport, Massachusetts, was the setting for the marriage of his daughter, Elizabeth, to William B. Reynolds, of Boston, on Tuesday, April 24, 1821. As related by Elizabeth's stepsister:

Now for the wedding assemblage. Parson Withington & two Sisters, Mrs. Frothingham in simple garb arrayed. E. Wheelwright, looking very neat & properly— Mrs. Baldwin starched & prim, Nursy Clark old & thin. Aunt Nabby displayed a long faded white ribbon. Mr. & Mrs. Tom Carter, with a phalanx of boys, in blue uniform & buff jackets. One broad grin diffused itself over the countenances of those last mentioned, & added much to my amusement, I promise you. Polly, Meribah, Catherine, Henrietta, Jemmy & black Clement witnessed the ceremony from the door. At 7 o'clock precisely, Mr. Reynolds led Miss Carter, Mr. Andrews led Miss Reynolds, Mr. Smith, Miss Lamb & Mr. Marquand Miss C. Carter in to their places, which was in front of the couch before mentioned, & the Bride Maids arranged themselves on one side, the groomsmen on the other, & the ceremony began.

Use of the church for weddings became more and more popular during the 19th century, with its heavy influx of immigrants from Roman Catholic countries, for whom there was the tradition of marriage as a sacrament. Similarly for those of Church of England tradition, where the Oxford Movement was reviving an emphasis on liturgy. Taking one's vows in front of the couch in the parlor became less and less common than walking to the altar.

When it comes to that final, ultimate observance of the cycle of life, the swing of the pendulum has been as complete as for the first. Just as few of us are born at home, few are borne from home.

One's house was once the almost certain site of one's funeral—as well as of the dying that preceded it:

> He [my brother] died [at home] as he had lived, beautifully, thinking of and sending messages to all his friends, and on his last day repeating passages of Scripture and even, weak as he was, joining in hymns sung at his bedside. . . . After services at the house, we walked to the church . . . [but] owing to the rain, none of us ladies were allowed to go into the cemetery. (Elizabeth Prentiss, 1872)

As opposed to the stricture and distraction of a hospital setting, there is a naturalness in falling into eternal sleep exactly where one is used to falling into nightly sleep, in one's own bed.

The immediacy of seeing death at home also gave immediacy to preparing for it. An 18th-century example: When Pennsylvania Germans built their homes, they frequently designated one room to be a *doed-kammer,* or 'dead room'—the site for the body to lie in; in the meantime the room would serve some other purpose. Its doors were often made wider to facilitate the carrying of the casket. Similarly where there were two parlors, the "best parlor" might be used for special occasions like a wedding or a funeral. (There was a connec-

tion between these two events also in the custom of setting aside a special bottle of wine to be opened at a wedding and then recorking it and saving some wine for the groom's funeral.) A *doed-kammer* or something comparable was the exception; normally, the living room was the place for the laying out and the funeral. Sometimes, however, the coffin was simply placed on top of the deceased's bed or even atop the dining room table.

The Victorian era, in the manner of its namesake, exalted mourning. The period between death and burial took on its own ritualistic gloom as survivors within a hushed household drew shut the curtains and draperies, dimmed the lights, spoke in softened tones, and even tiptoed about the house (lest Death spot them also).

Preparations for funerals during the colonial period and into the 19th century were the job of the family, usually with the help of friends or neighbors who would do the actual washing and readying of the body for burial. The funeral normally was held in the home. Following the service there, the coffin was covered with a pall and carried to the burial ground.

That done, the mood changed, for in those days of great scarcity of entertainment the completion of a funeral was an excuse for letting go. A funeral repast in Boston in 1797 included beef, ham, bacon, baked meats, fish, oysters, 150 eggs, peas, onions, potatoes, cheese, fruit, and sweetmeats in addition to copious quantities of rum, wine, beer, gin, and brandy. A diary kept by William Nutting, of Groton, Massachusetts, shows twenty-five entries written down between April 1785 and March 1790; every single one is a reference to a death or a funeral. The focus of all this festivity, of course, was the home.

From earliest colonial times, after the funeral service at home or church it had been the responsibility of mourners to bear the casket to the burying ground. As towns and cities grew, the distance to burial sites increased. Hand bearing of the casket gave way to conveyance by carriage. But since only the well-to-do owned carriages, people of ordinary means had to rent them, along with the necessary horses. Rentals of coaches complete with black horses for funeral processions date back to at least 1750 in Boston. Livery owners doing the renting eventually realized a greater potential for business by also offering the services of helpers to carry the coffin from the house to the carriage to the church to the burying ground, and so on; and in time these entrepreneurs offered to "undertake" for the family of the deceased the preparation of the body and all the arrangements for the funeral. An 1824 Baltimore city directory has a notice from a livery-stable owner offering these various additional services. Coroners, city and town registrars, and even messengers began to make themselves available as undertakers.

Even so, the home remained the focus of the funeral observance throughout the 19th century. The undertaker simply came in and took over those tasks that family and friends had performed. After 1900, embalming became more and more standard. Now, as part of his services, the undertaker would bring with him a portable cooling board, embalming cabinet, dressing case with hard rubber pump, arterial tubes, trocar, needles, forceps, scalpel, scissors, eye caps, razor, and so on—all of which he set out in the bedroom, thence to

proceed with his work. For the funeral he would bring in folding chairs to set up in the parlor and perhaps direct relatives and friends to sit in accordance with their relationship to the departed.

Clearly all this attention to detail, which was intended to make things easier for family and friends, was adding to the confusion and stress of an already difficult time. Instead of using the deceased's bedroom or parlor, why not let the undertaker undertake it all in his own parlor? Hence the funeral parlor (or funeral home, once "parlor" became anachronistic), an institution that began emerging around the 1880s and multiplied to profusion in the 20th century, eventually, except where religious preference dictated otherwise, superseding the home as the place for bidding the departed farewell.

## ANOTHER VANTAGE POINT

These various changes in society reflected in the American house: We have looked at them within the house itself, yet we have another vantage point just slightly removed from which to calibrate our outlook. And that is the front porch, which, despite having to take its bow to succeeding customs and traditions, remains a unique place in American life. As an outdoor room of the house, the front porch in its high season was a curiosity to visiting Europeans, who chided Americans for "living on the street" (*Craftsman* magazine, March 1906). That high season spanned only a finite period of American life, roughly from the early to mid 1800s through the early to mid 1900s, but its

*The American front porch: an "intimate connection of the life of the street." The place is Boston, c1890.* (Library of Congress, Prints and Photographs, Currier Collection)

coming and going sheds light on the evolution of the house both before and beyond and, more importantly, on the interaction of house and society.

That the popularity of the front porch is largely past is necessarily a subjective judgment; there are no statistics as to how many houses have front porches, let alone how many are used. The author, in an attempt to be at least somewhat empirical, conducted an informal survey using as his database the town of Great Bend, Kansas, which is quintessential Middle America, not only in its demographics but in its geographics. To draw a line through a map of the United States about halfway between north and south and halfway between east and west, given a stubby enough pencil point, is to bisect at Great Bend. Seemingly a fair enough site. It was August; it was a Saturday night, presumably the most suitable night of the week for porch sitting; it was between eight and nine-thirty, neither too early nor too late in the evening; it was pleasant weather, neither too hot nor too cool; and Great Bend is full of typically middle-class homes of the late-19th and early-20th centuries, nearly all of them with front porches. The author strolled by perhaps fifty or sixty homes, keeping a running tally of the number of people sitting out. The grand total was one—one man, lately retired from the local utility company, sitting alone in the quiet of a summer's night. Where was everyone else? inquired the author. "Wull," said the gentleman, sniffing the night air, "in watchin' TV, I guess."

Porchlike structures go back to antiquity—to the colonnaded terraces of Queen Hatshepsut's temple in ancient Egypt; to the stoa of a Greek temple from which those philosophers later called Stoics addressed their followers. Or to the Middle Ages, to the cloisters of monasteries, where monks often studied or meditated. These places were porchlike, not porches, and palaces, temples, and monasteries were not the vernacular house. In India, by the 1600s, there was something porchlike, as documented by Charles Lockyer in his *Account of the Trade in India* (London, 1711). Lockyer recorded details of a building in Madras that "is very ancient, two Story high, and has a paved Court, two large Verandas or Piazzas. . . ." Meanwhile, a countryman of his, halfway around the world, was recording evidence of a porch in the New World. Sir Hans Sloane, as physician to the duke of Albemarle, visited the West Indies in 1688. Of Jamaica he wrote: "The Buildings of the Spaniards on this Island were usually one Story high, having a porch. . . ."

A porch, by name; and we may guess, the climate of the West Indies being what it is, perhaps a place for getting some shade or catching a breeze. About this same time porches had appeared in Charleston, South Carolina—and probably elsewhere in the South—and they were likely used from time to time as a place to sit. Known in Charleston as piazzas, they were there at least by the late 1600s inasmuch as an act of the colonial legislature in the year 1700 regulated them: Owners of lots adjacent to the wharf who "shall hereafter build a brick house at least two stories high, are hereby permitted and impowered to build piazzas, not exceeding six foot [presumably in depth]." The earliest piazzas were destroyed by a disastrous fire in 1740, but later ones remain. English physician George Milligen, visiting in the early 1760s, wrote that Charleston's approximately eleven hundred homes were "generally incumbered with Balconies and Piazzas." A further indication of popularity was the usefulness of the piazza in selling real estate:

TO BE SOLD . . . three-story house, in Meeting street, having two good rooms on a floor with a fire place in each, also a cellar, and a piazza fronting to the south and east . . . (*South Carolina Gazette,* December 13, 1751)

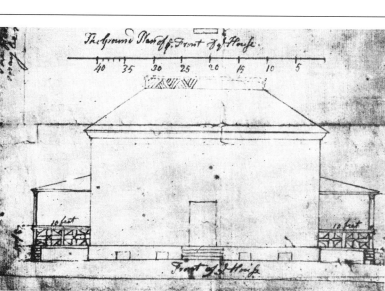

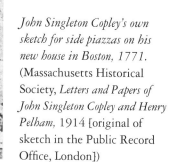

*John Singleton Copley's own sketch for side piazzas on his new house in Boston, 1771.* (Massachusetts Historical Society, *Letters and Papers of John Singleton Copley and Henry Pelham,* 1914 [original of sketch in the Public Record Office, London])

By the middle of the 18th century, porches were beginning to appear beyond the southeastern colonies. Homes of Dutch colonists in New York and New Jersey had their *stoep,* or 'stoop,' and this was documentably a place to sit. The Swedish scientist Peter Kalm, visiting the American colonies at midcentury, recorded the first clear evidence of the porch in its later, traditional role:

> The houses are covered with shingles. Before each door is a stoop to which you ascend by steps from the street; it resembles a small balcony, and has benches on both sides on which the people sit in the evening to enjoy the fresh air and to watch the passers-by.

Ah, the quintessential front porch! Yet lacking quintessence to this degree: The *stoep* of the mid 18th century was too small for anything except sitting on, and then only on built-in benches; and usually there was no roof over it—at most, a small overhang. But the "small balcony" in rather short time became a fully roofed porch extending the length of the house, the likes of which the Reverend Manasseh Cutler told of seeing in Rye, New York, in 1787: ". . . a large, well-built house, with a piazza extending the whole length of the front." The artist John Singleton Copley, while in New York, also noticed an increasing interest in porches; and when he married and was having a home built in Boston, he directed that his half brother Henry Pelham, who was supervising construction, make sure that piazzas (by whatever spelling) be included.

> I would have the windows put in the north side of my Rooms as above, for should I not add Wings I shall add a peazer when I return, which is much practiced here [in New York], and is very beautiful and convenient. (Copley, July 14, 1771)

> I don't comprehend what you mean by a Peazer. (Pelham, July 28, 1771)

> Peazas are cool in Summer and in Winter break off the storms so much that I think I should not be able to like a house without. (Copley, August 3, 1771)

> The Peaza's which you describe, appear to me, to be very convenient, as well as pleasant. (Pelham, August 25, 1771)

Copley's piazzas, it should be noted, were at the side of the house. Porches in front were also appearing in Philadelphia by this time and by late in the century had become common enough that it appeared there was "a porch to every house door, where it was universally common for the inhabitants to take their occasional sitting" (John F. Watson, *Annals of Philadelphia,* 1830).

## INDOORS OUTDOORS

So far we have seen the porch evolve by the late 18th century into a not uncommon appendage to the house. We have documented evidence that people went out on the porch to sit and catch a breeze or wave to passersby. Yet this was not a "living room" of the house; it was not yet what architect Alexander Jackson Davis had in mind when he advised that

a deep porch would be useful as a shelter, and in the mild season would be used instead of a sitting room. (*Rural Residences,* 1837)

Perhaps the first documentable porch that is indoors turned outdoors—an outside sitting room in which to read the paper or entertain friends or otherwise do outdoors what one had traditionally done indoors—is the great piazza at Mount Vernon. Here, just before the turn of the 19th century, on what George Washington modestly called the "long open Gallery in front of my house" did they, in fact, read the paper and take tea and entertain friends.*

*The piazza at Mount Vernon: the "long open Gallery in front of my house."* (Library of Congress, Prints and Photographs)

We know the diverse usefulness of the Washingtons' front porch in several ways. From an inventory, for example. After the deaths of both George and Martha, a complete inventory of Mount Vernon was made pursuant to settlement of their estate. The inventory included, "In the Piazza, 30 Windsor Chairs." Clearly the Washingtons meant to entertain company, and lots of it. And it wasn't only by sitting and talking. They also ate light meals and took tea out in the fresh air. There is evidence uncovered by a curator in the 19th century of bellpulls connecting the piazza with the kitchen—obviously to expedite refills of tea and the like.

---

* The piazza at Mount Vernon is on the east, or Potomac, side; it is the west side that faces the road. But because Mount Vernon is so commonly depicted from the river side, the piazza has taken on the aura of a front porch.

*Benjamin Latrobe's sketch of Martha Washington serving tea on the piazza at Mount Vernon, 1796.* (Benjamin Latrobe, *Journal of Latrobe* [New York, 1905])

(Below) *Washington receiving Lafayette on the piazza at Mount Vernon.* (Library of Congress, Prints and Photographs)

The architect Benjamin Latrobe visited Mount Vernon on July 16, 1796, and made several sketches of Mrs. Washington entertaining on the piazza. He also recorded in his journal that the president, dressed in a plain blue coat, met him on the piazza; that they seated them-selves on two of the Windsor chairs and talked for about an hour; that they joined the rest of the family in the dining room at half past three in the afternoon; and that, after dinner, "as I drink no wine and the President drank only three glasses, the party soon returned to the portico." The Polish poet Julian Ursyn Niemcewicz, also a guest at Mount Vernon about this time, added other details about porch sitting:

It is there [the piazza] that in the afternoon and evening the Gl. [general], his family and the guests go to sit and enjoy the fine weather and the beautiful view. . . . After dinner one goes out onto the portico to read the newspaper ["of which he receives about ten of different kinds" . . . and] in the evening seated under the portico, he often talked with me for hours at a time.

Would that Washington could have enjoyed it more. During his eight years as president, he averaged fewer than two visits a year to Mount Vernon; and they included many days on which, owing to the season, the piazza was of little use. But clearly, to the extent that they could sit out there, especially after retirement from public life, the Washingtons loved their front porch.

Even before the age of mass media, depictions of Mount Vernon (almost always emphasizing the "front porch") reached Americans by the masses. Newspapers, magazines, calendars, prints, even the painted dials of clocks prominently displayed the great temple on the Potomac. Furthermore, the 19th century was a time of increasing mobility, vastly accelerated by the coming of railroads. And while many people never got far beyond their own towns and villages, many others did travel; a familiar destination was Mount Vernon. A correspondent for the *Southern Literary Messenger,* writing in January 1852 about a trip there, had his destination already vivid in his mind's eye:

We had seen the "portrait" of this edifice an hundred times or more: we had seen it in rude prints upon the walls of village bar rooms, in the far distant valley of the Mississippi; we had noticed it often as a frontispiece upon the clocks of New England manufacture, such as find their way multitudinously over the broad regions of the American domain; we had had it in our observation in many forms and varieties of pencilling . . . [And now] here it was, the thing itself, standing palpably before our eyes; need we say, we recognized it at once?

Veneration of Mount Vernon, and its great piazza, was clearly an important element in the popularization of the front porch. Architectural, geographic, social, and creature-comfort factors also came into play. As for architecture: The first major change in architectural style in America was the classical revival that began virtually with the new nation itself, reflecting identification with the democracies of ancient times that this new American experiment in democracy emulated. The senates of the federal government and some state legislatures, for example, were the first governing bodies so named since the *senatus* of the Roman republic. And then there were the Greek wars of independence in the 1820s, which echoed America's own experience of less than half a century earlier. Classical revival architecture made use of the columned portico that, porchlike, adorned the facade. What was more natural than that countless Americans would want to make their own homes fashionable and stylish by turning them into little Greek or Roman temples? Indeed, the process seems to be celebrated in the second verse of "My Country, 'tis of Thee" (Samuel Francis Smith, 1832):

> *My native country, thee,*
> *Land of the noble free,*
> *Thy name I love;*
> *I love thy rocks and rills,*
> *Thy woods and templed hills . . .*

Successive architectural fashions were likewise wholesome to the development of the front porch—Romanesque at first and then Gothic Revival and a whole assortment of other styles generally regarded as "Victorian." One trend in this succession of styles was an increasing obsession with ornamental detail. Indeed, detail was added to detail, and decoration

*Design books like A. J. Downing's* Cottage Residences *(1842) helped to popularize the front porch. Shown here: "A suburban cottage for a small family."*

became so profuse—bargeboards, swags, cresting, battens, turrets, balconets, finials, eyebrow dormers, and the like, all decorating an already ornate structure of fish-scale shingles, multicolored slates, patterned tiles, and polychromatic brickwork—that the largest decorative addition to the house of the 19th century was the least obvious: the front porch.

Yet, over and above its intended use, the porch was decoration in its own right: a showcase for the builder's art, stage front to show off his skill, particularly with gingerbread. Parenthetically, the front porch also had the effect of making a small house look larger, more important, and more flattering to its owners' station. "The exterior of [a] cottage would be raised in character as well as comfort, by a veranda," observed A. J. Downing in *The Architecture of Country Houses* (1850). And of course, pretentiousness was hardly inimical to Victorian values. A notable example, though at the tail end of the period, is the home of Warren G. Harding in Marion, Ohio. It figured prominently

in the presidential campaign of 1920; indeed, Harding ran practically his entire campaign from the front porch. The basic house is a rather modest place that was given the air of a mansion with a huge, surrounding porch interspersed with Ionic columns.

As for increasing leisure time: In the 19th century, working hours were changing significantly. Farmers and many factory workers might still be laboring sunup to sundown, but the trend was toward more leisure time. The movement to a ten-hour day had begun in the late 1820s, and by the end of the century the eight-hour day was law in nearly half the states. Hence that most elementary of encouragements to porch sitting: more time to do it.

In another wise: vacations. Even midway through the 19th century the vacation was a luxury available only to the business owner (when he could spare the time) or to the long-standing employee (as a reward for loyalty). After the Civil War the vacation became more common, and even the clerk and junior employee, if not yet the factory worker generally, were coming to expect a fortnight of freedom as a matter of right and not of favor. When vacation time came—and it was a heady occasion in the grand age of the railroad—where did newly liberated workers speed themselves and their families to partake of this precious fortnight? The seashore, perhaps. Or the mountains. Or some healthful spa. Wherever they went, the resort hotel was there, waiting to be their home away from home; and the first of its many accommodations that was likely to be noticed was its capacious veranda. Capacious, indeed: The "front porch" of the Grand Hotel at Mackinac Island, Michigan, was nearly a sixth of a mile long, the longest

*A modest house made to look twice its size with a huge front porch: the Warren G. Harding Home in Marion, Ohio.* (Photograph by the author)

such structure in the world. The resort veranda was comfy with its rocking chairs and wicker settees, fragrant with honeysuckle climbing its latticework, and scenic with vistas that made remote the humdrum of life back home. What could be more natural, once at home, than to want to preserve a little of that honeysuckled reverie? To have a veranda of one's own?

In art, the period of the ascendancy of the front porch coincided with the turn to nature; American painting, heretofore predominantly portraiture, shifted in particular to landscape painting. The porch likewise, both symbolically and literally, led out into nature. It is not that no one had ever sat outside before. Jefferson, in a 1793 letter written while in Philadelphia, took note of his delight in reading, writing, entertaining friends, and even dining outdoors; Franklin was fond of setting up his tea table under a mulberry tree in his garden. The porch institutionalized the trend by making it practical to be outside: One could readily leave one's chairs and tables there, one could sit out in inclement weather; and this outdoor room was just outside the door, making trips in and out easy.

*The Grand Hotel, Mackinac Island, Michigan (1887): a "front porch" a sixth of a mile long.* (Library of Congress, Prints and Photographs)

Creature comfort was still another factor in the popularity of the front porch. The early colonists and the pioneers of westward expansion may have had a certain stoic hardiness about their lack of comfort, but 19th-century man and woman were rather more prone to feeling the sharpness of the seasons. Central heat was coming into use; so if one were beginning to expect a greater degree of comfort in winter, why not in summer too? The homes of the wealthy had high ceilings, ventilators, cross ventilation, and louvered doors and were often located in sylvan settings, all of which contributed a certain amount of cooling. The middle-class home of Victorian times had its own form of air conditioning—the porch, front or otherwise, where one could sit and catch a breeze on a sultry evening or perhaps, in the ease of a hammock, sleep away the whole of a suffocating summer's night.

That hammock might be on an open ground-floor porch; but if there was a separate sleeping porch, it was usually on the second floor. The most common accommodation there was a hammock, although some such porches were formal enough to possess a bed and, just

*The front porch in its high season: a place "of good will . . . an intimate connection" . . . but sometimes a bit stuffy with a photographer present. (Left, author's collection, no date, somewhere in Virginia; below and page 148, Library of Congress, Prints and Photographs, Currier Collection, c1890, places unknown)*

inside, a separate dressing room. By the turn of the 20th century, the typical sleeping porch had evolved essentially into a room of the house, albeit one that was all windows for maximum ventilation. It was very much analogous to the first-floor sun porch, another hybrid that was more room than porch.

Finally, the front porch was a part of the communications network of the 19th century.

In that telephoneless, radioless, televisionless, Internetless yesteryear, it was necessary to rely on more fundamental forms of communication to keep in touch. Antenna-like, the front porch extended out into that most immediate of worlds, the street, to transmit or receive word of what was going on. As recalled by Elizabeth Paxton Forsling of her street in Independence, Missouri:

The porches of the houses on Delaware Street [were] where the people sat in the evening, their voices were part of the evening. Friendly voices of good will between neighbors, an intimate connection of the life of the street.

## A CASE OF PORCH-ITIS

With uses so diverse and virtues so obvious, one pauses to wonder why the front porch hasn't remained a permanent fixture of the American home. In fact, even before its high season had waned, symptoms of "porch-itis" began to appear.

The high season began roughly at the time of Alexander Jackson Davis's advice that the porch be used "instead of a sitting room of the house" (1837) and continued until roughly the end of World War I. After that, to be sure, people continued to sit on their porches; but all the currents of social and architectural change were now running in the other direction, and it would be only a matter of time until the porch packed up and went back indoors.

Before getting to these various currents, let us see what happened to the porch in the latter 19th century. In brief, the porch grew and multiplied. What was once a simple appendage became larger and larger, and then a complexity of appendages: front porch, side porch, back porch, upstairs porch, children's porch, sitting porch, eating porch, garden porch, servants' porch, and so on. And why not? If a front porch was so good to have, why not others elsewhere with their own special uses? The various types enumerated above have all existed somewhere or another; and while no one house had all, the house with

three or four was not uncommon, and five was not unheard of.

As new architectural styles emerged about the turn of the century—the Bungalow and the Prairie, for example—the trend away from the porch began to show itself. Whereas almost all architects had been touting the virtues of the porch for half a century, a few now began to protest that the porch was a mixed blessing. It had become, in all its diversity, an encumbrance that in winter excluded sunlight and in summer had only the indifferent advantage of allowing one to sit outside—which predilection, they said, a would-be porch sitter might satisfy simply by picking up a chair from inside the house and taking it outside. At least retrench to just one simple front porch, they advised; or move the principal porch to the back; or better yet, do away with it altogether.

Early in the new century the style-setting home magazines began taking up the cause. For example:

> The up-to-date porch is really another living room. . . . Why should we not, therefore, make [comfort and convenience] changes in the living-room itself and omit the porch? (*House Beautiful,* August 1914)

> The large veranda which is to be used as an outdoor living-room should be at the side or back of the house, if possible. In front we do not need more than a little square porch with two prim settees for a bit of talk with the parting guest. (*The Delineator,* July 1913)

Even that prim little porch would become old-fashioned. For a time, not many people took such advice seriously. But a portent of things to come was literally advancing down the street, and this was something people did take seriously: the automobile.

In 1908 the Model T began to revolutionize personal transportation. Having an automobile meant, for example, that one might take a pleasant, rolling ride about the countryside to cool off on a hot summer's night, instead of sitting on the front porch hoping for a breeze to stir. The car was a form of recreation in its own right, and it could carry porch sitters of old to new forms of recreation and amusement—the music hall, the ball game, the city park, the country club. It was a place to date and court, as opposed to the front porch. If *you,* say, didn't want anything to do with this newfangled contraption and just wanted to sit home on your front porch as in the old days, well, fine; except that those neighbors of yours who used to come strolling by, always stopping for a chat—*they* were probably out wheeling about the countryside. As *House Beautiful* observed in August 1915, with no trace of lament:

> House after house along any great summer highway shows its porch, gay with all the trappings of outdoor elegance—vacant. They have hung their harps upon the willows, and gone a-motoring.

Alas, the car and the front porch were inherently antithetical. The automobile was born with the new century and was so much a part of it, so much a symbol of newness, that it was bound, sooner or later, to make old-fashioned anything that wasn't rolling into the new times with it.

Much the same was the telephone, which also came into its own with the new century. Now, instead of strolling by your neighbors' houses and stopping for a front-porch chat, you could crank up a box on the wall and chat with them from your own house.

The post–World War I period was a time of profound change generally. Where people lived, where they worked, where they went to school, where they shopped—all began changing to reflect new mobility. Paradoxically, this was a time of isolationism as national policy. Even as Americans were moving about to a degree unparalleled in the past, they were also (symbolically in terms of national posture) picking up their chairs and newspapers and novels and teacups and moving inside.

In the wake of World War I, architecture went through profound alteration. The Victorian era, already diluted by changing preferences, was officially dead. House styles, like the arts, and music in particular, began heading in two directions at once. On the one hand, there was the trend toward the avant-garde, in which case the house had nothing resembling even a vestige of a front porch. On the other hand, there was a return to earlier times—to period revival styles like Tudor, Dutch Colonial, New England Colonial, Spanish Colonial, and so on; and since all of these in their original forms preceded the age of the front porch, so too were their revivals prominently porchless. Suppose, however, you had a Victorian era home with a big front porch. Who said you had to keep it? Spurred on by such wielders of influence as *House Beautiful,* some people paid workers to come and pull down their old-fashioned porches. The classic admonition was a photograph in *House Beautiful* (April 1925) showing a forlorn-looking old

Victorian house recently shorn of its front porch. The accompanying caption tersely observed: "Passers-by exclaim, 'They have taken off the old porches! Why can't we too?' Thus the good work grows."

Not everyone agreed, of course. Said Mrs. F.P.L., of Chicago, for example, in a letter to the editor of *American Home* in April 1941:

Ever since the architects and "home" magazines started the epidemic of "lopping" off front porches, I have threatened to voice my opinion on the subject. Now my husband urges me to do so as he feels the interesting old and middle-age homes are being regimented by the present vogue for "face-lifting"; all are being "modernized" in similar Colonial design. We have an old house (70 years) with a front porch and you just try to remove our porch! . . . In June I gave a luncheon for twenty-eight ladies on our front porch and am still hearing complimentary things about it. One guest who lives in a grand new house with no front porch said my luncheon could not have been done in any other house but mine.

The postwar period also brought in a new attitude toward health and sunlight, with a resultant change in personal fashion. The Victorian woman prided herself on the paleness of her skin. The shade of the porch, like that of the sunbonnet and parasol, helped her to maintain that look. In the 1920s everything did an about-face, literally. The suntan was in. Articles in magazines advised the modern woman to heed "Doctor Sunshine" and get "Health via Sunlight." In time, of course, there would come another about-face as medical experts warned of the risks of too much exposure to the sun.

Creature comfort again played a role in the porch's history, but an adversarial one this time. It may be recalled that as central heating became common and one expected to be comfortable in winter, one also became more aware of the need to be cool in summer; hence, the air conditioning of Victorian times, the porch. In the late 1930s the home air conditioner made its first appearance, although it did not become widespread until after World War II. A turn of a knob made comfort available on a sultry night: no need to hope for a breeze now.

Yet none of this was yet the final blow; that would come with what had lured indoors all those porch sitters of old in Great Bend. They were in "watchin' TV" now. The front porch had survived radio, which was compact enough to take outside and did not demand one's total concentration. One could watch the passersby, as in the days of the *stoep,* and still listen to radio. Television needed undivided attention.

The age of the front porch was over, but hardly the use of the outdoors as an extension of the house. Now it was to the back. The backyard deck has never superseded the front porch in the fullness of indoors-life-outdoors, but it has had the virtue of being literally "laid-back" in an era known for a more easygoing, relaxed, casual style than was the formal era of the front porch. Indeed, the deck's very lack of structure overhead and at the sides makes it a literal interpretation of times less structured. Parenthetically, the unceremonious deck allows for simpler and scantier attire than convention dictated when one was sitting on the front porch in full view of all who passed by.

The deck also has paralleled technological changes in house building. Modern techniques permit use of terrain that the Victorian builder would not have thought of building on—sloping hillsides, woodland settings, and so on, places ideally suited to decks. The deck also works well with such modern building materials as pressure-treated lumber that can be left in its natural state, without need for painting. The deck thus requires far less maintenance than exquisitely painted gingerbread, and this feature only adds to its attractiveness to a more "natural state" generation of home owners.

The front porch came and went; hence, it is not a part of the continuing evolution of the house. But in retrospect, recalling the *stoep* that was a place where people could sit in the evening and watch the passersby, the front porch is symbolically a vantage point from which to observe the passing by of many profound changes in American life.

CHAPTER 5

# The Comfortable House

*I like the house more and more, and think it will be convenient.*

SARAH DAVIS, letter, November 7, 1871

## THE COMING OF CONVENIENCE

Comfort and convenience. For those who could afford them in 1871 they included a kitchen with hot and cold running water, a large stove, and an icebox . . . at least one bathroom with tub, sink, and water closet . . . central steam heat . . . gas lighting with remote-control battery-powered ignition . . . plenty of closets for storage . . . a built-in laundry . . . and an "intercom" of bellpulls and speaking tubes.

Such were the conveniences that made Sarah Davis's new house—under construction in Bloomington, Illinois, in 1871—comfortable indeed. But as the wife of U.S. Supreme Court justice David Davis, a lawyer who had amassed a considerable fortune in real estate, she could well afford the latest in home technology. We have also seen, on a lesser scale, something of

the same at Harriet Beecher Stowe's house, but she was ahead of her time. Elsewhere in the 1870s, among the middle-class homes that have been our primary focus, there was often not yet running water and only sometimes central heating. The outdoor privy was still very much in use, and kerosene lamps were the primary means of lighting. Iceboxes were coming into use, but only where there was an affordable supply of ice.

By 1900 industrialization had caught up with supply and demand sufficiently that the comfortable and convenient house was beginning to exist for the middle-class family as well, and with it came an increasing amount of leisure time that had a profound impact on how people spent their lives.

How I spend Sundays [and nonschool days] generally. Rise at 7, bring pail of water &

*Harry Lewis, aged seventeen, at his graduation from Sauk Centre High School, 1902.*

armful of wood; then breakfast. Read till between 11 and 12. . . . During afternoon I read, walk & fill wood box. (Harry Lewis, aged seventeen, Sauk Centre, Minnesota, 1902)

There was a time when the leisure of walking and reading were the domain of the wealthy who had servants to make life comfortable; otherwise, one had to generate one's own comfort. What constituted comfort for the Fairbanks family of 1637 was what they did to make themselves comfortable, and it was a time-enveloping process. To be warm, to be dry, to have light, to have clothing, indeed to have food—these were attained by personal initiative. Jonathan and Grace, John, George, Mary, and Susan, and Jonas and Jonathan, Jr.,

as they grew—each had his or her tasks to do around the house or on the farm. If any slackened, all were a little colder, or a little wetter, or left to see more dimly, or made to leave the table a little hungrier. Furthermore, these tasks were obligations that left precious little time for anything else.

Harry Lewis's family by 1905 had a kitchen with hot and cold water, an icebox, a furnace in the cellar, electric light, and a bathroom with water closet and tub. Though not as sumptuous as Sarah Davis's (only one bathroom, and no marble fireplaces here), the Lewises' house represented much the same degree of comfort and convenience. And this was clearly a middle-class house. Harry's father, Dr. E. J. Lewis, was a doctor with a very middling income. This was the comfortable home as it was coming to exist on middling streets throughout America.

Of course, Harry didn't spend all his time reading and walking (or "tramping" the woods and shooting rabbits and squirrels, his other favorite diversions). Besides bringing in the wood, he had other chores to do, typical of boys then and since—like sweeping the walk, mowing the lawn, shoveling snow in winter. And that wood he lugged inside for the woodbox next his mother's big cast-iron stove: It had to be cut first. But whereas the Fairbanks boys made firewood out of trees, Harry at least had only to make it out of a cord of wood delivered to the backyard woodshed. Nevertheless, it was onerous enough work that he thought fit to include a brief essay on it in his diary, that his hard work be a matter of written record:

[Thursday, January 23, 1902] . . . how wood is bought and prepared for stove. It is

Dr. E. J. Lewis.

bought in "cords" 8 [feet long] × 4 [feet high] × 4 [feet wide], sticks being 4 ft long. Each stick is cut into 3 pieces by the saw, the stick being placed on the "saw-buck" [here follows a crude diagram of a sawbuck]. Then each stick is split, by means of the axe.

This particular chore, which devolved upon young Harry, had fairly frequent reference in his diary; for example, Thursday, November 14, 1901: "Cord of poplar wood" delivered; Saturday, the 16th: "Finished that cord of wood. Another bought today"; Friday, December 27: "I have sawed all this winter's poplar wood except one cord." No wonder by the spring of 1902, now a senior at Sauk Centre High School and bound for college, he took obvious delight in exclaiming:

[Tuesday, April 8, 1902] Finished my 4 cords of iron wood today [last of the winter's

supply]. This is *possibly* the last wood I'll ever saw; very *probably* the last I'll ever saw here at home.

Furthermore, even this was changing. The wood Harry was cutting was only for the kitchen. In the cellar was a coal-burning furnace that provided central heating by means of a hot-water system. "Eventually," Harry wrote in his diary on January 23, 1902, "everyone will use coal." Meanwhile,

Wood is much used around here. I think that every family uses it in the kitchen-range, many use it in their [heating] stoves, and some use it in their furnaces. We use it only in the dining-room & kitchen, having hot-water heating in the rest of the house.

His antipathy to woodcutting notwithstanding, Harry was a beneficiary of the new times and their freeing up of time . . . time, for instance, to walk or to read.

It was Harry's leisure time that is the root of what makes it possible to see his house today, just about as it was when he went off to college. For the home of Dr. E. J. Lewis in Sauk Centre, Minnesota, is that rarity of rarities: the not-old-enough, not-new-enough in between of houses that otherwise, virtually without exception, has been so rekitchened and rebathroomed (probably a number of times), so vinyled and fiberglassed, so generally modernized, that the significance of what it looked like in, say, 1905, is forever lost. Here, as if frozen in time—thanks to Harry's predilection for reading books over cutting wood—is the comfortable house of 1905. Let us take a closer look at it.

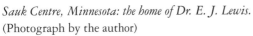

*Sauk Centre, Minnesota: the home of Dr. E. J. Lewis.*
(Photograph by the author)

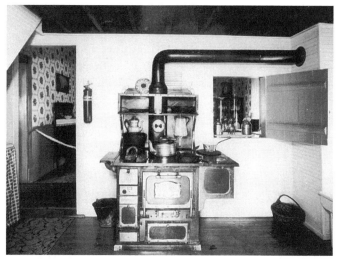

*The Lewis house, as it looked in 1905:*
*(opposite, top right)* the hallway, with its
phalanx of heating pipes, and the stairway, from
which a boy might eavesdrop on conversation
below; *(opposite bottom)* the parlor, suitably
prim; *(above left)* the dining room, its table set
with the family's best Blue Willow china; *(left
middle)* the kitchen, dominated by its Monarch
cast-iron stove; *(above)* the bathroom, in 1905
one of the first in town; and finally *(bottom
left)*, the boys' bedroom—Harry's is the little bed
by the window.

We are welcomed by the outstretched embrace of the front porch. Since this house was built in 1889, in the high season of porch sitting, we have no doubt it was put to proper use. The doorbell is on the front door and is the old kind that twists, releasing a low sound, something between a clicking and a clanking. That gains us entrance. In the hallway we find on the left a staircase with a wooden banister that looks as much meant for sliding kids down as for guiding upward the footsteps of elders. On the right is a corridor whose wall opposite the stairs is dominated by a phalanx of horizontal pipes. This is part of the original hot-water heating system. To our eyes it is an intrusion of now mostly hidden technology; to those who lived here nearly a century ago, it was a visible and very practical presence of comfort.

The room to our right is the parlor. Before the days of the "living room," the Victorians had their parlors—always two unless you could only afford one. The one in front was usually the formal parlor, corresponding to the "best room" of colonial times. This was the place for best furniture, best bric-a-brac, best wall hangings, and best manners . . . the place for receiving guests. The parlor in back, here known as the sitting room, was the more informal gathering place for the family. A clear demarcation between the two was summed up in a strict rule about children's limiting themselves to the sitting room and never, *ever,* trespassing into the front parlor unless invited. On the walls of the parlor are portraits of Lewis family members; on a table, a stereopticon. The back room is notable for bookcases full of books. Across the hall, in front, is the dining room, typically the largest room in a house of this kind and this period. As if expecting guests for dinner, the table is set with the family's best china, the Blue Willow pattern; Dr. Lewis insisted on using it day in, day out, and not needlessly saving it just for company. In the far corner is a china cupboard in which is safely kept a sugar bowl that came over on the *Mayflower* with family forebears.

The kitchen is dominated by a Monarch cast-iron stove with a reservoir for hot water. In a house that is a bridge to the home of the 20th century, this appliance is a link to the past. It can do everything a more modern-looking stove can do, but it seems old-fashioned for a house that otherwise signifies a new era. When the Lewis family first moved in, a pump in the kitchen accessed water stored in a cellar cistern, filled with rainwater from the roof via an eaves trap. This was the soft-water supply, used for washing. Drinking water came from a well across the street and was hauled into the house by hand, usually by Dr. Lewis himself. By 1905 Sauk Centre had city water and sewerage, and Dr. Lewis was among the first in town to take advantage by adding running water to the kitchen and installing a full, modern bathroom on the second floor, complete with sink, tub, and water closet; it replaced an outdoor privy. Three bedrooms—the master, the guest, and the boys' room—complete the upstairs.

So here we have the comfortable, convenient middle-class house of 1905—a reasonably modern kitchen, a bathroom with all the conveniences, central heat, electric light: everything to make life a little easier and create a little extra time for doing whatever one might like.

## REINTERPRETING HOME

In the case of Harry Lewis, "whatever" was reading. As for how this should preserve his home for us to see, let us begin by retracing our steps through the house, starting with the room last visited, the boys' room. The boys, besides Harry, were Fred, the oldest, and Claude, three years his junior. Red-haired Harry was the youngest by nine years. In the boys' room are two beds. The larger and more comfortable was shared by Fred and Claude; next to it is something looking like a child's bed, barely larger than a cot, which was Harry's sleeping place. It is next to the window. From here late one night Harry peered out to detect a light that he decided surely must signify a huge army preparing to invade Sauk Centre. He reported the alarming news to his father. The precise, exact, methodical Dr. Lewis explained that it was a farmer chasing home his cows with a lantern.

The stairs with that banister. From here Harry sometimes eavesdropped on a study group that his stepmother, Isabel, had organized, and that met regularly in the Lewis home. It was known as the Gradatim Club for a poem titled "Gradatim," by J. G. Holland, which was popular at the turn of the century and reflected on the reaching of heaven by gradations of good works. Was it genuine, this dialogue going on in the sacrosanct front parlor?

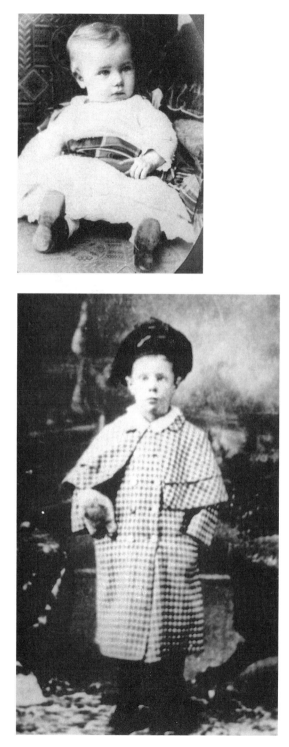

(Above) *Harry Lewis, aged four months, and* (right) *aged four. Archival photographs of the Lewis family are all courtesy of the Sinclair Lewis Foundation. Photographs of the house, unless otherwise indicated, are from the Historic American Buildings Survey.*

*Isabel Warner Lewis.*

---

Or was it a cover for so much old-fashioned gossiping? So wondered the eavesdropper on the stairs, a boy just beginning to turn skeptic.

The back parlor, or sitting room, with its bookcases. Harry devoured whatever was there that looked interesting and then turned his voracious appetite on the town library, checking so many books in and out that it was taken for granted he would eventually read everything. Favorites included Dickens, Sir Walter Scott, Washington Irving, Thoreau's *Walden,* and stories about King Arthur.

And then there is the backyard, where Harry did battle with cords of wood and where he also had a certain penchant (much to a pre-

cise and methodical father's chagrin) for sitting under a tree and dreaming.

That Harry liked to read and dream disposed him also to write—fiction, of course. He tried his hand at Sauk Centre High School, with no remarkable results. Following graduation—increasingly restless, more and more turning skeptic, determined to escape the bounds of what he saw as Midwestern provincialism—he spurned his father's advice about the University of Minnesota and went off into the world by way of Yale. He shed home, shed small-town life, shed older brothers, shed gradations to heaven, and then—officially with the first entry in his diary for his junior year at Yale—shed the name Harry. Adopting his middle name, he would hereafter be Sinclair Lewis.

In years to come, Sinclair Lewis had no real permanent home, living here and there, there and here, in America and Europe. He made his mark as a novelist and qualified as the first American to win a Nobel Prize in literature by vilifying his hometown with *Main Street,* whose Gopher Prairie, depicted as a place of hopeless despair, was only a thinly disguised Sauk Centre and whose Thanatopsis Club (from the Greek for 'vision of death', apparently from William Cullen Bryant's poem of that name) was nothing more than a demonic re-creation of Gradatim. And here the irony: In so doing, Lewis made Sauk Centre famous. Townspeople who were at first shocked came to recognize the useful side of it. They eventually renamed the main street Original Main Street, retitled the Lewises' quiet street Sinclair Lewis Avenue, built a museum in honor of the infamous famous son, and, most fitting of all, saw to the meticulous restoration of Dr.

E. J. Lewis's home to just the way it looked when Harry lived there.

Harry never returned but Sinclair did. He visited not infrequently and never seemed to mind all the attention or a certain sense of being back home. Indeed, the farther he went on his long walk about the world, the more he seemed to warm to the symbolism of home. Even in his scathing portrayal of hometown life, he gave in to a certain nostalgia. Warmth, to which he contributed by cutting wood, was central to his remembrance of home. In *Main Street* there is this presciently autobiographical passage:

He [Kennicott] was standing before the furnace. However inadequate the rest of the house, he had seen to it that the fundamental cellar should be large and clean, the square pillars whitewashed, and the bins for coal and potatoes and trunks convenient. A glow from the drafts fell on the smooth gray cement floor at his feet. He was whistling tenderly, staring at the furnace with eyes which saw the black-domed monster as a symbol of home and of the beloved routine to which he had returned—his gipsying decently accomplished. . . .

## KEEPING WARM . . .

Winters in Lewis's central Minnesota often range from bad to brutal, but anywhere in America outside the Deep South and the Southwest the temperature in winter can hover around freezing for lengthy periods and frequently drop well below. What was it like living through winter before the comforts of modern technology?

If we stop and think about it, we should conclude that one simply got used to being cold all winter long. The modern standard is an environment kept at roughly 68 to 70 degrees Fahrenheit, at least during the day.* Before the age of modern heat, there was basically nowhere one could go in winter and find 70 degrees of warmth—not at home, not wherever one worked (say, barn or workshop), not at a store or shop, not at church, not at the local inn, and certainly not driving in one's carriage (if one were fortunate enough to have one, and walking or riding horseback meant being even more exposed). Probably the snuggest place was in bed, wearing a sleeping cap and heavy garments, curled up under layer upon layer of blankets. There was also, of course, that wondrous, roaring fire in the hearth; one could go and sit immediately before it and be not merely warm but hot—on one's front, and quite the contrary in back. As recalled by novelist William Dean Howells of his youth:

We sat up late before the big fire at night, our faces burning in the glow, and our backs and feet freezing in the draught that swept in from the imperfectly closing door. . . .

The fireplace was a very inefficient room heater. Even with a good fire going, much of the room might barely be in the forties, and the farther

---

* Maintaining a room temperature of about 70 degrees seems to have been the ideal since central heating became common: "I am well pleased with the Gurney Heating Apparatus. We have experienced no difficulty in keeping our twelve rooms at 70° with the Mercury at 32°" (testimonial in ad in *Scribner's Magazine,* June 1889); "The house can be kept steadily at the uniform temperature of about 72 degrees by merely setting the indicator-hand [on the thermostat] at that point" (sales booklet of American Radiator Company, c1911).

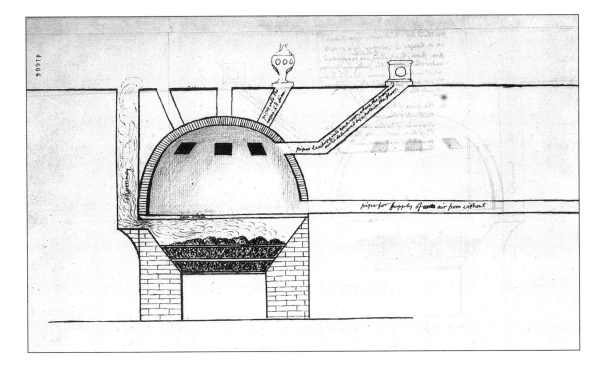

*"Method by which every apartment in a house is warmed by a single fire" is the inscription on the back of this drawing by Thomas Jefferson, c1790. Here was the concept of hot-air central heating just ahead of its time. Jefferson used fireplaces at Monticello, but a gravity-flow hot-air system like this one, albeit heating only the State Dining Room, was in use at the White House by 1812, three years after Jefferson had left office. In this illustration cold air via the horizontal pipe at right is heated in the furnace and rises through "pipes leading into each room, where the warmed air is delivered by a hole in the floor." At left is the chimney. This is essentially the modern hot-air heating system without a forced-air blower.* (Library of Congress)

reaches nearly at freezing. The Franklin stove gained popularity for keeping the room temperature at a relatively comfortable 50 degrees or so. And without a fire, one might just as well be out of doors. The Reverend Thomas Robbins, then a pastor in Mattapoisett, Massachusetts, observed as much in his diary on January 4, 1835: "Thermometer this morning at 4° in a back chamber, and did not exceed 14° through the day." The Reverend Mr. Robbins was fond of recording temperature extremes, and 1835 was not his coldest winter. While tending to a congregation in East Windsor, Connecticut, he noted on January 19, 1827: "Thermometer at sunrise, viewed carefully, was 20° below zero [presumably outside]. I believe I have had this instrument eight or nine years, and I think it has never been so low." The temperature inside was apparently not much better. The next day, a Saturday, hand numb with chill, poor Pastor Robbins lamented: "Could not write a sermon."

Those were cold times, ameliorated by wearing layers of heavy clothing and praying for an early spring. And gathering around the hearth. Regardless of its inefficiency, the fireplace was the mainstay of household heating from earliest colonial times through much of the 19th century and into the 20th, depending on one's means and where one lived. But that is not to say that nothing was changing. The fireplace had the dual function of both cooking and heating. As we have seen in exploring the changing kitchen, the most significant single factor in its transformation from postmedieval to modern was a reduction in the size of the heat source. The fireplace elsewhere that was intended just for heating likewise went through a gradual process of reduction in size and a resulting increase in efficiency. The rela-

tively cavernous fireplace of early colonial times let most of its heat go up the chimney. One means of improving efficiency was to plaster and whitewash the interior surfaces of the fireplace, which, being smoother and more reflective, conveyed more heat into the room.

The most significant change came at the end of the 18th century, notably through the influence of that same Count Rumford who had

*Count Rumford's redesign of the fireplace took the traditional box shape* (left) *and slanted the sides and back while also making the throat smaller* (right). *The result was more heat with less use of fuel.* (Rumford, Complete Works)

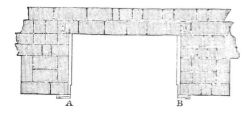

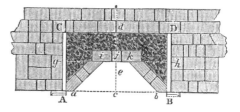

*An early example of the influence of Rumford is this fireplace at Gore Place, Waltham, Massachusetts (1806).* (Photograph by the author)

been helping to create the modern kitchen. Traditionally, the fireplace was box-shaped: everything vertical or horizontal, all squared off. This, argued Rumford, accounted for the basic inefficiency of the fireplace. He slanted both the sides and the back toward the front and made the throat smaller. The result was more heat with less use of fuel.

A fundamental deficiency of the fireplace is that, in effect, it is a single plane: Only what is immediately in front of it gets warmed. A heating stove, even if it is flush against a wall, has a top and three sides radiating heat. Furthermore, once its shell is hot, the radiation continues despite the fluctuating intensity of its fire; the fire may grow low, but heat continues to be given off. In a fireplace there is only as much heat emanating as there is fire within.

Stoves were in use in Europe (sheet-iron stoves in Germany in the 16th century, for example) before the first permanent settlers arrived in America. That they were used here during the 17th century is largely forgotten. Little has been written about them; what evidence there is comes from an occasional reference in a will or a diary. Dr. John Clarke, a surgeon who moved to America from London and died in Boston in 1664, included three stoves, valued at £3 each, in the estate that he left to his wife. The diary of Samuel Sewall, of Boston, offers some detail about actual use:

> Friday, January 16 [1702] Comfortable moderat wether: and with a good fire in the Stove warm'd the Room.

There are references to stoves in newspaper ads of the same period; for example:

> To be sold at a reasonable price, a very good and large Holland stove. (*Boston Gazette,* October 7, 1723)

Stoves had been used in Holland for at least a century before the Pilgrims stayed there prior to settling in America; and similarly used elsewhere in northern Europe. So it is not surprising that there was some use of stoves in the colonies, particularly among Dutch, German, and Swedish settlers, and more so in the 18th century than in the 17th. At Schifferstadt in Frederick, Maryland, the home of German settlers we saw in chapter 2, stoves were the primary means of heating in all rooms other than the kitchen at the time the house was built in 1756. A cast-iron stove dated 1756, made in Pennsylvania, remains in one upstairs room. Originally one large room, it was subdivided by means of a partition as the children grew and needed some measure of privacy; the partition left a small opening so the stove could heat both sides of the room.

The Franklin stove (which Franklin called the Pennsylvania Fireplace) was developed in the early 1740s. It was not so much a stove as a fireplace insert that projected into the room, thus contributing greater warmth than the hearth alone. Further improvements to stoves were made during the 19th century, and use became widespread. Compact and inexpensive units were used in bedrooms and parlors in cold weather and then, in spring, taken out, cleaned, and stored away for the next heating season. Stoves were manufactured in abundance throughout the 19th century.

Despite the improvement of heating stoves, it was only with central heating that a modern standard of comfort began to evolve. And yet central heating was not a new concept. It was essentially the effect produced by the hypocaust of the ancient Roman home. There, small furnaces beneath the floor warmed not only the floor itself but the walls, which held the flues that conducted the smoke out. An early conceptualization of central heating in modern times, proposed in 1653, was a system using steam, not for a dwelling but for a greenhouse:

> To have Roses or Carnations growing in Winter, place them in a roome that may some way be kept warme, either with a dry fire, or with the steam of hot water conveyed by a pipe fastened to the cover of a pot, that is kept seething over some idle fire. . . . (Sir Hugh Plat, *The Garden of Eden,* London, 1653)

*Although heating stoves were used occasionally in the 17th century, it was the 19th with its capacity for mass production that made them common. Here, the Dr. Alfred Paige House, Bethel, Vermont (1833): a stove believed to be original to the house made by R. and J. Wainwright, Middlebury, Vermont.* (Historic American Buildings Survey)

Curiously, it was for a similar purpose, rather than for comfort in the home, that the concept of central heating is first found in America. Among the very wealthy of the latter 18th century, notably in Maryland, the growing of oranges, lemons, limes, pineapples, and the like afforded the luxury of having exotic fresh fruits otherwise unobtainable; parenthetically, it also firmly demonstrated one's affluence, for there was no way to grow these

*The orangery at Hampton, in Towson, Maryland.* (Photograph by the author)

delicacies other than to possess great wealth. The project required the construction of a greenhouselike structure, known as an orangery, with walls full of windows and a hypocaust system using a wood-burning furnace in a separate small structure outside; ductwork under the floor generated warmth, supplemented by the radiant heat of the sun. A reconstruction of one such orangery, originally built around 1825, is on the grounds of Hampton (1790) in Towson, Maryland.

Central heating for humankind began to emerge in America just after the turn of the 19th century. One of the first systems was that installed by inventor Daniel Pettibone in 1810 at Pennsylvania Hospital in Philadelphia. It was an experimental hot-air system using a central furnace to heat six rooms. It worked well enough that the hospital's board of managers soon directed Pettibone to extend it throughout the hospital.

An early instance of household central heat-

ing is that installed in 1820 in Wyck, also in Philadelphia. Wyck, built about 1710, had relied on fireplaces for more than a century. In 1820 sixth-generation owner Reuben Haines III decided to try central heating and in November of that year hired a mason to build "a furnace in front cellar for Schuylkill coal." Brief though it is, Haines's reference tells us basically what we need to know: There was a furnace only in the front cellar, central heating being limited to only a few rooms; it had to have been a gravity-flow hot-air system utilizing a masonry enclosure with ductwork to the rooms heated; and the furnace was coal-fired. Was this similar to the system Pettibone installed at Pennsylvania Hospital? Probably, and perhaps even modeled on it. In any event, it is one of the earliest domestic heating systems of which there is any record.

This was the simplest form of central heating and the one that popularized it for domestic use. A hot-air system was relatively easy to install and simple to use. But this was not yet the hot-air furnace that became commonplace in the late 19th century. Let us look at an early installation, first recalling the evolution of house heating beginning with the open hearth of the medieval house. There it was virtually an open fire in the middle of the room, its smoke trailing up through an opening in the roof. In time the fire was moved to the side so that a canopy could direct the smoke out through the wall; and then the fire was partly enclosed by a fireplace connected to a chimney—that half-enclosed bonfire. The fireplace was steadily reduced in size while continuing to be a half enclosure. Early hot-air central heating symbolically completed the cycle by making the enclosure complete. What was in the cellar of the early to later 19th-century home was, in effect, a fully enclosed fireplace with a furnace in the middle. The enclosure was an air chamber, through which cold air came in from outside, was warmed, and then rose through ducts to the rooms upstairs.

How much heat? By modern standards these early central-heating systems would seem wholly inadequate. But as technology improved, a new level of comfort and convenience was achieved. Thomas Tredgold in his *Principles of Warming and Ventilating Public Buildings {and} Dwelling-Houses* (London, 1824) took note of how little an increase in warmth really was needed to make a difference: "Where it is proposed to warm a supply of fresh air for an apartment, the air [in the room] should not be warmed beyond 56 degrees."

Hot-air systems grew somewhat more commonplace during the 1840s and 1850s as new and improved furnaces became available. A state-of-the-art installation at midcentury was

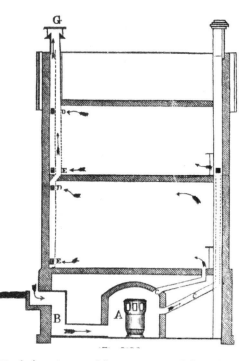

*Early hot-air central-heating systems differed from later ones in that the furnace was not a self-contained unit. The essential feature was a brick enclosure, or "air chamber," that surrounded the actual furnace. As shown in this diagram from A. J. Downing's* Architecture of Country Houses *(1850),* A *is the air chamber and furnace; cold air enters through* B, *is heated within the chamber, and then rises through the warm-air ducts,* C, *to the rooms above. In this installation there is also a ventilating system using a "ventiduct" on the wall opposite that from which warm air enters the room. The ventiduct has vents top and bottom,* D *and* E, *and allows for release of stale air through a ventilator,* G. *The diagram does not include the flue from the furnace.*

the 1854 furnace placed in the cellar of the home of Martin Van Buren in Kinderhook, New York. It remained in use until 1937, and the original ductwork is still used with a modern forced-air furnace.

It should be noted that early central heating

*Essentially the same system was in use in the 1850s, as is evident from the illustration on this statement for installation of a Boynton furnace in the home of William Reynolds in Meadville, Pennsylvania, in 1857. This is almost certainly the same furnace that was used by Martin Van Buren (see chapter 3). (Reynolds Collection, courtesy Crawford County Historical Society, Meadville, Pa.)*

*Basement detail, architect's drawings for home of Elias Baker, Altoona, Pennsylvania, 1844; Robert Cary Long, Jr., architect. Detail shows installation of central hot-air heating, with ductwork (clockwise from 12 o'clock) going to parlor, second parlor, hall, dining room, second floor (hall), and library. The dotted lines at lower right (5 o'clock) are the flue from the furnace. This (or possibly a later) coal furnace remained in the home until the 1940s, when it was sold for scrap as part of the war effort. (Blair County Historical Society, Altoona, Pa.)*

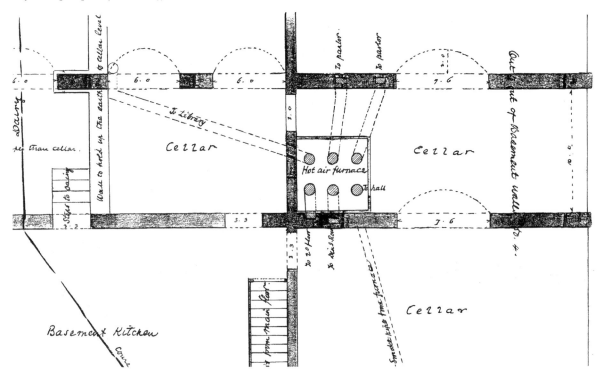

did not necessarily encompass all rooms of the house; indeed that was rarely the case. The most expedient approach was to heat only the rooms on the first floor, in which case all the necessary ductwork could be located within the basement; if there was heat to the second floor, it might only reach the hall (the duct being built into the stairwell). It was also commonplace to connect the furnace only with rooms on the north (colder) side of the house, letting room fireplaces provide for the remaining rooms. But the rooms with central heating often had fireplaces too; they provided supplemental warmth, and their flues helped to draw hot air through the room from the heat registers.

At the mid 19th century, central heating was still relatively rare and still found mostly in the homes of the wealthy. Cost of installation was a principal factor. There was also concern about purity of air. Furnaces were cast iron and intentionally designed (use of corrugated surfaces, gas-recirculation pipes) to have a maximum of surface area. This area was heated close to red-hot to generate a maximum of heat. A. J. Downing's *Architecture of Country Houses* (1850) argued that these furnaces were constantly pouring deleterious air through the house; that air passing over red-hot cast iron with carbon, sulfur, phosphorus, and even arsenic in its composition, once in the room, was "stifling and close [and] its atmosphere produces languor, debility, head-ache, and sooner or later, pulmonary diseases."

So dire a scenario was not generally agreed upon. Even Downing himself, in his *Cottage Residences* (1842; "A Cottage in the Italian or Tuscan Style"), had unselfconsciously advocated the use of "hot-air flues, which proceed from the furnace in the basement, and by means of registers, warm all the apartments [rooms] in the house." With increased availability of coal through the proliferation of railroads, the hot-air furnace became more and more common—so much so that in 1880 *American Architect and Building News* declared that the "furnace in the cellar [is nearly] universal where anthracite is used in America."

Universality was probably considerably overstated, even for those parts of the country having an abundance of coal; but in colder climates the furnace was commonplace by the early 20th century. By now it was the self-contained hot-air type familiar today, the

*By the 1880s the self-contained hot-air furnace was in use in essentially its modern form. Ductwork extended out of the furnace itself; the masonry enclosure was now a thing of the past. (Scribner's Magazine, June 1889)*

GREATEST RADIATION SMALLEST COAL CONSUMPTION REQUIRES LEAST CARE

PALACE KING.

PALACE KING.

Send for Catalogue covering all the scientific points and Price-List.

RUSSEL WHEELER SON & CO.,
Utica, N. Y.

furnace itself having an internal heat exchanger as opposed to requiring a brick enclosure. The next step was to attach a blower and force hot air into the rooms, a much more fuel-efficient system in that not as great a volume of heat need be generated; relatively less heat provides as much warmth, and faster. Blowers came into general use during the later 1930s, along with the automatic coal stoker. Stokers existed earlier for industrial and commercial furnaces. With the shift away from coal to the use of oil and gas, stokers largely disappeared in the post–World War II period; otherwise, except for more efficient oil or gas burners, forced hot air remains essentially as it was in 1940: a relatively simple, inexpensive, efficient system well suited to the house of small to moderate size.

Steam heat was in use in England at the turn of the 19th century; in America its first known application was at the Harmony Society's woolen and cotton factories in Old Economy Village, Ambridge, Pennsylvania, where steam was being used jointly for power and heat at least by 1826. It was not until after the mid 19th century that steam began to gain popularity for domestic use, and then largely for the well-to-do because of the greater expense of installation. As a fairly early example we have Sarah Davis's home in Bloomington, Illinois. A central steam-heating system was part of the original construction in 1872. It consisted of an A. L. Winne and Company "Gold's Patent" low-pressure steam boiler connected with radiators for rooms on the first floor. There was no direct heat on the second, the rooms there having floor registers that allowed some small amount of heat to rise from the first floor. Many of the radiators, as was typical of this period, were mounted horizontally just below floor

*One of the most welcome of all developments in heating technology was the room thermostat, which, according to promotional material for this "Ideal Sylphon Regitherm" (c1911), saved the householder "many laborious trips up and down the cellar stairs to readjust the weights, draft, and check dampers."* (American Radiator Company, *Ideal Sylphon Heating Specialties* [Chicago? 1911?]. Science, Industry and Business Library/New York Public Library/Astor, Lenox and Tilden Foundations)

level, conveying heat upward through floor registers similar to, though somewhat larger than, those used for a hot-air system. The radiator was thus not visible. The principal reason appears to be the precedent of hot air and the fact that many steam-heat installations were conversions of existing hot-air systems. Where there were already cutouts in the floor for hot-air registers, it only made sense to put them to use for the new type of heat; even if the home was a new one, keeping the radiator out of sight appears to have had aesthetic appeal. But setting the radiator below floor level was less efficient. It was only a matter of time until radiators assumed their now traditional above-floor position, even if often disguised by some form of enclosure.

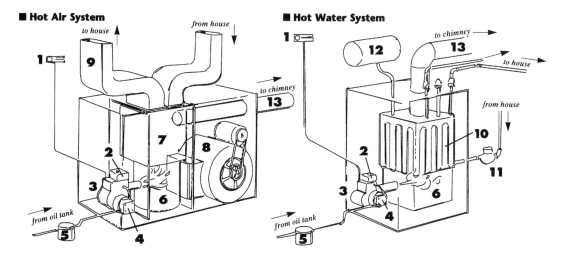

*The modern hot-air heating system* (left) *differs from that conceptualized by Thomas Jefferson c1790 chiefly through use of a high-efficiency burner (oil in this case) instead of a simple fire and through utilizing a blower to force air through the ductwork rather than waiting for the hot air to rise. In this system,* 1 *is the room thermostat;* 2 *and* 3, *the controls and burner; and* 4, *the fuel pump that draws fuel through the filter,* 5. *The fuel, mixed with air, is ignited in the combustion chamber,* 6, *creating heat in the heat exchanger,* 7. *The blower,* 8, *pumps the heat through* 9 *to ducts throughout the house. In a hot-water system* (right), *water is heated as it circulates around a heat exchanger,* 10, *and is then pumped through the house to radiators, baseboard or otherwise;* 12 *is the expansion tank that adjusts to varying pressures. Combustion gases are emitted through the flue,* 13. (By permission. © Warm Thoughts Communications)

A variation of steam is hot-water heat, which in the later 19th century and well into the 20th used radiators virtually identical to those for steam. In modern applications there is a hardly noticeable finned pipe running along the baseboard, and water is circulated by means of a pump. In its early form, as with hot air, there was not yet a pump. Water was heated in a boiler and, being lighter by volume than cold water, rose up through the pipes and radiators as cooled water in the system came back down through return pipes—a process that was continuously repeated as long as a fire was burning in the boiler. A Montgomery Ward heating catalog of 1915 described hot-water heat as the best all-around choice for a residence: ". . . the most economical from a fuel-burning standpoint . . . the most reliable system, and the simplest and easiest to take care of." Steam is best for large installations, the catalog said, and hot air the simplest and least expensive to install. For the most part, the same observations remain true today.

Electric heating was actually conceived in the mid 1800s but given up as too impractical and too expensive. There were the likes of G. B. Simpson's patented (1859) all-purpose "electro heater . . . to warm rooms, boil water, cook victuals, etc." It consisted of an 8-inch soapstone frame with twenty-one wire coils in parallel grooves across the surface. In principle, it was like a modern electric-coil heater. But it was too small to be effective in heating a room, and the only supply of electricity at the time was the galvanic battery. As for cooking, that old superstition about the necessity of an open flame persisted.

In more recent times there has been a wide range of developments, including radiant heating, convection heat, heat pumps, solar heat, and the like. What has not changed, since technology made it possible, is the American predilection for having a warm house. As Salomon Rothschild, visiting from France, observed in 1860:

> . . . you do not suffer as much from the cold here as in Europe. The air is purer, more invigorating, and it would be an excellent climate if inside the house one were not suffocated by hot-air stoves, gas heaters, or coal stoves. Everybody lives here all day long in a temperature very like what we put up with in the old days at poor grandfather's house.

## AND STAYING COOL

Although what is warm or what is cool is a highly subjective assessment, coping with this basic fluctuation in levels of human comfort has been a necessary preoccupation of humankind throughout recorded history.

Keeping warm has always held priority; it is the more crucial to survival. One can beat the heat by finding the shade of a tree or the cool of a river or lake; or within the bounds of custom and modesty, one can take off clothing down to . . . well, nothing. Keeping warm is a more complex task. Adding clothing requires a sufficient wardrobe, and even the most sufficient

coat can be insufficient without shelter. And even shelter can be insufficient without a source of warmth to compensate for the cold outside.

The priority of keeping warm over staying cool goes back to earliest recorded history; appropriately, the same pattern follows in the evolution of the house. Relatively sophisticated means of keeping warm existed before the technology of keeping cool had significantly transcended so simple a device as the hand-held fan, which in mid-19th-century America was only as much technological development as had been achieved in ancient Egypt.

Attempts at keeping cool, while not as crucial as keeping warm, have nearly as long a history of improvisation and invention. For an example in colonial American history:

> He also showed us . . . his great armed chair, with rockers, and a large fan placed over it, with which he fans himself, keeps off flies, etc., while he sits reading, with only a small motion of his foot. (The Reverend Manasseh Cutler, of a visit with Benjamin Franklin in Philadelphia, July 1787)

That master of inventiveness had already revolutionized (at least in name) the process of keeping warm with the Franklin stove. There is no record that he likewise sought to revolutionize keeping cool with what might have become known as the Franklin chair. But this cooling device powered by a small motion of the foot provides us with an index to the cooling technology of the late 18th century. There was as yet nothing to equate with the progress, such as it was, in heating. Basically, one opened

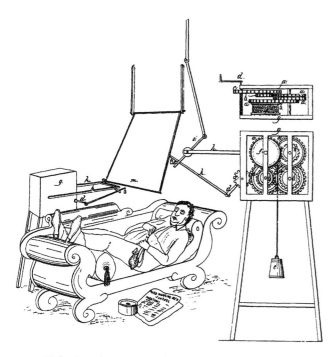

(Right) *Half a century later, a patent was issued for this "portable cooling apparatus for houses." Ice was placed in the urn atop the maiden's head. As the iced melted, it supposedly produced a cooling sensation if one were close enough. The runoff trickled down through the figure's arm and out of the pitcher in her hand into a reservoir at the bottom.* (U. S. Patent Collection, "Portable Cooling Apparatus for Houses," No. 387,954, Aug. 14, 1888)

*Technology for staying cool lagged well behind that for keeping warm until the 20th century, when mass production of the compact electric motor made possible the mechanical fan, and subsequent technology the air conditioner. But the search for comfort had long since started, even if it amounted to little more than wishful thinking. Patented in 1830, this "automatic fan" (above) surely vies for some kind of record as to maximum contrivance for minimum of comfort. There is no record that it was ever produced.* (U.S. Patent Collection, "Automatic Fan," Nov. 27, 1830)

the windows on a hot day and hoped for a breeze.

The turn of the 19th century produced the first great wave of technological change in the house, generally speaking; but as to keeping cool, the progress was as elementary as recognizing that heat rises. This being so, let it rise right out of the house. Hence, an early form of "air conditioning": Provide a vent of some sort in the roof. One example is Gore Place (1806) in Waltham, Massachusetts, whose cupola doubled as a vent. (There was also the relative comfort that came with windows providing cross ventilation and a first-floor ceiling height of 17 feet 9 inches.)

Even so, nearly half a century later: "It is only very lately that any attention has been paid in this country to the important subject of ventilating houses," declared A. J. Downing in his *Architecture of Country Houses.* Downing described an all-season system that consisted of a rooftop *ejecting ventilator* to vent air, coupled with an *injecting ventilator* to supply fresh, outside air to the furnace during the heating season. "With an equal and agreeable temperature," he said, "a pure and healthy atmosphere is at all times maintained." While not necessarily using Downing's system, houses of midcentury began experimenting more and more with better ventilation. Hillforest in Aurora, Indiana (1853–1855), in the fashion of Gore Place, used a belvedere as a vent. The Gallier House in New Orleans (1857–1860) had two air vents ingeniously concealed in decorative plasterwork in the ceiling of the master bedroom; the vents could be opened or closed with a pole. For most people of moderate means, said Downing, "the Venetian blind, with the open window, is the active ventilation of most of our apartments."

By midcentury the furnace in the cellar, while not yet common, was at least an accepted part of household technology. What about the application of technology to keeping cool? We may recall here Dr. John Gorrie, who developed the first machine for artificially producing ice. The ice was a by-product. The machinery he patented in 1851 was really intended to cool the rooms of his tropical-fever patients in Apalachicola, Florida.

Air conditioning was still half a century away; but there were other inventors and other searchers for solutions. Some of their ideas barely exceeded pure gimmickry; some were contrivances of a highly imaginative order, as for example the fanning device illustrated on page 173. Others were ahead of their time: An electric fan was first patented in the United States in 1854; it was conceptually the equivalent of later fans except that the electric motor was still too large to make its use practical and the only source of electricity was a battery, which was low-voltage and still crude and ex-

pensive. Electric fans only began to proliferate in the 1890s as electric power became more widely available.

Yet the electric fan was no more than a mechanized version of the hand-held fan. The revolution in comfort was the air conditioner, which could make spring out of summer much as the furnace made autumn out of winter. Gorrie had shown how to cool; but cooling alone is not enough to assure comfort, which also depends on the amount of moisture in the air. The breakthrough was the development of dehumidification by Willis H. Carrier in 1902. The earliest installations were for industrial plants where control of moisture was essential; for example, in cotton and silk mills. In coming years, office buildings, department stores, and theaters would follow. For many people, their first tryout of air conditioning was the movie house, which was often actually kept too cold for comfort.

A few room air conditioners for offices or the homes of the very wealthy began to appear in the late 1920s, but a typical unit was both expensive and bulky (and at that needed a remote compressor, usually placed in the basement). Practical room units were a post–World War II development; indeed with the war winding down, this technology was something else to look forward to as part of a new era. "Air conditioning—" headlined *Life* magazine on a story in July 1945: "After the war it will be cheap enough to put in private homes." And sure enough. "Air Conditioning: Booming Like Television," reported *Newsweek* in July 1950. That same month, the *Digest* informed its *Readers* that the price of a unit was down to three hundred dollars, with three years to pay, and that the typical unit used only as much current as an electric iron. Sales doubled in two years. By the 1970s central air conditioning was becoming common. The hot-air furnace provided a big advantage: Its existing duct-work was a ready-made distribution network for cool air throughout the house.

## LIGHTING

| Old great Candles | | |
|---|---|---|
| of our own | burned | $4^h 45'$ |
| Bayberry Wax | " | $6^h 34'$ |
| New gt Candles | " | $7^h 20'$ |
| New Small Candles | " | $3^h 10'$ |

So recorded the Reverend Edward Holyoke in his diary in 1755—the burning times of various kinds of candles, anywhere from three hours and ten minutes to nearly seven and a half hours. A few years later, he found that spermaceti candles lasted eight hours and forty-nine minutes per candle, on average, but cost nearly four pence an hour to burn.

Such concern with hours and pence owed to the necessity of being economical about candles: Candles were expensive to buy and a bothersome chore to make. That the Reverend Mr. Holyoke had a choice was a reflection of his status: He was president of Harvard College. Many families had only one kind of candle—tallow. These were made from beef or mutton fat, usually in the fall when cattle and sheep were being slaughtered for meat for winter. Most candles were dipped; some were poured into molds, a more time-consuming process but one that yielded candles with greater uniformity of shape. Where there was a choice, mutton tallow was preferred for its relative

*Snuffing the candle. A necessary nuisance of early candles was the frequent snuffing, or cutting of the charred end of the wick to keep it from falling into the molten wax and thus lessening the light. Modern candles make this chore unnecessary. (Harper's Weekly, Mar. 17, 1866)*

whiteness, compared with yellowish beef tallow. Beeswax might be added to provide greater firmness, unless, of course, one had the means to use beeswax alone, for it was costly.

Yet whether one had only a tallow candle or was the Reverend Mr. Holyoke with a choice, the amount of light generated was essentially one candlepower. Often the light of that one candle was the only light in the room, or even the house. The whole family might cluster around this one precious source of light in the evening; if there was a full moon, they might gather near a window, the candle with them, and luxuriate in twice the light by which to do whatever simple tasks or diversions were possible. During the day, unless it was extraordinarily dark outside and the need extraordinarily great inside, one simply never lit a candle.

Such economizing did not apply to the wealthy in anywhere near the same degree; indeed, for entertaining the well-to-do might use a considerable number of candles to express their hospitality (while subtly proclaiming their affluence).

Such displays of opulence were few compared with the nightly ritual of the many for whom one or a few candles constituted the norm. There were also those for whom even a solitary candle was a luxury. Their nightly light was often that of just the fireplace, supplemented, at hearthside, by a knot of pitch pine known as candlewood that sputtered brightly.

Many homes even in the 17th century also used a simple lamp—the Betty lamp, as it was often called—that burned fish oil or animal fat. The Fairbanks House used both candles and lamps, although whether both were used in the earliest days is not a matter of record.

Roughly paralleling other forms of technology—recalling here the emergence of technology in England in the 1790s—was the first breakthrough in lighting, the Argand lamp, so called for Aimé Argand, of Switzerland, who in 1783 devised a new type of burner that produced light on a magnitude unknown before—ten times or more the brightness of any existing lamp. Argand's solution was a cylindrically shaped wick instead of the usual flat one, rising between two concentric metal tubes, the inner of which directed a flow of air upward to create a wider area of combustion. A glass chimney, which increased the draft, was an important feature of Argand's design.

By the 1850s the usefulness of the lamp was greatly enhanced by the use of kerosene—particularly after Edwin L. Drake's discovery of oil in Pennsylvania in 1859, marking the beginning of plentiful (and thus cheap) supply. As a fuel, kerosene, also known as lamp oil and coal oil, was so much better than the types of oil used heretofore that lamps simpler and cheaper in construction than the Argand were possible; and the kerosene lamp remained a mainstay of lighting until the days of electrification. The sixteen-room Carson City, Nevada, mansion of L. S. "Sandy" Bowers, first known millionaire of the Comstock Lode, had kerosene lamps and candles when it was built in 1864 and was still using nothing else in the 1930s.

Meanwhile, the third major form of lighting had already begun coming into use—gas. The development of gas for lighting had begun in that crucible of modern household technology, late 18th-century England. The first commercial company in the United States was established in Baltimore in 1816. The New York Gas Light Company, serving the tip of lower Manhattan, was organized in 1823, followed in 1833 by the franchising of the Manhattan Gas Light Company, with operating territory to the north. A merchant, Seabury Treadwell, house hunting in New York City in 1835, found a home on East Fourth Street that had been built in 1832 with gaslight in mind, even though gas was not yet available there: Two floors were fully piped. Having seen gaslight in use farther downtown, Treadwell chose this house; and once Manhattan Gas Light had run its mains to Fourth Street, he made his home one of the first in the area to be gaslit. (Treadwell's house is preserved as the Merchant's House Museum.) By 1855 there were 297 companies in the United States selling manufactured gas to more than a quarter-million customers.

Gaslight advanced the magnitude of candle-power still further but also allowed for a new flexibility of lighting in the average house. Candles and lamps lit relatively small areas—tables, chairs, and so on. General room lighting with chandeliers using candles and lamps was possible but was too expensive to be practical for most people. The gasolier, on the other hand—a chandelier that used gaslight—made room lighting feasible for the average house. Gas lighting continued to be popular into the 20th century, usage trailing off as electricity became available.

Among early experimenters trying to harness electricity for light was Professor Moses G. Farmer, who in 1859 devised an electric incandescent lamp for the parlor of his home in Salem, Massachusetts. The lamp consisted of an open-air strip of platinum through which flowed electric current from a battery. The amount of light barely equaled that of a candle. Thomas Edison's lightbulb of 1879, the result of thousands of experiments, used a high-resistance filament within a glass bulb; it was the prototype that launched a whole new era.

Early electric fixtures were often converted gaslights. In many cases the fixture was both gas and electric. Suspicion often existed about the reliability of electric power supply, as indeed it had about gas when it was beginning to supersede the kerosene lamp. The Alexander Ramsey House in St. Paul, Minnesota, had gas fixtures when it was built in 1872, but the family also kept using kerosene lamps, partly in case the

*As gas came into use for lighting, eventually succeeding the oil lamp, many people continued to use their lamps for reasons of economy and because they distrusted the dependability of the gas supply. The same cycle was repeated with the coming of electricity, and it was not unusual to have dual fixtures using both forms of energy. Shown here: a combination gas/electric fixture in the Parker House, Davenport, Iowa.* (Historic American Buildings Survey)

supply of gas failed and partly because kerosene was cheaper. By 1891, St. Paul also had electricity, and the James J. Hill House, built that year, was accordingly wired for electric light—along with being piped for gas. The chandeliers were electric; the wall sconces, dual fixtures using both gas and electric.

With widespread use of electricity a certain democratization had been accomplished. The lavish glow of dozens of expensive candles in the 18th-century mansion could now be duplicated with a couple of lightbulbs in the everyday home.

## ATTIC AND CLOSETS

The attic is a unique combination of the practical and impractical. On one hand, it is a useful place for keeping things one will need, say, a season hence—for storing winter clothing and winter blankets during the summer. But it is also a practical place for what would be impractical to keep if one didn't have an attic—things one doesn't need day to day, or even year to year, but might need sometime and doesn't want to throw away:

> Well, we might need it some day. [The attic] is for things we don't dare throw away and yet have no room for downstairs. (Harry I. Shumway, *House Beautiful,* 1918)

It is also practical for nothing practical at all:

> An attic is one of those rare places where time ceases to exist, the hours wheeling by so smoothly that we have no sense of motion. [It is] a castle of quietude and mysterious romance where, the gray rain making a gossamer of mist on the windows and pattering on the sloping roofs, the long afternoons pass with a dignified and gentle grace. (Ruth Adele Sampson, *Country Life in America,* 1919)

The attic is a room that came into being by default. It was not created out of specific necessity, as were the other rooms of the house. The attic emerged because the house had a roof,

*The attic. This one is Schifferstadt, in Frederick, Maryland.* (Photograph by the author)

usually gabled for the efficient shedding of rain and snow. With the gabled roof came a space—indeed a void—that, like a vacuum in nature, was to be abhorred. So the attic (or garret or loft, as this space was more commonly known in the early colonial period) filled the void as a storage area. In the Fairbanks House it was called the garret and was used for storing things, albeit a bare minimum of them. The inventory of the house made after Jonathan's death in 1668 recorded the totality of the attic's contents as "some Indian Corne & an old fann" (here meaning a farm implement for winnowing grain) with a total valuation of four shillings. Inventories of other Dedham attics of the same period showed much the same: in one, just "grain" (1649); in another, "grain, wool, hops, bedding" (1658); and another, "bedding, provisions" (1658). The bedding was presumably there for out-of-season storage; the provisions were probably dried fruits and vegetables.

The Fairbankses' garret had two windows to let in light and serve as ventilation in the heat of summer. Were the leaded panes of these windows occasionally gossamered to the eyes of some family member seeking solitude on a rainy afternoon? Ruth Sampson also recalled her childhood attic as a place where, with siblings and friends, "battles and games flourished"; or where, playing alone, one might indulge in some spectacular fantasy prompted by what was discovered there:

I found an ancient sword and a plumed hat [and] one day in an ecstasy of courage I donned them both, and inflated with pride, promenaded. [It] was a rare and awful moment of solemnity . . . a pinnacle of sensation in my life.

Did John, George, Mary, Susan, Jonas, and Jonathan, Jr., have battles and games in their garret in the early 1600s? Or George, William, Catherine, Gunning, Charles, John, and Mary—did they promenade about in makeshift costume in the fourth-floor storage area that was the "attic" of the Read home in the early 1800s? Alas, we do not know; but there is no more evidence they did *not* than that they did.

In time, the attic subdivided to offer a use-fulness beyond that of mere storage. Additional bedrooms or servants' rooms began to appear in what had heretofore been an open area the length and breadth of the house, but at first only in the houses of the well-to-do. By the mid 1800s house plans of Beecher and Vaux and others included fully subdivided attics in relatively modest houses. A "Suburban Cottage" in Vaux's *Villas and Cottages* (1857) had the attic floor divided into two bedrooms (each with a closet), a storage room, and a hallway-landing with a large closet. The bedrooms, being in the attic, were more likely intended for servants than family; this was still the uninsulated attic of the 19th century. By the 20th, the rafters could be insulated so as to make the attic more comfortable in both cold and hot weather, and it became a more attractive place for family members when needed.

Before public water supply, the attic was also sometimes the place for a cistern filled with rainwater that provided a supply of water within the house. Attic cisterns had appeared at least by the early 1800s; there was one in Gore Place (1806) in Waltham, Massachusetts. Subdivision of the attic into one or more bedrooms and/or servants' rooms remained common into the 20th century, until changes in the overall size and structure of the house, as well as evolving domestic technology, diminished the size and importance of the attic or even eliminated it altogether.

The most fundamental use of the attic is for storage. So from here, let us consider storage in the household generally, and particularly that most taken-for-granted of modern inventions, the closet. It is hard to fathom its almost total absence in most homes until the latter part of the 19th century. There were no closets anywhere in the Fairbanks House—or in other homes of the early 17th century. Among the Fairbankses of this world, there was not the need. Although clearly a middle-class family in the context of the times, they had an accumulation of personal possessions that amply fitted into a few chests or were hung on a few pegs about the house. Given the lack of stuff to put there, closets would have been superfluous; and given the rugged nature of the post-and-beam construction of the Fairbanks House, they would have been incongruous to the basic structure. It has also been said that closets were rare in the 17th and 18th centuries because they were taxed, either as luxuries or as "rooms" of the house. In the absence of any documentation, this contention should be regarded as spurious at best.

Even by the early 19th century, personal wealth had not changed materially. The scantiness of what needed closet space in pre–industrial revolution America is poignantly evident in the last page of a diary kept for the year 1819 by Harriet P. Bradley of Watertown, Connecticut:

*List of Expenses for the Year 1819.*

Bought 1 Skein of yarn 16 pence.
half a yard of Muslin ___ pence.
1 Pair of Leather gloves ___ pence.
1 skein of Hacks ___ cents.
Pen knife {for cutting quills} ___ pence.
1 Pr of Morocco Shoes 2 dollars Strings
   2 Shillings
1 Pr of Leather Shoes 10 sixpence
Half a paper of pins 6 pence 1 Leno Ruffle
   7 pence

All in all, what Harriet Bradley bought in the course of a whole year was barely more than what a woman might buy on a day's outing at the mall at the turn of the 21st century. For what belongings there were in the Bradley household, there was plenty of storage space in highboys, chests, barrels, and trunks under beds; for clothes, there were hooks and pegs about the house. The typically closetless house prevailed for much of the 19th century. Two good examples are the boyhood homes of Henry Ford (Detroit) and Orville and Wilbur Wright (Dayton, Ohio), both moved to and restored as part of Greenfield Village in Dearborn, Michigan. Both are modest dwellings, presumably typical of the vast majority of middle-class American homes of the mid 19th century. The Ford home has no closets at all; the Wright home, only a hall closet added as part of a renovation in 1892.

In the homes of the wealthy or relatively well-to-do who had more in the way of worldly goods, closets or built-in cupboards had been appearing in the late 17th to early 18th centuries, but only in modest size. The usual location was the fireplace wall—a logical place inasmuch as space is automatically generated by the plane established by the front of the fireplace wherever it is of internal construction. By making that plane a paneled wall, an area to the side of the fireplace becomes potential storage space accessible through a door within that plane. Although Susanna Wright (1697–1784) was only relatively well-to-do, her home, later known as Wright's Ferry Mansion, in Columbia, Pennsylvania (1738), made the most of this principle. There were ten closets when the house was built (one subsequently being sacrificed to become a "hidden entranceway"); at least one closet adjoined each fireplace, and other closets made use of other nooks and crannies in a remarkable utilization of space for its time.

Among the knowing or the affluent, closets became more numerous. The house that Joseph Priestley built (1796) in Northumberland, Pennsylvania, after settling in America had closets in all three full-size bedrooms as well as a large linen closet in the upstairs hall. Similarly the Read House (1804) in New Castle, but on an even grander scale: four closets in the master bedroom alone. In Philadelphia the John Todd House (1777) incorporated closets into virtually every wall with a fireplace. (It was here that John Todd's widow, Dolley, became Dolley Madison when she married the future fourth president.) By the mid 19th century the homes of the affluent commonly had closets in the kitchen, dining room, upstairs hall, and bedrooms. What went into these closets usually can only be speculated; for while diaries illuminate many aspects of changing household life and probate inventories list the totality of the contents of a house, neither provides much help with the content of closets. An exception is Sidney George Fisher's diary recording life in and around Philadelphia during the years 1834 to 1871, wherein the account of a break-in affords us a peek:

*Although closets were relatively rare in the colonial period, they were to be found occasionally. Here: the John Todd House, Philadelphia (1777), with its typically shallow, hooks-only bedroom closets.* (Photograph by the author)

> *April 5, 1858.* An unpleasant affair occurred last night. About 2 o'clock, I happened to be awake and . . . it was evident that robbers had been in or were in the house. I looked into the dining room, all the closets were open & things scattered over the table; into the parlor, Bet's secretary and other drawers were open and letters & papers, &c,

were lying about the floor. . . . In the entry upstairs is a closet in which all the silver in common use is put every night. It escaped. There is also a linen closet there, in which two chests of silver are kept. It was not opened. The robbers no doubt heard me speak to Bet & rise and they went downstairs at once to get away.

These closets of the mid 19th century generally were not yet fully developed by modern

*The built-in wardrobe* (below) *is one of the amenities of well-closeted Gore Place, Waltham, Massachusetts (1806).* (Right) *A half century later Catharine Beecher's* American Woman's Home *(1869) was championing more efficient utilization of space in the more modest dwelling with such devices as this room divider/closet on rollers.* (Photograph *below* by the author; sketch *right,* The American Woman's Home, p. 29)

standards, the exceptions being linen closets and dining room cupboards. Clothes closets were generally in the range of 14 to 18 inches deep and were for garments stowed on hooks or pegs. What dictates the depth of the modern closet (the standard is 24 inches) is the length of the hanger, which did not come into use until the latter 19th century. One of the earliest known references to the use of hangers is in the *Young Englishwoman,* February 1873, an observation that "hangers . . . will be found very advantageous for hanging up heavy articles of dress, as winter cloaks, etc." The coming of hangers and rods set the size of the modern closet.

An increasing proliferation of consumer goods, including clothing, brought about by the industrial revolution was also making closets more and more important in the average home. Among the first to see the need and incorporate closets in their model home plans were Catharine Beecher and A. J. Downing at mid 19th century, although Beecher also had open pegs in the hallway for overgarments. Calvert Vaux included bedroom closets and a large linen closet even in a "Suburban Cottage" in his *Villas and Cottages* (1857). By the 20th century, closets had become a standard feature of every house, large or small; today they are so essential to daily life that no house seems to have enough of them. Closets are not only deeper but wider (the ideal is at least 48 inches per person just for hanging clothes), and many today are walk-in. Many also have built-in lights that turn on when the door is opened, and in children's bedrooms a frequent practice is to make closet rods and hooks movable, so that they can be raised as the child grows taller.

## CELLAR AND GARAGE

Although a cellar was rarely part of the basic English home that served as the model for the early house in America, colonists, almost from the start and especially in New England, sought to cope with a harsher climate by building their houses with small storage cellars underneath. A cellar below ground provides natural refrigeration in summer; but it also has usefulness in winter: It is actually somewhat warmer than an unheated room above and hence can keep provisions cold, but not frozen, in subfreezing temperatures.

These cellar storage areas were hardly comparable to the full basements of later times. For example: The overall dimensions of the Fairbanks House were roughly 34 by 17 feet, and

the cellar was only a corner of this, measuring approximately 10 by 14 feet. Its purpose was storage of food, primarily fruits and vegetables (if a true root cellar, a place for root crops like potatoes, turnips, and beets); perhaps salted meat was kept there as well. Typically of the 17th century (and into the 19th century for some homes), its entrance was through outside steps. Inside cellar stairs began to appear later in the 17th century; elsewhere, hatchways also came into use.

There were good reasons for having only a small cellar. Excavation was difficult and expensive, and also time-consuming when the need was to get a roof over one's head as quickly as possible; and there was no real reason for anything more than a small storage area. Full basements began to appear by the 18th century and were relatively commonplace by the 19th. During the same period, the cellar began to subdivide into areas of use. Let us look, for example, at the cellar of the house Benjamin Franklin built in Philadelphia in 1765. It was here he had his kitchen. There was also a cold-storage area, a continuation of the cellar's early use for storage of food and one favoring proximity to the kitchen; a general storage area; and a storing place for wood used in the kitchen fireplace. The cellar was connected to the first floor by means of an inside staircase.

When a cellar was first used for kitchen purposes is not clear—probably sometime in the 18th century, obviously by 1765. There was a certain logic to it in the desirability of separating the living area from the heat and smell of cooking. By the late 18th century, cellar kitchens were relatively common in Philadelphia but less so elsewhere. Moreau de

Saint-Méry, visiting New York in 1794, said cellars there were poorly built and very damp and at high tide often had water in them; thus, he found fewer cellar kitchens than in Philadelphia. Occasionally, there was a cellar dining room adjacent to the kitchen; one such is shown in Calvert Vaux's *Villas and Cottages* (1857), but it existed only because the terrain sloped so as to allow windows in the dining area.

Midway through the 19th century there were still cellar kitchens—for example, in the Greek Revival Elias Baker Mansion in Altoona, Pennsylvania (1849), which used a dumbwaiter to convey meals to the first-floor dining room. But the basement of the Baker Mansion, in proportion to the house's generous size, could accommodate both a kitchen and a central-heating system (along with coal room, bake room, herb room, refrigeration room, and ice room). Central heating at this time was almost invariably hot air, necessitating octopus-like duct work flaring out from the furnace in as many directions as there were rooms above to be heated. In a house of modest size, this virtually precluded a kitchen in the cellar. But lack of convenience also tended to limit whatever popularity there was; the cellar kitchen never became predominant and in time largely disappeared.

The ideal cellar of the average home of the mid to late 19th century, in the eyes of Catharine Beecher, had no kitchen but did employ that other major element of domestic life that remains a part of many a basement to the present time—the laundry, including tubs, ironing table, and a stove just for heating wash water. A. J. Downing's *Cottage Residences* (1847) had a basement laundry earlier still.

By the 20th century, food storage was being taken over by the icebox or refrigerator upstairs in the kitchen or pantry or on the back porch. This allowed more room in the cellar for doing laundry or other household chores—as in a basement workshop. This seemingly modern adaptation of cellar space also has its antecedents. The inventory that was made of the Fairbanks House in 1668 following Jonathan's death showed the cellar to contain "2 vises and one turning lath[e] and other small things."

Two trends in the 20th century further modernized the cellar and made it into additional living/working space. These were modernization of heating and new techniques for waterproofing and insulating.

Coal was the predominant fuel for central heating early in the 20th century, and its use meant not only the necessity for coal bins but the inevitability of dirt. One way to minimize the latter was suggested by *House Beautiful* in 1913:

> If you can only afford one partition in the whole cellar, let that form a good tight room around the furnace and coal bins, so that all of the dirt is kept from settling over everything. Don't waste any space in the furnace room; make it just large enough to allow for shoveling coal and a narrow passage around the furnace.

Although "dirty" coal would continue to predominate for the coming decades and remain a common fuel through roughly the first half of the 20th century, it was "modern heating" that would liberate the cellar. "We are now planning basements that form part of the living quarters of the house," proclaimed *House and*

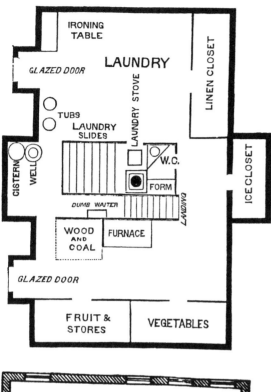

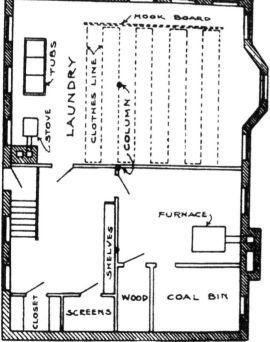

*The cellar in transition. The earliest American cellars—the Fairbanks, for example—were primarily storage areas for food. By the mid to late 19th century* (top left) *the model cellar as depicted in Catharine Beecher's* American Woman's Home *(1869) continued to save space for fruits and vegetables but devoted more space to incoming technology, including an ice closet for cold storage of food, a furnace for central heating, and a water closet. More than a third of the space is given over to laundry use. By the 20th century* (bottom left) *food storage was being taken over almost entirely by the icebox or refrigerator, upstairs in the kitchen or pantry or on the back porch. The cellar's original use was now confined to a few shelves for preserves or canned goods. Laundry use, including indoor clotheslines, took up fully half the cellar. This model cellar is from* House Beautiful, *October 1913.*

*Garden* in 1929. "With the general adoption of modern heating systems the basement has taken on a new importance."

"Modern" meant "a plant for hot water and house heating operated by gas or oil." Gone now would be not only the dirt inherent in a heap of coal but also the soot inherent in its residual ashes; gone now would be the space-consuming bins for storing coal. Oil required only a tank, in the cellar or sunk underground outdoors; gas, nothing but a pipeline. There had also been considerable progress in how to make a cellar waterproof—by proper drainage outside (avoiding a buildup of water pressure that might force moisture through the walls) and by making the basement walls impervious through the use of asphalt or a coating of cement mortar mixed with proprietary waterproofing compounds.

By the late 1920s the basement was becoming additional living space quickly known as the recreation (or "rec") room. "The cellar has been transformed into a glorified place of amusement whose popularity seriously threatens the more formal rooms of the house," wrote Harriet Sisson Gillespie in *American Home,* December 1929. "The evolution has been short and swift." For a time, as *Woman's Home Companion* observed in October of that same year, the recreation room's sociability was enhanced "with the player piano and gramophone, as well as a loud speaker to reproduce dance melodies from the radio upstairs." A virtue to the basement rec room, said the *Companion,* was that "here can be given the jolliest kind of parties, for there's plenty of room and the noise doesn't disturb the quieter members of the household." In time, however, the gramophone would be succeeded by high-tech audio equipment that could drown out a whole roomful of player pianos.

Meanwhile, above ground, around and about the house, there was an even more significant transformation going on:

As the companion of man, he [the horse] would be fit to be cherished even if there were no work left for him to do; but there is, and always will be. . . . ("E.S.M.," *Harper's Weekly,* 1899)

Man has no more hard working or serviceable friend than his automobile. (Henry Humphrey, *American Home,* 1931)

The role of the horse in American life changed dramatically in the first decades of the 20th century, as so amply exemplified in these two quotes barely a generation apart; and with that change came the emergence of the garage not merely as successor to the stable but as part of the house.

The horse had his place in the order of things—his work to do, notably around the farm or in town hauling a buggy; and he had made himself seemingly indispensable over the ages. But in 1899 the *Harper's Weekly* correspondent identified only as E.S.M. examined "The Status of the Horse at the End of the Century" and, while guardedly professing perpetuation of the status quo, allowed forebodings about the future of the most servile of beasts. "Every year," he observed, "more and more of the world's heavy drudgery is done by machinery. . . . We must expect, as electricity and steam and gasoline and compressed air are more and more used to propel all sorts of vehicles, that the number of horses will diminish." And diminish they did, although during roughly the first two decades of the automobile age the number of horses remained relatively constant. The sharpest decline began in the mid 1920s.

And although he was cherished by some, the horse was kept in his place: a barn or stable. In town, where space was scarce, a backyard stable of one's own was a sign of affluence. Common to a degree almost totally forgotten today was the public stable, where, lacking the space or means for a private stable, one could board one's own horse or rent a horse and perhaps a buggy as well for some particular purpose or occasion.

If a horse was kept on one's property, the house and stable were traditionally separate. A stable inevitably smells and is best kept a distance from one's living quarters. Yet need generated exceptions; there was the so-called continuous house that evolved in New England in the 18th century: house and outbuildings (barns, sheds, stable, and sometimes the privy) connected in one continuous chain; the stable was usually at the far end. The continuous house was an adaptation to New England's climate; it allowed the farmer to tend to many of his chores without going outside on a cold winter morning.

The concept of attaching the stable to the house also emerged on rare occasion in the city. One of the earliest instances is the third Harrison Gray Otis House (1807) designed by Charles Bulfinch. The carriage house is attached at the rear, as is the privy; both are separated from the family's living space by servants' quarters and such facilities as kitchen, wash room, and shed; one of New England's continuous houses may have been a conscious or unconscious inspiration. Another example later in the century is the J. J. Glessner House in Chicago (1885–1887, H. H. Richardson, architect). The Glessner was, and is, one of Chicago's grand homes, a fortresslike granite structure monumental in size. Its very size facilitated the attaching of the stable; four rows of rooms,

including butler's pantry, kitchen, servants' hall, storeroom, and cold closet, insulate the family's living quarters from the stable.

These were the exceptions. The horse might be cherished, but not to the point of living in the house and certainly not to being one of the family. But the automobile!

My automobile is one of my family and I like to treat it as such. Therefore, it has its own room in the house [that] I may pay it a visit in its own private boudoir. (Clare Briggs, *Country Life in America,* 1920)

And so the stable became the garage and moved into the house. And the car became one of the family. So complete has been the assimilation of the automobile into American life that we now have only a hazy notion of what personal transportation was like before its coming; and without finding some discernible form within this haze, it is difficult to appreciate the transition from stable to garage.

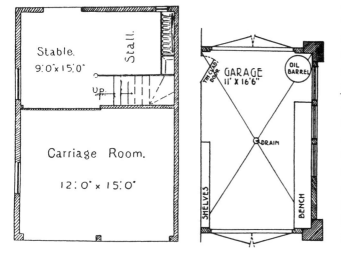

*From stable to garage: a saving in space. The stable at left (1889) and the garage at right (1911) each housed one vehicle, so they serve as a fair basis of comparison. The stable required a stall for the horse in addition to the space for a carriage, just on the first floor. There was also a second floor for storage of hay. The same degree of transportation in the automobile age required less space, all on one floor. Illustrations to same scale. (Left, R. W. Shoppell, Stables and Carriage Houses [New York, 1889], No. 590, courtesy Art and Architecture Collection/Miriam and Ira D. Wallach Division of Art, Prints and Photographs/New York Public Library/Astor, Lenox and Tilden Foundations. Right, House Beautiful, Aug. 1911, p. 87)*

It was not a one-for-one transition; that is, not every stable became a garage and not every garage was a former stable—in the latter case, particularly so. Whereas today, as a generality, every family has at least one car, in the pre-automobile era not every family had a horse, let alone a horse and buggy; nor was the ratio even close to one for one. As recalled of Newburyport, Massachusetts, in the early 1800s:

> A stable was attached [here almost certainly meaning part of the grounds as opposed to part of the house] to the better class of houses, and many of the more common had a barn for the accommodation of a cow if not a horse. . . . The more prominent citizens usually had a horse, and some kept a coach and span. (Sarah Anna Emery, *Reminiscences*)

In the country the horse was considerably more common and was readily available for transportation as well as other work. Travel from farm to town, or farm to market, or town to town, was by saddle horse, horse and buggy, or horse and wagon. Up to about 1840 the primary vehicle was the two-wheeled chaise, a descendant of the chariot of the ancient world. The four-wheeled coach was almost exclusively the province of the well-to-do. The invention of the elliptical spring in 1825 and its use in carriage building after 1830 led in the 1840s to the development of the four-wheeled buggy, a distinctly American vehicle. Such improvements, coupled with advances in road building (the federally funded National Road between Maryland and Illinois, built between 1806 and 1852, was the first fully engineered, macadamized highway in America), resulted in increased production and sales

of buggies and carriages during the 1840s and 1850s. Although the wealthy continued to have their coaches, along with coachmen in livery, the vast majority aspired at best to buggies but more often settled for wagons or for riding horseback.

In cities and towns, where everything was relatively close by, walking was the usual means of transportation; one often spent one's life only rarely going anywhere except by walking or, later in the century, taking the train. For special occasions or where circumstances required it more routinely, there was the hired carriage or, more often, the common hack. The carriage was for special occasions and was commensurately priced; even the hack was beyond the day-to-day means of many people. New York City in the 1860s ostensibly limited hack fare to fifty cents for a mile or less and seventy-five cents for two miles. Yet British author George Sala recorded his astonishment at having to part with five dollars for a five-mile drive in a carriage he had to share with others picked up along the way. By way of comparison, the ferry to Brooklyn was one cent a ride, and even getting to Staten Island cost only six and a quarter cents.

Maintaining one's own horse, and even more so a carriage or buggy, involved both expense and effort. There was the responsibility of daily care of the horse—feeding, watering, grooming, emptying the stall of manure and soiled straw. Those who had the means could employ a stable boy to do the drudgery and a chauffeur to do the driving. But those of lesser means, if they could afford to own a horse and buggy at all, had to do these chores for themselves. Hence, another example of the fallacy that "life was simpler then." How more simple than turning a key in the ignition? And then there was the maintenance of the stable itself, almost a small house in size. A garage need only be somewhat larger than the vehicle it houses; the stable required a comparable space for the carriage and roughly that much again for just one horse, plus a loft for storing hay.

Where one had the means to own a horse but not the space on one's property for a stable or not the disposition to care for a horse, there was the public stable. Virtually every small town and village had a livery stable where one boarded one's own horse or rented a horse much as one rents a car today. In Chicago in the 1860s a coach with two horses and a driver cost five dollars a day; a smaller vehicle with a single horse, three dollars.

This was the status of the stable at the time it began its transition to garage. The most noticeable aspect of the transition was the substantial contraction in size, making it feasible to attach the garage to the house. Where so depended on various factors. The most logical place was at the side, like another room, sometimes balanced out by an addition of comparable size (a sun porch, for example) on the other side. As part of a two-story house the garage wing might have a room, say a den, above the garage. If the house was being built on a slope, it might be more practical to make the garage part of the basement.

There were numerous advantages to an attached garage, convenience being the most obvious. There was an inherent saving in cost—stated as roughly the cost of three walls instead of four. Attachment made it more feasible to provide the garage with electrical service (lighting and other applications), heat (easier starting of the engine in cold weather),

and water (for refilling the radiator, washing one's hands). And by no means least of all, the attached garage, like the large front porch, had, and has, a unique capability for making a modest home look more prestigious. As for disadvantages: Adding an attached garage to an existing home might compromise its architectural integrity, and insurance was costlier. Furthermore, by the 1920s some local building codes flat out prohibited attached garages.

As of the 1930s, Burton Bugbee, writing in *House Beautiful,* still saw the influence of the stable in "the distressing rows of auto kennels along the rear property lines of the American scene"—an influence that continued past mid-century in some places. But over the years the

*The convenience of opening one's garage door without getting out did not entirely await the age of the battery-powered remote. Here in 1920 in the magazine* Country Life in America *was a device, actuated by pulling a chain, by which "the necessity for getting out into the open air in adverse weather is reduced to the vanishing point." (*Country Life in America, *Jan. 1920. Courtesy New York Public Library/Astor, Lenox and Tilden Foundations)*

advantages of the attached garage have clearly won out. It is probably safe to say that the vast majority of garages at the time of this writing are part of the house.

Perhaps the most notable advance has come in the convenience of not even having to leave your car to get the garage door up. A 1920 device let one driver do it by pulling a chain. In 1929 *Architectural Record* noted that the door might be operated "by means of a switch placed on a post which the driver can reach without getting out of the car." By the 1960s this had become the remote control, operable without even rolling the window down.

The early 1960s also produced another unique interaction between home and society, combining such traditional American gratifications as getting a bargain, cleaning up the house, and meeting new friends—that commercial/social phenomenon known as the garage sale.

## WINDOWS AND SCREENS

Bring paper and linseed oil for your windows. (Edward Winslow, letter from the Plymouth Colony, 1621, to prospective colonists in England)

It was deemed a spacious and elegant mansion; and the size of the panes of glass, fourteen inches by ten, excited the admiration and curiosity of the neighborhood. (Eliza Quincy, of the house Josiah Quincy built in Braintree, Massachusetts, in 1770)

Create breathtaking, beautiful, wide-open spaces. (1990s window catalog)

*Not all windows are for seeing through. The late 19th century's fondness for stained glass and the sheer beauty of light streaming in is exemplified by the front door of the Parker House, Davenport, Iowa.* (Historic American Buildings Survey)

So simple a part of the house's evolution in comfort and convenience as the window—and all that the window means for protection from the elements, ventilation, observation, assimilation of outdoors-indoors, architectural fashion and style—has had its own evolution.

It was probably only a very few of the earliest houses that had oiled-paper windows and more that may have had nothing other than simple, unglazed openings protected by shutters. But there was glass wherever it could be obtained and afforded. Although glass windows were briefly manufactured in the colonies (a glassworks was part of the Jamestown settlement and one was established at Salem in 1638, but neither lasted very long), it was generally necessary for the first colonists to bring their panes with them. Glass was also expensive, so windows were kept relatively small and few in number. Just as compelling was the fact that windows were efficient dissipaters of what little heat was generated by those inefficient fireplaces. Hence, the use of shutters to help retain heat in winter or block out heat and light in summer (the latter being more aptly carried out by louvered shutters properly known as blinds). To some degree shutters also added to security, or at least to a sense of security, against Indian attack, though it is probably fair to surmise that a raiding party using torches to burn down a settler's house would have found shutters less a deterrent than just so much additional flammable material to suit their purpose.

The common window of 17th-century homes was the leaded casement with diamond-shaped panes measuring roughly 6 by 4 inches. The overall sash was considerably smaller than the modern-day type owing both to the high cost and scarcity of glass and to the necessity of avoiding heat loss. While diamond-shaped panes held in place with lead cames, or joints, are perhaps the most familiar, casements with square panes, also leaded but otherwise styled like later double-hung windows, were also in use (for example, a window surviving from the

Governor William Coddington House, Newport, Rhode Island, c1641, demolished in the 19th century).

The casement remained common in the 17th century. By about 1700 the double-hung sash of all-wood construction began coming into use, although there were some earlier instances; Inigo Jones, in England, used vertical sash windows in houses at Raynham (1636) and Coleshill (1650). The double-hung claimed virtually universal acceptance in a very short time. Old-fashioned leaded casements were quickly replaced, and in most cases destroyed, so that very few authentic examples remain. Federal architecture of the turn of the 19th century also favored slimmer muntins (the wooden structural elements between panes); together with the larger panes now in use (Josiah Quincy's were steadily eclipsed in size), the trend was clearly toward greater openness and more light. Production of plate glass for residential use by roughly the mid 1800s made single-pane windows popular (at least for the lower sash), and by the 1880s virtual picture windows were a possibility (Frederick Church's Olana in Hudson, New York, for example).

The real picture window was a development of the 1930s. For example, what was then known as the Andersen Frame Corporation in 1932 offered a single unit frame with casement windows at both sides and a large picture window in the middle. Casements, meanwhile, began to regain popularity early in the 20th century, championed by such architects as Frank Lloyd Wright, who liked their visual and mechanical simplicity. The Gropius House (see chapter 6), completed in 1938, had virtual window walls in the living and dining rooms.

Although Walter Gropius used single-pane plate glass (seeking to solve the problem of heat loss by a hot-water perimeter heating system at the base of the windows), the breakthrough, literally, in turning walls into windows was the development of glass that had inherent heat-retaining rather than heat-dissipating properties (the availability of "thermopane" glass was announced by *Scientific American* in October 1934). The key was double glazing—the use of double sheets of glass, making a sandwich of air sealed to become one unit. Eventually, thermal glass would be used in windows of all sizes as an expedient way of avoiding on the one hand drafts and chills and on the other the necessity of storm windows. Yet, though panes of glass might easily encompass the full size of almost any window opening, clearly denoting a technological accomplishment of the 20th century, window manufacturers came to offer optional snap-in, square-paned grid work to make windows look 18th-century or even diamond-paned to simulate casements of the 17th century.

Apropos windows are window screens, a relatively recent addition to the house but one now so taken for granted that it is difficult to comprehend life before them. Harriet Connor (Grandmother) Brown reminds us by recalling her childhood in Ohio in the 1830s and 1840s. Flies, she observed, would try to spoil everything but . . .

My mother just would n't [*sic*] have it so. We were n't allowed to bring apples into the house in summer, because apples attract flies. If any of us dropped a speck of butter or cream on the floor, she had to run at once for a cloth to wipe it up. . . . At mealtime someone stood and fanned to keep the flies away while the others ate.

Another means of defense was to place some tall object in the middle of the table, drape a cloth over it, and slip the food under the cloth until everyone sat down at the table. A more stylish alternative was small round screens placed over each plate.

Nighttime left one more vulnerable. There is perhaps no simple nuisance so formidable as a mosquito on a summer's night. Until the latter 19th century, one generally had no choice but to put up with it—windows open to let in a breath of air, along with the invader, or windows closed, both to the nuisance and to whatever respite might come by way of a gentle breeze.

A few people in colonial America were finding some recourse by the mid 18th century; an advertisement in the *Maryland Gazette* in 1759, for example, listed an assortment of household goods just imported from England, including "green Musketo Knitting for Bed Curtains, or Blinds for Windows." This was obviously a fiber netting of some kind. Such netting had been used in India and elsewhere when sleeping outside. Here now was the same mode of protection for the bedroom: Placed around one's bed in the manner of bed curtains, it provided a reasonable degree of comfort. But it was a luxury available only to a few, and it provided respite only during the hours of sleeping. The netting, as the ad suggests, might also be placed as a covering over one's bedroom window; this would make it the fore-

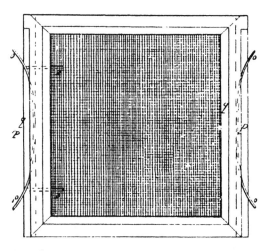

*"Window Screen" patented in 1866 by E. A. G. Roulstone of Massachusetts. The screen was described as "netting material."* (U.S. Patent Collection)

*"Improved Screen Attachment for Windows,"* 1890. *With the window closed, the screen was folded below the sash; as the window was raised, the screen rose with it. According to an announcement in* Scientific American, *the screen could be either fabric or woven wire.* (Scientific American, July 26, 1890)

*For one who could afford it, this canopy of netting was the solution to summertime sleeping before the use of window screens. Shown here: the master bedroom of Gore Place, Waltham, Massachusetts (1806).* (Photograph by the author)

runner of the window screen, but it was probably a rather makeshift arrangement.

By the mid 19th century there was still usually just the choice of an open window or stifling heat. *Harper's Magazine* in 1856 recounted the story of a newly opened summer resort built in the mosquito-infested Dismal Swamp of Virginia and North Carolina. There was obviously nothing to separate the guests from the mosquitoes, and "before the month of August visitors, servants, and proprietors had all cleared out and left the place in full possession of the mosquitoes and yellow flies. . . . The hotel was taken down."

The earliest known patent for a window screen was issued in 1854 to Benjamin B. Webster of Boston for a "mosquito curtain." It was a rather ingenious device for its day, employing a frame affixed to the window. At the bottom of the frame was a roll of netting, the end of which was attached to the bottom of the lower window sash. As the sash was raised, the netting rose with it. It was probably something wondrous to show one's neighbors, but its impregnability is rather suspect. A similar device was marketed in 1890, presumably reflecting some degree of refinement.

Wire screen also existed in the 18th century but was advertised for pantries and dairies to keep out flies. Use for houses otherwise was rare, although Jefferson is believed to have used wire screens for both the White House and Monticello. This, of course, was all handmade screening. A patent was issued in 1866 for a "mosquito bar" consisting of a fixed frame fitted with "either iron wire or cloth"; it looked much like a modern screen, but the iron wire was still primitive. Another patent was granted in 1866 for a frame of netting spring-loaded

so as to fit relatively snugly within the window frame.

Window screens did not come into general use until the mass production of "steel wire cloth" late in the 19th century, although fabric netting continued to be offered as an option for a time. Woven wire of steel, copper, or brass was considerably more durable than fabric, and it allowed for a finer mesh. By 1897, Sears Roebuck offered not only an assortment of window screens but screen doors as well, and the would-be customer was advised that "Screen doors [let alone screen windows] are no longer considered a luxury but one of the necessities of modern life."

Comfort was only part of the matter, however. The late 19th century, as reflected elsewhere in the house, was a time of unprecedented awareness of public health, including the identification of factors contributing to the spread of disease. For example, Dr. H. Gradle in *Popular Science Monthly,* September 1883:

> Scourges of the human race . . . are no longer invisible creatures of our imagination, but with that omnipotent instrument, the microscope, we can see and identify them. . . . The germ theory of disease . . . can not be ignored.

In the same 1883 issue there appeared an article by Dr. A. F. A. King titled "Insects and Disease." Dr. King in 1883 was dean of the faculty at the National Medical College in Washington and was perhaps the first knowledgeable authority to link the mosquito with the spread of disease. His finding was reported in a paper read before the Philosophical Society of Washington in 1882, excerpts of which constituted the *Popular Science* article. Having drawn the connection between the mosquito and disease, Dr. King urged a threefold counterattack: by government, through the destruction or draining of swamps and pools that produce mosquitoes; outside the house, "with fires, lamps, or electric lights, to act as traps for the attraction and destruction of such winged insects as may approach"; and inside the house, by "the use of smoke or of some volatile aromatic oil, as of camphor" but chiefly "by gauze curtains, window-screens, or clothing impenetrable to their [mosquitoes'] probosces."

"The reading of this notable paper," according to the *Dictionary of American Biography,* "produced little impression upon an audience which was skeptical and unconcerned." For a time, the scientific community dismissed Dr. King's findings. It was still supposed that contagion was only possible through contact, direct or indirect, with an infected person, as was so graphically recorded of an epidemic that struck Philadelphia in 1793:

> People uniformly and hastily shifted their course at the sight of a hearse coming toward them. Many never walked on the footpath, but went into the middle of the street, to avoid being infected in passing houses wherein people had died. Acquaintances and friends avoided each other in the streets, and only signified their regard by a cold nod. The old custom of shaking hands fell into such general disuse that many shrunk back with afright at even the offer of a hand. (Mathew Carey, 1793)

Ironically, all the handshaking in the world would not have made a difference. The epidemic was yellow fever, the worst ever in America; and yellow fever is not contagious. As was proved to the satisfaction of the scientific community late in the 1890s and firmly established in the mind of the public by Walter Reed in the early 1900s, yellow fever is transmitted by the mosquito.

While window screens evolved chiefly to satisfy creature comfort, the confluence of technology and emerging medical knowledge in the late 19th century made them a standard part of the American home.

## THE BEDROOM

> Of all the rooms in the house, the bedroom has changed least. It would almost be accurate to say that the only essential difference between the sleeping chamber of today and one of the post-Civil War period is the absence of the chamber pot. (George Nelson, *Tomorrow's House,* 1945)

To conclude this look at comfort and convenience, we turn now to that ultimate place of ease, all the more appropriate for a conclusion since it is the last place seen each day—the bedroom.

Is it true the bedroom has changed the least of all the rooms of the house? It depends on what we mean by bedroom. In the Fairbanks House there were two definitions. Upstairs were the two chambers where the children slept (though they may all have shared the one that had a fireplace). Downstairs was the parlor that, with its "best bed," was also the master bedroom as well as the "best room" for receiving guests—a virtually universal configuration of living and sleeping space among the middle class in the 17th century. The master bedroom was commonly on the first floor into the 18th century.

So if by "bedroom" we mean a room devoted solely to sleeping, there is change or not depending on which definition we apply. Yet additional uses have been common, further complicating the question. Before the bathroom, the bedroom was a place for washing and for using a chamber pot (hence the logic of having the bathroom, once it became a fixture of the house and especially if there was only one, more accessible to the bedroom than to any other room). Before the kitchen became the nerve center and command post of the house, the bedroom was sometimes the place from which household affairs were directed. Before industrialization, it was a place for spinning yarn and looming cloth; in more recent times, the principal place for storing clothes as well as assorted other worldly goods produced by that industrialization. With modern light, it has become a primary place for reading . . . with modern sound, for listening to music . . . with modern communications, for watching late-night television or waking up to the weather forecast. It can also be something of a miniature gymnasium: The bedroom is a common place for keeping an exercise machine.

Yet it is still primarily for sleeping that one comes here. Hence, how the bedroom has not changed at all and yet changed the most: in the comfort of the bed. The Fairbanks children, if they had a bed, probably doubled up, or even tripled up; or maybe they had no bed and used straw mattresses on the floor or bedding that had been rolled up and stored away during the day, in which case they were only once removed in comfort from the common people who slept on rushes strewn about the medieval great hall. Father and mother, Jonathan and Grace Fairbanks, almost certainly had a real bed, but how comfortable it was defies modern judgment.

Mattresses were made of ticking full of straw, or anything else suitable, piled on cords, sacking, or perhaps wooden slats stretched across a bed frame. By the mid 19th century, comfort was still basically at this same level. The mattress was still a straw-filled tick that was supposed to be emptied out, washed, and refilled once a year, preferably in the spring. Underneath were still cords, sacking, or wooden slats. Comfort came from using a feather bed on top of the straw tick. Made of some substantial fabric, it was filled with thirty to fifty pounds of feathers and down, it was often a family's most prized possession, and it was the first removed in an emergency. The feather bed needs to be distinguished from modern-day down comforters, which are used to cover the sleeper; the feather bed provided comfort underneath, with layers of blankets above the person.

Another form of comfort, this one against the cold, was the four-poster with its bed curtains. It was in use at the time of the Fairbankses, though usually only on the best bed in the parlor. The curtains, especially heavy ones in winter, kept in body warmth during the cold season. They continued to be popular through roughly the mid 19th century. By then, changing ideas of healthfulness prompted second thoughts about curtained sleeping. Did these fabric canopies harbor dust and vermin? Did they block the flow of fresh air that was

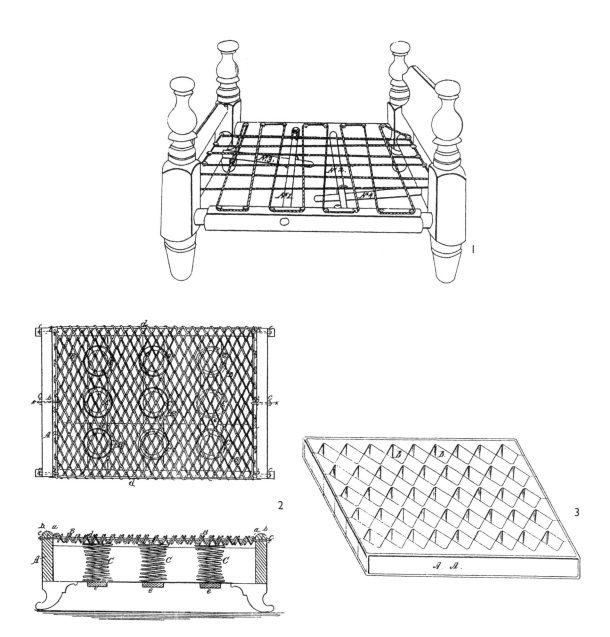

*In search of a better night's sleep. Prior to development of the modern bed, the corded bed (Fig. 1) was a common form of support for whatever straw ticking might suffice for a mattress. This is one that was patented in 1839. Beginning in the 1850s there were more determined efforts to improve sleeping comfort, notably with the box spring. An improved version (Fig. 2) of 1869 is shown. Although most people were still using cording, sacking, or wooden slats as support for straw-filled ticks, there were also attempts at the comfortable mattress. Fig. 3 is one patented in 1859 that made use of baffled sections of stuffing to divide the mattress into partitions, ostensibly increasing comfort and producing ventilation within the mattress. (U.S. Patent Collection)*

considered so important to good health? And needless to say, reading in bed with a candle or gas lamp, though bad enough, posed a danger of exponential degree with curtains all around. The use of bed curtains declined steadily in the second half of the 19th century, in part also as a result of improved systems of heating.

The eventual successor to the bed curtain as a close-in form of comfort was the electric blanket. It first appeared on the market in 1946 and became popular in the 1950s. Weighing the equivalent of one light blanket, the electric blanket gave the warmth of two or three heavy coverings while also assuring that, no matter how much the room temperature might fluctuate overnight, the degree of warmth within would remain the same.

Comfort in the bed itself began to change at about the same time as the bed curtains were coming down. Inventors of the 1850s looked at ways of replacing the cording, sacking, and wooden slats. Springy metal lath or combinations of wires and springs were among the solutions tried. Far more promising in the long run was the equivalent of the modern box spring, first developed during the 1850s, using spiral or coil springs much as the modern version does.

Similarly, there came the evolution of that sack of straw into the comfortable mattress of today.

Over the years, comfort and convenience have come in many shapes and forms:

- For Susanna Wright of Columbia, Pennsylvania, it was having ten closets in 1738, when most people had none.
- For Dr. Francis LeMoyne of Washington, Pennsylvania, it was having a roof garden in 1812 so as to grow herbs for his apothecary shop without leaving the house.
- For the Lymans of Hilo, Hawaii, it was getting a steel roof in 1855 to replace the thatch roof with which their house was built in 1839.
- At the Hixon House, La Crosse, Wisconsin, it was a built-in central vacuum-cleaning system with outlets in downstairs and upstairs halls, installed c1908.
- At the Lindbergh home in Little Falls, Minnesota, in 1917 it was a gasoline motor to pump well water, rigged up by a boy of fifteen named Charles, whose faith in gasoline motors later took him across the Atlantic.

*The comfortable house of the early to mid 20th century: Two birthplaces of famous 20th-century Americans, preserved as historic sites, also preserve a segment of American life that is otherwise almost entirely obliterated by a fast-changing century. The Brookline, Massachusetts, birthplace of John F. Kennedy (Figs. 1–9) is restored to the way it looked at roughly the time of his birth in 1917, but its comfy, middle-class appearance is typical of many an American home through midcentury. The birthplace of the Reverend Martin Luther King, Jr., in Atlanta (Figs. 10–11) is restored to its state in 1929, the year of his birth. (Historic American Buildings Survey)*

1

2

3

4

5

6

7

8

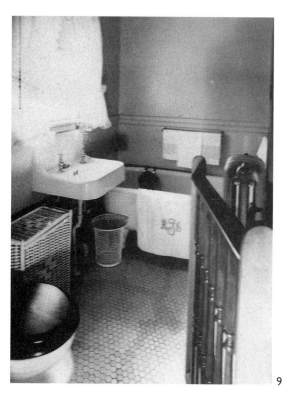

9

10

11

## A Latter-Day Joshua Hempsted

24 South Main Street, Milford, Mass., as it appears today.

All the "what now?'s" of keeping up a house in the 18th century were uniquely recorded in the diary of Joshua Hempsted II (excerpts, chapter 2). Hempsted started his diary in 1711 at the age of thirty-three and, day in, day out, set down his life and times until his death at eighty in 1758. There is a remarkable 20th-century counterpart in the account book of Lucius R. Dodge, begun in 1889 when he was twenty-six and kept until shortly before his death in 1947 at the age of eighty-three.

Dodge was first a blacksmith and carpenter but spent most of his life working as a railroad conductor, retiring at seventy-three. With the same punctilious attention to schedule that characterized the grand age of railroading, he kept a meticulously regular account of all personal and household expenses for more than half a century. While it is not a diary in the traditional sense, as is Hempsted's, Dodge's record is nevertheless a rich reflection of daily life—including all that needed doing for a home owner to stay up-to-date in the age of modernization. The following, in his own words, are highlights of a section titled, "Brief History." Like a hobbling and stooping Hempsted fixing his roof in his seventies, Dodge was apparently still doing painting around the house at age eighty.

| | |
|---|---|
| 1889 | L. R. Dodge and Marie A Goddard married in Grafton Mass. |
| 1899 | Moved to 24 So Main St Milford Mass buying same |
| 1904 | Shingled house |
| | Made bathroom and connected same with both hot and cold water |
| 1912 | Connected house with town sewerage and dug cellar under kitchen and put in bulkhead |
| 1913 | Painted house in and out |
| | House connected with gas and using same in range |
| 1914 | Had 25 marriage anniversary at our home |
| | Electric lights put in house and use elec. fan and Elec Vacuum cleaner. |
| 1918 | Built an open piaza on south side house |
| 1919 | Built Garage and bought a Hudson Automobile |
| 1922 | Built dormer window in [daughter] Dorothy's room and shingled with paper [asphalt?] shingles, south sid[e] house |
| 1925 | Built dormer windows on North side of house |
| 1926 | Built . . . driveway to Garage. |
| 1927 | May. raised roof over kitchen Ell making good storeroom |
| 1928 | Marie A. Dodge (wife) died March 27. |
| | Painted kitchen and, bath room, varnished |
| 1930 | New hotwater boiler and plumbing bill $57.87 |
| 1930 | Painting and papering Front, Dining, Bedrooms, 2 halls $58.84 |
| | Linoleum for Dining room and two halls $80.00 |
| | Shingled one sid[e] [work]shop. Roof |
| | [Daughter] Dorothy and family here all year. John no work |
| 1937 | Sheathed backroom and new cupboards. |
| 1938 | Built 6′ × 8′ addition to [work]shop. Cement floor there. Shingled North side shop. |
| | New linolium in Den and back room |
| 193[?] | Have now new oil heater in living room. Use coal *no* more |
| 10/44 | Lu[cius himself, apparently, at age eighty] paints Shed, garage, Kitchen, Den, Pantry and Bathroom |
| 10/45 | House painted [by someone else] 2 coats, south side roof shingled 4 new windows, New gutter |
| 1946 | [End of account book] |

# CHAPTER 6

# The House as Architecture

## VISITING THE MODERN HOUSE

Just outside Lincoln, Massachusetts, more or less around the corner from Lexington and Concord and down the road from Walden Pond, is a house that is historic for reasons having nothing to do with its historic location.

And it was so at the beginning. This house, at 68 Baker Bridge Road, perhaps had more visitors when it was built than any other private home in America, before or since. The visitors came by the thousands—many just to stare from the main road, others to see inside, some to be entertained, a select few to occupy for a night or more the guest room on the second floor. One who was among the first to be an overnight guest later recalled of that first burst of curiosity:

While I was staying [there] in the autumn of 1938 crowds of visitors used to come over every weekend, and often on weekdays as well, to see the newly finished "modern house"; for up till then not a single example could be found within a radius of upwards of a hundred miles.

People had to have a look. It was as if a Martian had landed in Boston Common. Was it friend or foe, this "modern house"? Besides the roadside onlookers, the curious from "upwards of a hundred miles" included groups sponsored by museums, universities, and sometimes churches—the organized explorers of modern living. There were also the spontaneous investigators. Sometimes on a quiet Sunday afternoon the doorbell would ring. The man of the house, making the most of a day off, might retreat upstairs, with his thirteen-year-old

*The "modern house": home of the Walter Gropius family, Lincoln, Massachusetts. People had to have a look.*
(Photograph by the author)

*The Gropius House: a view from the garden side.*
(Photograph by the author)

daughter just behind him, she to take refuge in the bathroom if need be, to have one last place of privacy from the curious. That would leave it to the woman of the house to answer the door.

And with no reservations. She knew full well why this house would be historic, and that seemed to make privacy pale against the opportunity to explain, here in its own hallowed presence, what this house was all about. If there was someone so interested as to depart the legions of the merely curious and actually ask to see inside, that was exactly the kind of visitor, she thought, to be welcomed.

That the explaining was being done by the woman of the house on a Sunday afternoon only reflected the fact that the man of the house—who was also the architect of the house—had been doing similar explaining all week long. Dr. Walter Gropius (1883–1969) was the newly appointed head of the Department of Architecture at Harvard University's Graduate School of Design. He had made his reputation in post–World War I Germany as an architect and as founder (1919) of that avant-garde school of the arts known as the Bauhaus. Integrating art and architecture with life sciences, the Bauhaus (in Gropius's own words) sought to "rouse the creative artist from his other-worldliness and to reintegrate him into the workaday world of realities . . . averting mankind's enslavement by the machine by saving the mass-product and the home from mechanical anarchy and by restoring them to purpose, sense and life." Such sense of purpose and life collided head-on with every dogma of Nazism. Gropius fled the country in 1934, taking refuge in England and practicing architecture there; and then he accepted a personal

invitation from Harvard president James B. Conant to come to America.

Gropius and his wife, Ise, arrived in Boston in March 1937 (to be joined in July by daughter Ati, then twelve) and took up temporary residence in Cambridge—much the same as another immigrant family had three centuries earlier. The Jonathan Fairbanks family lived in Boston before settling down and building a home in Dedham in 1637. For the Gropiuses the choice in 1937 was Lincoln, roughly as distant from Boston as Dedham is and a rural haven from the citified life they had known in Berlin and London.

The decision to build a house was not foreordained. Like most newcomers to a new place, the Gropiuses first went house hunting; and like most newcomers, recalled Ati years later, they found it a "very chaotic time." The chaos was abated by the rental of a small Colonial-style house adjacent to a farm outside Lincoln. Country life—cows, barns, orchards, ponds, and all—took hold; it was here, still within reasonable commuting distance of Harvard, they would remain, and build. Philanthropist Helen Storrow, of Boston, provided the land and the financial wherewithal: She would be the owner of record of the house the Gropiuses would construct, renting it to them on generous terms. Here near Lincoln, on a gentle rise within the sight of an orchard and the sound of cows, in April 1938 began the digging of the foundation; here, over the coming months, proceeded the construction, sometimes viewed with great curiosity by students in Gropius's spring classes at Harvard; and here in September emerged the "modern house" that all those people came to see.

## REDEFINING
## ARCHITECTURE

As did Jonathan Fairbanks, Walter Gropius brought with him the conception of the house as it existed in his homeland, although Gropius had a more individualized idealization of his own design than Fairbanks, who transplanted a more generic concept from England. But just as Fairbanks adapted the house as he had known it (notably with the addition of its clapboard overcoat), so too did Gropius in reinventing the home he had left behind in Dessau, Germany. "I made it a point," he later explained,

> to absorb into my own conception those features of the New England architectural tradition that I found still alive and adequate. This fusion of the regional spirit with a contemporary approach to design produced a house that I would never have built in Europe with its entirely different climatic, technical and psychological background. I tried to face the problem in much the same way as the early builders of the region had faced it when, with the best technical means at their disposal, they built unostentatious, clearly defined buildings that were able to withstand the rigors of the climate and that expressed the social attitude of their inhabitants.

Yet clearly this was not the typical New England house; people would not have come from miles around to stare at what they could see next door. Adaptation notwithstanding, this was the "modern house"—so had said Siegfried Giedion, architectural historian and Harvard colleague of Gropius, the early guest who had recorded his personal observation of the "crowds of visitors" in the autumn of 1938. One then must ask: What *is* the modern house? and what is modern architecture?

For that matter, what is architecture? Let us recall, far earlier in time, so primordial a manifestation of domesticity as the piling of branches against the portal of a cave. Here was adaptation for the purpose of protection from the elements: the first step, the sine qua non, but surely not the essence, of architecture itself. Architecture transcends the merely functional; it gives form to function and does so in a form that signifies those who are sheltered there.

We don't know, but were there perhaps some cave dwellers who tied their branches together with vines rather than merely heaping them, thereby unconsciously imparting some small sense of permanency to their dwellings? Or those inhabitants of late-prehistoric Glastonbury who placed flat stones at their entrance ways: Did some of them unwittingly view the size and shape of the stones as an opportunity to make a statement about the individuality of those living within?

Architecture takes a finite amount of space and makes of it an infinite expression of that which transcends the merely spatial—one's own self, one's own being, one's own sense of the infinite.

In much the same vein, there is a definition by Frank Lloyd Wright: "Architecture extends the bounds of human individuality." From that point we have a stepping-stone from which to peer about this house. What was it those crowds of visitors could see that generated such fervent curiosity?

There was seemingly no roof . . . and the house was very plain and horizontal-looking . . . with windows strangely placed in long bands like ribbons . . . a wall of glass blocks supporting something that looked like a porch roof, yet there was clearly no front porch . . . a spiral, wrought-iron stairway, but on the outside? . . . and wood sheathing running vertically? . . . and instead of a prominent front door something that looked like a simple back door, yet this was the front, wasn't it? . . . and all of this grouped with no apparent sense of arrangement, no formal and symmetrical pattern, no apparent concern for all those niceties of architectural design that had been the hallmark of homes hereabouts for countless generations. Modern house, indeed!

Yet was there some underlying logic to this?

*At the Gropius House in 1940.* (Left to right) *Marcel Breuer, Mrs. James Plaut, James Plaut, director of the Institute of Contemporary Art, Boston, Frank Lloyd Wright, and Walter Gropius. A gathering of redefiners.* (Courtesy of the Society for the Preservation of New England Antiquities)

## WHY "MODERN" IS MODERN

Let us observe more closely this well-looked-at house, examining in particular those features that made it then (and still do) "modern," keeping in mind what to expect, as Gropius himself reminds us:

It will no longer be like the earlier fortress, a rigid monument with expensive facades placed representationally, but instead a place flooded with sun passing through. . . . The modern home, which corresponds to our modern life, functions through simple, clear form, through the harmonic mass of all building parts, through open walls that make possible a maximum intrusion of light, through the beauty and reliability of its materials. . . . It should adapt to its requirements and make possible a relaxed and natural life by providing an elastic and unburdened atmosphere. It should strengthen the self-confidence of the inhabitant, create harmony of body and soul.

## The Basic Plan

Although the modern house hardly does away with rooms, it attempts to redefine the relationship both of room to house and of inhabitant to room. Not long after the Gropius house was built, Elizabeth B. Mock, curator of architecture at New York's Museum of Modern Art (MOMA), explained the new emphasis on openness this way in *House & Garden* (August 1946):

> Instead of cooping up each activity in a tightly circumscribed room of its own—a practice which made sense only in pre-central-heating days—modern architects like to give their clients as much freedom as can be made consistent with quiet and privacy. This they accomplish by open planning, by treating space as continuous and allowing it to flow freely, not only from one room to another, but from inside to outside, so that the exterior too will contribute to the feeling of expanding space.

Stepping through that unceremonious front door into the entrance hall of the Gropius House, we begin to feel that new sense of openness. There is a circular stairway that has a

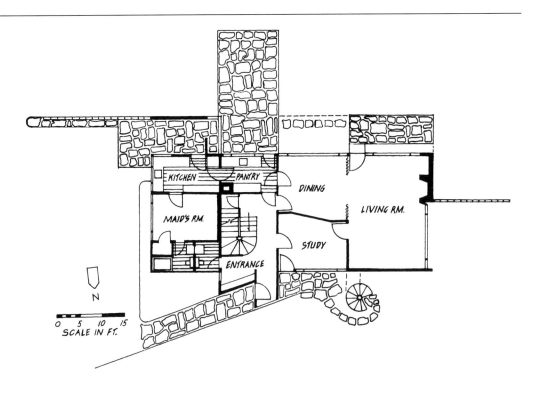

(Left) *Walter Gropius at home, 1960.*
(Below) *Gropius House, the stair hall, first floor, partly bathed in the soft light of glass block that borders the entryway.* (Courtesy of the Society for the Preservation of New England Antiquities; photograph *below* by David Bohl)

(Facing page) *The first-floor plan of the Gropius House. The coil shape at the lower right is the outside spiral staircase and the flagstone path leading to it; the large flagstone extension at upper center, a screened-in terrace; the horizontal extensions at right and upper left, trellises. Although the trellises and flagstone areas are exterior and technically outside the scope of a floor plan, they are included here as a way of emphasizing the integration of indoors and outdoors that is a key element of Gropius's design.* (Drawing by Dolores Malecki-Spivack)

*Gropius House. The dining and living rooms: free-flowing space.* (Courtesy of the Society for the Preservation of New England Antiquities; photograph by David Bohl)

grace and lightness reminiscent of the Federal period, but this is much more open. There is no more to it than what is necessary to get from one floor to another safely. Instead of a traditional railing, there are simple chrome-plated tubes serving as balusters, stretching, with each successive step, in inverse increments from tread to floor above. A simple handrail winds along the inner circumference. (Here it should be noted that the exterior wrought-iron spiral staircase, though some early observers may have wondered, is *not* the principal means of getting to the second floor; it was built for daughter Ati as a secondary access, so her friends could visit without intruding on the family.)

Immediately to the right of the entrance

hall is a small study. It is separated from the living area by a glass-block wall that provides privacy while also admitting light. Beyond it, reached separately from the hall, is the largest interior space—the free-flowing living-dining area that is also enveloped in light. There are wall-size windows that extend the concept of open design to make outdoors indoors. The panorama is broken only by the fireplace, which is brick (traditional) painted gray (not so). Off the dining area are the pantry and kitchen, both only as large as necessary, and the maid's quarters, a common pre–World War II amenity that disappeared from the middle-class house after the war.

On the second floor are the master bedroom with dressing room, a sewing nook, the guest room, and Ati's room with a separate small alcove for her bed. There are two bathrooms on this floor, one accessible only from the master bedroom and the other opening onto the central hall. A look in one of the bedrooms helps to explain those ribbon windows: There is a certain sense of openness and yet privacy as well, since the windows are generally at shoulder height. Beyond Ati's room is a sun deck connected to the spiral staircase.

## Windows

The windows, which look out in all directions on the countryside that lured the Gropiuses here in the first place, further help to explain the design of the house.* The entrance is on the north side, facing the road; on the south is the living-dining area. In summer this area would be beastly hot with sunlight pouring in. In fact, it is not, because the room is shaded by the large overhang of the flat roof. Since the summer sun is much higher in the sky, the rooms beneath, with sufficient overhang of the roof, remain mostly in shade all day. In the winter the reverse is true, given the lower angle of the sun, and sunlight pours inside, providing much natural warmth owing to the overly large size of the windows—an instance of underlying logic, of form following function. Form and function also explains the bands of windows on the front of the house. The road side wants a degree of privacy not needed on the garden side; and the winter sun has nothing to offer the north side in the way of warmth, so there is no need for window walls on the north. Small ribbon windows suffice quite well there, as well as for second-floor bedrooms in the interests of privacy. The windows, with the exception of large panes fixed in place, are swing-open casements. One of the first targets of 20th-century modernists was the double-hung sash that itself was a new symbol of the "modern" house at the turn of the 18th century. Frank Lloyd Wright claimed credit for helping to lead the attack on the "guillotine window," as he called it, at the turn of the 20th century.

## Materials

By the late 1930s, construction materials unknown or still merely exotic only a few years before—plywood, glass block, reinforced concrete, stainless steel, chrome, acoustical plaster, fiberglass—were available for the modern house, and they impelled experimentation, inevitably producing results that looked modern. James and Katherine Ford, who also lived in Lincoln in a Gropius-designed house, made a point of this in *The Modern House* (1940):

> Materials and fixtures derived from modern technology lose value when encased in traditional forms. Modernists consider it absurd that concrete should be made to look like natural stone, or electric light fixtures like candlesticks. . . . The new materials make possible thinner walls, lighter construction, new proportions, and new textures.

Gropius was notable for using new materials in his own house. But for reasons of economy, and as a way of demonstrating use in everyday homes, he made it a point generally to employ

---

*Earlier in time, there was Benjamin Henry Latrobe's explanation of the modern-for-its-day appearance of the John Markoe House, Philadelphia, completed in 1811: "As to the exterior, it is created by the *interior*, and was with me a secondary thing altogether." (Letter of December 5, 1810).

materials readily available. In large part, he ordered stock items from catalogs or local suppliers. Manufacturers included Revere Copper and Brass, Sanitary Company of America, Pittsburgh Plate Glass, Armstrong Cork, Kohler, and General Electric. The dining table was illuminated from overhead by a theater spotlight ("klieg light") ordered stock from Kliegel Brothers. The spiral stairway to Ati's room came from a supplier of fire escapes. Gropius's use of acoustical plaster (sound-absorbing as opposed to sound-reflecting) for first-floor ceilings was one of the first domestic uses ever.

At the same time Gropius also made a point of using such time-honored New England building materials as clapboard and fieldstone. The walls of the downstairs hall are an innovative combination of the traditional and the nontraditional—clapboard of the kind found on the outside of untold numbers of houses, set *vertically* instead of horizontally *inside*. The resulting effect of gentle corrugation produces subtly changing shadows as light filters in and out during the day. The exterior consists primarily of redwood sheathing painted white.

## A Crisp, Clean Look

Absence of ornamentation is another hallmark of the modern house. As the Fords explained it to their contemporaries, modern architecture "seeks not style but substance, not ornament or ostentation but rational simplicity." The emphasis here should be on the word rational, which reflects a redefinition of house that is the essence of the new form. The Gropius House has nothing on it that is not functional.

## A Flat Roof

Although a shallow roof had been a familiar sight on private residences since the early 19th century, it was 20th-century modernism that effectively introduced the flat roof, with the rationale that the pitched roof was just so much waste of space and material and hence failed the test of functionality. The Gropius House has a roof that is just slightly concave, so that water, instead of running off the side, flows to the center; here a pipe runs down the center of the house to a dry well.

One objection to a flat roof, in the public's mind, was the absence of an attic; another was that such a roof was unsafe. The real test of the structural rigidity of Gropius's unorthodox design turned out to be something else unorthodox to New England—a hurricane. The infamous hurricane of September 21, 1938, which killed nearly seven hundred people in New England, howled in just after the Gropiuses had settled down. It caused hardly any harm to them but extensive damage to countless houses with traditional pitched roofs. Skeptical neighbors nonetheless came by the day after the storm to see if the Gropius house was still there.

## Location

As much as possible, the modern house takes advantage of its location. Where there is a good view, that is where the largest and amplest windows (indeed window walls) go; where privacy is important, there are smaller windows, or advantage is taken of the landscape—the seclusion afforded by trees and shrubbery. Placement of decks and windows pays attention to the sun.

## "AS IF A STARTLING INNOVATION"

Was it friend or foe, this modern house? "The important thing," advised MOMA's Elizabeth B. Mock, when people were still wondering about the Gropius house, is

> to try to see each house as freshly as if the very idea of domestic shelter were a startling innovation, as if one had heard of houses and never before seen any. (*House & Garden,* August 1946)

"Trying to see" has to take into account the times. The modern house was a product of a modern age—post–World War I. It was a time of radical change, epitomized by speed . . . undreamed-of speed, on land, in the air . . . speed not only in transportation but in communication . . . people doing old things faster—or if not faster, more conveniently, more comfortably. All this emphasis on speed and mobility and convenience called for new shapes, shapes connoting speed; for streamlining, to get the most speed possible or at least to look speedy in a speedy age. Even science, in a sense, was becoming streamlined: What constituted matter was now relative. Architecture likewise. No longer was it tied to "Greek space," wrote Frank Lloyd Wright in the *Architects' Journal* in August 1936; architects were now "free to enter into the space of Einstein."

The basic conception of house had to change at least somewhat apace. With increasing mobility there was less need to stay at home, less need for space. With new technology in the kitchen less space was required for food storage and preparation. And by now the transforma-tion of the house from producer to consumer had long since been consummated. With changing construction technology came those new substances—plywood, reinforced concrete, plastic, glass block, stainless steel, chrome, fiberglass—that by their clean and streamlined appearance inspired clean and streamlined architecture. The result was the final overthrow of the Victorian predilection for spatial saturation.

But change in domestic architecture did not come easily. It was one thing to look in wonderment and say nice things about the "house of the future," as long as one could go home to one's comfortable old house; it was one thing to visit, but did one really want to live there? Gropius's colleague Marcel Breuer, also of the Bauhaus and a collaborator on the planning of the Gropius house, as well as of his own nearby, conceded as much at the time:

> [Any house is] the type of design nearest to ourselves. Its atmosphere of privacy is composed of the most various functions: sleeping, eating, working, leisure, social life. . . . As it is the oldest type of building, it is the most overloaded with feelings for tradition. Nearly everyone has some personal ideas about it and nearly everyone associates his opinions with past styles.

Personal ideas. They both created and set apart the Gropius house. Yet as unique as it was, as much an extension of the bounds of individuality, this modern house was not the individual creation of Gropius. It was a family project: father, mother, and daughter (the last sometimes with indifference befitting her age) all putting their heads together to make this a house for all. The months preceding adoption

*"We should cultivate individualism, but also the attitude that we all enrich each other"—Walter Gropius. As a maxim, it was certainly true of the family house's being a family project. Here: Walter, Ati, and Ise Gropius at the house they rented nearby in 1937–1938 while their modern house in Lincoln, Massachusetts, was being built.* (Collection of Ati Gropius Johansen, courtesy of the Society for the Preservation of New England Antiquities)

that . . . And I was principally bored, with the exception of being asked what did I want for my room.

In fact, she fared well, with what amounted to a two-room suite with private entrance (room, bed alcove, and that ever-so-neat spiral staircase). And indeed the whole family fared well. This was not a showplace, despite the thousands of visitors. It was, first of all, home. A very comfortable home. A very pleasant home. And individuality was not lost by its being a family project. "We should cultivate the strongest possible individualism," said Gropius, "but also the attitude that we all enrich each other." This was not simply a home, but *their* home—their conception of harmony of body and soul.

## "THE MOST LOGICAL HOUSE"

At about the same time the Gropius house was attracting so much attention, a young journalist in Washington, D.C., captivated by the work of Frank Lloyd Wright, sought out the country's most famous architect about designing a house for him.

Most of the houses associated with Frank Lloyd Wright (1867–1959) are showplaces of the wealthy, but Wright also made a point of the need to design affordable, middle-class housing—the kind that has been our primary focus here—and indeed looked on it as a major challenge. "The house of moderate cost is not only America's major architectural problem, but the problem most difficult for her major architects," Wright remarked in 1938, the

of plans in fact made the new house the overwhelmingly predominant matter of talk, at the dinner table and otherwise. As Ati, then twelve, recalled it many years later:

I think it was being discussed at every meal. I mean, the endless discussion . . . whether the windows should be here . . . and all of same year Gropius completed a very middle-class home for himself.

Describing a genre, Wright coined the word "Usonian," loosely based on "United States of North America," a term that also had a vague but not unintended ring of "utopian" to it. This was one of his conceptions of the modern house, but scaled to the needs and price range of the middle class—the affordable utopian house. A quintessential example is the Pope-Leighey House, built originally in Falls Church, Virginia, but since moved to the grounds of Woodlawn Plantation in nearby Mount Vernon.

The journalist who welcomed Wright's interest in a house of moderate cost—and even more, Wright's conception of the house as "a spiritual place"—was Loren B. Pope, a few years out of college and then assigned to the copy desk of the *Washington Evening Star.* Recently married, he had bought a 1½-acre lot in Falls Church on which he and his wife were about to build a Cape Cod house complete with picket fence and rambling rose bushes. It was just about then that *Time* magazine ran an article on Wright's Fallingwater (the Edgar J. Kaufmann house, in Mill Run, Pennsylvania), completed in 1938. Cantilevered over a stream in the mountains of western Pennsylvania, it was (and is) a remarkable conception of the integration of nature and habitation. Pope, intrigued with the creative energy behind it, borrowed Wright's biography from the library, read a few chapters, then went out and bought his own copy and read it through twice.

A friend convinced Pope to stop dreaming and build his own Fallingwater. In August 1939 he sent Wright a six-page letter explaining what it would mean to him to have a Frank

*Charlotte and Loren Pope, c1940.* (By permission. From the collections of Frank Lloyd Wright's Pope-Leighey House, a property of the National Trust for Historic Preservation)

Lloyd Wright house. Wright agreed to the project and two months later completed preliminary sketches. In September Pope journeyed to Wright's celebrated home, Taliesin, in Spring Green, Wisconsin, to see the sketches and conclude a formal agreement.

What happened next, Pope may not have foreseen: Every lending institution he turned to refused him a mortgage. Bankers generally were leery about financing modern homes, and they were being very choosy: How "modern" was it? What was the neighborhood like? Was this the only "modern" house in a neighborhood of comfortably traditional houses? In Pope's case, even though the house would be in a wooded area separate from other homes, a building-and-loan official told Pope flat out, "This house would be a white elephant."

Finally, Pope turned to his employer, and

the *Star* in March 1940 agreed to provide a loan, deducting repayment at the rate of twelve dollars a week from Pope's salary of fifty dollars. The total cost of building and furnishing the house was roughly seven thousand dollars. Construction, which began in late spring of 1940, posed difficulties comparable to those of the financing. Contractors were generally wary of modern construction and suspicious of Wright in particular. Original bids were so high that Pope gave up on hiring a general contractor. Instead, relying on one of Wright's apprentice architects, Gordon Chadwick, for overall supervision, Pope contracted individually with the separate crafts. Howard Rickert was the carpenter. Rickert was enthusiastic about the plans when he first saw them, saying it looked like a logical house. One day during construction, even more convinced, Rickert turned to Pope and exclaimed, "This is the most logical house I ever built."*

Shortly before the house was completed in March 1941, there came a defining moment eerily reminiscent of the Gropius's new house during the hurricane of '38. This time it was snow, 16 inches of it, bearing down on the flat roof. It was the biggest snowfall in northern Virginia in twenty years. As Pope recalled later, "As soon as the road was open, there was a procession of architects to the scene of the anticipated disaster and thus triumph." But the

structure of the house was more than up to the test, and the architects left shaking their heads much as had those neighbors on Baker Bridge Road.

The house into which Loren and Charlotte Pope and their young son, Ned, moved early in 1941 appears much more at one with its surroundings than the Gropius House, which, by intent, is a clearly defined structure and, painted white in deference to New England tradition, stands out against the gentle hills and orchards that are its living space. In more wooded terrain and typically for its architect, the Pope-Leighey House seems to grow out of its surroundings, to be part of them, to have an organic connection with the land. There is a strong emphasis on the horizontal, further demonstrating oneness with the land; and this accentuation of earthiness comes through still more in the earthy tones and textures of the materials—unfinished cypress, brick, and red-colored concrete. Like the Gropius, this house dispenses with what Wright called the usual "fussy lid" and has a flat roof. That is not to say that Wright disliked roofs: It was the look of the roof that was important. The house, said Wright, should materially represent shelter, and this was most noticeably accomplished by a low-spreading or flat roof with projecting eaves. The eaves also serve to control the amount of sunlight entering in summer. In-

---

* Loren Pope sold the house for seventeen thousand dollars in late 1946 and bought a 150-year-old farmhouse once owned by one of the Lees of Virginia in Loudoun County, Virginia, with the hope of replacing that structure with a Frank Lloyd Wright farmhouse. It never came to pass. Pope later returned to journalism, eventually retiring as education editor of the *New York Times*. As of this writing he was living in Alexandria, Virginia, not far from the original site of his Frank Lloyd Wright house, and was the author of two recent books on edu-

cation. Robert and Marjorie Leighey purchased the Pope house in February 1947. In 1964, with the house threatened with condemnation for construction of Interstate Route 66, Mrs. Leighey, by then a widow, appealed to the National Trust for Historic Preservation. The Trust took ownership of the house, giving Mrs. Leighey life tenancy, and moved the house to the grounds of Woodlawn Plantation, near Mount Vernon. What is now known as the Pope-Leighey House is preserved as a house museum and is open to the public.

*The Pope-Leighey House photographed in its original location in Falls Church, Virginia.* (Historic American Buildings Survey)

stead of the usual garage, there is a simple carport, another Wright innovation. Nor is there a basement; the house is constructed on a poured concrete slab. Both of these omissions were essentially cost-saving measures. Heating is radiant, using hot water flowing through wrought-iron pipe laid under the concrete-slab floor.

The house is L-shaped and, though one story, is on two levels because the original lot sloped. For its relatively modest size, it has a living room of unexpected spaciousness owing to a ceiling 11½ feet high and windows nearly the same. Inside, there is the same combination of cypress and brick that characterizes the exterior. The plan of the interior is even more open than that of the Gropius House, the small kitchen being essentially an alcove and only bath and bedrooms being fully separate. Like the Gropius, openness is dramatized by windows linking inside with outside. The fireplace is shared by both living and dining areas.

In preplastic, previnyl, pre-Formica days, this was a remarkably easy house to maintain. There was no paint and no plaster. The floor was red-colored concrete requiring nothing more than sweeping or mopping. The only maintenance needed for the cypress and brick walls was an occasional coat of clear wax.

Although designed for one particular family and place, this house was inevitably meant as a model for the modern, middle-class, American home . . . anywhere. But is it comfortable? Is it really a livable place? Is it home? Or is it just so much abstract stylishness? By the last year of World War II, Pope had risen through the ranks to become the *Washington Evening Star*'s national news editor and thus the designated target of a daily barrage of wire-service bulletins coming in like bullets on the battlefield. Here was the story of global conflict unfolding, but in bits and pieces, and it was his responsibility to see that these bits and pieces were taken in, sorted out, weighed, counted, and

2

3

*The Pope-Leighey House interior: kitchen, Fig.1,
and the living-dining areas, Figs. 2 and 3, with their
unexpected spaciousness, the result of a ceiling 11½ ft.
high. The interior finish is the same combination of
cypress and brick that characterizes the exterior.*
(Historic American Buildings Survey)

then almost instantly turned into accurate and easily comprehended accounts of a war that inevitably touched the life of everyone who would be reading and trusting that day's *Star.* It was high-stress . . . adrenalin flowing all day, and often into the night.

Pope remembered that intensity in reflecting, years later, on whether the house that Frank Lloyd Wright created was really a place to call home.

Home, as a place of creature comfort? Yes,

but more. "It was a spiritual place," recalled Pope, "it spoke to the spirit." He remembered coming home from the newsroom and finding a place of great tranquillity: "The horizontal flow that ties the house to the earth gives it great repose. And it is only the thickness of a brick to the grass outside, and beyond that the trees and woods."

Wright visited the Popes at the house several times after they were living there, and architect and home owner sometimes had breakfast together. Both the house itself and the knowingness of its architect left Pope in reverence: "It was a spiritual and religious experience. Frank Lloyd Wright meant as much to me spiritually as Emerson, Tao, or Jesus." In keeping with that spiritual feeling, it may be said that Pope, during the designing of the house, scrupulously left every detail to Wright. "Would *you,*" he explains, "tell Mozart how to write a symphony?"

Just as there is no one "modern" style, neither is there any one architect who singlehandedly accomplished the transition to the house that broke with the lineage of generations immemorial. Wright, however, came closer than any other to being the dominant innovator, and he is probably the most identifiable to the most people as the creator of the modern house in America. He himself considered the house the most creative challenge in architecture. Not all architects do. In his early twenties Wright was hired by the celebrated firm of Adler and Sullivan in Chicago. Since the firm's principal partners were more interested in major building projects, they let Wright handle whatever requests for dwellings came along. Among the first house jobs he got was designing the home of his mentor, Louis Sullivan. Wright subsequently set out on his own, contributing to American architecture such monumental projects as New York's Guggenheim Museum as well as houses large and small; in the course of a career of some seventy years he saw the remarkable total of more than four hundred of his designs built.

## FINDING PARALLELS

The Fairbanks and Gropius Houses, both clearly middle-class dwellings, were built in the same geographic area by recently arrived immigrants, three centuries apart to the year. In terms of appearance, these structures are about as different as two houses can be. But as we have seen, architecture is more than outer image; if we take the two houses apart and look at their components side by side, we will find not merely some similarities but some remarkable parallels.

### Adaptation of Design

Each of these immigrants, Jonathan Fairbanks and Walter Gropius, brought with him the image of a house as he had known it in his

*The floor plans, same scale, of the Fairbanks House* (top) *and the Gropius House* (bottom); *photographs, opposite page, of the living-dining area of the Gropius House* (left) *and the all-purpose hall of the Fairbanks House. There is comparison to be made in the similarity of free-flowing space in the Fairbanks hall and the Gropius living-dining space as well as in the fact that both are hearth-oriented. On the other hand, also to be observed is the effect of condensation of the heat source. The Fairbanks House is virtually dominated by its massive chimney stack, which, while taking up a significant amount of space, also provided a certain degree of radiant heat within the house. In the Gropius House, an efficient, modern heating system leaves just that much more room for living space.* (Floor plans by Dolores Malecki-Spivack, architect. Gropius House photograph by David Bohl, courtesy of the Society for the Preservation of New England Antiquities. Fairbanks House photograph, Historic American Buildings Survey)

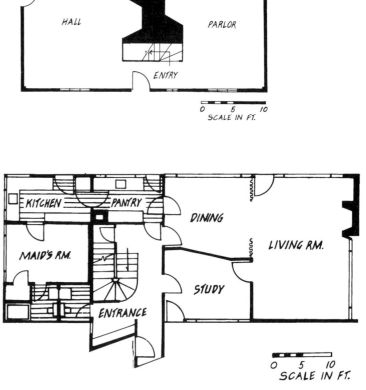

homeland, yet each made no attempt to keep that image intact. In the case of Fairbanks the change was notably that overcoat he gave his half-timber house for its colder new home. Gropius, as we have seen, went to a greater degree of adaptation, consciously seeking to infuse elements of New England construction. Similarly . . .

## Functionality

"Unostentatious . . . clearly defined" (quoting Gropius) describes either the Fairbanks or the Gropius House. Certainly Gropius thought it was so, and for him it was part of a conscious awareness, indeed an appreciation, of the basic integrity of style and structure of the early New England house. He said so in words that might as well as have been written by the builder of Fairbanks's house:

> I tried to face the problem in much the same way as the early builders of the region

had faced it when, with the best technical means at their disposal, they built unostentatious, clearly defined buildings that were able to withstand the rigors of the climate and that expressed the social attitude of their inhabitants.

On another occasion Gropius wrote of a strong parallel between early New England architecture and the "spirit [of] simplicity, functionality, and uniformity" that was likewise a hallmark of the Bauhaus. There is also an ironic twist to this affinity between the modern and the colonial. A dinner guest of the Gropiuses in 1938 was one John Adams, a descendent of *the* Adamses. As recalled by Ise Gropius, Adams tempered his conspicuous distaste for modern architecture after visiting the Gropius's house, allowing that there was indeed something of New England tradition preserved in it and that therefore it couldn't be all bad.

## Materials

The Fairbanks and Gropius Houses both have wood exteriors. Gropius's affinity of spirit was matched by his conscious use of materials characteristic of New England, especially clapboard, brick, and fieldstone, as well as by the use of white paint, which he considered an American invention.

## Construction

The Fairbanks House was notable for its rugged post-and-beam construction—summer beams 10 by 10 inches, roof plates 7 by 7 inches, rafters 5 by 5 inches, studs 4 by 6 inches. Frames gradually became lighter, and by the mid 19th century the balloon frame, using small-dimension lumber, was becoming common; by the early 20th century it was nearly universal. Gropius, however, returned to a rugged timber frame—sills 4 by 8 inches, corner posts 4 by 6 inches, all cut to specification—that was reminiscent of houses of Fairbanks's time. This heavy framing, supplemented by steel I beams, was his choice to accommodate the oversize windows that provided a panoramic view of those fields and orchards.

## Open Plan

Much is made, and rightly so, of the open plan of the modern house. Yet essentially the same was true of the hall of the Fairbanks House. Here was one space that was free-flowing with family activity. It was also the site of . . .

## The Hearth

The nucleus of life in the Fairbanks House was the hearth. Fireplaces continued to be the principal means of cooking and heating through the mid to late 19th century. As central heating became common from the early 1900s on, the fireplace was an expensive option that was increasingly omitted. Its appearance in the

*Frank Lloyd Wright's Fallingwater, Mill Run, Pennsylvania (1937): centrality of the hearth. Paradoxical to the outspoken modernism of the house (although not inadvertently so, given the significance of the hearth) is the link with early tradition to be found in the swinging arm and kettle, so reminiscent of an 18th-century fireplace.* (Historic American Buildings Survey)

*Fallingwater.* (Historic American Buildings Survey)

Walter Gropius House thus makes it an emphatic link with tradition. Frank Lloyd Wright was something of a fanatic about including fireplaces in his houses, regardless of size or locale, for the psychological value of the hearth. Wright's Fallingwater—as strikingly "modern" a house as has yet been built anywhere—has a fireplace with a swinging arm and kettle attached, ever so reminiscent of an 18th-century hearth.

## Windows

The windows of the Fairbanks House were leaded casements, the predominant type of window in use. By the early 18th century the casement was going out of fashion; many new houses were fitted with double-hung sashes, and older dwellings were "modernized" as fast as the new sashes could be installed. This was true even of the Fairbanks House, where only fragments of some of the original casements remain. The modern house, as exemplified in both the Gropius and the Pope-Leighey, disdains the "old-fashioned" double-hung in favor of the visual and mechanical simplicity of casements or awning windows.

## Minimal Storage

Unlike the modern house, the Fairbanks has an attic and a cellar, but *no* closet space whatsoever. The Gropius and Pope-Leighey, dispensing with attic and cellar, immediately keep storage to a minimum but provide a very finite amount of closet space. One basically equals the other.

## Appearance

Of course one can find dissimilarity, and here the parallels seem to break down. The Gropius and Fairbanks houses don't look anything alike. They are of two very different eras and represent two very different but equally valid conceptions of what a house should look like.

And yet . . . viewing these two structures from a great distance, squinting so as to make out objects but not details, one would see something darkly somber and something else light-colored. Approaching, one would be able to define the two as houses. In their present form, the Fairbanks would be darkly colored— indeed, austere; and the Gropius, bright against its backdrop of woods and meadows. Were this 1937, the latter would surely be so; were this 1637, or let's say a few years later, to allow for getting settled down, the former might not be so at all. It has been taken for granted that the American house of the early 17th century, especially in New England, must have been a bleak and gloomy and colorless place befitting Puritan virtues. In fact it was probably much more cheerful, and historical perception has been changing in this direction with the help of more modern and scientific methods of analysis. The Fairbanks House for years was meticulously stained dark brown to keep up its image of austerity. The staining has ceased. Existing clapboard siding is being allowed to fade back to something approaching its natural patina; new clapboard will be left untreated. This, now, is understood to have been the original order of things. The clapboard of the Fairbanks House, when new, was left simply to age to gray. Furthermore, there is a possibility that the exterior window frames were painted some bright color or another. There is recently uncovered evidence elsewhere of bright colors—reds and blues and perhaps others—on the chamfering of interior posts and beams of 17th-century houses, and indeed even of some of the beams and posts themselves.

Now, squinting through the mist of time, wherein gray and white become indistinguishable, we might see two houses side by side and detect one as monochromatic and the other as reflecting bright hues. Which is the modern house?

## EARLY ARCHITECTURAL TRADITIONS

Of houses built in Jonathan Fairbanks's time, there is arguably no other as old still standing

and only a few approaching it in age (see footnote at the beginning of chapter 1 for other early examples). It is hardly surprising that there are so few remaining, since there were relatively so few built; colonial settlement in 1637, when Fairbanks raised his house, probably totaled less than fifty thousand. Those houses that were constructed were mostly very modest in size; the house of Arthur Allen that has come to be known as Bacon's Castle (c1655, in Surrey, Virginia) was larger and more ornate, with its angled chimneys and curved gables, but was in a small minority compared with what the Fairbankses were building. Likely the largest structure in America at that time was a continent away, in Santa Fe, the timber and adobe Palace of the Governors (c1610), which, still standing and continuously occupied, antedates the Fairbanks House as a structure but not as a house, let alone a middle-class home.

American houses of the 1600s likewise retained their medieval mien, as did houses generally in England. London itself was still essentially a medieval city at the time of the Great Fire of 1666 and its great cathedral, Saint Paul's, still a Gothic structure, although there had been attempts to modernize it with a classical front, and plans for a dome by Christopher Wren (1632–1723) were on the drawing board at the very time that fire destroyed not only the cathedral but two-thirds of London.

This matter of doming a Gothic cathedral gets us to a point: It was during the 17th century that England went through its first wave of classicism in architecture, beginning conspicuously with Inigo Jones (1573–1652). Jones had traveled in Italy and observed firsthand the Roman antiquities that were the substance of Renaissance architecture. Following his return, as surveyor of the king's works he produced what is generally regarded as his masterpiece—the sumptuous Banqueting House in Whitehall, with elaborately painted ceilings by Rubens, built (1619–1622) at precisely the same time the settlers at Plymouth were coping with the wilderness and were happy to have a roof of any kind over their heads.

It was more or less a century later that the basic principles of classicism would penetrate the architecture of the Colonies. A notable but mysterious example of classicism is a house in Boston that was demolished in 1833 and is thus preserved only as a woodcut published in 1836 by the *American Magazine of Useful Knowledge*. What is known is that it was built about 1688 by John Foster, who became rich as a merchant after emigrating from England, and that the house eventually passed into the hands of his wife's nephew, Thomas Hutchinson, hence to be known as the Foster-Hutchinson House. As portrayed in *American Magazine*, it had such astounding features, given the prevailing postmedieval architecture of the time, as three-story pilasters of the Ionic order, a roof of fairly shallow pitch with a balustrade over the eaves, a balustraded balcony over the front entrance way, carved stone trim, and formal, symmetrical composition. These were features ranging generally from a half to a full century ahead of their time in America. It may, of course, be argued that these were add-ons of some 18th-century remodeling that also involved a lowering of the pitch of the roof. And all of that is *possible*, except that the pilasters are made of stone and set 2 inches deep into the brick of the facade. To

*Mystery house: the Foster-Hutchinson House, Boston, believed to have been built c1688. It was demolished in 1833. (American Magazine of Useful Knowledge, Feb. 1836)*

*From medieval to "modern": the Isaac Royall House, Medford, Massachusetts. The sketch (facing page) shows the original brick farmhouse of the later 1600s, with its steeply pitched roof, in solid black. A lean-to of somewhat later construction is the area shown in medium shading.* (Right) *The house as completed by 1737 is an early and notable example of the Georgian style that was the "modern" of the 18th century.* (Photograph, Historic American Buildings Survey; sketch, *Medford Historical Register,* 1900)

do that retroactively would have taken chiseling of a laboriousness beyond anything that is credible. Because the house is long since gone, the mystery remains; that the house may well have existed in the late 17th century exactly or mostly as portrayed in 1836 is at least evidence of profound change taking place.

Another early example, also no longer extant, is the William Clarke House in Boston (c1712). This was a three-story, twenty-six-room mansion built of brick, perfectly symmetrical in appearance, with dormers carefully placed in vertical alignment with the windows on the floors below, each dormer capped with either a classical arch or a classical pediment. The formal entryway was surmounted by a broken pediment. The windows were all of the new fashion—double-hung sashes, with rectangular panes instead of the increasingly old-fashioned leaded casements. A somewhat later instance does survive—the Isaac Royall House in Medford, Massachusetts. Its nucleus is a brick farmhouse of the later 1600s. Over and around this was built (see illustration, page 229) a considerably larger house for Royall, who acquired the farmhouse along with six hundred acres of farmland in 1732. Royall's new house—completed by 1737, the year he moved in—was clearly of the new fashion. Notable in particular is its west facade, which is of simulated stone evocative of the Renaissance and has colossal (ground to roof) fluted pilasters, pedimented double-hung sash windows, and an entryway of Ionic pilasters capped by a segmented arch—all combined with obvious deference to classical rules of symmetry.

This infusion of classical detail and symmetry early in the 18th century produced what

is generally known as Georgian architecture. Inspired by a new English translation of the highly influential Italian architect and scholar Andrea Palladio (1508–1580), builders quickly picked up on the new fashion from the turn of the 18th century on, almost overnight stigmatizing anything of medieval appearance as ignorant in this, the Century of Enlightenment.

This new architecture flourished among the affluent, who had both the knowledge and the means to use it. But the trickle-down also came quickly, as we have already seen in New London, Connecticut. The house that Joshua Hempsted built in 1678 (see chapter 2) had the same rather austere, steep-roofed, leaded-window postmedieval ambience as the Fairbanks House. When grandson Nathaniel, exactly fifty years later, built an addition to

accommodate the starting of a family, he chose the new style, or at least what semblance of it he could afford. Perhaps the most noticeable difference was Nathaniel's roof; it was a less steeply pitched roof typical of Georgian rather than what had still been prevalent in 1678. Noticeable, indeed. Here was half a house with one kind of roof and half with another, and one roof higher than the other. It was a troubling enough disparity that Joshua II, living in the original house, rebuilt his roof to more or less equalize the two. Nathaniel's addition also included the new fashion in windows—rectangular-paned double-hung sashes. There was also now some sense of symmetry; what had been a house one room wide with a chimney at the end now became a central-chimney house two rooms wide.

Beyond windows and roof lines, new features of Georgian architecture included paneled doors instead of batten, concealment of beams, full interior plastering, and increasing use of classical details (columns, pilasters, pediments, architraves). There was also a trend toward larger buildings. Virtually all the houses in the English colonies of the 1600s were one room deep under the main roof, which is to say, single pile (the so-called saltbox is one-room deep with a separate room under an essentially separate roof over the rear). The Georgian era characteristically produced double-pile (two-room-deep) houses, more often than not with a central chimney but also with end chimneys in warmer climates. Unlike other changes in detail, however, chimneys tended to remain the same rather massive structures that they were in the postmedieval period.

*The Benjamin Hall,
Jr., House, Medford,
Massachusetts, 1785:
later Georgian.*
(Historic American
Buildings Survey)

In its logic and simplicity, Georgian is a material reflection of the Age of Reason, and if there is a single epitome, it is perhaps Williamsburg, Virginia. It was one of the smallest of the colonial capitals, and, given the nature of colonial plantation society and the absence of a port (such as made possible the grand and imposing homes of Newport, Philadelphia, Annapolis, and Charleston), Williamsburg was a city of mostly modest homes. These were sufficient for the tradesmen, craftsmen, and artisans who were its permanent population and even for wealthy planters while staying in town for business or when the legislature was in session (this coinciding also with the social season). Yet paradoxically Williamsburg in the early 18th century was also the site of what was probably the largest structure yet built in the colonies, what is now known as the Wren Building (1699) at the College of William and Mary.

Despite the modest size of most of its houses, it is Williamsburg that uniquely captures the Age of Reason in brick and clapboard. Owing in part to a town plan adopted soon after its becoming the capital of Virginia in 1699 and in part to the tradition of its early builders, the impress of Reason is evident in the symmetry and proportion that is often accomplished in subtle ways: in geometric balance, for example, and in use of the square and triangle in particular. The Orrell House is an exact square—28 by 28 feet in area, and 28 feet from the top of the basement wall to the ridge

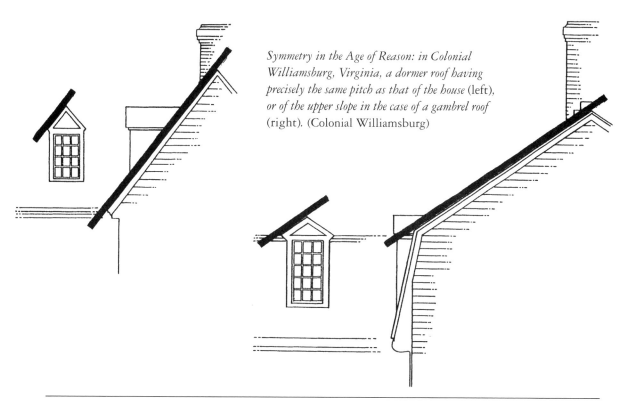

*Symmetry in the Age of Reason: in Colonial Williamsburg, Virginia, a dormer roof having precisely the same pitch as that of the house* (left), *or of the upper slope in the case of a gambrel roof* (right). (Colonial Williamsburg)

of the roof. A coincidence? Not likely. The builder of the Archibald Blair House used a triangle to determine its height. The chimney tops are at the apex of an equilateral triangle whose sides are the same as the length of the house. A Williamsburg characteristic virtually unknown elsewhere, except for a few examples in Maryland and the Carolinas, is the custom of making the pitch of the roof of the dormer precisely the same as the pitch of the main roof (if a gambrel, the upper slope). The town's original building act set a minimum of "ten foot pitch" (height of the first floor) and a square and a half 20 feet by 30 feet as the smallest permissible house on Duke of Gloucester, the main street. Other regulations dictated house orientation (all to "front alike" on the main

street), house location, and fence lines. Though not a matter of requirement, Williamsburg's many gardens were probably also full of geometric patterns and have been restored accordingly.

Not all 18th-century buildings were so carefully thought out. There was ever-increasing proliferation of architectural pattern books arriving in the Colonies from London, dozens of different titles before the Revolution. Readers ran the gamut from builders, charged with executing contracts for specific projects, to men of learning. Sometimes houses were built almost completely from given designs; more often, details were borrowed from this design or that, from one book or several.

*Changing forms of construction: The early timber house was a post and beam structure made up of massive framing components—studs 4 by 6 in., roof plates 7 by 7 in., summer beams as large as 11 by 11 in.—assembled entirely with mortise-and-tenon joints. Shown here (Fig.1) is a section of the Fairbanks House as portrayed in its entirety on page 15. Atypically, the Fairbanks uses two-story posts and studs, a practice going back to the medieval period when the hall was open to the ceiling. Generally speaking, timber houses of the 17th century, though of the same massive construction, were using single-story framing components. By the 19th century the process reversed itself. The balloon frame (Fig. 2) that came into use in the 1830s and dominated house construction for more than a century was a natural for the building boom that accompanied the rapid growth of the nation in the 19th century. It made use of lightweight studs (lumber now instead of timber, owing to mechanized sawmills) and nails rather than mortise-and-tenon joints (another result of industrialization). Posts and studs were once again two-story. The net result was a frame that was much cheaper and easier to build than the old post and beam. But evolution once again reversed the cycle in the 20th century. The so-called platform frame (Fig. 3), now virtually universal, is assembled floor by floor with one-story posts and studs, generally two-by-fours and two-by-sixes. It is actually simpler to build than the balloon frame; it is also more rigid and is more fire-resistant because each floor is a separate box.* (Fairbanks House adapted from illustration on page 15 by June Strong, © Fairbanks Family in America Inc.; balloon and platform frame illustrations by Dolores Malecki-Spivack, architect)

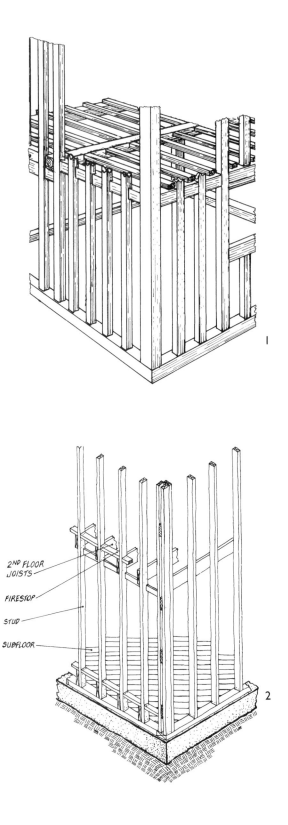

1

2ND FLOOR JOISTS

FIRESTOP

STUD

SUBFLOOR

2

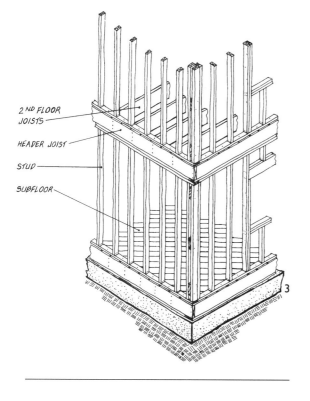

2ND FLOOR
JOISTS

HEADER JOIST

STUD

SUBFLOOR

## A DEVELOPING DIVERSITY

In Frederick, Maryland, we saw Schifferstadt, the home built in 1756 by German immigrant Elias Brunner. Look at it again from the perspective of this review of architecture and styles. Although not Georgian, it has similarity in its symmetry, carried out to the degree that windows and doors on one side match those on the other, creating cross ventilation. And it has a center hall, like a typical Georgian plan, although the stairs use a separate well to the side rather than the hall itself. The windows are double-hung sashes. There is a kitchen, complete with an early version of the kitchen sink. In short, this is clearly a house of the 18th century, not the 17th. And yet with

its stove heating and its massive stone walls to retain heat, it must have been a rather comfortable place in winter, much more so than the typical house of its time.

In the George Read II House (1804) in New Castle, Delaware, there is an intermix of late Georgian and Federal. Its interior plan is basically Georgian, as is the rather massive chimney structure. The Palladian window is likewise an old favorite but will continue to remain in fashion. The massive entrance way, with its fanlight and sidelights, is Federal and is more imposing close up than from a distance by virtue of being raised significantly from street level, another device of the Federal period. The somewhat slender windows, capped with splayed lintels, are similarly of the new era.

Quintessentially of the new is Gore Place (1806), in Waltham, Massachusetts, the work of the prominent Paris architect J.-G. LeGrand in collaboration with Rebecca Gore. There is an intriguing balance between its overt horizontality, enhanced by the shallow roof, and the verticality of the very slender chimneys and tall windows of the central section. The other windows are actually units including the half-rounds, each within a relieving arch that adds to the sense of verticality when seen up close. The elliptical form at the center is a clue to what is going on inside: This house is also modern in its freer use of space. The oval room on the first floor is the drawing room; on the second, the family parlor. In Williamsburg geometry was used to determine proportions; now there is overt use of geometry—forms that are elliptical, triangular, octagonal, and curved. Classical orders are still in vogue, but less massive, more delicate, the columns or pilasters often attenuated. The Octagon, in

*Quintessentially Federal: Gore Place (1806), Waltham, Massachusetts.* (Photograph by the author)

Washington, D.C., and Jefferson's Monticello, already seen for their technology, possess these same qualities. Overall, the Federal style imparts airiness, lightness, gracefulness, tastefulness, harmony. In its larger expanse of glass, and in the oval room that literally protrudes into the outside world, the Federal house represents an architectural opening up of the house to the outdoors that is paralleled by the front porch's emerging as a living room of the house.

Sometimes it was a matter of retrofitting. There is a good example in a house we have al-

ready seen briefly in another light, and that is Wyck, in Philadelphia, which was notable for its very early use of central heating (see chapter 5). Likewise, its definition of interior space. In a letter written in May 1824, Reuben Haines III, sixth-generation owner of Wyck (built c1710 and already twice enlarged), described a major feature of a remodeling undertaken in 1824 by architect William Strickland:

We have a folding door cut through the wall of the hall opposite the niche. Another is to be cut into the entry and another into the front parlour the two latter so arranged as to meet together across the entry, cut the stairs off on one side and a vestibule on the other, and throw the parlour Hall and dining room into one complete suit of rooms. This plan is due to Strickland who was up to see us last week.

Strickland, a protégé of Benjamin Latrobe and perhaps the most prominent architect practicing in Philadelphia at the time, had taken interior space that was cramped and poorly ventilated and opened it up, both through a new layout with larger rooms and by an ingenious use of doors pivoting as much as 180 degrees. The effect was something of a forerunner of what Frank Lloyd Wright proposed. Strickland also installed larger windows that could open up more scenic views of the garden on one side and a parklike setting on the other, the effect of which was obvious to Haines as he talked fondly about "bringing outside in." Strickland's remodeling also gave Wyck an assortment of closets, including built-in cupboards in the kitchen and dining areas.

That the Federal style (sometimes also referred to as Adamesque) only became popular in America in the late 18th century and into the first decades of the 19th is another example of transatlantic delay. The brothers Adam (Robert, 1728–1792, in particular, the most significant architect of his day in England) had set in motion a new wave of classical influence

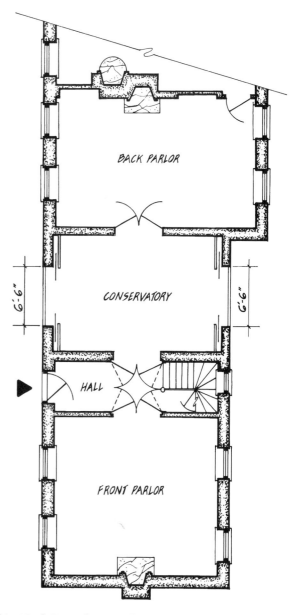

*Wyck, in Philadelphia, as remodeled by William Strickland in 1824. Formerly cramped and poorly ventilated space in a house built c1710 was opened up to "throw the parlour Hall and dining room {parlors and conservatory here, using later nomenclature} into one complete suit{e} of rooms." The key was the use of doors pivoting 90 degrees or, in the case of the back parlor, 180, to provide flexible use of space—sealing off the hall, stair hall, conservatory, and/or front parlor, as appropriate, for social occasions. Owner Reuben Haines III also liked to talk about "bringing outside in." The exterior walls of the conservatory are virtually window walls, with the window area extending from floor to ceiling and nearly wall to wall (6 ft. 6 in.), an unusually wide expanse for the early 19th century.* (Drawing by Dolores Malecki-Spivack)

Greek Revival was the first architectural style to find popularity from coast to coast and was similarly broad in that it might be anything from the very simple to the grandiose. (Left) *The Archibald Yell House, Fayetteville, Arkansas (c1830);* (facing page left) the *D. F. Weaver House, Weavers, Alabama.* (Historic American Buildings Survey)

in England at midcentury, emphasizing grace and harmony and movement within interior spaces. This wave of interest in classicism went beyond English translations of Palladio and Roman antiquities already well known in Italy and southern France. Adam, for example, went to see firsthand the Palace of Diocletian in what is now Croatia. Archaeology was emerging as a new tool to understanding the past. Excavations at Herculaneum in 1783 and Pompeii in 1793 marked the beginning of modern archaeology. From these and other studies came new architectural models and a keener understanding of classical architecture, including the realization, in Adam's words, that the ancients were not strictly bound by rigid rules but adjusted them "as the general spirit of their compositions required." Likewise adjusting to a general spirit of the times was this new domestic architecture with its Adamesque imprint.

Something of an American Adam was Thomas Jefferson, who while serving as U.S. minister to France took to studying Roman antiquities there and was a good friend of Charles Louis Clerisseau, who had accompanied Adam to the Palace of Diocletian a quarter century earlier. Clerisseau collaborated with Jefferson on his design for the capitol of Virginia, modeled on a Roman temple of Augustus (by then known as the Maison Carrée) at Nîmes, in southern France. In Monticello as enlarged and remodeled between 1796 and 1809, Jefferson evoked the features of a Roman villa as described by Cicero and Pliny the Younger while using a basic Palladian scheme.

While Jefferson and some others were continuing to look to Rome for their inspiration, others were turning to ancient Greece. Studies of the ancient world had concentrated largely on Rome because it was nearer in distance and, as a civilization, closer in time than ancient

*At its grandest, Greek Revival was the essence of the southern plantation house. Here* (above), *one of the grandest of them all: Windsor, near Port Gibson, Mississippi, completed in 1861 and destroyed by fire in 1890. All that remains are twenty-four of its massive Corinthian columns and occasional stretches of wrought-iron railing.* (Photograph by the author)

Greece. Rome through its occupation, furthermore, had left a direct and lasting imprint on Western Europe, with an abundance of relics and traditions intact.

Greek Revival architecture began to take hold in America in the second decade of the 19th century and continued until past mid-century, helped along in popularity by America's identification with the cause of the Greeks in their own war of independence in the 1820s. Greek Revival is significant as the first style with national impact: There were examples in California almost as early as in the East. The most immediate distinction between Greek Revival and Roman-inspired designs is the absence of the arch, which was not used in Greek temple architecture. (Likewise the dome, though with the exception of Monticello this is irrelevant to domestic architecture.) All windows and doors are thus squared off; if there is a transom it is oblong, as opposed to the semi-

elliptical Adamesque fanlight and the semi-circular Georgian, with their Renaissance (Roman) inspiration. The Greek Revival roof is of very shallow pitch or flat. There is virtually no external ornament. Orders follow Greek rather than Roman tradition (for example, the Doric has no base). A further identifying feature (and the significance of this will be seen forthwith) is that wherever the structure is made of wood and thus to be painted, it is almost invariably painted white, the color that evokes the marble of the temple prototype. Greek Revival was the choice for many a stately mansion, not least of

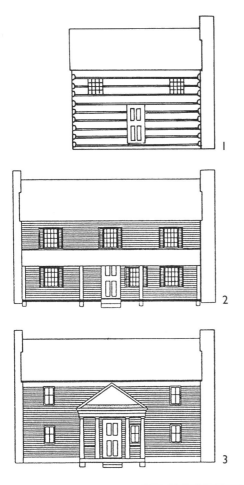

1

2

3

*The evolution of a house: When John Tipton settled in the wilderness of eastern Tennessee in 1784, he bought property on what had once been a buffalo trail. For the sake of expediency, like many another pioneer, he built the simplest kind of dwelling: a log cabin (Fig.1) that consisted of one large room with a loft. Perhaps to make it more secure against Indian attack, he built the cabin high, with windows only in the loft area. German stonemasons built the chimney of limestone and used stone chips as chinking between the logs. By sometime in the early 19th century, the cabin, now owned by John Tipton, Jr., had been expanded (Fig. 2) by knocking out the wall opposite the chimney and stretching the one large room into a sitting room and parlor downstairs and three bedrooms upstairs. The log exterior was now covered with clapboard. A porch with a shed roof was also added. In 1831 the house came into the ownership of Landon Carter Haynes, who further changed it (Fig. 3) by knocking down the shed porch and, in the fashion of the times, replacing it with one of modified Greek Revival style. He took off the shutters, made the windows narrower, and added an ell in the back that included a kitchen, dining room, and pantry. This is the house essentially as it is today. The original limestone chimney is on the right, more massive than its 19th-century counterpart on the left, and underneath the stylish facade is still that original log structure of 1784. (Drawings courtesy of the Tipton-Haynes Historical Association)*

all the Southern plantation house. But it was easily adaptable to modest dwellings. Built with its gable fronting the street and given a shallow-pitched roof and a few columns out front, a modest house at least seemed fashionable. Especially if painted white. Visiting Worcester, Massachusetts, during his American tour of 1842, Charles Dickens found, "All the buildings looked as if they had been painted that morning. . . . Every house is the whitest of white."

## SEEING IN CONTRAST

But times were changing, and this matter of color gets right to the point:

There is one colour . . . we feel bound to protest against most heartily, as entirely unsuitable, and in bad taste. This is *white*, which is so universally applied to our wooden houses of every size and description. The glaring nature of this colour, when seen in contrast with the soft green of foliage, renders it extremely unpleasant to any eye attuned to harmony of colouring, and nothing but its very great prevalence in the United States could render even men of some taste so heedless of its bad effect. No painter of landscapes, that has possessed a name, was ever guilty of displaying in his pictures a glaring white house. . . . (A. J. Downing, *Cottage Residences,* 1842)

American painting, heretofore predominantly portraiture, had been shifting to landscape during the early decades of the 19th century. By the 1820s Thomas Cole and others were finding their inspiration in the romantic beauty of the American outdoors, particularly the craggy vistas of the Hudson River valley. Their colors were those of nature—the colors of earth, grass, stone, wood, moss, and all flowering things. That the color white was not on their palette (except for bright touches) was due not only to its rarity in nature but to its absence as a quality of romanticism. To be perfectly symmetrical and logical was to be the color white, as in the marble of a perfectly symmetrical, perfectly logical Greek temple. To be gray, brown, or mossy green was to have feeling, to have sentiment, to have emotion, to be worshipers at that great asymmetrical temple we call nature.

This was the age of romanticism, defined not only in architecture but in music, by such bucolic excursions as Beethoven's Pastoral Symphony (1808), and in art, by Cole and his followers.

A. J. Downing was America's first great landscape architect (he was chosen to lay out the grounds of the U.S. Capitol, White House, and Smithsonian Institution in 1851 but died before he could carry out the project) and was practically as significant in the architecture of houses. His *Cottage Residences* (1842) was one of various such books that helped to popularize this new era. And as romanticism by its nature represented individuality and diversity, so did the architectural styles it encompassed. *Cottage Residences* included houses in the "Gothic," "Tudor," "Old English," "Rhine," "Italian, or Tuscan," and "Italian, Bracketed" styles. Downing's own favorite seemed to be "Gothic," or what is more accurately known as Gothic Revival, the earliest and in many ways most expressive, most individual, most emotional of these picturesque new styles.

Gothic Revival is most frequently to be seen in the architecture of churches dating from roughly the 1840s through the late 19th century. Among houses it dates to Benjamin Latrobe's Sedgeley, built near Philadelphia in 1790 (the first Gothic Revival domestic structure in America). Sedgeley in turn was based on occasional, recent use of Gothic in and around London, dating back to Strawberry Hill, an English countryside cottage that Horace Walpole romanticized into a pseudo-Gothic castle in the mid 1700s, generally regarded as the first such use of neo-Gothic stylization for a house.

In its usefulness in provoking emotion—the literature of the time had the Gothic novel, with its evocation of the grotesque and mysterious—Gothic architecture was an ideal vehicle for moving romanticism into the mainstream. It was also easily adaptable to the use of stained glass. And its bargeboards and other trim worked wonderfully well jigsawed into delicate reminiscences of the tracery of real Gothic stained-glass windows—into ornamentation called gingerbread, a virtual art form that proliferated along with technological development of the mechanical scroll saw from the 1840s on. With its usually steeply pitched roof and often somber color, Gothic was the medieval, revived and romanticized.

As applied to houses in America, Gothic began to gain popularity in the 1830s; and including its Victorian high style phase, it continued to be popular until late in the century. We have met (see chapter 4) two examples, one extant and one not, in Hartford. The earlier and no longer existing is Oakholm, the dream house that Harriet Beecher Stowe built with the profits of *Uncle Tom's Cabin.* It was too big, too expensive, too costly to maintain, insisted Calvin Stowe. And in the end he was right. The Stowes eventually moved to another house in Hartford, this one already built, this one also Gothic Revival. For Harriet, and for countless others in this century of Victorian piousness, Gothic was a fitting symbol of how the house might go beyond mere bricks and lumber to be a symbol of the lodging of the soul. In designing Oakholm, Harriet made the most of the Christian symbolism inherent in Gothic as the "architecture of Christianity," summed up in finials in the shape of crosses on each of the house's eight gables.

Oakholm the mansion, of course, is no more; it was demolished sometime after the Stowes abandoned its grandeur for the more modest and more practical house into which they moved in 1874 and with which we are far more familiar. Here on Forest Street in Hartford we have a house architecturally mirroring the essential mood of the mid to late 19th century yet paradoxically also hinting at the house of the 20th century. For here, more than in most dwellings of its time, we see the house striving to incorporate technological change. We have observed that Harriet was somewhat ahead of her time in the degree to which her house reflected changing concepts of comfort and convenience. Through both personal predisposition to cleanliness and religious attitudes (cleanliness and godliness) she was adamant about personal hygiene and so saw to it that this house had a bathroom with tub, sink, and water closet—at a time when just running water to a kitchen was modern enough. Through personal commitment to the changing role of women, she modernized the kitchen, presumably (some of these details are conjectural; see chapter 4) with an efficient work center that included a built-in sink, continuous counter, and lots of shelves, all adjacent to a modern cast-iron coal stove yet also handy to a nearby pantry with an icebox that automatically emptied itself of melted ice.

Here was technological change, yet here also was architectural change, for now there was a conscious effort to design (or at least remodel, since Harriet was not the first owner) a kitchen so that efficiency and usefulness were inherent qualities. In terms of interior space and function generally, we have here the house in recognizably modern form. Besides the kitchen and bathroom, we have central heating—a furnace in the cellar supplying central heat to at least some rooms, although fireplaces continued to be used for supplementary effect. Central heating, particularly as it becomes common early in the 20th century, will have more impact on room use and layout. When only room heat existed (by fireplace or stove), the effort necessary to tend the fire made it common for various family members to share the one or two rooms being heated for an assortment of purposes. Central heating helped to expand room use, a process leading to the open plan of Wright, Gropius, and so many others in the 20th century.

## FULL CIRCLES

Rooted in a romanticism that exalted individualism and diversity, this was an age that produced a diversity of styles. These others were frequently found:

### Italianate

Derived from the picturesque Italian villa, or farmhouse, with its characteristic square tower, or cupola. The roof is low-pitched and noticeably overhanging, supported by brackets. Windows are usually rounded. A piazza is common. Popular from roughly the 1840s to the 1880s.

### Second Empire

A style based on what was popular in Paris during the reign of the emperor Napoleon III (1852–1870), the so-called Second Empire. The most distinctive feature is its mansard roof. Usually symmetrical, commonly with a projecting central pavilion. Very ornate; for example, in the cresting on the roof. Popular between the 1860s and 1890s.

### Queen Anne

An eclectic style notable for its tall chimneys, turrets, towers, steep roofs, and imaginative use of surface texture (notably bricks and shingles). The name is a misnomer since the style has nothing to do with the reign of En-

gland's Queen Anne (1702–1714) but rather evokes qualities of medieval architecture. Popular from the 1880s until after the turn of the century.

### Shingle Style

A more formal working of contemporary forms, especially of Queen Anne, with which it has much in common while more subdued. Emphasis on uniformity as opposed to the rampant eclecticism characteristic of Queen Anne. Popular from the 1880s to World War I.

The first two of these forms, Gothic Revival and Italianate, were waning in popularity when E. J. Lewis, M.D., moved his family across the street to the new home he built in Sauk Centre, Minnesota, in 1889. Hence we have in the Sinclair Lewis House a structure reminiscent of the Stowe House but with a lessening of all those elements that made the latter more "Victorian." Here is a roof less steeply pitched; indeed, with an angle of about 45 degrees at the apex, it is virtually a definition of average. The gingerbread is mostly gone, except for tiny vestiges atop the front-porch posts. Gone the evocation of Gothic verticality. Gone any pointed windows; they are all squared off now. As a style, the house is what might be summed up as "late-Victorian Eclectic Vernacular," a sufficiently vague and inclusive term to account for what is probably the great majority of middle-class homes built in America in the late 19th and early 20th centuries. These were houses that held on to essentially Victorian forms but with obvious self-consciousness about all the excess.

Much more substantive and demonstrable reaction to Victorian styles showed itself in the

(Upper left) *Italianate: Rensselaer Russell House, Waterloo, Iowa (1862–1863).* (Historic American Buildings Survey)

*Second Empire: J. Monroe Parker House, Davenport, Iowa* (lower left and right). (Historic American Buildings Survey)

Colonial Revival, or what might more properly be called the Georgian Revival, since it is the Georgian phase of the colonial era rather than the postmedievalism of the 17th century that is being celebrated. Its origins were in the Philadelphia Centennial Exposition of 1876, which, celebrating the declaring of independence one hundred years earlier, focused new attention on the nation's colonial roots. As architecture, Colonial Revival invoked the integrity inherent in classical forms, but often with exaggerated detail and exaggerated mass.

The first wave had popularity between the 1880s and the 1920s, but the "colonial" has been a fixture of residential architecture ever since. Early Colonial Revival was followed by reincarnations of Spanish, French, Dutch, and Tudor architecture.

A separate current was the Arts and Crafts Movement, a rejection of the industrialization of the Victorian era and its mass-production impress on the house in favor of a purity and honesty of style reflecting handcrafted workmanship. Although primarily applicable to

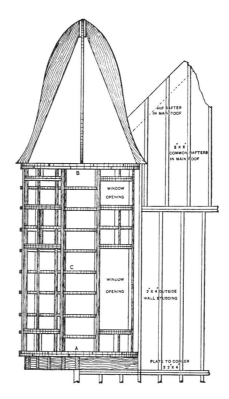

*Lightweight framing techniques of the 19th century also made feasible some of the decorative elements so characteristic of Victorian architecture. A popular feature, especially of Queen Anne style, was the turret. Here is how it was done. (Hodgson, Light and Heavy Framing [1909])*

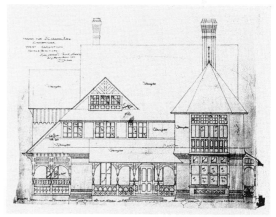

*Queen Anne: Edward S. Dodge House, Cambridge, Massachusetts (1878). The ink-on-linen drawing is by the architects, Longfellow and Clark, and shows a few minor modifications in the course of construction.* (Historic American Buildings Survey)

furniture, Arts and Crafts translated into the Craftsman house (so called for its popularization by *Craftsman* magazine, published by furniture designer Gustav Stickley) and the Bungalow style, both of which took root in southern California and flowered by the hundreds of thousands throughout the country in the first decades of the 20th century.

While *Craftsman* was popularizing one form of very middle-class house, the *Ladies' Home Journal* in 1900–1901 was letting various architects take turns at the "Model Suburban House Which Can Be Built at Moderate Cost." In February 1901 it was the turn of a young and still not widely known architect named Frank Lloyd Wright. What he supplied was "A Home in a Prairie Town." That it reflected his prairie roots is clear in the accompanying text: "The exterior recognizes the influence of the prairie, is firmly and broadly associated with the site, and makes a feature of its quiet level." Here we see already a sense of the organic that will characterize Wright's work in the half century ahead. The exterior finish is cement on metal lath for durability and

economy of construction. The interior is, in some ways, more interesting, for here we have a virtual open plan. On the first floor there is continuous space from one end of the house to the other, a distance of 56 feet, encompassing living room and overhead gallery, library, and dining room—what otherwise at this time would still have been separate and clearly defined rooms and yet is almost exactly what William Strickland had in mind nearly a century earlier at Wyck with his plan to "throw the parlour Hall and dining room into one complete suit[e] of rooms." In Wright's plan the central section of this considerable area, what is labeled living room with gallery above, is two stories high. Here, instead of looking back, we preview the living room of Loren Pope's house nearly four decades later: a space 11½ feet high in contrast to the lower-ceilinged space around it—a familiar characteristic of Wright houses. The "gallery feature" here is optional. Wright thought it desirable "because of the happy sense of variety and depth it lends to the composition of the interior, and the sunlight it gains from above," ac-

*Near mirror images: the prairie country—low and wide and gently terraced—just outside Spring Green, Wisconsin, Frank Lloyd Wright's birthplace, and the Prairie House (an early example, Wright's contribution to a series of designs for model homes of moderate cost in the* Ladies' Home Journal *in 1901). In the roots of one architect, the roots of a new perspective of the house in America. (Left,* photograph by the author; *right,* Ladies' Home Journal, *Feb. 1901)*

cording to the *Journal*'s text. If this design were adapted to the needs of a large family, however, the living room might be one story, the gallery eliminated, and two additional bedrooms constructed above the living room. Otherwise to be noted in Wright's design is the use of casement windows of a style not merely evocative but almost duplicative of the casement of the 17th century.

The concept of open plan in Wright's suburban house makes the first-floor living area practically one very large 17th-century hall, complete with massive fireplace as its focal center. We have already observed that Wright liked fireplaces for the psychological value of the hearth. Just as we found parallels between the Gropius House and the Fairbanks, so too in this instance. It all comes together as expressed in the text: The 1901 plan

> is arranged to offer the least resistance to a simple mode of living, in keeping with a high ideal of the family life together.

It is a description that works equally as well for the Fairbanks family's hall of 1637 . . . or, for that matter, the Pope family's living room of 1940. Architectural evolution, like architectural design, runs not only in straight lines but in angles and, here and there, full circles.

# The Focus Houses

The focus houses included in this book are all active house museums open to the public. Their locations and governing agencies are given here. Some may be open only seasonally. They are listed in the order in which they appear in the book.

**FAIRBANKS HOUSE,** 511 East Street, Dedham, Massachusetts. Fairbanks Family in America, Inc., 511 East Street, Dedham, MA 02026. Telephone (617) 326-1170.

**JOSHUA HEMPSTED HOUSE,** 11 Hempsted Street, New London, Connecticut. Antiquarian and Landmarks Society, 66 Forest Street, Hartford, CT 06105. Telephone (860) 247-8996.

**SCHIFFERSTADT,** 1110 Rosemont Avenue, Frederick, Maryland. Frederick County Landmarks Foundation, 1110 Rosemont Avenue, Frederick, MD 21701. Telephone (301) 663-3885.

**HEYWARD-WASHINGTON HOUSE,** 87 Church Street, Charleston, South Carolina. The Charleston Museum, 360 Meeting Street, Charleston, SC 29403. Site telephone (803) 722-0354.

**GEORGE READ II HOUSE AND GARDENS,** 42 The Strand, New Castle, Delaware. Historical Society of Delaware, 505 Market Street, Wilmington, DE 19801. Site telephone (302) 322-8411.

**MONTGOMERY PLACE,** Annandale-on-Hudson, New York. Historic Hudson Valley, 150 White Plains Road, Tarrytown, NY 10591. Site telephone (914) 758-5461.

**MONTICELLO,** Charlottesville, Virginia. Monticello, Home of Thomas Jefferson, P.O. Box 316, Charlottesville, VA 22901. Telephone (804) 984-9822.

**GORE PLACE,** 52 Gore Street, Waltham, Massachusetts. Gore Place Society, 52 Gore Street, Waltham, MA 02154. Telephone (617) 894-2798.

**RUNDLET-MAY HOUSE,** 364 Middle Street, Portsmouth, New Hampshire. Society for the Preservation of New England Antiquities, 141 Cambridge Street, Boston, MA 02114. Site telephone (603) 436-3205.

**JOSEPH PRIESTLEY HOUSE,** 472 Priestley Avenue, Northumberland, Pennsylvania. Pennsylvania Historical and Museum Commission, Box 1026, Harrisburg, PA 17108-1026. Telephone (717) 473-9474.

**THE OCTAGON,** New York Avenue and 18th Street NW, Washington, D.C. American Architectural Foundation, 1799 New York Avenue NW, Washington, DC 20006. Telephone (202) 638-3105.

**LINDENWALD,** Route 9-H, Kinderhook, New York. National Park Service, Martin Van Buren National Historic Site, P.O. Box 545, Kinderhook, NY 12106. Telephone (518) 758-9689.

**HARRIET BEECHER STOWE HOUSE,** 73 Forest Street, Hartford, Connecticut. Stowe Day Foundation, 77 Forest Street, Hartford, CT 06105. Telephone (860) 522-9258.

**DAVID DAVIS MANSION,** 1000 East Monroe, Bloomington, Illinois. State of Illinois, Illinois Historic Preservation Agency, Division of Historic Sites, Old State Capitol, Springfield, IL 62701. Site telephone (309) 828-1084.

**SINCLAIR LEWIS BOYHOOD HOME,** Sinclair Lewis Avenue, Sauk Centre, Minnesota. Sinclair Lewis Foundation, Highway 71 and I-94 South, Sauk Centre, MN 56378. Telephone (320) 352-5201.

**WYCK,** 6026 Germantown Avenue, Philadelphia, Pennsylvania. Wyck Association, 6026 Germantown Avenue, Philadelphia, PA 19144. Telephone (215) 848-1690.

**GROPIUS HOUSE,** 68 Baker Bridge Road, Lincoln, Massachusetts. Society for the Preservation of New England Antiquities, 141 Cambridge Street, Boston, MA 02114. Site telephone (781) 259-8098.

**POPE-LEIGHEY HOUSE,** 9000 Richmond Highway, Mount Vernon, Virginia. National Trust for Historic Preservation, 1785 Massachusetts Avenue NW, Washington, DC 20036. Site telephone (703) 780-4000.

# The American Home and the Emergence of Technology

Relative to time and place, the Fairbanks House was a comfortable home in which to live in 1637; likewise the Gropius House in the 20th century—clear evidence of how much standards of comfort and convenience had changed.

In the following pages, using a cross-section of homes, the emergence of technology is revealed house by house. Most of this data was obtained from a survey, "The American Home and the Development of Domestic Technology," prepared by the author and sent from Henry Holt and Company to a sampling of historic houses throughout America. Additional data was obtained directly by the author through personal contacts and visits as well as through research in general for this book.

There is not space to include all houses for which replies were received. Priority was given to data significantly helping to date the early use of technology as well as ampleness of detail (dates, documentation, descriptions, and original cost figures, for example). All focus houses in the text (those introducing chapters) are automatically incorporated here. Some of these, as well as others reached through the survey,

have virtually nothing in the way of evolving technology and serve simply as benchmarks against which the overall process can better be gauged. Chronological organization produces such a juxtaposition as that of the well-to-do Merchant's House in New York, fitted out for gaslight and coal heat and running water in the kitchen, appearing in sequence with a primitive log cabin in New Salem, Illinois—simply because they were both built around 1832.

The survey focused primarily on houses constructed between the 1790s, the time of the onset of significant domestic technology, and the 1920s, from which time on the chronology of new technology is well-known and amply documented, air conditioning being an obvious example. Built-in technology (as opposed to appliances generally) was emphasized. Lighting, which is both built-in and appliance in nature, is included because its importance overrides the distinction. Closets are here in part because the survey was an opportunity to obtain data on this usually overlooked feature of the house. Yet the information is also relevant in that the evolution of the closet mirrors the impact of the industrial revolution, as manifested in the accumulation of goods needing storage space. Closets also reflect an increasing complexity of the house and a sharpening sense of utilization of space, both of which also demonstrate technological evolution. Similarly, garages. Specific inquiries on the survey included Water Supply, Water Use in Kitchen, Means of Cooking, Refrigeration, Laundry, Bathroom, Lighting, Heating, Other Technology (ventilation, bellpull systems, as examples), Stable/Garage, Closets, and the usual Is There Anything Else?

Although questionnaires were sent throughout the country and houses from Maine to Hawaii are represented here, a disproportionate number will be found to be from the East. This is inevitable, in that the unfolding of new technology began in the East, and there are probably more historic homes east of the Mississippi than west.

As for sources: Material on houses not mentioned in the text may be assumed to have come from the technology survey or from the personal knowledge of the author. Otherwise sources will be as acknowledged in the text. Houses discussed in the text are indicated by an asterisk.

Some entries contain considerable information. Others that, for whatever reason, supply only one or two details are just as important; for it is the overall picture that emerges that is vital to us here.

*Abbreviations used in this appendix; state, month, and other common abbreviations are not listed here.*

| | |
|---|---|
| cent. | century |
| co. | company |
| E | east, eastern |
| Eng. | England |
| ft. | foot, feet |
| gal(s). | gallon(s) |
| in. | inch(es) |
| min. | minute(s) |
| N | north, northern |
| orig. | original, originally |
| S | south, southern |
| w/ | with |
| W | west, western |
| w/o | without |
| yd(s) | yard(s) |

| 1600–1700 | 1800 | 1850 | 1900 |
|---|---|---|---|
| **\*FAIRBANKS HOUSE**<br>Dedham, Mass.<br>*1637*<br><br>(Built 1637; substantially enlarged early 19th cent.)<br><br>Well and privy (although not necessarily at time of construction); water carried into house; small cold cellar for food storage; large hearth for cooking; 2 additional fireplaces for heating<br>*1637*<br><br>Barns, other outbuildings<br>*1637 or later*<br><br>Opening of kitchen fireplace reduced in size and bake oven built in at side<br>*18th cent.* | Kitchen fireplace covered over, stove installed for heating and cooking; indoor privy built into new section; 3 closets added<br>*19th cent.* | | Habitation of house discontinued though it continues in possession of Fairbanks family and eventually becomes a museum; up to present time no gas, electricity, indoor plumbing ever installed<br>*c1906* |
| **\*DR. JOHN CLARKE HOME**<br>Boston, Mass.<br><br>Use of stoves for heating (per will, leaving to his wife an estate that included 3 stoves valued at £3 each). Clarke was a surgeon who had moved to America from London and died 1664 in Boston.<br>*1664* | | | |
| **\*JOSHUA HEMPSTED HOUSE**<br>New London, Conn.<br>*1678; enlarged 1728*<br><br>Separate kitchen in lean-to in back superseding all-purpose hall typical of middle-class 17th-cent. house (probably orig. to house, and if not, added very early); leaded casement windows; fireplaces for heating and cooking; full cellar; eelgrass insulation (naturally fire retardant) between lath/plaster interior and clapboard exterior<br>*1678*<br><br>New wing added in style of early Georgian architecture; double-hung sash windows<br>*1728* | | | |

| 1600–1700 | 1800 | 1850 | 1900 |
|---|---|---|---|
| **\*ADAM THOROUGHGOOD HOUSE**<br>Virginia Beach, Va.<br>*c1680*<br><br>Primitive heating/cooling technology: chimney stack on S end external to dissipate heat; that on N end internal to retain heat<br>*c1680* | | | |
| **PHILIPSBURG MANOR**<br>North Tarrytown, N.Y.<br>*1690–1720; reconstructed c1940*<br><br>Well water hauled in; cooking and heating by fireplace; outdoor privy<br>*1690–1720* | | | |
| **\*SAMUEL SEWALL HOME**<br>Boston, Mass.<br><br>Use of stove for heating. From diary of Samuel Sewall, Jan. 16, 1702: "Comfortable moderat wether: and with a good fire in the Stove warm'd the Room"<br>*1702* | | | |
| **\*WRIGHT'S FERRY MANSION**<br>Columbia, Pa.<br>*1738*<br><br>10 closets (1 since turned into "hidden" entryway), utilizing space aside chimneys as well as assorted nooks and crannies about the house; cellar stairs under main staircase<br>*1738* | | | |
| **SISTERS' HOUSE (SARON)**<br>Ephrata Cloister<br>Ephrata, Pa.<br>*1743*<br><br>(Cloister founded in 1732; while it is notable for austerity of lifestyle it presents the paradox of a probable "oldest" in household convenience)<br><br>As part of remodeling, in German tradition, kitchen on each of 3 floors is fitted w/ hollowed-out sandstone slab draining through wall to outdoors; albeit lacking running water, these are probably the oldest extant kitchen sinks in America<br>*c1745* | | | |

| 1600–1700 | 1800 | 1850 | 1900 |
|---|---|---|---|
| **SHIRLEY-EUSTIS HOUSE**<br>Roxbury, Mass.<br>*1747–1751*<br><br>Indications of basement cistern fed through hollowed-out pilasters from roof (evidence lost when house moved and old foundation demolished 1867); 14 closets believed to be orig., including 3 w/shelves in room traditionally used as library<br>*1751* | Carriage house<br>*c1800* | Hot-air central heating<br>*Pre-1860* | |
| **PALMER-MARSH HOUSE**<br>Bath, N.C.<br>*c1751*<br><br>Basement kitchen w/fireplace (iron crane, oven in back, warming oven at side) for cooking; fireplaces for heat; candles for light; well for water; root cellar<br>*c1751* | | | |
| ***SCHIFFERSTADT**<br>Frederick, Md.<br>*1756*<br><br>Cast-iron heating stoves except kitchen, which is heated by hearth (one stove dated 1756 in situ); cross ventilation; spacious *keller* under kitchen for cold food storage; sandstone windowsill basin serving as primitive kitchen sink<br>*1756* | | | |
| ***WHITEHALL**<br>Annapolis, Md.<br>*c1765*<br><br>(Built by colonial Governor Horatio Sharpe)<br><br>Water closet, probably the earliest in America and possibly the only one of its time; located in extension at side of house; used water from roof-fed cistern and discharged into cesspool underneath; of a type found in England by c1730 (Osterly House, London); of simple design using a marble trough, with water admitted by turning a cock; emptied by pulling up a handle, thus raising a plunger device sealing a hole at the bottom of the trough<br>*c1765* | | | |

| 1600–1700 | 1800 | 1850 | 1900 |
|---|---|---|---|
| **\*SILAS DEANE HOUSE**<br>Wethersfield, Conn.<br>*1766*<br><br>Stone sink, dated 1771, in kitchen beneath window adjacent to fireplace; sink drained through hole under window<br>*1771* | | | |
| **\*WYCK**<br>Philadelphia, Pa.<br>*c1710; alterations and additions 1736, 1771, 1824*<br><br>Fireplace w/oven in back for cooking<br>*By 1771*<br><br>2 shallow closets w/hooks (armoires otherwise)<br>*1771 addition*<br><br>Coach house, stone barn, brewery<br>*1796* | Coal-burning stove in kitchen for cooking and heating<br>*c1815*<br><br>Central heating (per account book record of hiring a mason to build "a furnace in front cellar," Nov. 1820; furnace coal-burning and served only part of house; some coal-burning stoves elsewhere (details unknown); also use of open fireplaces, at least in sitting room<br>*1820*<br><br>Attic cistern; wash shed next to summer kitchen (used until 1910s)<br>*1820s*<br><br>Coal grates added to fireplaces in rooms served by central heating, suggesting system was inefficient; remodeling by architect William Strickland anticipates 20th-cent. concepts of space with use of doors pivoting as much as 180 degrees to create "movable" walls and vary configuration of space; numerous closets and built-in cupboards<br>*1824*<br><br>Icehouse<br>*1836* | Gaslight<br>*By 1860*<br><br>Public water; bathroom w/water closet and copper-lined tub (but no hot running water)<br>*1860s*<br><br>Icebox<br>*1870s*<br><br>2nd bathroom<br>*1890s* | Hot running water<br>*1912*<br><br>Electric light<br>*1918*<br><br>Electric refrigerator<br>*1920s*<br><br>Coal furnace, hot-water heat<br>*1926*<br><br>Connection to public sewers<br>*1930s* |
| **\*HEYWARD-WASHINGTON HOUSE**<br>Charleston, S.C.<br>*1772*<br><br>Coal-burning fireplaces; many closets, 2 in each fireplace wall; high ceilings, spacious windows for comfort in summer<br>*1772* | | | |

| 1600–1700 | 1800 | 1850 | 1900 |
|---|---|---|---|
| **\*TODD HOUSE**<br>Philadelphia, Pa.<br>*1775*<br><br>(Built by a local carpenter, Jonathan Dilworth, who never lived there and sold house to John Todd)<br><br>Efficient utilization of space to create small closets in fireplace wall of virtually every room<br>*1775* | | | |
| **\*BISHOP WHITE HOUSE**<br>Philadelphia, Pa.<br>*1786*<br><br>Indoor privy at back of house, accessible through kitchen. It is believed the privy emptied into a brick-lined sewer that drained into Dock Creek by a sort-of flushing action of water dumped into the privy vault by servants using wooden buckets. Almost, but not quite, a water closet.<br>*1786* | | | |
| **\*PRESTWOULD**<br>Near Clarksville, Va.<br>*1795*<br><br>Bellpulls, using bells, springs, wires, and "bell slides" shipped from Birmingham, Eng.<br>*1795* | | | |
| **ROBERT E. LEE BOYHOOD HOME**<br>Alexandria, Va.<br>*1795*<br><br>Bell-call system<br>*1795*<br><br>Oven made by Stratton Co., 73 Cheapside, London, installed at side of kitchen fireplace<br>*c1795* | Running water<br>*1833*<br><br>Gaslight<br>*1848* | Central heating<br>*1853* | |
| **\*MONTICELLO**<br>Charlottesville, Va.<br>*1768–1784; enlarged 1796–1809*<br><br>3 indoor privies vented through sophisticated system using 160-ft.-long "air tunnel" at basement level and shafts venting through flue in chimney; 3 closets; plans for a bathing house<br>*Enlargement of 1796* | Water-collection system using cisterns and fed from roofs of main house and dependencies (calculated by Jefferson as having capacity to supply more than 1,000 gals. a day)<br>*As of 1808*<br><br>See also FARMINGTON, p. 262 | | |

| 1600–1700 | 1800 | 1850 | 1900 |
|---|---|---|---|
| **\*JOSEPH PRIESTLEY HOUSE**<br>Northumberland, Pa.<br>*1796*<br><br>2 copper kettles adjacent to kitchen hearth heated by charcoal fire for hot water; well inside kitchen; linen closet plus closets in 3 of 4 bedrooms<br>*1796* | | | |
| | **\*THE PRESIDENT'S HOUSE**<br>(Subsequently and more familiarly known as the White House)<br>Washington, D.C.<br>*1800*<br><br>Water from wells; outdoor privy; fireplaces for heat<br>*1800*<br><br>Water closet (ordered 1801) installed<br>*1804*<br><br>Gravity-flow hot-air heating system using furnace in basement, but heat supplied only to state dining room directly above<br>*c1810–1812*<br><br>Spring in Franklin Square tapped as source of water, which flowed to pondlike reservoir on grounds; water pumped into house, primarily for bathing room in basement of East Colonnade<br>*1833*<br><br>More comprehensive version of central heating, using coal-burning furnace in basement, to heat additional rooms and some hallways<br>*1840*<br><br>Installation of gaslight<br>*1848* | Bathtub with hot/cold running water, 2nd floor<br>*c1855*<br><br>Potomac River supersedes Franklin Square spring as source of water<br>*1861*<br><br>Electricity<br>*1891* | Room air conditioner in Oval Office<br>*Early 1930s*<br><br>Full central air conditioning<br>*1952*<br><br>Solar panel for heat<br>*1979* |

| 1600–1700 | 1800 | 1850 | 1900 |
|---|---|---|---|
| | **\*THE OCTAGON**<br>Washington, D. C.<br>*1799–1801*<br><br>(Col. John Tayloe III House;<br>William Thornton, architect)<br><br>Sophisticated water-collection<br>system using conduits in cellar<br>floor to fill cistern for basement<br>kitchen (or if well instead of<br>cistern, to supplement its supply;<br>as of this writing, archaeological<br>investigation was in process of<br>determining if there is a masonry<br>bottom, in which case the<br>enclosure is a cistern, and if not, a<br>well); Rumford-like kitchen range<br>plus stewing range, both probably<br>coal-fired; exhaust hood connected<br>to main chimney flue over stewing<br>range; water boiler on kitchen<br>range; baking oven; possibly a<br>water closet, judging by<br>Thornton's design studies for<br>house, as well as earlier proposal<br>(not accepted) by Benjamin<br>Latrobe that clearly included a<br>water closet; fireplaces w/coal<br>grates; underground coal storage<br>vault filled through hatch from<br>street; bellpull system; numerous<br>closets; flat roof constructed of<br>layered, tar-soaked canvas over<br>wooden planks<br>*1801*<br><br>New roof (hipped) to replace<br>original, which leaked almost<br>from the start<br>*1815–1817*<br><br>Icehouse<br>*By 1817* | Installation of heating ductwork<br>suggesting central furnace<br>*1850s* | |
| | **MENARD HOUSE**<br>Ellis Grove, Ill.<br>*c1802*<br><br>Spring water; water hauled in to<br>sink in kitchen, drain tube to<br>outside; fireplaces for heating and<br>cooking; candles, possibly oil<br>lamps; "lots of windows" for<br>ventilation; no closets<br>*c1802* | | |

| 1600–1700 | 1800 | 1850 | 1900 |
|---|---|---|---|
| | **HOMEWOOD**<br>Baltimore, Md.<br>*1801–1803*<br><br>Probable Rumford-type kitchen, but all evidence lost; evidence of roof-fed cistern above kitchen fireplace wall, w/water presumably available at hearth; indications of sink beneath window in wall opposite hearth; also outside well in proximity to kitchen; privy (extant) of 2 rooms with total of 7 seats; bathhouse as outbuilding; evidence of at least 1 room orig. heated by a stove; a number of closets, all with shelves for household articles or books<br>*1803* | Gaslight<br>*Late 1800s* | |
| | **\*HENRY DRINKER HOME**<br>Philadelphia, Pa.<br><br>A "bathing Tub [obviously portable] bought yesterday for 17 Dollars—made of wood, lined with tin and painted—with Castors under ye bottom and a brass lock to let out the water"<br>*1803* | | |
| | **\*GARDNER-PINGREE HOUSE**<br>Salem, Mass.<br>*1804*<br><br>Connection to public water supply (Salem water system constructed 1796); water from street main through wood pipe to pump in back of house, thence to kitchen; open hearth for cooking and heating and boiler for hot water for laundry use in back (summer) kitchen; Rumford roaster (authentic one on site but not orig. to house) plus hearth plus built-in boiler for stew, soup and/or heating water, in main kitchen; wood-burning Rumford-style fireplaces for heat; closets, including 1 in master bedroom and 1 w/shelves (apparently for books) in room traditionally used as library; wine cellar; outdoor privy; wood frame stable in back<br>*1804*<br><br>Franklin stove purchased, presumably for 2nd-floor library (per receipt)<br>*1812* | Gaslight<br>*c1850s*<br><br>Brick stable to replace orig. wood-frame structure<br>*1860s*<br><br>Electric lighting (sometime soon after establishing of Salem Electric Light Co., c1883)<br>*c1880s* | |

| 1600–1700 | 1800 | 1850 | 1900 |
|---|---|---|---|
| | **\*GEORGE READ II HOUSE**<br>New Castle, Del.<br>*1804*<br><br>Pump room adjacent to kitchen; water from well pumped into 30-gal. boiler (in situ) in back of kitchen fireplace; "steam table" supplied by steam from boiler; Rumford-type oven (in situ) heated by flues from fireplace; bellpull system connecting virtually all rooms w/kitchen (mostly in situ); remote control mechanisms to unlock passage doors from inside (as from in bed); many closets (4 in master bedroom alone)<br>*1804*<br><br>"Steam kitchen" adjacent to kitchen fireplace to replace steam table and perhaps also Rumford-type oven (no details extant); hot running water to 7½-ft. bathtub with shower bath in bathing room, 2nd floor<br>*1811*<br><br>Coal-burning grates in fireplaces<br>*By 1818* | | |
| | **\*MONTGOMERY PLACE**<br>Annandale-on-Hudson, N.Y.<br>*1804*<br><br>Stewing stove, but no evidence as to whether part of orig. construction<br>*1804 or later*<br><br>Bathing tub (apparently a portable device of some kind)<br>*By 1806*<br><br>Evidence of installation of heating stove or stoves<br>*c1811*<br><br>Possible additional stove or stoves for heating<br>*By 1816*<br><br>Purchase of "4 Boiler" stove, presumably for cooking<br>*1820*<br><br>Purchase of "Large Franklin Stove" for $30<br>*1822* | | |

| 1600–1700 | 1800 | 1850 | 1900 |
|---|---|---|---|
| | **VANN HOUSE**<br>Chatsworth, Ga.<br>*1804*<br><br>(Built by Chief James Vann of the Cherokee Nation)<br><br>Water from spring, heated in fireplace; springhouse for refrigeration; fireplaces for cooking and heating; privy; candles for lighting; closets in bedrooms plus 1 closet under stairwell; main stairway oldest example of cantilevered construction in Georgia<br>*1804* | | |
| | **WOODLAWN PLANTATION**<br>Mount Vernon, Va.<br>*1800–1805*<br><br>(William Thornton, architect)<br><br>Inside well (primarily for laundry use); open hearth for cooking; fireplaces for heat; outside privies<br>*1805* | | |
| | **ASHLAND**<br>Henry Clay Estate<br>Lexington, Ky.<br>*1806; rebuilt 1853–1856; remodeled 1883*<br><br>Open well 10 yds in back of house; kitchen outbuilding w/open hearth for cooking; candles for light<br>*1806*<br><br>Pump (in situ) installed at well<br>*1811*<br><br>Cistern fed from roof gutters; 2 icehouses and dairy cellar; run-off water from icehouses channeled through underground pipes to trough in floor of dairy cellar, dairy products in ceramic crocks placed in water to keep cool (system in use until at least 1910; icehouse and dairy cellar restored and in situ)<br>*1830s* | 2 additional roof-fed cisterns; coal/wood-burning iron stove in kitchen, now part of rebuilt house; by now oil lamps in addition to candles; fireplaces w/coal grates for heat<br>*1853*<br><br>Bellpull system (mostly intact) connecting principal rooms w/servants' hall<br>*c1856*<br><br>Running water in kitchen via attic cistern; ceramic kitchen sink; new coal-fired kitchen range w/copper water heater attached; 2 small closets; 2-sided bathroom installed, 1 side w/water closet and sink, the other w/water closet and tub, all fed by attic cistern; water closets emptied into privy pit dating to 1853; gaslights including gasoliers using on-site gas generator; coal-fired hot-air central heating for principal rooms<br>*1883*<br><br>Electricity for lighting (though gas fixtures also remain in use)<br>*1892* | City water; city gas<br>*1900*<br><br>Icebox in kitchen<br>*c1900*<br><br>Full central heating system (supplementing partial system of 1883)<br>*1917*<br><br>City sewers; existing bathroom connected and 2nd bathroom added<br>*1929*<br><br>Gas range in kitchen superseding 1880s coal/wood-burning iron stove<br>*1920s*<br><br>1st electric refrigerator<br>*Late 1940s*<br><br>Gas-fired forced-air heating and cooling system installed using ductwork and floor grates of 1883 and 1917 systems<br>*1964*<br><br>Glycol HVAC installed using 1883, 1917, and 1964 grates but new ductwork and sensor system<br>*1992* |

| 1600–1700 | 1800 | 1850 | 1900 |
|---|---|---|---|
| | *GORE PLACE<br>Waltham, Mass.<br>*1806*<br><br>(Country seat of Gov. Christopher Gore)<br><br>Account book for construction includes following details: "Rumford kitchen," $148.11; copper-lined bathtub, $27; installation of Rumford kitchen and bath and laundry tubs, $88; stove (unknown whether heating or cooking), $22.50. Additionally: cistern, presumably roof-fed, in attic; numerous closets, including walk-in wardrobe adjacent to master bedroom; spacious linen closet; cupola for ventilation as well as light in upper hallway<br>*1806*<br><br>Water closet, $103.75; stove, $120<br>*1807*<br><br>Purchase and/or installation of pipe, $104.25<br>*1808* | Iron cook stove inserted, 1st-floor hearth<br>*c1850*<br><br>Water pump (Walker & Pratt, Boston) installed in basement<br>*1850–1860*<br><br>Hot-air central heating (Wm. Lumb & Co., Boston)<br>*1896* | |
| | *HARRISON GRAY OTIS HOUSE<br>Boston, Mass.<br>*1807*<br><br>(Charles Bulfinch, architect; 3rd in series of Otis houses)<br><br>Attached privy; attached carriage house; washroom adjacent to kitchen<br>*1807* | | |
| | JOHN GREENLEAF WHITTIER HOME<br>Amesbury, Mass.<br>*1810; additions 1847, 1884*<br><br>Kitchen w/fireplace for cooking, brick oven for baking; fireplaces for heat<br>*1810*<br><br>Sink w/hand pump in small room adjoining kitchen; room also had small fireplace, presumably for heating water, for both kitchen and laundry purposes<br>*c1810–1830*<br><br>2nd floor w/2 bedrooms added, 1 closet (apparently hooks only) in each room (no closets in orig. 1-story structure)<br>*1847* | 2nd-floor addition includes 2 more bedrooms, each w/ hooks-only closet<br>*1884* | New wing added, including kitchen w/gas range and hot/cold running water; bathroom; central heating<br>*c1900*<br><br>Electric refrigerator<br>*1930s* |

| 1600–1700 | 1800 | 1850 | 1900 |
|---|---|---|---|
| | **\*JOHN MARKOE HOUSE**<br>Philadelphia, Pa.<br>*1808–1811*<br><br>(Benjamin Latrobe, architect; *demolished c1880*)<br><br>Bathtub w/heated cistern, water closet w/cistern, in separate chambers, 2nd floor<br>*1811* | | |
| | **\*RUNDLET-MAY HOUSE**<br>Portsmouth, N.H.<br>*1807–1811*<br><br>Rumford roaster, Rumford range, fireplaces designed on Rumford principles; set kettle for hot water for laundry and other household uses; indoor well; 2 indoor privies in ell; bellpull system<br>*1811* | | |
| | **FARMINGTON**<br>Louisville, Ky.<br>*1810*<br><br>(Built for John Speed to a design, only slightly modified, of Thomas Jefferson)<br><br>2 indoor necessaries apparently making use of chamber pots emptied by house slaves; although not water closets and not having a direct connection to a privy vault, these 2 small rooms off a central hall nevertheless represent an early use of a specialized place for elimination and are thus a significant step in the evolution of the "bathroom"; also outdoor privies for slaves; spring water carried to house and kitchens from spring house that served for cool storage of food; also ice house for food preservation and storage of ice; winter kitchen w/open hearth fitted w/rotisserie, crane, and warming oven; summer kitchen with open hearth and bake oven; owing to a symmetrical plan, excellent cross ventilation making use of large windows; wooden slat vents in walls for circulation of air in basement; fireplaces for heat<br>*1810*<br><br>Coal-burning fireplace insert in music room<br>*Early 1830s* | | Electric light<br>*Early 1900s*<br><br>Modern plumbing<br>*1940s* |

| 1600–1700 | 1800 | 1850 | 1900 |
|---|---|---|---|
| | **\*LEMOYNE HOUSE**<br>Washington, Pa.<br>*1812*<br><br>(The home of a physician)<br><br>Roof garden, a kind of notch in roof, as place for planting herbs and flowers, the former used by Dr. LeMoyne in his practice as physician<br>*1812* | | |
| | **DR. MOSES MASON HOUSE**<br>Bethel, Me.<br>*1813*<br><br>Well water; arch kettle for kitchen and laundry use; cold cellar; fireplace for cooking and heating; candles for lighting; bedroom closets; attached stable<br>*1813* | | |
| | **AVILA ADOBE**<br>El Pueblo de Los Angeles<br>Los Angeles, Calif.<br>*c1818; restored after earthquake 1971*<br><br>Water from Los Angeles River via Zanja Madre (Mother Ditch) flowing through property; water kept cool by storing in a large olla; outdoor beehive oven; tallow candles for light; braziers for warmth; outdoor privy; pegs for hanging clothes, plus trunks for storage<br>*c1818* | | |
| | **\*GAY MONT**<br>John H. Bernard House<br>Rappahannock Academy, Va.<br><br>"Shower bath pan and watering pot" ($3)<br>*1818*<br><br>Washing machine ($13.75)<br>*1832*<br><br>Cistern ($70); bathing tub (no record of cost); 575 ft. of lead pipe ($196.13)<br>*1838*<br><br>"Boiling machine" (presumably hot water heater, $20); pump and additional lead pipe ($47.56, this and the above apparently to bring water from well into house, thence to kitchen, dressing room, library)<br>*1839*<br><br>"Refrigerator" (icebox, $15)<br>*1844* | Niagara Shower Bath (Patent No. 5993, E. Larrabee, 1849, wood frame, canvas sides, pull-chain overhead cistern, lead-pan bottom) purchased from E. Larrabee, Baltimore, for $20<br>*1854* | |

| 1600–1700 | 1800 | 1850 | 1900 |
|---|---|---|---|
| | **THE HERMITAGE**<br>Home of Andrew Jackson<br>Hermitage, Tenn.<br>*1819; remodeled 1836*<br><br>Spring (plus well behind house, probably of later date) for water carried into house; water heated in fireplace; chamber pots and privy, never any indoor plumbing installed (house became museum 1889); fireplaces for heating<br>*1819*<br><br>Icehouse and springhouse for refrigeration; Franklin stove inserts for fireplaces<br>*Dates uncertain*<br><br>4 linen closets in upstairs hall<br>*1836 remodeling*<br><br>Stove purchased (may have been kitchen stove or perhaps additional heating stove)<br>*c1840* | "Clark's Patent Refrigerator" and shower bath purchased by Andrew Jackson, Jr.<br>*c1850* | Electricity<br>*c1950* |
| | **BRYANT HOMESTEAD**<br>Cummington, Mass.<br>*1785/1865*<br><br>(The boyhood home of William Cullen Bryant, who returned there in 1865, considerably enlarged it, and used it as a summer retreat)<br><br>Using water-supply system consisting of small spring-fed stone basin on nearby hillside and pipe, presumably wood, leading to homestead, running water available at least to barn by this time<br>*1821*<br><br>Running water to house as well at least by this time<br>*1829* | Kitchen sink w/running water (reconstruction in situ); separate boiler for hot water; wood-burning kitchen stove; bathing room w/tub; various closets added (orig. structure had none)<br>*1865*<br><br>Bathing room converted to full bathroom w/addition of water closet and ceramic sink with hot/cold running water; terra-cotta waste pipe drains into pasture downhill from house<br>*1894* | |

| 1600–1700 | 1800 | 1850 | 1900 |
|---|---|---|---|
| | **\*WAYNE-GORDON HOUSE** Savannah, Ga. *1818–1821; enlarged 1886* <br><br>Wood-burning kitchen range; fireplaces for heat; Argand, oil, kerosene lamps and candles *1821* | Gaslight; fireplaces converted to coal *1850* <br><br>Piped-in public water (superseding use of public pumps and cisterns); kitchen sink w/cold running water; water heated at cast-iron range; bathroom w/water closet, sink, and mahogany and copper bathtub installed *c1855* <br><br>Kitchen range converted to coal *c1870* <br><br>Icebox *c1875* <br><br>Coal-burning hot-air central heating *1883* <br><br>Bathroom modernized w/new water closet, cast-iron tub, and cast-iron/enamel sink; 3 additional bathrooms installed; opening skylight installed for ventilation; closets of modern dimensions added *1886 renovation* | Kitchen range converted to gas *c1900* <br><br>Electric lighting, electric refrigerator *1903* |
| | **HART-CLUETT MANSION** Troy, N.Y. *1827* <br><br>Roof-fed cistern in back of house; oil lamps and candles *c1827* <br><br>Gaslights—connection to Troy Gas Light Co. for service begun Nov. 8, 1849 (per bill for $5.52 dated Dec. 1, 1849) *1849* | | |
| | **CARTER HOUSE** Franklin, Tenn. *1828–1830* <br><br>Well; water carried to outside kitchen; open hearth cooking; fireplaces for heat; food lowered into well for refrigeration; Argand lamps, candles, for light; outside privy *1830* | | |

| 1600–1700 | 1800 | 1850 | 1900 |
|---|---|---|---|
| | **HERMANN-GRIMA HOUSE** New Orleans, La. *1831* Roof-fed cistern; washroom with set kettle and dry sink in addition to kitchen; open hearth; stewing range similar to Rumford (reconstructed); fireplaces for heat; washhouse in addition to washroom; outdoor privy; indoor bathing room (restored); Argand lamps; no closets *1831* Gaslight *Late 1830s* | Stable added *c1870* | |
| | **\*MERCHANT'S HOUSE** Seabury Tredwell House New York, N.Y. *1832* In anticipation of adaptation to new technology, 2 floors fitted for gaslight during construction even though gas not yet available in this area of Manhattan; roof-fed underground cistern for water supply; water pumped to sink in kitchen; open hearth plus bake oven for cooking; wood-burning fireplaces for heating but, in anticipation of conversion to coal, built-in chute (existing) from hatch at curb presumably to coal bin (no longer existing) in basement; outdoor privy; bellpull system throughout house Conversion to gas for lighting, presumably with Manhattan Gas Co. *c1835* | Coal grates in fireplaces for heating *By c1850* | Electricity *1930 or later* |
| | **LOG CABIN** New Salem, Ill. *1830s* (Typical cabin in reconstructed old town of New Salem, Petersburg, Ill., where Lincoln lived 1830s) Outside well, water hauled inside; dry sink; portable tubs for laundry; fireplace(s) for heating and cooking; cold cellar; outdoor privy; no closets; typical cabin might be 1 room or 2, possibly with loft above *1830s* | | |

**HYDE HALL**
Near Cooperstown, N.Y.
*Begun 1817; first occupied 1819;
completed 1835*

Running water in kitchen by
means of gravity-flow system from
small reservoir on adjacent Mount
Wellington; house connected to
reservoir by lead pipe; two
limestone sinks for kitchen
purposes; wood-burning range in
kitchen; Bramah water closet,
imported from Eng. 1827,
installed off 1st-floor hallway
under staircase (largely extant
except for bowl, some orig. lead
pipe also still in place); evidence
of unusual heating system for
drawing room and dining room
consisting of 6-in. iron pipe
running under floor to circulate
fresh, outside air through air
chambers behind fireplaces, the
heated air thence exiting through
holes on sides of chimney breast
creating convection; wood for
drawing room and dining room
fireplaces kept in adjacent storage
boxes filled through trap doors
from rear hallway; supplementary
central heating system with
soapstone plate stove in
semienclosed, basement-level
furnace room using tile pipe
running under floor to provide
additional heat in drawing room,
dining room, entrance hall, water
closet, and pantry, the heat exiting
through "heat regulators"
(adjustable metal louvers 6 in.
in diameter); entrance hall also
heated by Greek Revival cast-iron
stove, fire in which was tended
through opening in rear hallway;
evidence of small stoves in other
rooms; oil lamps for light,
generally; in dining and drawing
rooms, suspended fixtures with
both candles and alcohol burners;
bell-call system (remnants
remaining); no bedroom closets
but several hall closets (use of
movable wardrobes for bedrooms)
*As of 1835*

| 1600–1700 | 1800 | 1850 | 1900 |
|---|---|---|---|
| | **\*SUNNYSIDE**<br>Washington Irving Home<br>Tarrytown, N.Y.<br>*1690s/1835*<br><br>(2-room 1690s Dutch farmhouse purchased by Irving 1835; rebuilt 1835, updated technologically 1847 after Irving's return from serving as ambassador to Spain)<br><br>Open hearth for cooking; wood-burning fireplaces for heat; large icehouse; opening skylight for ventilation; whale-oil lamps and candles<br>*1835*<br><br>3-compartment privy adjacent to house<br>*Probably sometime after 1835*<br><br>Sophisticated plumbing system supplying hot/cold water to kitchen and laundry sinks; gravity-fed piped-in water from freshwater spring uphill from house (remote from privy) directly to sinks (cold water) and to coils in kitchen stove for heating and thence to adjacent holding tank for storing; bathing room w/tub and cold running water; kitchen sink with hot/cold running water; laundry w/separate tubs for soaking, scrubbing, rinsing (all with hot/cold running water); wood-burning kitchen stove inserted into hearth for cooking<br>*1847–1849*<br><br>Fireplaces updated with coal grates for heating<br>*Probably 1848–1849* | | |
| | **CLARKE HOUSE**<br>Chicago, Ill.<br>*1836*<br><br>Heating by fireplaces on 1st floor and stoves in two 2nd-floor bedrooms; shallow, hooks-only closets in bedrooms and two 1st-floor rooms<br>*1836* | Gaslight (gasoliers) on 1st floor; cupola and wagon-wheel window installed in ceiling on 2nd floor for ventilation<br>*Mid 1850s* | |

| 1600–1700 | 1800 | 1850 | 1900 |
|---|---|---|---|
| | **\*LYMAN HOUSE**<br>Hilo, Hawaii<br>*1838–1839*<br><br>(Home of missionaries David and Sarah Lyman)<br><br>Thatch roof; no inside water; although undocumented, water supply from rain-filled cistern likely; kitchen in separate building; cooking by means of wood-fired stone hearth; lighting by oil lamps; outdoor privy; no provision for heating owing to tropical climate; no closets<br>*1838–1839* | Addition of steel roof, replacing thatch and creating attic; also new wing<br>*1855*<br><br>Electric lighting, closets<br>*After 1885* | Bathroom with running water<br>*Before 1931* |
| | **LINCOLN HOME**<br>Springfield, Ill.<br>*1839*<br><br>(Orig. 3-room cottage, 1839; 5 successive enlargements created 10-room house by 1860)<br><br>Candles and oil lamps for light; fireplaces for heat and cooking; outdoor privy; backyard shed for laundry<br>*1839* | Wood-burning stove purchased for kitchen<br>*1853*<br><br>Larger "Royal Oak" No. 9 wood-burning stove (Jewett & Root, Buffalo, N.Y.) purchased for kitchen; by now, heating stoves instead of fireplaces; roof-fed cistern plus well pump for water, which is hauled into kitchen and heated on stove for kitchen and bathing purposes (portable tub); icebox in pantry; laundry now done in or near kitchen (outdoor shed having been removed); carriage house in back<br>*1860*<br><br>Gaslight<br>*1877*<br><br>Central heating<br>*1889–1890*<br><br>Electric lights<br>*c1899* | Connection to public sewer<br>*After 1900*<br><br>City water<br>*c1910* |
| | **CHARLES B. AYCOCK BIRTHPLACE**<br>Raleigh, N.C.<br>*1840s*<br><br>Well water brought into house in wooden buckets; water heated at open fireplace; open-hearth cooking; milk and butter kept cool in well; laundry done in large pot outdoors, w/fire burning under pot; privy, plus chamber pots indoors; heating by open fireplace; no closets; pegs on walls for hanging clothes<br>*1840s* | | |

| 1600–1700 | 1800 | 1850 | 1900 |
|---|---|---|---|
| | **\*BALDWIN-REYNOLDS HOUSE** Meadville, Pa. *1841–1843* Water to house from spring via wooden pipes; oil lamps *1843* | Installation of Boynton wood-burning furnace (hot-air central heating) *1857* Gaslight *1866* New kitchen in basement w/Barstow multiburner wood stove; kitchen sink w/running water, possibly both hot and cold; dumbwaiter to dining room on 1st floor *1869* Installation of lightning rods *1870* Conversion to steam heat *1873* 2 icehouses *By 1878* | Electricity *c1900* New kitchen on 1st floor *1912* Electric refrigerator *c1912* |
| | **MURRELL HOME** Park Hill, Okla. *c1845* Kitchen fireplace for cooking; fireplaces in 7 of 8 rooms for heat; rooftop cupola for ventilation; closets in parlor, kitchen, bedrooms; whale-oil lamps (later kerosene) for light; water hauled to house from springhouse 30 yds away; outdoor privy *c1845* | Icebox *By 1850* Smokehouse *c1896* | Declared historic site (still no indoor water or electricity) *1948* Electricity *c1950* |
| | **TULLIE SMITH FARM** Atlanta, Ga. *c1845* Well water; fireplace (no oven) in detached kitchen; root cellar; privy; candles for light; fireplaces for heat; closet under stairs may or may not have been part of orig. house *c1845* | Oil/kerosene lamps *c1860* | Running water *c1950* |

| 1600–1700 | 1800 | 1850 | 1900 |
|---|---|---|---|
| | **BOWEN HOUSE**<br>Woodstock, Conn.<br>*1847*<br><br>(Also known as Roseland Cottage; built as summer home in Gothic style)<br><br>Basement cistern, water then pumped to attic cistern for gravity flow to kitchen and bathing room; water heated in kitchen for use there (copper tank in situ, but not necessarily orig.); bathing room adjacent to principal chamber had tub with drain to outdoors but no apparent connection to water supply for filling (presumably filled by pail w/water from kitchen water heater); probably a laundry (specifications unknown) in cellar at time of construction; bake oven ("Eagle Furnace," Stafford, Conn.) in kitchen hearth, latter also being available for cooking; fireplace in each room for heat; oil lamps; one outdoor privy plus indoor privy in ell in rear of kitchen; closets (hooks and shelves, some w/built-in chests of drawers) in nearly every room including hallways<br>*1847* | Icehouse<br>*c1850*<br><br>Outbuilding added including 2nd privy and woodshed w/loft above<br>*c1870*<br><br>Laundry room (3-section granite tub, ironing boards, tables) added to kitchen ell, replacing one in cellar<br>*1870–1875* | "Palace Crawford" (Canada) wood-burning range installed in kitchen<br>*c1900*<br><br>Small rooms on 1st, 2nd floors converted into bathrooms (WC, tub, and sink)<br>*Early 1900s/possibly 1890s*<br><br>Electric lighting (superseding kerosene lamps); electric buzzer "intercom"; 1st central heating consisting of hot-air furnace ("Perfect No. 3482 Warm Air Heater") w/ducts to 1st floor only<br>*c1920*<br><br>Conversion to steam heat: H. B. Smith Model No. 25–50 oil-burning boiler<br>*1940–1950* |
| | **\*ELIAS BAKER MANSION**<br>Altoona, Pa.<br>*1844–1849*<br><br>Gravity hot-air central heating consisting of coal furnace in basement and ductwork leading to all 1st-floor rooms plus 2nd-floor hall; kitchen in basement, dumbwaiter to 1st-floor dining room; speaking tube from dining room to kitchen; basement ice room filled w/ice in winter, runoff gradually melting into trough leading outside; adjacent refrigeration room utilizing natural spring flowing through trough in room, into which butter, milk, etc., could be placed to keep cool; herb room and laundry also in basement<br>*1849* | | Indoor plumbing<br>*1904*<br><br>Electricity<br>*1905* |

| 1600–1700 | 1800 | 1850 | 1900 |
|---|---|---|---|
| | | **\*LINDENWALD**<br>Martin Van Buren<br>National Historic Site<br>Kinderhook, N.Y.<br>*1797; remodeled 1849–1850*<br><br>Kitchen cook stove w/separate cooking and warming ovens also provides heat for kitchen; indoor pump to cistern supplying kitchen, bathroom, and laundry w/running water; tub w/running water; water closet (all above in situ, theoretically in working condition)<br>*1849–1850*<br><br>Boynton cast-iron furnace (patented 1854), central hot-air heating system (in situ)<br>*c1855* | |
| | | **ANDREW JOHNSON**<br>**HOMESTEAD**<br>Greenville, Tenn.<br>*1849–1851*<br><br>Water from spring hand-carried to house; springhouse and cold cellar for refrigeration; kitchen fireplace for cooking; chamber pots, privy; candles, kerosene lamps; fireplaces for heat; no closets<br>*1851*<br><br>2 rooms w/small closets added on 2nd floor<br>*c1869*<br><br>City water; running water to kitchen sink<br>*1890*<br><br>Hot-air central heating; wood bathtub lined w/tin (but w/o running water)<br>*1890s*<br><br>Electric lighting<br>*1898–1899* | Icebox in basement<br>*c1900*<br><br>Garage for car bought by Andrew Johnson Patterson, grandson of the president<br>*1920s*<br><br>Electric refrigerator<br>*By early 1930s*<br><br>Bathroom installed on 1st floor (chamber pots still used upstairs)<br>*1930s*<br><br>Bathroom upstairs<br>*1940s* |
| | | **COX-DEASY HOUSE**<br>Mobile, Ala.<br>*c1850*<br><br>1 original cast-iron wood-burning heat stove (#19 Rose Garland "E") in situ; otherwise fireplaces for heat, one apparently w/fireplace insert; probably well for water; detached kitchen; outdoor privy<br>*c1850* | |

| 1600–1700 | 1800 | 1850 | 1900 |
|---|---|---|---|
| | | **CAMPBELL HOUSE**<br>St. Louis, Mo.<br>*1851*<br><br>Cooking presumably at open hearth; heating by coal-burning fireplaces and perhaps also by coal-burning hot-air furnace to heat 1st floor (though this may have been added sometime later); use of washbowls, pitchers for personal washing in bedrooms; chamber pots and closetools; no clothes closets (use of wardrobes only); house apparently piped for gaslight when built (pair of Cornelius & Co. gasoliers in situ, along w/other lighting devices from this or later time, including an astral lamp, kerosene lamps, candelabra)<br>*1851*<br><br>Kitchen enlarged; coal-/wood-burning cast-iron range apparently built into fireplace (replaced early 20th cent. w/gas or electric range)<br>*1855* | |
| | | **DUKE HOMESTEAD**<br>Durham, N.C.<br>*1852*<br><br>Detached kitchen; water hauled from spring<br>*1852*<br><br>Kitchen added to house; fireplace for cooking; kerosene lamps, candles<br>*c1860*<br><br>Well dug and well house built; cook stove added to kitchen<br>*1870* | Last occupied as residence; still no electric or running water; privy, chamber pots still used<br>*1931* |
| | | **HILLFOREST**<br>Aurora, Ind.<br>*1853–1855*<br><br>Belvedere for ventilation; coal fireplaces for heat; bedroom closets; 3-hole privy, rear of freestanding carriage house; possibly up to 11 cisterns, 7 verified; 1 under basement believed fed from roof through front porch columns; others fed from pond and ravine<br>*1855* | |

| 1600–1700 | 1800 | 1850 | 1900 |
|---|---|---|---|
| | | **LAWNFIELD**<br>James A. Garfield House<br>Mentor, Ohio<br>*c1832; enlarged 1880* | Bathroom added on 3rd floor<br>*1904* |
| | | Heating by fireplaces and stoves, the latter documented by 1857 patent stove<br>*1857 or later* | |
| | | Hydraulic water ram for irrigation of fields<br>*1876* | |
| | | Icehouse (12 by 15 ft.) constructed; also, privy w/brick vault<br>*1877* | |
| | | Diary record of kitchen water pipes being overhauled, showing running water available in kitchen by this time; 2 new sinks installed in butler's pantry<br>*1878* | |
| | | Enlargement of house includes bathroom, 1st floor (details unknown); electric doorbell operating off battery in basement; clothes closets w/hooks (2 including built-in drawers); temporary private telegraph line installed in conjunction w/Garfield's campaign for presidency<br>*1880* | |
| | | Drilling produces on-site natural gas; conversion to gaslight, superseding candles, kerosene lamps; gas heating (12 gas fireplaces), superseding coal stoves and fireplaces; new kitchen w/gas range and water heater, plus pantry and butler's pantry, plus laundry; 2nd bathroom added on 1st floor, 2 on 2nd floor; windmill built for pumping water<br>*1885* | |
| | | Detached carriage barn constructed<br>*c1893* | |
| | | New windmill built for pumping water, 300-gal. in-house holding tank constructed for supply (holding tank in situ, windmill destroyed 1930)<br>*1894* | |

| 1600–1700 | 1800 | 1850 | 1900 |
|---|---|---|---|
| | | **THE WILLOWS**<br>Fosterfields<br>Morristown, N.J.<br>*1854*<br><br>(Quintessential Gothic Revival house built in 1854 by Joseph Revere, grandson of Paul Revere; purchased in 1881 by Charles Foster, a New York City commodities broker; the home of his daughter, Caroline, for 98 years, from infancy until her death in 1979 at age 102)<br><br>Ice house sufficient for storing 20 tons of ice harvested from nearby pond<br>*1854*<br><br>Elaborate water supply system consisting of mounded reservoir on nearby hill, filled w/spring water pumped to it, the water then being gravity-fed to cistern outside of kitchen and pumped from there to cistern in the attic, from which it was gravity-fed for use w/in house, in kitchen and perhaps bathing room (but no evidence of water closet)<br>*Possibly 1854, perhaps later* | Telephone<br>*1907*<br><br>Garage to house Caroline Foster's first car, a 1922 Model-T Ford<br>*c1927*<br><br>Electricity<br>*1930s* |
| | | **PERSHING BOYHOOD HOME**<br>Laclede, Mo.<br>*1857–1858*<br><br>Well water; wood-fired cook stove in kitchen (a relatively early instance of a house built w/o a kitchen fireplace for cooking); root cellar; kerosene lamps; 2 bedroom closets documented as part of orig. construction<br>*1858* | Electric service available (no documentation of use in home)<br>*c1910*<br><br>Public water supply<br>*1950s*<br><br>Gas-fired boiler installed for heat<br>*1957* |
| | | **\*MOSES G. FARMER HOME**<br>Salem, Mass.<br><br>Use of primitive electric light apparatus. (Professor Farmer devised and tried out in the parlor of his home an electric incandescent lamp consisting of an open-air strip of platinum through which flowed current from a battery. It produced light barely the equivalent of a candle.)<br>*1859* | |

| 1600–1700 | 1800 | 1850 | 1900 |
|---|---|---|---|
| | | **MEIGHEN HOUSE**<br>Forestville<br>Preston, Minn.<br>*Late 1850s*<br><br>Hand-dug well with pump; water hauled inside; wood-burning stove w/hot-water reservoir; outdoor privy; kerosene lighting; wood/coal stoves in individual rooms<br>*Late 1850s*<br><br>(The building of the Southern Minnesota Railroad in 1868 bypassed Preston, leaving the town struggling to survive while other towns prospered; hence no further technological progress for this house.) | |
| | | **GALLIER HOUSE**<br>New Orleans, La.<br>*1857–1860*<br><br>Roof-fed 5,000-gal. brick cistern for household use; cold water supplied from this cistern or separate pump-fed attic storage tank; hot water via boiler attached to cast-iron kitchen range; hollow brick base of cistern also provided cool storage area for food; cypress icebox also; bathroom w/copper-lined tub (hot/cold running water) and water closet (hand-painted porcelain bowl) that emptied into cesspool beneath courtyard; outdoor privy for servants; coal-burning fireplaces in dining room, parlors, bedrooms, bathroom, 1 servant's room; gaslight, candles; pole-operated air vent disguised in decorative plasterwork of ceiling of master bedroom; skylight in upstairs library for ventilation and light; decorative cast-iron gate on front entrance for additional ventilation; 2 large walk-in closets in master bedroom; armoires otherwise; no stable—horses kept at public stables<br>*1860* | |
| | | **MABRY-HAZEN HOUSE**<br>Knoxville, Tenn.<br>*1858*<br><br>Coal-burning fireplaces for heat (the original owner was a railroad president, making coal easily obtainable); cisterns for water, apparently roof-fed; transoms over interior doors for ventilation<br>*1858* | |

| 1600–1700 | 1800 | 1850 | 1900 |
|---|---|---|---|
| | | **\*HIXON HOUSE**<br>La Crosse, Wisc.<br>*1860*<br><br>Heating stoves in 1st floor living areas; large closet in master bedroom; lean-to in back for storage<br>*1860*<br><br>Gaslight installed (sometime before payment of 1st gas bill in Dec.; gas bills paid every 6 months)<br>*1879*<br><br>House connected to city water supply, household water system installed; property owner billed by city for "842 ft. of 8″ water pipe" laid in public street in front of house; telephone service installed (40 private lines in town; service began late 1870s)<br>*1880*<br><br>Renovations to house include master bathroom w/skylight plus 2nd bathroom for children and guests on 2nd floor, each w/water closet, tub, sink; coal furnace installed in basement; closets, generally deep enough for hangers, built into bedrooms<br>*1881*<br><br>Electric lighting, including some dual gas/electric fixtures; bathroom added on 1st floor<br>*1883*<br><br>Battery-ignition gas-heating unit installed, presumably as supplement to coal furnace; battery-operated bell-call system (manufactured by Julius Andrae, Milwaukee) installed<br>*1885*<br><br>Construction begins on carriage house w/elevator by which, according to season, carriages and sleighs might be raised to overhead storage area<br>*1892* | Built-in central vacuum-cleaning system (engine patent dated 1908), w/2 outlets each on 1st and 2nd floors<br>*c1908* |

| 1600–1700 | 1800 | 1850 | 1900 |
|---|---|---|---|
| | | **ELI SLIFER HOUSE**<br>Lewisburg, Pa.<br>*1861*<br><br>Fireplaces for heat; gaslight using on-site carbon gas generator (probably very sparingly and primarily for guests owing to cost of operation); no indoor plumbing; main kitchen plus summer kitchen; icebox ("D. Eddy & Son, Boston, est. 1847"); 4 bedrooms, each w/large closet (hooks only)<br>*1861* | |
| | | **RENSSELAER RUSSELL HOUSE**<br>Waterloo, Iowa<br>*1861*<br><br>Evidence of cistern in basement directly under kitchen, from which water was presumably pumped upstairs; also evidence of outside cistern close to back door; probably well in yard; outdoor privy; wood-burning stove in front parlor; no clothes closets<br>*1861*<br><br>Electric lighting<br>*c1890* | |
| | | **BOWERS MANSION**<br>Carson City, Nev.<br>*1863–1864*<br><br>(16-room mansion of 1st known millionaire of the Comstock Lode)<br><br>Outside well; cold cellar for root crops, butter, milk, wine; hot water from wood/coal kitchen stove (in use until 1940s); no closets; candles/kerosene lamps for light (until 1930s); 4 small coal-burning fireplaces on 1st floor for heat (none on 2nd)<br>*1864* | Indoor water for kitchen purposes<br>*1927*<br><br>1st bathroom (sink, toilet) replacing chamber pots, privy<br>*Late 1930s* |

| 1600–1700 | 1800 | 1850 | 1900 |
|---|---|---|---|
| | | **HARRY S. TRUMAN NATIONAL HISTORIC SITE** Independence, Mo. *1867/1885*<br><br>(House built 1867 by George P. Gates, grandfather of Bess Wallace Truman, out of small farmhouse; expanded into 2½-story mansion 1885 w/14-room addition; Harry and Bess Truman moved in after marriage in 1919, sharing house with Bess's mother, grandmother)<br><br>Wood-burning kitchen range; fireplaces for heat *1867*<br><br>Gaslight, running water; notwithstanding availability of city water in 1884, cistern built under rear porch for storage of water from spring under property, thought to be part of "very fine spring" in nearby park (quoting Gates) *1885*<br><br>Electric lighting *1888 or later* | Bathroom *By 1907*<br><br>Central heating *Probably 1907–1910*<br><br>Telephone *c1910*<br><br>Use of cistern built 1885 discontinued after new housing in area raised suspicion of contamination and Truman had it tested *1926*<br><br>Construction of closets in attic to store clothing acquired while in Washington (bedrooms generally had closets, probably dating to 1885 enlargement) *1953* |
| | | **CARL SANDBURG HOUSE** Galesburg, Ill. *c1868*<br><br>(A small workman's cottage)<br><br>Well and pump outside; dry sink in kitchen; coal/wood-burning kitchen stove for cooking, also as source of heat for whole house; cold cellar; privy; kerosene lamps *1870s* | |
| | | **CLARA BARKLEY DORR HOUSE** Pensacola, Fla. *1871*<br><br>(An architectural curiosity in that the front and back of the house do not match, either in style or in roof line. Although built all at once, with continuous floor joists from front to back, the front is Greek Revival while the back is Pensacola Vernacular.)<br><br>Water supply presumably from well; coal-burning range in kitchen; privy; kerosene or oil lamps; fireplaces w/coal grates in every room; high ceilings and very large windows to exploit sea breezes for natural ventilation; no closets (very shallow closets in 2 bedrooms not orig. to house) *1871* | |

| 1600–1700 | 1800 | 1850 | 1900 |
|---|---|---|---|
| | | **\*DAVID DAVIS MANSION**<br>Bloomington, Ill.<br>*1872*<br><br>Using 2-man Goulds force pump in basement (capable of 47 gals. per min.), water from well pumped to attic cistern (pump in situ); gravity flow to 3 bathrooms, each w/water closet, tub, sink; 6 bedrooms w/sinks; central steam heat using A. L. Winne & Co. "Gold's Patent" low-pressure, coal-fired steam boiler; some radiators mounted horizontally under floor, w/registers similar to those for hot-air systems to convey heat into rooms; gas lighting (city gas) using Cornelius & Sons fixtures, plus use of kerosene lamps and candles<br>*1872*<br><br>Some gaslight fixtures have flexible hoses by means of which tabletop lamps can be moved about and ceiling fixtures can be raised and lowered (the latter referred to as "droplights" in letter of Sarah Davis, Nov. 1874). The net result is considerable flexibility in lighting for the time.<br>*By 1874 (probably orig. to 1872)*<br><br>Automatic ignition system for gaslights, powered by batteries in basement<br>*1889* | Garage<br>*1915* |

| 1600–1700 | 1800 | 1850 | 1900 |
|---|---|---|---|
| | | **\*ALEXANDER RAMSEY HOUSE**<br>St. Paul, Minn.<br>*1868–1872*<br><br>Public water supply just recently made available, connection from house to main in street via lead pipe; hot/cold running water, hot water from 40-gal. copper boiler connected to wood/coal kitchen stove; icebox; laundry in basement; 2 bathrooms 2nd floor, each w/Excelsior valve water closet, marble-top washstand, bathtub; waste released into recently constructed city sanitary sewer system (thence dumped raw into Mississippi River); all bedrooms on 2nd floor have sinks; gaslight using city gas (but kerosene lamps also used because of high cost of gas); hot-air heat using Lawsons No. 24 coal furnace and tin hot-air pipes to registers (Tuttles & Bouley, sizes ranging from 10 by 14 in. to 15 by 20 in.) in rooms on 1st and 2nd floors; cooling by means of cross ventilation, opening skylight, and interior shutters w/louvres; many closets<br>*1872*<br><br>Carriage house constructed<br>*1884* | |
| | | **\*HARRIET BEECHER STOWE HOUSE**<br>Hartford, Conn.<br>*1871*<br><br>Central heating plus fireplaces for supplemental heat; kitchen sink w/running water built into wooden countertop; cast-iron kitchen stove for cooking and heating; icebox in pantry w/pipe for emptying melted ice outdoors; bathroom consisting of water closet and combination bathtub-sink w/built-in kerosene water heater<br>*c1874*<br><br>(Kitchen and bathroom are 20th-cent. reconstructions using period equipment; some details conjectural) | |

| 1600–1700 | 1800 | 1850 | 1900 |
|---|---|---|---|
| | | **OLIVER H. KELLEY HOUSE**<br>Elk River, Minn.<br>*1876*<br><br>Water pumped from well, hauled inside; dry sink with slop pail for waste; root cellar w/2 entrances; wood stoves for heat; hand laundry w/scrub boards, tubs; privy<br>*1876* | |
| | | **STEVES HOMESTEAD**<br>San Antonio, Tex.<br>*1876*<br><br>Cistern on roof for gravity feed to sinks in upstairs bedrooms; possibly also cistern in ground near rear porch; wood/coal stove for cooking; gaslight (fixtures later converted to electricity); evidence of wood/coal stoves for heat; closets in bedrooms thought to be orig.<br>*1876* | Bathroom w/water closet, sink, tub installed on 2nd floor<br>*c1900*<br><br>Artesian well dug, indoor swimming pool (filled from well) built on site<br>*1910*<br><br>2nd bathroom created by closing in part of a porch<br>*c1930* |
| | | **ASA PACKER MANSION**<br>Jim Thorpe, Pa.<br>*1861*<br><br>On 1st and 2nd floors, remote-control push-button panels to control gas-burning lights; central heating<br>*c1877* | |
| | | **BLOOM MANSION**<br>Trinidad, Colo.<br>*1882*<br><br>City water (available since 1879); coal-burning stove for cooking; icebox; bathroom w/water closet, sink, tub; kerosene lamps; closets w/hooks (bedrooms only)<br>*1882* | |
| | | **COMSTOCK HOUSE**<br>Morehead, Minn.<br>*1882–1883*<br><br>Roof-fed cistern w/connection to 1st-floor kitchen, bathroom; hot water via kitchen stove; orig. sink in situ; wood-burning stove; icebox on back porch; water closet; tub but cold running water only; central hot-air heat (wood or coal); closet each bedroom<br>*1883*<br><br>Conversion to steam heat<br>*1886–1888 (based on dates on radiators)* | Bathroom added on 2nd floor<br>*1924* |

| 1600–1700 | 1800 | 1850 | 1900 |
|---|---|---|---|
| | | **SEPULVEDA HOUSE**<br>El Pueblo de Los Angeles<br>Los Angeles, Calif.<br>*1887*<br><br>Wood-burning stove in kitchen<br>for cooking; copper water heater<br>connected to stove for hot water;<br>coal-burning stoves for heat;<br>icebox for refrigeration; bathroom<br>w/tub, water closet, washbasin<br>*1887* | |
| | | **LEAR-ROCHBLAVE HOUSE**<br>Pensacola, Fla.<br>*1888*<br><br>Coal-burning range in kitchen;<br>icebox; oil/kerosene lamps;<br>outdoor privy; coal fireplaces<br>*1888* | Connection to public water<br>*c1915–1920*<br><br>Kitchen sink with hot/cold<br>running water; gas range;<br>bathroom w/water closet, hot/cold<br>bath; electric light; evidence of<br>use of gas heaters in front of<br>fireplaces<br>*1920s* |
| | | **\*SINCLAIR LEWIS<br>BOYHOOD HOME**<br>Sauk Centre, Minn.<br>*1889*<br><br>Basement cistern filled w/<br>rainwater from eaves trap on roof<br>(soft-water supply for washing);<br>water from cistern pumped<br>upstairs by means of hand pump<br>in kitchen; drinking water hauled<br>from well across the street; central<br>hot-water heat (some orig. piping<br>in situ); Monarch wood stove<br>w/hot water reservoir in kitchen;<br>summer kitchen on porch behind<br>kitchen w/kerosene stove,<br>washtubs, wooden wringer;<br>outdoor privy<br>*1889* | Electricity<br>*1901*<br><br>Connection to city water and<br>sewerage; bathroom w/water<br>closet, tub, sink<br>*1905* |

| 1600–1700 | 1800 | 1850 | 1900 |
|---|---|---|---|
| | | **\*JAMES J. HILL HOUSE** St. Paul, Minn. *1888–1891* (The mansion of a railroad baron) City water, city sewers; also roof-fed cistern, primarily for grounds care; kitchen sink with hot/cold running water; kitchen gas range w/oven, charcoal broiler; 2 iceboxes (Wickes Refrigerator Co., Chicago) in pantry plus cold storage room in basement; 13 bathrooms w/water closet, hot/cold running water at sink and tub (some bathrooms also w/shower); gas and electric lighting (some fixtures combination, gas fixtures w/ Welsbach mantles); heating system consisting of coal-fired boiler and gravity circulation radiators plus 16 fireplaces w/gas-fired porcelain "logs" and 6 fireplaces either coal- or wood-burning; telephone, 2nd floor; many closets, some apparently meant to accommodate hangers; security system utilizing electric contact alarms on many windows and doors *1891* | Installation of intercom consisting of 4 "intercommunicating telephones" *1906* |
| | | | **\*LUCIUS R. DODGE RESIDENCE** Milford, Mass. (House at 24 South Main Street purchased by Dodge and his wife Oct. 15, 1899. Dodge was a railroad conductor.) Bathroom with hot/cold running water installed *1904* Connection to municipal sewer system (above may have been for bathing only) *1912* House connected to gas for use in kitchen range *1913* Electricity added for lighting as well as for use of electric fan and vacuum cleaner *1914* Garage built to house Hudson automobile purchased secondhand *1919* |

| 1600–1700 | 1800 | 1850 | 1900 |
|---|---|---|---|
| | | | **DRUMMOND HOME**<br>Hominy, Okla.<br>*1904–1905*<br><br>Roof-fed cistern (still intact) next to house, water hauled inside in bucket; coal/wood cast-iron range; icebox; privy; wooden washing machine and many accessories (clothespins, bluing, etc.) in situ; kerosene lamps; fireplaces, coal/wood stoves, and at least 1 kerosene heater for heat<br>*1905*<br><br>Telephone in downstairs hall<br>*Later in 1905*<br><br>Bathroom w/water closet (emptying into nearby creek), 1st floor<br>*After 1905*<br><br>Acetylene generator near back door for gaslight<br>*c1910*<br><br>Gas and electric added; Charter Oak gas range installed in kitchen; electric lights<br>*1914*<br><br>Detached garage (boys had just gotten cars); city sewers, bathroom connected<br>*c1914*<br><br>Sleeping porch added to back of house, 2nd floor<br>*c1915–1916*<br><br>Upstairs bathroom added<br>*c1918*<br><br>Serval gas refrigerator<br>*1920s*<br><br>Maytag electric washing machine; radiant heater w/firebricks added to parlor fireplace<br>*1930s* |

| 1600–1700 | 1800 | 1850 | 1900 |
|---|---|---|---|
| | | | **\*CHARLES A. LINDBERGH HOUSE**<br>Little Falls, Minn.<br>*1906*<br><br>Water from well pumped into house by 1½-horsepower Fairbanks Morse gasoline engine, heated in tank on side of wood stove, thus allowing for hot/cold running water at kitchen sink; "Majestic" wood stove for cooking (taking advantage of local sawmill and cheap leftover chips); icebox in pantry supplied by icehouse built 1901 storing ice cut in winter from nearby Mississippi River; bathroom w/water closet, hot/cold running water for sink, tub; kerosene lamps; closets in bedrooms<br>*1906*<br><br>Singer sewing machine for sewing room<br>*c1913*<br><br>Attached garage added for family's new Saxon Six automobile<br>*c1916*<br><br>Wood-fired hot-air furnace installed (but since consumption of fuel turns out to be excessive, family continues to spend as much of winter as possible huddled around kitchen wood stove)<br>*1917* |

**MCFADDIN-WARD HOUSE**
Beaumont, Tex.
*1905–1906*

Public water supply apparently
from the beginning (also roof-fed
cistern, 1907–c1919); probably
wood-fired stoves for cooking;
steam central heat w/coal-fired
"Ideal Steam Heater No. S-30-5"
boiler in basement (later oil-fired,
still later gas); also fireplaces
w/coal grates; all-electric lighting,
most orig. push-button switches
still in use; 4 bathrooms w/water
closet, sink, tub (at least 2 also
w/shower apparatus) plus
downstairs bathroom w/water
closet, sink only; closets w/hooks
in all bedrooms; all 3 floors
equipped w/standpipe and hose
(earlier home on same property
had burned down); bell-call
system connecting various rooms
w/kitchen
*1906*

Freestanding carriage house
includes gymnasium, servants'
quarters w/2 bathrooms, and
garage for family's first
automobile, purchased July 1907
*1907*

Icebox
*By 1912*

Remodeling includes electric
ceiling fixtures specified to use
16-candlepower lamps; 2
bathrooms added, 1 w/footbath
and tiled shower (shower
apparatus extant); bedroom closets
remodeled or added, all now with
rods for hangers
*1912*

Kitchen w/1938 Westinghouse
electric refrigerator, 1940s sink,
and 1955 Roper gas stove (all in
situ)

**DANA-THOMAS HOUSE**
Springfield, Ill.
*c1868/1902–1904*

(A complete rebuilding of a house
of c1868 by Frank Lloyd Wright,
*1902–1904*)

Hot/cold city water plus water
from cistern (some sinks
accordingly have 3 faucets); 2
kitchen stoves: 1 coal/wood-
burning for cooking, the other a
small gas stove for heating water;
icebox; laundry room w/small
stove to heat water,
supplementing that available from
hot-water tank; 5 bathrooms, each
w/water closet, sink, tub (master
bath w/tile shower, sitz bath);
both gas and electric for light
(first fully electrified house in
Springfield); 1 electric socket and
1 gas jet in each major room (gas
considered necessary in case
electric power failed); steam heat
using private steam line in street;
battery-powered intercom system
w/9 stations in house, 2 in
carriage house; closets w/hooks
only (no hangers until c1920);
bowling alley in basement;
carriage house rebuilt from
original stable
*c1910*

**SWAN HOUSE**
Atlanta, Ga.
*1928*

Public water, public sewers; hot-
water heater in basement; 1928
Magic Chef gas range in kitchen
(in situ); electric refrigerator;
bathrooms with toilet, sink, tub
or shower stall; electric light;
steam central heating (coal, later
gas); telephone closet; numerous
closets; freestanding garage
*1928*

Electric chair lift
*c1960*

| 1600–1700 | 1800 | 1850 | 1900 |
|---|---|---|---|
| | | | **\*GROPIUS HOUSE**<br>Lincoln, Mass.<br>*1937–1938*<br><br>Floor-to-ceiling windows, ribbon windows (fixed, casement, and combinations thereof); flat roof; use of such modern materials as acoustical plaster, chrome, stainless steel, and glass block; flow-through interior planning; fireplace; overhanging eaves for shade in summer coupled with overlarge windows for warmth in winter; additional shade via exterior venetian blind controlled from inside; 2 joint heating systems: hot air supplying all rooms and hot water for bathrooms and a perimeter system under windows; garbage disposal<br>*1938* |
| | | | **\*POPE-LEIGHEY HOUSE**<br>Falls Church, Va.<br>*1939–1941*<br><br>(Frank Lloyd Wright, architect)<br><br>Open-plan interior; compact, efficient kitchen (stove, sink, refrigerator all within steps of each other); mostly recessed lighting; radiant heat by means of hot water flowing through iron pipe laid in concrete-slab floor; fireplace for psychological value of hearth; low-maintenance exterior of unfinished cypress, brick, concrete; low-maintenance interior consisting of walls of cypress and brick and floors of red-colored concrete; no attic, no cellar; carport instead of garage<br>*1941* |

# Source Notes

Source notes are grouped under chapters and then their subheads in the text. Full citations, other than periodicals, will be found in the bibliography. The following abbreviations are used: CUR (archival and other material received directly from curator or curatorial staff of house or agency indicated); HABS (Historic American Buildings Survey); TECH (data received in response to survey "The American Home and the Development of Domestic Technology"—see appendix 2 for details).

## Chapter 1: The Genealogy of the House

A FORTUITOUS ANCESTOR: Cummings, *Framed Houses,* 22–30, 44, 61–63, 95–97, 168, 203–204 [Fairbanks House and English precedent generally], 203 [1648 tax assessment]; CUR, Fairbanks House; Dedham Historical Society, *Plan;* Deetz, *In Small Things,* 99; Fairbanks, *Genealogy,* 9–17, 31–40, 869–873; Hill, *Dedham Records,* III, 25, 28, 32, 45; HABS, Fairbanks House; Holinshed, *Chronicles,* 2nd book, "On the manner of Buylding and furniture of

our houses," 85; Johnson, *Wonder-Working Providence,* 113 ["burrow in earth"]; Neve, *Builder's Dictionary,* "Thatching" [50–60 years]; Smith, *Dedham History,* 10–18; Fletcher, *Architecture,* 691 [burgages]; TECH, Fairbanks House. The discussion about the Fairbanks House being of mildly grayish appearance, as opposed to the dark and austere appearance traditionally associated with early New England frame dwellings, is based on recent and continuing research by the curator of the Fairbanks House as well as other curators. More on this appears in "Finding Parallels," chap. 6 of this book. See also Cummings, *Framed Houses,* 136, regarding red paint, possibly original, on exterior trim of Ross Tavern, Ipswich, Mass. (late 17th century) as well as chap. 9 of *Framed Houses* for passim references to use of color as well as whitewash for interior finish.

FROM HALL TO HOUSE: Addy, *Evolution,* chap. 2 passim; Barley, *English Farmhouse,* 18–20 [Colchester assessments], 21–37 [evolution of medieval house]; Barley, *House and Home,* 31–46; Barley, *Houses and History,* 49–50; Carew, *Survey of Cornwall,* as quoted in Mercer, *English Vernacular Architecture,* 8; Cummings,

*Framed Houses,* "The English Background"; Fletcher, *Architecture,* 691–692; Foster, *Architecture,* 67–70; Gies, *Medieval,* 33–34; Helm, *Homes,* 21–23; Holinshed, *Chronicles,* 2nd book, "On the manner of Buylding and furniture of our houses," 85–86; Innocent, *English Building,* passim; King, *Vale-Royall,* 19 [chimneys]; Mercer, *English Vernacular Architecture,* 8–9, 22–23 [evolution of hall]; Platt, *Medieval England,* 230; Salzman, *Building,* 187–209; Wood, *English Mediaeval,* chap. 15 passim

STILL EARLIER BUILDERS: Addy, *Evolution,* 6–8; Bulleid, *Glastonbury,* primarily vol. 1, chap. 3, passim (illustrations are 57, 124 [mortised joints], 333 [oak front door]); Holinshed, *Chronicles,* 2nd book, "On the manner of Buylding and furniture of our houses," 84; Innocent, *English Building,* chap. 2, passim; Page, *Anglo-Saxon England,* 144–151 [buildings in the time of King Alfred]; Quennell, *Prehistoric,* 182–193 [Glastonbury]; Yarwood, *Architecture,* "Early Architecture in Britain until 1066." Trans. of excerpt from Alfred's preface to Saint Augustine's *Soliloquies* by M. I. The significance of Glastonbury is summed up in Thomas, *Guide to Prehistoric England,* p. 184: "The remains of [Glastonbury and Meare] have been so well preserved . . . that the objects recovered from them tell us more about everyday life in the last century B.C. than do those of any other sites of this period."

## Chapter 2: The House A-Building

THE BUILDING OF A HOUSE, 1729: The diary account is in *New England Historical and Genealogical Register* XIII (1859), 31 (some minor editing); for reference in annotating Fessenden's journal, over and above general research: Cummings, *Framed Houses,* passim; Underhill, *Woodwright's Companion,* 179–189

BLOWS OF MALLETS AND HAMMERS: CUR, Antiquities and Landmarks Society, Hartford, Conn.; "Diary of Joshua Hempstead," New London County (Conn.) Historical Society, *Collections,* I (1901)

ANOTHER TRADITION: CUR, Schifferstadt Museum; National Heritage Corp., *Schiefferstadt*

THE EVOLVING TOWN HOUSE: Chiefly, CUR, Charleston Museum; Herold, *Preliminary Report;* Zierden, *Archaeological*

## Chapter 3: The House and the Coming of Technology

GETTING MORE COMFORTABLE and A VERY MODERN HOUSE: CUR, Historical Society of Delaware/Read House; Delaware Federal Writers Project, *New Castle,* 89–93; John Dornberg, "Count Rumford," *Smithsonian,* Dec. 1994; Mullin, *Read House Guide Manual;* Munroe, *Federalist Delaware,* 146, 232; Nylander, *Fireside,* 114; Rumford, *Works,* III, 152–162; Wise, *Read House,* 3–4; *The Times,* London, selected dates, 1785–1815

CHANGERS AND NONCHANGERS: Adams, *Monticello,* 52, 130, 139, 187; CUR, Gore Place, Historic Hudson Valley (Montgomery Place), Monticello, National Park Service (Bishop White House), Priestley House, Society for the Preservation of New England Antiquities (Rundlet-May House); Drinker, *Not So Long Ago,* 30; Jefferson, *Garden Book,* "Water Supply at Monticello," 629–631; Rice, *Langeac,* 15; Willich, *Encyclopedia,* "Vault"; Wright, *Clean,* 102–103. Credit goes to William L. Beiswanger, director of restoration at Monticello, for calling my attention to Jefferson's sketch proposing the piping of water into Monticello; similarly the sketch included with the section on central heating in chap. 5.

SHAPING THE FUTURE: Cohen & Brownell, *Latrobe,* 117–119 [plans for house for Tayloe]; CUR, Octagon, White House [Hoban letter of Jan. 4, 1816]; Hamlin, *Latrobe,* 266 [Latrobe letter Jan. 26, 1805, to John Lenthall, his superintendent at the Capitol, referring to problems involving the water closet cistern at the White House, indicating that a water closet was by now installed]; Latrobe, *Correspondence,* I:532n [Latrobe letter Aug. 5, 1804, to Benjamin King, an iron craftsman, requesting him to complete his work on the President's House, especially the water closet, showing it was not yet installed]; Seale, *President's*

*House,* 90 [Adams's privy], 90–91 [water closet ordered by Jefferson], 126–127 [water supply under Madison], 198–200 [wells, water supply, and bathing room under Jackson], 215–216 [heat, bathtubs under Van Buren], 268–269 [gaslight], 316–317 [bathtub, hot/cold running water under Pierce], 379 [water supply under Lincoln]. Material on The Octagon is derived chiefly from a detailed response to the TECH survey by Lonnie J. Hovey, A.I.A., then preservation coordinator for The Octagon; credit is due him for the explanation of "Octagon" as the name by which the house has come to be known.

TECHNOLOGY IN AND AROUND THE KITCHEN: Appert, *Art of Preserving,* xxi–xxiii, 41–43; S.S. Block, "New Foods to Tempt Your Palate," *Science Digest,* Oct. 1944 [early microwave oven]; Brown, *Hundred Years,* 56–57; Celehar, *Kitchens,* 8–11, 22, 37, 49, 53, 63–65; Fred L. Church, "The Tin Can," *Modern Metals,* Feb. 1991; Cohen, *Franklin,* 195, 200 [electricity for cooking]; DeBono, *Eureka!* 195–196; Giedion, *Mechanization,* 512–627 passim; Grow, *Kitchens,* 10–31 passim; Harrison, *Kitchen,* 125; Lupton, *Bathroom, Kitchen,* 56–60; Moore, *Ice-Houses,* passim; Nylander, *Fireside,* 96–97 [reference to Stowe quote]; Randolph, *Virginia House-Wife* (1825 ed.); Roth, "The Kitchen"; Saint-Méry, *Journal,* 155 [New York market, 1794]; Smallzried, *Everlasting Pleasure,* 104–107; *Time,* "Help in the Kitchen," Dec. 20, 1954, 64 [TV dinners]; Watson, *Annals,* 202 [icehouses "have all come into use"]; Williams, *Frozen Foods: Biography,* passim

CONCENTRATING THE HEAT SOURCE: Brown, *Hundred Years,* 56–58; Celehar, *Kitchens,* 22–23; Dow, *Domestic Life,* 15–17, 15 [Captain Denney]; Du Vall, *Domestic Technology,* 114–115 [gas as a fuel for stoves]; Giedion, *Mechanization,* 527–542; Grow, *Kitchens,* 10–15; William J. Keep, "Early American Cooking Stoves," *Old-Time New England,* XXII (Oct. 1931), 72. The concept of concentrating the heat source as a factor in the evolution of the kitchen was chiefly explored by Giedion.

THE BATHROOM AND ITS CONNECTIONS: Bennett, *King without a Crown,* 319–20 [Prince Albert]; Bridenbaugh, *Wilderness,* 239 [Newport; public necessary house in New York]; Colden, "Observations," 325–326; Drinker, *Not So Long Ago,* 23–28, 25 [Rush quote], 26 [Drinker quote]; Du Vall, *Domestic Technology,* 226–227; Kane, *Facts,* 540–541; Kranzsberg, *Technology,* 219–220; Lambton, *Temples,* 11 [Prince Albert "would be plumber"]; Fred Landon, "Excerpts from the Diary of William C. King," *Michigan History Magazine,* XIX (1935), 68–70; Longmate, *Cholera,* 13–14, 148–149, 169, 204–207; McNeil, *Technology,* 956–957; Metcalf and Eddy, *Sewerage,* passim, 5–6 [cholera]; *New York Times,* Jan. 1, 1866, Jan. 23, 1867; Palmer, *Water Closet,* 16 [Proclamation of Richard II], 23–24; Winkler, *Bath,* 15–16. *Not So Long Ago,* the diary (1758–1807) of Elizabeth Drinker of Philadelphia was edited and extensively annotated by Cecil K. Drinker, M.D., dean of the School of Public Health, Harvard University, making it a particularly authoritative source in this instance.

AND THEN THROUGH PIPES: Acrelius, *History,* 405–406 [Bethlehem water works]; *American Almanac, 1850,* 187–188 [Philadelphia, 1799–1822], 193 [Boston, 1834–1846], 200–201 [Boston, 1850]; Benson, *Kalm's Travels,* 26 [Philadelphia, 1748]; CUR, Fairbanks House; Dedham Historical Society, *Plan* (1892); Du Vall, *Domestic Technology,* 218–219; Hill, *Dedham Records,* III, 4; Kane, *Facts,* 651 [Boston, 1652]; Levering, *History,* 288–290 [Bethlehem water works]; Lupton, *Bathroom, Kitchen,* 22–23; Martin, *Standard,* 38–42 [public water supply, c1800–1860], 111 [Boston 1860], 112 [New York 1856]; Nylander, *Fireside,* 114 [early water supply]; Ripley, *Social Life,* 38–39; Saint-Méry, *Journal,* Roberts tr., 262 [use of public pumps in Philadelphia]; Smith, *Dedham History,* 156, 406–407, 417–418; Watson, *Annals,* 191 [Union Fire Co. 1744]

FROM OUTHOUSE TO IN-HOUSE: Allen, *Rural Architecture,* 123–124; *American Architect and Building News,* Aug. 18, 1883, 76 ["Niagara"]; Barlow, *Vanishing Outhouse,* passim; Bayles, *House Drainage,* 268 ["In dry summer weather"], chap. 5, "Water-Closets," passim; Brown, *Water-Closets,* passim; Cohen and Brownell, *Latrobe,* 117–119 [plans for house for

Tayloe], 500–501 [White House], 508–512, 521–522 [Markoe]; CUR, Gore Place; Drinker, *Not So Long Ago,* 28 [early water closet as increased hazard to health]; Gerhard, *Water Supply,* 135–151 [development of the water closet from the pan closet to 1910]; 455; Hamlin, *Latrobe,* 341–342 [Markoe House]; Hardyment, *Home Comfort,* 180–183; *House Beautiful,* October 1925, 424 ["flush closet"]; *House and Garden,* July 1911, 378 ["toilette"]; Lambton, *Temples,* 5–12; Lupton, *Bathroom, Kitchen,* 28; Martin, *Standard,* 89–90 [plumbing and sanitary facilities generally], 111–112 [water closets in New York], 127 [water closets in Baltimore], 424; Palmer, *Water Closet,* 13–19, 26–31; Waring, *Sanitary Drainage,* 101 [Edinburgh 1872]; Winkler, *Bath,* 12, 17–19, 21–22; U.S. Patent No. 441,268 (1890), "Siphon Closet-Bowl" [illustration and description]; Wright, *Clean,* 200–205 [water closets in 19th cent.]. I am indebted to Orlando Ridout V, Maryland Historical Trust, for the reference to Whitehall and its c1765 water closet. See Charles Scarlett, Jr., "Governor Horatio Sharpe's Whitehall," *Maryland Historical Magazine,* March 1951.

SCRUBBING AWAY OLD ATTITUDES: Richard L. Bushman and Claudia L. Bushman, "The Early History of Cleanliness in America," *Journal of American History,* LXXIV (March 1988), passim; Drinker, *Not So Long Ago,* 28–31 [but note: quote about "28 years" is from typescript of complete diary in Historical Society of Pennsylvania as quoted in Bushman, 1214]; Farrar, *Young Lady's Friend,* 160–161 ["It may shock the feelings"]; *Godey's Lady's Book,* May 1860, 464; Lewis, *White House,* 161; Lupton, *Bathroom, Kitchen,* 18–19, 29–30, [Cromie quote], 19; Lynes, *Domesticated,* 218–221; McNeil, *Technology,* 918–919; Martin, *Standard of Living,* 111–112, 127 [1860 statistics]; May N. Stone, "The Plumbing Paradox: American Attitudes toward Late Nineteenth-Century Domestic Sanitary Arrangements," *Winterthur Portfolio,* XIV (Autumn 1979); Winkler, *Bath,* 11–13, 18

THE MODERN BATHROOM: Bushman, "Cleanliness," passim, 1226 [Nathaniel Waterman]; Downing, *Country Houses,* 326; Fowler, *Home for All,*

132–33; Kira, *Bathroom,* 6–9, 156–163; Williamson, *American Hotel,* 55–62 [hotels cited]

## Chapter 4: The House as a Reflection of a Changing Society

THE HOUSE A CABIN BUILT: CUR, Stowe House; *Drake's Magazine,* VII (August 1889), 440–442 [description of interior of Stowe house]; *Hartford Times,* May 16, 1863; Hedrick, *Stowe,* 232–234 [success of *Uncle Tom's Cabin*], 310, 311–312 [Oakholm, "house of eight gables"], 316, 385 [sale of Oakholm, "If it please God"]; Johnston, *Runaway,* 384–385, 415–416

A HOUSE MORE PRACTICAL: Beecher/Stowe, *American Woman's Home,* 33, 34, 40 [model kitchen]; CUR, Stowe House; Hedrick, *Stowe,* 385

THE HOUSE AND THE STATUS OF WOMEN: Beecher, *Treatise,* "On the Construction of Houses," 258–277; Frederick, *Household Engineering,* vii–viii; Hedrick, *Stowe,* viii–ix, 385; Reich, *Colonial America,* 201 ["Everie marryd woeman"]; Sklar, *Beecher,* xii–xiii, 151–154, 162, 164–165; Strasser, *Never Done,* 168 [servants]

WOMEN AS THEIR OWN ARCHITECTS: Almost entirely archival material furnished by curators of the houses cited. Also: Edward Chappell and Willie Graham, "Prestwould: Architecture," *Antiques,* January 1995, 158

THE QUEST FOR EFFICIENCY: Beecher/Stowe, *American Woman's Home,* 32–36, 371–375, 222 ["sovereign of an empire"]; Beecher, *Treatise,* passim; Mary C. Francis, "Saving Steps in the Kitchen," *Woman's Home Companion,* September 1911; Frederick, *Household Engineering,* passim; Giedion, *Mechanization,* 512–521; Harrison, *Kitchen,* 126; Lupton, *Bathroom, Kitchen,* 41–51; Strasser, *Never Done,* 214–218

FROM PRODUCER TO CONSUMER: Barck, *Colonial America,* 336; Bishop, *American Manufactures,* I,

411–417, 413 [Coxe quote], 414 [fulling mills in N.J.]; Brown, *Hundred Years,* 59–61; Degler, *At Odds,* 5; Hayden, *Domestic Revolution,* 12, 13, 80–82, appendix; Holmes, *Account,* 208; Howe, *Houses,* 138–139; Howells, *Recollections,* 122–126; Keir, *Epic of Industry,* 17–21; Tryon, *Household Manufactures,* 370–376

THE KITCHENLESS HOUSE: Hayden, *Domestic Revolution,* 12–13, 80–82, appendix; Sinclair Lewis, Diary 1900–1908 (Yale Collection of American Literature, Beinecke Rare Book and Manuscript Library, Yale University); [Melusina Fay Peirce], "Cooperative Housekeeping," *Atlantic Monthly,* December 1868

FROM CONSUMER TO DISPOSER: Blake, *Public Health Boston,* 1–22 [Boston, 17th cent.], 14 ["City-like Towne"]; Blumberg, *War on Waste;* Capes, *Municipal Housecleaning,* 134–135 [Camden, Passaic, Cleveland]; Eliot C. Clarke, "City Scavenging at Boston" (paper read at Seventh Annual Meeting of the American Public Health Association, Nov. 18, 1879) [Boston 1870s]; Deetz, *Small Things,* 124–127 [colonial times, sheet refuse, trash pits]; "The Disposal of New York's Refuse," *Scientific American,* Oct. 24, 1903 [Waring, New York to 1903]; Gerhard, *Household Waste;* Geoffrey P. Moran, "Trash Pits and Natural Rights in the Revolutionary Era: Excavations at the Narbonne House in Salem, Massachusetts," *Archaeology,* July 1976; Harry A. Mount, "A Garbage Crisis," *Scientific American,* January 1922; Pyne, *Costume,* "The Dustman" [recycling in London early 1800s]; Rathje, *Rubbish!,* passim; Sala, *America Revisited,* I, 205 ["The garbage-boxes"]; Snow, *Boston,* 167 [house with recycled bottles in plaster]

RECYCLING THE LIFE CYCLE: Arms, *Immaculate,* 18 [Semmelweis]; Coffin, *Death,* 73 [*doed-kammer*]; Degler, *At Odds,* 57 [midwives, 1910]; Fischer, *Albion's Seed,* 80–83, 282–283, 489 [wedding customs]; Garrett, *At Home,* 227–231; Habenstein and Lamers, *History of Funeral Directing,* 232 [Boston 1750, Baltimore 1824], 242 [coming of "undertakers"], 393–397 [customs generally], 394 [walk on tiptoe], 396 [embalming procedures], 404–407 [use of home for

funerals]; Mitford, *American Way,* 198–201; Nash, *Augusta,* 284–285 [Ballard diary]; "A Newburyport Wedding One Hundred and Thirty Years Ago," Essex Institute, *Historical Collections,* LXXXVII (October 1951), 324–325; "Wm. Nutting's Diary," *Groton Historical Series* [Groton, Mass.], III (1893) 386–387; Prentiss, *Prentiss,* II, 154; Caesar Rodeney, "Fare Weather and Good Health" (The Journal of Caesar Rodeney), Harold B. Hancock, ed., *Delaware History,* X (April 1962), 54–55; Shorter, *Women's Bodies,* 127–135 [Semmelweis, birth and antisepsis], 156–160 [shift from home to hospital for birth]

ANOTHER VANTAGE POINT: Bailey, *Dutch Houses,* "Addenda"; Benson, *Kalm's Travels,* 121; *Craftsman,* magazine, "Porches, Pergolas," March 1906, 840 [quoting German visitor]; Lockyear, *Trade in India,* 20; Massachusetts Historical Society, *Copley Letters,* 131, 134, 136, 137, 147; Charles E. Peterson, ed., "American Notes," *Journal of the Society of Architectural Historians,* May 1951, 19–20 [colonial piazzas]; Simons, *Charleston,* 19; Sloane, *Voyage,* I, xlvii; Watson, *Annals,* 199 [porches in Philadelphia]

INDOORS OUTDOORS: *American Architect,* Nov. 13, 1880, 231 [increasing use of central heating]; *Century* magazine, February 1902 [Niemcewicz]; Dodge, *Mount Vernon,* 155 [bellpulls]; Davis, *Rural Residences,* Part 2, "American House" [porch as a "sitting room"]; Downing, *Country Houses,* 96 ["raised in character"]; Fitzpatrick, *Writings of Washington,* XXVII, 303; Elizabeth Paxton Forsling, "Remembering Delaware Street," *Jackson County {Mo.} Historical Society Journal,* May 1962, 11; Freeman, *Washington,* VII, 283 [visits to Mount Vernon]; Garrett, *At Home,* 30 [Jefferson, Franklin]; *Inventory of Mount Vernon,* 6 ["30 Windsor chairs"]; Latrobe, *Journal,* 54–59; *Nation,* Aug. 7, 1873, 90 [vacations]; *Putnam's Magazine,* January 1870, 30 [resort hotels]; Frederick N. Reed, "The Evolution of the Porch," *House Beautiful,* August 1914, 85 [vacations]; Estelle H. Ries, "The Evolution of the American Porch," *Garden Magazine & Home Builder,* August 1925, 481; Thomas P. Robinson, "Piazzas," *House Beautiful,* July 1918, 74 [leisure as a factor]; *Southern Literary Messenger* January 1852,

53; Wilstach, *Mount Vernon,* 149–150 ["paced before bedtime"]

A CASE OF PORCH-ITIS: *American Home,* April 1941, 13 [letter from Mrs. F. F. L., Chicago]; Richard C. Davids, "Glorifying a Great American Tradition," *Better Homes & Gardens,* February 1941, 16 [lopping off]; Ruby Ross Goodnow, "Pleasures and Purposes of Porches," *Delineator,* July 1913, 21; *House Beautiful,* August 1914, 85 ["up-to-date porch"]; Alice M. Kellogg, "New Ideas for Porch Furnishing," *Delineator,* August 1904, 280 [diversity of porches]; Frederick N. Reed, "The Evolution of the Porch," *House Beautiful,* August 1914, 85 [architects of 1890s opposing front porch]; Edith Dunham Smith, "Porches Past and Present," *House Beautiful,* April 1925, 402 [lopping off]; John Gilmer Speed, *Cosmopolitan,* June 1900, 139 [contemporary concept of automobile ushering in new age]; Lillian Hart Tryon, "Piazza Conversation," *House Beautiful,* August 1915, xi ["hung their harps upon the willows"]

**Chapter 5: The Comfortable House**

THE COMING OF CONVENIENCE and REINTERPRETING HOME: The Davis House is based almost entirely on archival and other material, CUR; the Lewis House, substantially so. In addition: Sheldon Grebstein, "Sinclair Lewis' Minnesota Boyhood," *Minnesota History,* Autumn 1954, XXXIV, 85; Sinclair Lewis, Diary 1900–1908, Yale Collection of American Literature, Beinecke Rare Book and Manuscript Library, Yale University; Lewis, *Main Street,* 177, 410; Olson, *Lewis,* 1–6; Schorer, *Lewis,* 4–5, 16–35 passim

KEEPING WARM: *American Architect and Building News,* Nov. 13, 1880 [as quoted]; Bishop, *American Manufactures,* 302 [Harmony Society and William Wheeler]; CUR, Hampton and Martin Van Buren National Historic Sites, Old Economy Village, Schifferstadt; Downing, *Country Houses,* 475–479 [hot-air furnaces]; Ford, *Franklin,* 355–358; Ford Museum research library [misc. catalogs, brochures, etc. from

which was derived dating of blowers and stokers]; Howells, *Years of My Youth,* 53; Kranzberg, *Technology,* Rotsch, "Home Environment," 226–227; *Life,* "Electronic Blanket," Feb. 11, 1946; Nylander, *Fireside,* 74–82, 76 [reference to Robbins diary]; Peirce, *Fire,* 36 [Clarke and Sewell]; Plat, *Eden,* 50; Rumford, *Works,* "Of Chimney Fireplaces," II, 222–307; Tarbox, *Robbins* [dates in diary as cited]; Rothschild, Diamond tr., *View of America,* 23 (diary entry is New York, Jan. 12, 1860); TECH, Davis Mansion, Wyck; Tredgold, *Principles of Warming,* 158–160

AND STAYING COOL: Cutler, *Life,* I, 269 [visit with Franklin]; Downing, *Country Houses,* 190–191 [ventilators], 473 [blinds]; Kranzberg, *Technology,* Rotsch, "Home Environment," 228–231; *Life,* "Air Conditioning," July 16, 1945; *Newsweek,* "Booming Like Television," July 10, 1950 [air conditioning]; Skolfield, *Electric Fans,* 6–13; TECH, Hillforest, Gallier House; Don Wharton, "Comfort for Millions," *Reader's Digest,* July 1950 [home air conditioners]

LIGHTING: CUR, Merchant House Museum; Garrett, *At Home,* 140–141, 145; Howell and Schroeder, *Incandescent Lamp,* 34 [Farmer's lamp]; *Holyoke Diaries,* 15, 24; Martin, *Standard of Living,* 94–97; Nylander, *Fireside,* 106–109; TECH, Bowers, Hill, and Ramsey Houses

ATTIC AND CLOSETS: Harriet P. Bradley, Diary, 1819, ms., Research Library, Old Sturbridge Village; Carson, *Consuming Interests,* 22 [18th-century cupboards]; Cummings, *Framed Houses,* 115 [Fairbanks House], 226 [other Dedham attics]; "An Inventory of the whole Estate of Jonathan Fairbank . . ." (Suffolk County [Mass.] Probate, V, 112) [Fairbanks's attic]; Fowler, *Home for All,* 119 [charcoal filtration], 132–133 [cisterns]; Richard LeGallienne, "Roofs, Gables and Garrets," *House & Garden,* April 1929, 100; Noble, *Wood, Brick, and Stone,* I, 13; Ruth Adele Sampson, "The Spell of the Attic," *Country Life in America,* February 1919, 32; Harry I. Shumway, "Might Need It Some Day," *House Beautiful,* Dec. 1918, 370; TECH, Fairbanks, Priestley, and Read Houses, Gore Place, and Wright's Ferry Mansion;

Wainwright, *Diary of Fisher,* 296–297; Watson, *Annals,* 184 [chests of drawers]

CELLAR AND GARAGE: Allen, *Rural Architecture,* 163; Theo Baer, "The Attached Garage," *House Beautiful,* September 1922, 189–190; Sherman R. Barnett, "How to have a bright basement," *Better Homes and Gardens,* September 1948, 229 [knotty pine]; Beecher/ Stowe, *American Woman's Home,* 40; Briggs, *Homes of the Pilgrim Fathers,* 155, 176; Clare Briggs, "My Car's Room in the House," *Country Life in America,* January 1920, 51; Burton Ashford Bugbee, "The Garage's Place Is in the Home," *House Beautiful,* February 1932, 134; Charles Alma Byers, "Keeping the Automobile in the House," *Keith's Magazine,* May 1920, 262–265; R. W. Carney, "A Recreation Room," *Woman's Home Companion,* October 1929, 58; CUR, Fairbanks House [cellar]; Emery, *Reminiscences;* Harriet Sisson Gillespie, "The basement becomes the games room," *American Home,* December 1929, 261; Jules Gregory, "The Cellar Becomes Livable," *House & Garden,* January 1929, 78; R. Horner, "The Cellar of a House," *House Beautiful,* October 1913, 159; Henry Humphrey, "House your Car," *American Home,* April 1931, 26; Jandl, *Yesterday's Houses,* 159 ["switch placed on a post"]; E.S.M., "Status of the Horse," *Harper's Weekly,* Nov. 18, 1899, 1172; Martin, *Standard of Living,* 265–267 [personal transportation c1860]; Saint-Méry, Roberts tr., *Moreau de St. Méry,* 146; Vaux, *Villas and Cottages,* 123, 214–215; Charles E. White, Jr., "Housing the Automobile," *House Beautiful,* August 1911, 84–87

WINDOWS AND SCREENS: Andersen Corp., "Making Window History" (privately printed, n.d.) [picture window of 1930s]; Briggs, *Building Crafts,* "Glazing" [use of vertical sash windows by Inigo Jones]; Brown, *Hundred Years,* 57–58; CUR, Fairbanks House, Society for the Preservation of New England Antiquities (Gropius House); Drinker, *Not So Long Ago,* 32–33 [public health aspects of mosquitoes early 1800s]; Garrett, *At Home,* 202 [Jefferson and screens at President's House and Monticello]; H. Gradle, M.D., "The Germ-Theory of Disease," *Popular Science Monthly,* XXIII (September 1883), 577;

"An Improved Window Screen," *Scientific American,* Sept. 10, 1892, 162; A. F. A. King, "Insects and Disease," *Popular Science Monthly,* September 1883, 656 [article cited, also Dismal Swamp Hotel]; *Maryland Gazette,* Annapolis, July 26, 1759, 3 [ad for mosquito netting]; Quincy, *Memoir,* 91, ["size of the panes excited admiration"]; Kathleen Catalano Milley, "Residential Casement Windows," *Cultural Resources Management,* National Park Service, XVI, no. 8 (1993), 20 [Governor Coddington House]; Charles E. Peterson, ed., "American Notes," *Journal of the Society of Architectural Historians,* May 1951, 20 [use of screens in the 18th century]; *Scientific American,* October 1934, 218 [announcement of double-glazed "Thermopane" window glass]; U.S. Patents 11,764 (1854) [Webster's "Mosquito Curtain"], 56,128 (1866) ["iron wire or cloth"], 56,994 (1866) [spring-loaded frame]; Young, *Pilgrim Fathers,* 237 [Winslow quote]

THE BEDROOM: Annabelle Voigt Dirks, "Comfort and warmth for winter nights," *Good Housekeeping,* December 1946, 126; "Electronic Blanket," *Life,* Feb. 11, 1946, 53; Garrett, *At Home,* 114–115, 118–119 [bed curtains]; *Missouri Historical Review,* vol. 47, p. 219 [featherbeds, 30 to 50 pounds; most prized possessions]; Nelson, *Tomorrow's House,* 114; U.S. Patent 12,111 (1854) ["Spring Bed-Bottom"]; Wright, *Warm and Snug,* 237–240 ["Springs and Stuffings"]

A LATTER-DAY JOSHUA HEMPSTED: "The Account Book of Lucius R. Dodge, 1889–1946." Ms., Baker Library, Harvard University Graduate School of Business Administration

## Chapter 6: The House as Architecture

VISITING THE MODERN HOUSE: Invaluable here was use of the master's thesis of Peter Gittleman (see bibliography, unpublished works), which includes the quotations attributed to Ati Gropius Johansen. Gittleman is director of interpretation and public programs for the Society for the Preservation of New England Antiquities, which owns and operates the Gropius House as a museum, and was of all possible help. Also: Beulah Brown Anthony, "The Massachusetts home of Dr. and Mrs. Walter Gropius," *American Home,* July 1939, 21; Giedion, *Space, Time,* 502 ["While I was staying in 1938"]

REDEFINING ARCHITECTURE and WHY MODERN IS MODERN: "American Modern Architecture," *House Beautiful,* September 1938, 22; Ford, *The Modern House,* Introduction, 8–14; Gittleman, thesis [passim, Gropius quote]; Elizabeth B. Mock, "Modern Houses: How to look at them," *House & Garden,* August 1946, 30; "Nine on Modern: Here Are the Questions Most Often Asked about Modern Houses," *House & Garden,* April 1946, 77; "Tell Me, What Is Modern Architecture?," *House & Garden,* April 1940, 46 [brief interviews with architects Marcel Breuer, John Ekin Dinwiddie, Walter Gropius, and William Wilson Wurster]; Wright, *Architectural Record,* March 1908. The footnote on p. 213 is from Latrobe, *Correspondence,* II, 929

AS IF A STARTLING INNOVATION: Breuer, in "Tell Me," *House & Garden,* April 1940, 71 ["type of design nearest to ourselves"]; Gittleman, thesis, (bibliography, unpublished works) [Ati Gropius quote]; Mock, "Modern Houses," *House & Garden,* August 1946, 30 ["as if a startling innovation"]; Wright, "Recollections," a series of articles in *Architects' Journal,* July–August 1936

THE MOST LOGICAL HOUSE: Primarily material furnished by the National Trust for Historic Preserva-tion, which administers the Pope-Leighey House, and correspondence and telephone interview with Loren Pope, the original owner, in August 1996. Also: HABS; Loren Pope, "The Love Affair of a Man and his House," *House Beautiful,* August 1948, 32; Naden, *Wright,* 125–130 [Usonian house]

FINDING PARALLELS: Chiefly a distillation of the above, going back to chap. 1 (see, in particular, source notes for "The Oldest Living Relative"). The 1938 John Adams quote is from Gittleman.

EARLY ARCHITECTURAL TRADITIONS, A DEVELOPING DIVERSITY, SEEING IN CONTRAST, and FULL CIRCLES: Likewise, much here is derived from the foregoing chapters. Additionally, besides quotations, the sources of which are clear from the text: Carley, *American Domestic Architecture,* McAlester, *Field Guide,* Whiffen, *American Architecture,* these in particular, all passim [evolution of architectural styles]; Colonial Williamsburg, *President's Report* (n.d., c1960s), "Beauty from Geometry," "Beauty from Simplicity" [Williamsburg]; CUR, Wyck; Dickens, *American Notes,* 29; Arthur L. Finney, "The Royall House in Medford: A Re-Evaluation of the Structural and Documentary Evidence," in Colonial Society of Massachusetts, *Architecture in Colonial Massachusetts,* 23–33 [Royall House]; Morrison, *Early American Architecture,* 475–477 [Foster-Hutchinson House]; Whitehill and Nichols, *Palladio in America,* 101–109 passim; Wright, "A Home in a Prairie Town," *Ladies' Home Journal,* February 1901, 17

# Bibliography

Acrelius, Israel. *A History of New Sweden.* Philadelphia, 1876.

Adams, Charles Francis. *Three Episodes of Massachusetts History.* Boston, 1892.

Adams, William Howard. *Jefferson's Monticello.* New York: Abbeville Press, 1983.

Addy, Sidney Oldall. *The Evolution of the English House.* London, 1898/1933.

Allen, Lewis F. *Rural Architecture.* New York, 1854.

*American Almanac.* Boston: Gray and Bowen, 1830–1861.

American Stove Company, *Lorain Cooking.* St. Louis: 1926.

Appert, M. *The Art of Preserving.* Translated from the French, Paris, 1810. London, 1811.

Arms, Suzanne, *Immaculate Deception.* Boston: Houghton Mifflin, 1975.

Bailey, Rosalie Fellows. *Pre-Revolutionary Dutch Houses and Families in Northern New Jersey and Southern New York.* New York, 1936/1968.

Barck, Oscar Theodore, and Hugh Talmage Lefler. *Colonial America.* New York: Macmillan, [1958].

Barley, M. W. *The English Farmhouse and Cottage.* London: Routledge and Kegan Paul, 1961.

———. *The House and Home: A Review of 900 Years of House Planning and Furnishing in Britain.* Greenwich, Conn.: New York Graphic Society, 1971.

———. *Houses and History.* London and Boston: Faber and Faber, 1986.

Barlow, Ronald S. *The Vanishing American Outhouse.* El Cajon, Calif.: Windmill Publishing, 1989.

Bayles, James Copper. *House Drainage and Water Service.* New York, 1880.

Beecher, Catharine E. *Treatise on Domestic Economy.* New York, 1845.

——— and Harriet Beecher Stowe. *The American Woman's Home.* New York, 1869.

Bemis, Albert F., and John Burchard. *The Evolving House.* Cambridge, Mass.: MIT Press, 1933.

Benjamin, Asher. *The American Builder's Companion.* Boston, 1827.

Bennett, Daphne. *King Without a Crown.* London: Heinemann, 1977.

Benson, Adolph B. ed. *The America of 1750: Peter Kalm's Travels in North America.* New York, 1937.

Bentley, William. *The Diary of William Bentley, D.D.* Salem, Mass., 1914.

Beverley, Robert. *The History and Present State of Virginia.* (1705) Chapel Hill, N.C.: University of North Carolina Press, 1947.

Bishop, J. Leander. *A History of American Manufactures from 1608 to 1860.* 3d ed. Philadelphia, 1868.

Blake, John B. *Public Health in the Town of Boston, 1630–1822.* Cambridge, Mass.: Harvard University Press, 1959.

Blumberg, Louis, and Robert Gottlieb. *War on Waste.* Washington, D.C.: Island Press, 1989.

Bradford, William. *Of Plymouth Plantation.* New York: Knopf, 1970.

Bridenbaugh, Carl. *Cities in Revolt.* New York: Knopf, 1955.

———. *Cities in the Wilderness.* (1938) New York: Capricorn Books, 1955.

———. *The Colonial Craftsman.* New York: New York University Press, 1950; London: Oxford University Press, 1950.

Briggs, Martin S. *A Short History of the Building Crafts.* Oxford: Oxford University Press, 1925.

———. *The Homes of the Pilgrim Fathers in England and America.* London/New York: Oxford University Press, 1932.

Brown, Alexander, ed. *Chronicles of the First Planters of the Colony of Massachusetts.* Boston, 1846.

Brown, Glenn. *Water-Closets: A Historical, Mechanical and Sanitary Treatise.* New York, 1884.

Brown, Harriet Connor. *Grandmother Brown's Hundred Years, 1827–1927.* Boston: Little Brown, 1929.

Buisseret, David. *Historic Architecture of the Caribbean.* London, 1980.

Bulleid, Arthur, and Harold St. George Gray. *The Glastonbury Lake Village.* [Glastonbury?]: Glastonbury Antiquarian Society, 1911.

Burchard, John, and Albert Bush-Brown. *The Architecture of America.* Boston: Little Brown, 1961.

Capes, William Parr, and Jeanne D. Carpenter. *Municipal Housecleaning.* New York, 1918.

Carley, Rachel. *Visual Dictionary of American Domestic Architecture.* New York: Henry Holt, 1994.

Carson, Cary, Ronald Hoffman, and Peter J. Albert, eds. *Of Consuming Interests: The Style of Life in the Eighteenth Century.* Charlottesville, Va.: University Press of Virginia for the U.S. Capitol Historical Society, 1994.

Celehar, Jane A. *Kitchens and Kitchenware.* Lombard, Ill., Wallace-Homestead Book Co., 1985.

Chappelow, A. C. *The Old Home in England, 1100 to 1830.* London: The Old Wooden Shop, 1953.

Cheever, George, ed. *The Journal of the Pilgrims at Plymouth.* New York, 1848.

Child, [Lydia] Maria. *Letters from New York.* New York, 1845.

Clark, Clifford Edward. *The American Family Home, 1800–1960.* Chapel Hill, N.C.: University of North Carolina Press, 1986.

Cloag, John. *The Englishman's Castle: A History of Houses, Large and Small, in Town and Country, from A.D. 100 to the Present Day.* London, 1944.

Coffin, Margaret M. *Death in Early America.* New York: Elsevier/Nelson Books, 1976.

Cohen, I. Bernard. *Benjamin Franklin's Experiments.* Cambridge, Mass.: Harvard University Press, 1941.

Cohen, Jeffrey A., and Charles E. Brownell. *The Architectural Drawings of Benjamin Henry Latrobe.* New Haven, Conn., and London: Yale University Press for the Maryland Historical Society and American Philosophical Society, 1994.

Colden, Cadwallader. "Observations on the Fever which prevailed in the City of New-York in 1741 and 2." *American Medical and Philosophical Register,* vol. 1 (1814).

Colonial Society of Massachusetts. *Architecture in Colonial Massachusetts.* Boston: Colonial Society of Massachusetts, distributed by University Press of Virginia, 1979.

Cousins, Frank, and Phil M. Riley. *The Colonial Architecture of Philadelphia.* Boston: Little, Brown, 1920.

Cummings, Abbott Lowell. *The Framed Houses of Massachusetts Bay, 1625–1725.* Cambridge, Mass.: Harvard University Press, 1979.

Cutler, Manasseh. *Life, Journals and Correspondence of the Rev. Manasseh Cutler.* Cincinnati, 1888.

Dahmus, Joseph H. *A History of Medieval Civilization.* New York: Odyssey Press, 1964.

Dankers, Jaspar, and Peter Sluyter. *Journey of a Voyage to New York.* Brooklyn, N.Y., 1867.

Davey, Norman. *A History of Building Materials.* New York: Drake, 1971.

Davis, Alexander Jackson. *Rural Residences.* New York, 1837.

De Bono, Edward, ed. *Eureka! An Illustrated History of Inventions.* New York: Holt Rinehart, 1974.

Dedham Historical Society. *Plan . . . of Dedham Village.* Dedham, Mass., 1892.

Deetz, James. *In Small Things Forgotten: The Archeology of Early American Life.* (Garden City, N.Y.: Anchor/Doubleday, 1977.

Degler, Carl N. *At Odds: Women and the Family in America from the Revolution to the Present.* New York: Oxford University Press, 1980.

Delaware Federal Writers Project, Works Progress Administration. *New Castle on the Delaware.* [New Castle]: New Castle Historical Society, [1937].

Dickens, Charles. *American Notes.* New York, 1842.

Disston, Henry, & Sons. *The Saw in History.* Philadelphia, 1921.

Dodge, Harrison Howell. *Mount Vernon: Its Owner and Its Story.* Philadelphia, 1932.

Dow, George Francis. *Domestic Life in New England in the Seventeenth Century.* Discourse delivered at the opening of the American Wing of the Metropolitan Museum of Art. Topsfield, Mass., 1925.

Downing, Andrew Jackson. *The Architecture of Country Houses.* New York, 1850.

———. *Cottage Residences.* New York, 1842.

Drinker, Cecil K. *Not So Long Ago.* Chiefly the diary of Elizabeth Drinker, 1758–1807. New York: Oxford University Press, 1937.

Du Vall, Nell. *Domestic Technology: A Chronology of Developments.* Boston: G. K. Hall, 1988.

Eden, Peter. *Small Houses in England, 1520–1820.* London: The Historical Association, 1969.

Emery, Sarah Anna. *Reminiscences of a Nonagenarian.* Newburyport, Mass., 1879.

Fairbanks, Lorenzo Sayles. *Genealogy of the Fairbanks Family in America, 1633–1897.* Boston, 1897.

[Farrar, Eliza]. *The Young Lady's Friend.* Boston, 1837.

Fessenden, Benjamin. "An Account of Getting up my frame." *New England Historical and Genealogical Register,* vol. 13 (1859).

Fischer, David Hackett. *Albion's Seed: Four British Folkways in America.* New York and Oxford: Oxford University Press, 1989.

Fitch, James Marston. *American Building: The Historical Forces That Shaped It.* Boston: Houghton Mifflin, 1947/1966.

Fitzpatrick, John C., ed. *The Writings of George Washington.* Washington, D.C., 1931–44.

Flaherty, David H. *Privacy in Colonial New England.* Charlottesville, Va.: University Press of Virginia, 1972.

Fletcher, Banister Flight. *The English Home.* London, 1910.

Fletcher, Sir Banister. *A History of Architecture.* 18th ed., revised by J. C. Palmes. New York: Scribner's, 1975.

Foley, Mary Mix. *The American House.* New York: Harper and Row, 1980.

Ford, Paul Leicester. *The Many-Sided Franklin.* New York, 1899.

Foster, Michael, ed. *Architecture: Style, Structure, and Design.* London: Quill Publishing, 1982.

Fowler, Orson S. *A Home for All, or The Gravel Wall Octagon Mode of Building.* New York, 1854.

Frederick, Christine. *The New Housekeeping: Efficiency Studies in Home Management.* New York: Doubleday, 1913.

———. *Household Engineering.* Chicago, 1919.

Furnas, J. C. *The Americans: A Social History of the United States 1587–1914.* New York: Putnam's, 1969.

Gardiner, Stephen. *The Evolution of the House.* New York: Macmillan, 1974.

Garrett, Elisabeth Donaghy. *At Home: The American Family 1750–1870.* New York: Harry N. Abrams, 1990.

Gerhard, William Paul. *Disposal of Household Waste.* New York, 1890.

———. *The Water Supply, Sewerage, and Plumbing of Modern City Buildings.* New York, 1910.

Giedion, Siegfried. *Mechanization Takes Command.* New York: Oxford University Press, 1948.

———. *Space, Time and Architecture.* Cambridge, Mass.: Harvard University Press, 1941/1982.

Gies, Frances and Joseph. *Life in a Medieval Village.* New York: Harper & Row, 1990.

Goodrich, S. G. *Recollections of a Lifetime.* New York, 1856.

Gowans, Alan. *Images of American Living: Four Centuries of Architecture and Furniture as Cultural Expression.* New York: Harper and Row, 1964/1976.

Grow, Lawrence. *The Old House Book of Kitchens and Dining Rooms.* New York: Warner Books, 1981.

Gutman, Robert, ed. *People and Buildings.* New York: Basic Books, 1972.

Habenstein, Robert W., and William M. Lamers. *The History of American Funeral Directing.* Milwaukee: National Funeral Directors Association, 1955.

Hall, Florence Howe. *Social Customs.* Boston, 1887.

Hamlin, Talbot. *Benjamin Henry Latrobe.* New York: Oxford University Press, 1955.

Handlin, David P. *The American Home: Architecture and Society, 1815–1915.* Boston: Little, Brown, 1979.

Hardyment, Christina. *Home Comfort: A History of Domestic Arrangements.* London/New York: Viking, 1992.

Harington, Sir John. *A New Discourse of a Stale Subject; Called the Metamorphosis of Ajax.* London, 1596.

Harrison, Henry S. *Houses.* New York: Scribner's, 1980.

Harrison, Molly. *The Kitchen in History.* New York: Scribner's, 1972.

Hayden, Dolores. *The Grand Domestic Revolution: A History of Feminist Designs for American Homes, Neighborhoods, and Cities.* Cambridge, Mass.: M.I.T. Press, 1981.

Hedrick, Joan D. *Harriet Beecher Stowe: A Life.* New York and Oxford: Oxford University Press, 1994.

Hellerstein, Erna Olafson, Leslie Parker Hume, and Karen M. Offen, eds. *Victorian Women.* Stanford, Calif.: Stanford University Press, 1981.

Helm, W. H. *Homes of the Past.* London, 1921.

Hill, Don Gleason, ed. *The Early Records of the Town of Dedham.* Dedham, Mass., 1892.

Hodgson, Fred T. *Light and Heavy Timber Framing Made Easy.* Chicago, 1909.

*Holinshed's Chronicles.* London, 1587; reprinted, London, 1807.

Holmes, Isaac. *An Account of the United States of America . . . during a Residence of Four Years.* London, 1823.

*The Holyoke Diaries, 1709–1856.* Salem, Mass.: Essex Institute, 1911.

Howe, Barbara J., Dolores A. Fleming, Emory L. Kemp, and Ruth Ann Overbeck. *Houses and Homes.* Nashville, Tenn.: American Association for State and Local History, 1987.

Howe, Philip. *Diary of Philip Howe.* New York: Dodd Mead, 1936.

Howell, John W., and Henry Schroeder. *History of the Incandescent Lamp.* Schenectady, N.Y., 1927.

Howells, William Cooper. *Recollections of Life in Ohio, 1813–1840.* Cincinnati, 1895.

Howells, W. D. *Years of My Youth.* New York, 1916.

Huger Smith, Alice R., and D. E. Huger Smith. *The Dwelling Houses of Charleston.* Philadelphia and London, 1917.

Innocent, C. F. *The Development of English Building Construction.* Cambridge, Mass.: Cambridge University Press, 1916.

*Inventory of the Contents of Mount Vernon.* Cambridge, Mass., 1909.

Jandl, H. Ward. *Yesterday's Houses of Tomorrow: Innovative American Homes, 1850 to 1950.* Washington, D.C., Preservation Press, 1991.

Jefferson, Thomas. *Thomas Jefferson's Garden Book.* Philadelphia: American Philosophical Society, 1944.

Johnson, Edward. J. Franklin Jameson, ed. *Johnson's Wonder-Working Providence, 1628–1651.* New York, 1910.

Kane, Joseph Nathan. *Famous First Facts.* New York: H. W. Wilson, 4th ed., 1981.

Kauffman, Henry J. *The American Farmhouse.* New York: Hawthorn Books, 1975.

Keir, Robert Malcolm. *The Epic of Industry.* New Haven, Conn.: Yale University Press, 1926.

Kimball, Fiske. *Domestic Architecture of the American Colonies and of the Early Republic.* New York: Scribner's, 1922; reprinted, Dover, 1966.

King, Daniel. *The Vale-Royall of England.* London, 1656.

Kira, Alexander. *The Bathroom.* New York: Viking Press, 1976.

Kirker, Harold. *The Architecture of Charles Bulfinch.* Cambridge, Mass.: Harvard University Press, 1969.

Kranzberg, Melvin, and Carroll W. Pursell, Jr. *Technology in Western Civilization.* New York: Oxford University Press, 1967.

Lafever, Minard. *The Modern Builder's Guide.* New York, 1841.

Lambton, Lucinda. *Temples of Convenience.* London: Gordon Fraser, 1978.

Lancaster, Osbert. *Homes Sweet Homes.* London, 1939.

Larkin, Jack. *The Reshaping of Everyday Life 1790–1840.* New York: HarperCollins, 1988.

Latrobe, Benjamin Henry. *The Correspondence and Miscellaneous Papers of Benjamin Henry Latrobe.* Edited by John C. Van Horne and Lee W. Formwalt. New Haven, Conn., and London: Yale University Press for the Maryland Historical Society, 1984.

———. *Journal of Latrobe.* New York, 1905.

Levering, Joseph Mortimer. *A History of Bethlehem, Pennsylvania 1741–1892.* Bethlehem, Pa., 1903.

Lewis, Ethel. *The White House: An Informal History.* New York, 1937.

Lewis, Sinclair. *Main Street.* New York: Harcourt, Brace & World, 1920/1948.

Light, Sally. *House Histories.* Spencertown, N.Y.: Golden Hill Press, 1989.

Lloyd, Nathaniel. *A History of the English House from Primitive Times to the Victorian Period.* London, 1931.

Lockyer, Charles. *An Account of Trade in India.* London, 1711.

Longmate, Norman. *King Cholera: The Biography of a Disease.* London: Hamish Hamilton, 1966.

Lupton, Ellen, and J. Abbott Miller. *The Bathroom, the Kitchen, and the Aesthetics of Waste.* Cambridge, Mass.: M.I.T. List Visual Arts Center, 1992.

Lynes, Russell. *The Domesticated Americans.* New York: Harper and Row, 1957.

Macdonald, Anne L. *Feminine Ingenuity.* New York, 1992.

Markham, Gervaise. *The English Hus-wife.* London, 1615.

Martin, Edgar W. *The Standard of Living in 1860.* Chicago: University of Chicago, 1942.

Massachusetts Historical Society. *Letters and Papers of John Singleton Copley and Henry Pelham, 1739–1776.* N.p., 1914.

Matthaei, Julie A. *An Economic History of Women in America.* New York: Schocken Books, 1982.

Mayhew, Edgar deN., and Minor Myers, Jr. *A Documentary History of American Interiors.* New York: Scribner's, 1980.

McAlester, Virginia, and Lee McAlester. *A Field Guide to American Houses.* New York: Knopf, 1984.

McNeil, Ian, ed. *An Encyclopedia of the History of Technology.* London and New York, Routledge, 1990.

Mercer, Eric. *English Vernacular Architecture: A Study of Traditional Farmhouses and Cottages.* London: Royal Commission on Historical Documents, England; Her Majesty's Stationery Office, 1975.

Metcalf, Leonard, and Harrison P. Eddy. *Sewerage and Sewage Disposal.* New York: McGraw-Hill, 1930.

Mitford, Jessica. *The American Way of Death.* New York: Simon and Schuster, 1963.

Moore, Thomas. *An Essay on the Most Eligible Construction of Ice-Houses. Also, a Description of the Newly Invented Machine Called the Refrigerator.* Baltimore, 1803.

Moreau de Saint-Méry. *Moreau de St. Mery's American Journal.* Translated by Kenneth Roberts and Anna M. Roberts. Garden City, N.Y.: Doubleday, 1947.

Morrison, Hugh. *Early American Architecture.* New York: Oxford University Press, 1952.

Munroe, John A. *Federalist Delaware, 1715–1815.* New Brunswick, N.J.: Rutgers University Press, 1954.

Naden, Corinne J. *Frank Lloyd Wright: The Rebel Architect.* New York: Franklin Watts, 1968.

Nash, Charles Elventon. *History of Augusta* [Maine]. Augusta, Me., 1904.

*National Trust Book of English Architecture.* New York and London: Norton, 1981.

Nelson, George. *Tomorrow's House: How to Plan Your Post-War Home Now.* New York: Simon and Schuster, 1945.

Neve, Richard. *The City and Country Purchaser's and Builder's Dictionary.* London, 1736.

Nichols, Frederick Doveton. *The Early Architecture of Georgia.* Chapel Hill, N.C.: University of North Carolina Press, 1957.

Noble, Allen G. *Wood, Brick, and Stone: The North American Settlement Landscape,* vol. 1: *Houses.* Amherst, Mass.: University of Massachusetts Press, 1984.

Nye, Russell B. *Society and Culture in America, 1830–1860.* New York, 1974.

Nylander, Jane C. *Our Own Snug Fireside: Images of the*

*New England Home, 1760–1860.* New York: Knopf, 1993.

Oliver, John W. *History of American Technology.* New York: Ronald Press, 1956.

Olson, Roberta. *Sinclair Lewis: The Journey.* Sauk Centre, Minn.: Privately published, 1990.

Osborn, Donald Lewis. *Joseph Brunner of Rothenstein, Schifferstadt and Frederick.* Lee's Summit, Mo.: Published by the author, 1991.

Page, R. I. *Life in Anglo-Saxon England.* London: B. T. Batsford Ltd; New York: G. P. Putnam's Sons, 1970.

Palmer, Roy. *The Water Closet: A New History.* Newton Abbot [England]: David & Charles, 1973.

Peirce, Josephine H. *Fire on the Hearth.* Springfield, Mass.: Pond-Ekberg Co., 1951.

Peterson, Merrill D. *Thomas Jefferson and the New Nation.* New York: Oxford University Press, 1970.

Phipps, Frances. *Colonial Kitchens, Their Furnishings and Their Gardens.* New York: Hawthorn Books, 1972.

Plat, Sir Hugh. *The Garden of Eden.* London, 1653.

Platt, Colin. *Medieval England: A Social History and Archaeology.* London: Routledge & Kegan Paul, 1978.

Prentiss, Elizabeth. *Life of Elizabeth Prentiss.* New York, 1898.

Pyne, W. H. *The Costume of Great Britain,* "The Dustman." London, 1808.

Quennell, Marjorie, and C. H. B. Quennell. *Everyday Life in Prehistoric Times.* New York: Putnam's, 1959.

[Quincy, Eliza S. M.]. *Memoir of the Life of Eliza S. M. Quincy.* Boston, 1861.

[Randolph, Mary]. *The Virginia House-Wife.* Washington, D.C., 1824.

Rathje, William, and Cullen Murphy. *Rubbish! The Archaeology of Garbage.* New York: Harper Collins, 1992.

Reich, Jerome R. *Colonial America.* Englewood Cliffs, N.J.: Prentice-Hall, 1984.

Rice, Howard C. *L'Hôtel de Langeac: Jefferson's Paris Residence/Residence de Jefferson à Paris, 1785–1789.* Paris: Chez Henry Lefebvre; Monticello, Va.: Thomas Jefferson Memorial Foundation, 1947.

Richardson, George. *The New Vitruvius Britannicus.* London, 1802–1808.

Rifkind, Carole. *A Field Guide to American Architecture.* New York, London, Scarborough, Me.: New American Library, 1980.

Ripley, Eliza. *Social Life in Old New Orleans.* New York, 1912.

Roberts, Robert. *The House Servant's Directory.* Boston, 1827.

Robinson, Solon. *How to Live.* New York, 1874.

Roth, Rodris. "Recording a Room: The Kitchen." *Historic America.* Washington, D.C.: Library of Congress, 1983.

Rothschild, Salomon de. *A Casual View of America.* Translated by Sigmund Diamond. Stanford, Calif.: Stanford University Press, 1961.

Rumford, Sir Benjamin Thompson, Count. *The Complete Works of Count Rumford.* (Boston, 1870–1875.) Reprinted as *Collected Works* by Belknap Press, Cambridge, Mass., 1968–1970.

Sala, George. *America Revisited.* London, 1882.

Salmon, Lucy Maynard. *Domestic Service.* New York: Macmillan, 1897.

Salway, Peter. *The Oxford Illustrated History of Roman Britain.* New York: Oxford University Press, 1993.

Salzman, L. F. *Building in England Down to 1540.* Oxford: Oxford University Press, 1952.

Schivelbusch, Wolfgang. *Disenchanted Night: The Industrialization of Light in the Nineteenth Century.* Translated by Angela Davies. Berkeley/Los Angeles/London: University of California Press, 1988.

Schlereth, Thomas J. *Victorian America: Transformations in Everyday Life, 1876–1915.* New York: Harper Collins, 1991.

Schorer, Mark. *Sinclair Lewis: An American Life.* New York: McGraw-Hill, 1961.

Seale, William. *The President's House: A History.* Washington, D.C.: White House Historical Association with the cooperation of the National Geographic Society and Harry N. Abrams, Inc., New York, 1986.

————. *Recreating the Historic House Interior.* Nashville: American Association for State and Local Government, 1979.

Sears, Roebuck and Co., Catalogs, 1897, 1908, 1927.

Sewall, Samuel. "Diary of Samuel Sewall." Boston: Massachusetts Historical Society, *Collections,* ser. 5, vols. 5–7 (1878–1882).

Shorter, Edward. *Women's Bodies: A Social History of Women's Encounters with Health, Ill-Health, and Medicine.* New Brunswick, N.J., and London: Transaction Publications, 1991.

Shurtleff, Nathaniel B., ed. *Records of the Governors and Company of the Massachusetts Bay.* Boston, 1854.

Simmons, Amelia. *American Cookery.* Hartford, Conn., 1796.

Simon, Maron J., ed. *Your Solar House.* New York: Simon and Schuster, 1947.

Sklar, Kathryn Kish. *Catharine Beecher: A Study in American Domesticity.* New Haven, Conn., and London: Yale University Press, 1973.

Skolfield, W. K. *A Century of Electric Fans.* (Bridgeport, Conn.: General Electric Co., 1957.

Sloane, Sir Hans. *A Voyage to the Islands.* London, 1707.

Smallzried, Kathleen Ann. *The Everlasting Pleasure: Influences on America's Kitchens, Cooks and Cookery, from 1565 to the Year 2000.* New York: Appleton-Century-Crofts, 1956.

Smith, Frank. *A History of Dedham, Massachusetts.* Dedham, Mass., 1936.

Snow, Caleb H. *A History of Boston.* Boston, 1828.

Stewart, George R. *American Ways of Life.* Garden City, N.Y.: Doubleday, 1954.

St. George, Robert Blair, ed. *Material Life in America, 1600–1860.* Boston: Northeastern Press, 1988.

Stowe, Harriet Beecher, and Catharine E. Beecher. *The American Woman's Home.* New York, 1869.

Strasser, Susan. *Never Done: A History of American Housework.* New York: Pantheon, 1982.

Tarbox, Increase N., ed. *Diary of Thomas Robbins, D.D., 1796–1854.* Boston, 1886.

Thomas, Nicholas. *A Guide to Prehistoric England.* London: Batsford, [1976].

Tredgold, Thomas. *Principles of Warming and Ventilating Public Buildings, Dwelling-Houses . . .* London, 1824.

Tryon, Rolla Milton. *Household Manufactures in the United States, 1640–1860.* Chicago: University of Chicago Press, 1917.

Underhill, Roy. *The Woodwright's Companion.* Chapel Hill, N.C.: University of North Carolina Press, 1983.

Upton, Dell, ed. *America's Architectural Roots: Ethnic Groups That Built America.* Washington, D.C.: National Trust for Historic Preservation, 1986.

[U.S. Census Bureau]. *A Century of Population Growth: From the First Census of the United States to the Twelfth, 1790–1900.* Washington, D.C., 1909.

Van Doren, Mark, ed. *Samuel Sewall's Diary.* New York, 1963.

Vaux, Calvert. *Villas and Cottages.* New York, 1857.

Wainwright, Nicholas B., ed. *A Philadelphia Perspective: The Diary of Sidney George Fisher Covering the Years 1834–1871.* Philadelphia: Historical Society of Pennsylvania, 1967.

Waring, George E., Jr. *Earth Closets and Earth Sewage.* New York, 1870.

———. *The Sanitary Drainage of Houses and Towns.* New York, 1876.

Watson, John F. *Annals of Philadelphia.* Philadelphia, 1830.

Wheeler, Gervase. *Homes for the People.* New York, 1858.

Whiffen, Marcus, and Frederick Koeper. *American Architecture, 1607–1976.* Cambridge, Mass.: M.I.T. Press, 1981.

Whitehill, Walter Muir, and Frederick Doveton Nichols. *Palladio in America.* New York: Rizzoli, 1978.

Williams, E. W. *Frozen Foods: Biography of an Industry.* Boston: Cahners Publishing Co., 1970.

Williamson, Jefferson. *The American Hotel.* New York: Knopf, 1930; reprinted, Arno, 1975.

Willich, A. F. M. *The Domestic Encyclopedia; or A Dictionary of Facts and Useful Knowledge.* Philadelphia, 1804. [1st American edition; first published in London in 1802.]

Wilstach, Paul. *Mount Vernon: Washington's Home and the Nation's Shrine.* New York, 1916.

Wineberger, J. A. *The Home of Washington at Mount Vernon.* Washington, D.C., 1860.

Winkler, Gail Caskey. *The Well-Appointed Bath.* Washington, D.C.: Preservation Press, 1989.

Winthrop, John. *The History of New England.* Boston, 1825–1826.

Wise, Herbert C. *The George Read II House at New Castle, Delaware.* (White Pine Series of Architectural Monographs, n.d.)

Wood, Margaret E. *The English Mediaeval House.* London: Phoenix House, 1968.

Woodward, George E. *Woodward's Country Homes.* New York, 1865.

Wright, Frank Lloyd. *Frank Lloyd Wright on Architecture.* New York: Duell, Sloan and Pearce, 1941.

Wright, Lawrence. *Clean and Decent: The Fascinating History of the Bathroom and the Water Closet.* New York: Viking, 1960.

————. *Warm and Snug: The History of the Bed.* London: Routledge & Kegan Paul, 1962.

Yarwood, Doreen. *The Architecture of England from Prehistoric Times to the Present Day.* London: Batsford; New York: Putnam, 1963.

Young, Alexander. *Chronicles of the First Planters.* Boston, 1846.

————. *Chronicles of the Pilgrim Fathers.* Boston, 1841.

## Unpublished Works

Gittleman, Peter. *The Gropius House: Conception, Construction, and Commentary.* Master's Thesis, Boston University Graduate School, 1996.

Herold, Elaine B. *Preliminary Report on the Research at the Heyward-Washington House.* Charleston Museum, Charleston, S.C., 1978.

Mullin, Timothy J. *Read House Guide Manual, 1987.* Revised 1991. Historical Society of Delaware/George Read II House, New Castle, Del.

National Heritage Corporation. *Schiefferstadt: A Restoration Study.* West Chester, Pa., 1974.

Zierden, Martha. *Archeological Testing and Mitigation at the Stable Building, Heyward-Washington House.* Charleston Museum, Charleston, S.C., 1993.

## Manuscripts

Bradley, Harriet P. Diary, 1819. Research Library, Old Sturbridge Village, Sturbridge, Mass.

Lewis, Sinclair. Diary, 1900–1908. Yale Collection of American Literature, Beinecke Rare Book and Manuscript Library, Yale University, New Haven, Conn.

## Technology Survey

In the spring of 1996 a questionnaire prepared by the author and titled "The American Home and the Development of Domestic Technology" was mailed from Henry Holt and Company to a cross section of curators, site administrators, and parent agencies of historic homes throughout the country. The questionnaire sought information on such aspects of household technology as water supply, water use in kitchen, means of cooking, refrigeration, laundry, bathroom, lighting, and heating. Data derived from the survey is incorporated into the text and serves as the basis of the appendix "The American Home and the Emergence of Technology." References to this survey in source notes are given as TECH.

# Index

*Page numbers in italics indicate illustrations.*